CW00460888

Adaptation Studies

Adaptation Studies

New Approaches

Edited by
Christa Albrecht-Crane
and Dennis Cutchins

Madison • Teaneck
Fairleigh Dickinson University Press

New hardcover printing 2013 by Fairleigh Dickinson University Press
Co-published with The Rowman & Littlefield Publishing Group, Inc.
4501 Forbes Boulevard, Suite 200, Lanham, Maryland 20706
www.rowman.com

Estover Road, Plymouth PL6 7PY, United Kingdom

978-0-83864-262-7 (cloth: alk. paper)

Originally published by Associated University Presses
2010 Eastpark Boulevard
Cranbury, NJ 08512

Copyright © 2010 by Rosemont Publishing & Print Corp.
All rights reserved. Authorization to photocopy items for internal or personal use, or the internal or personal use of specific clients, is granted by the copyright owner provided that a base fee of $10.00, plus eight cents per page, per copy is paid directly to the Copyright Clearance Center, 222 Rosewood Drive, Danvers, Massachusetts 01923. [978-0-83864-262-7 /09 $10.00 + 8¢ pp, pc.]

Library of Congress Cataloging-in-Publication Data
Adaptation studies : new approaches / edited by Christa Albrecht Crane and Dennis Cutchins.
     p.   cm.
     Includes index.
     ISBN: 978-0-83864-262-7 (alk. paper)
     1.   Film adaptations—History and criticism. 2. Motion pictures and literature.
        I. Albrecht-Crane, Christa, 1967–   II. Cutchins, Dennis R. (Dennis Ray),
        1963–
     PN 1997.85.A319 2010
     808.2'3071—dc22

     2009045506

♾™ The paper used in this publication meets the minimum requirements of American National Standard for Information Sciences—Permanence of Paper for Printed Library Materials, ANSI/NISO Z39.48-1992.

Printed in the United States of America

Contents

Acknowledgments

SEVERAL OF THE CHAPTERS IN THIS VOLUME BEGAN AS PRESENTA-tions at various national and regional Popular Culture Association/ American Culture Association meetings. Both editors would like to thank those associations for their continued support of adaptation studies. Dennis Cutchins would like to thank the Charles Redd Center and the BYU English department for their generous support of his research.

Adaptation Studies

Introduction:
New Beginnings for Adaptation Studies
Christa Albrecht-Crane and Dennis Cutchins

The study of adaptation needs to be joined with the study of recycling, remaking, and every other form of retelling in the age of
mechanical reproduction and electronic communication. By this
means, adaptation will become part of a general theory of repetition, and adaptation study will move from the margins to the center of contemporary media studies.

—James Naremore, *Film Adaptation*

You can't say the same thing with a moving picture as you can with
a book any more than you can express with paint what you can
with plaster.

—William Faulkner

FILMS AND NEW MEDIA HAVE, IN LARGE MEASURE, ASSUMED MANY OF
the roles novels and short stories used to occupy in Western society.
J. Hillis Miller argues that "forces of economic, political, and technological globalization" have eclipsed the traditional value of literature:
while the novel used to provide society with the primary means of delivering "narratives," Miller argues that in recent decades new media
have increasingly taken up that role.[1] In the process, film and other
media have not only assumed the role of literature in delivering narratives, they have also adapted and incorporated a great deal from works
of literature. Since 1995, for instance, more than half of the sixty-five
films nominated for Best Picture by the Academy of Motion Picture
Arts and Sciences were based on works of literature.[2] In the fourteen
years between 1995 and 2008, eight of the winners were adaptations.
Despite the dominant role adaptation has played in the film industry,
however, adaptation theory has progressed very little since the 1950s.
Recent works by Robert Stam notwithstanding, adaptation studies has
steadfastly resisted adopting critical new insights offered in literature
and media studies, particularly by poststructural theories.

Most noticeably, scholars in adaptation studies continue focusing

11

on the issue of "fidelity" to a precursor text as a means to understand an adaptation's scope and worth. Following George Bluestone's seminal (and still dominant) study of adaptation, *Novels into Film* (1957), the field has emphasized a uni-directional analysis of literature and cinema's essential natures. The operative assumption in much of this work is that fiction's "essence" may be somehow captured in a film. Moreover, Bluestone took the term "adaptation" to mean strictly the transformation of highly valued, literary "novels" into the mass entertainment of "cinema." Thus, Bluestone's close readings of six literary "masterpieces" and their transformation into film—*The Informer, Wuthering Heights, The Grapes of Wrath, Pride and Prejudice, The Ox-Bow Incident*, and *Madame Bovary*—confirm James Naremore's suggestion that Bluestone validates "the intellectual priority and formal superiority of canonical novels, which provide the films he discusses with the sources and with the standard of value against which their success or failure are measured."[3] This implicit privileging of canonical literature persists despite the fact that Bluestone, even in this early work on adaptation, laments the prevalence of fidelity criticism. His intentions notwithstanding, his method of analysis perpetuated a reliance on fidelity as a primary criterion for judgment. As Bluestone notes, his focus was to "assess the key additions, deletions, and alterations revealed in the film and center on certain significant implications which seemed to follow from the remnants of, and deviations from, the novel."[4] Unwittingly, he defines an adaptation's scope and quality in terms of its allegiance to the primacy of the source text. With Bluestone as their intellectual progenitor, many contemporary scholars in adaptation studies likewise claim to reject "fidelity" as a marker of an adaptation's success, but more often than not perpetuate a dedication to the literary values underlying "adaptation."

A stubborn insistence on fidelity certainly has kept adaptation theory from maturing, but another central reason for this failure must be its unwillingness to allow the term "adaptation" to broaden and expand. It is simple enough to suggest that an adaptation is a film based on a novel, play, or short story, but what about a novel that is based on a film, or a video game based on either a novel or film? What about a film based on a video game, and a Broadway play based on a movie? This expansion of meanings for the term "adaptation" may be a bit confusing but it's also exciting. Contemporary culture, to put it mildly, loves to adapt. It is quite possible that adaptation has become so much a part of our daily lives that we have learned to ignore the important role it plays in all of our media experiences. We are familiar, for instance, with film and television adaptations of literary works. But several of the shows recently appearing on Broadway are also adaptations from various sources. *Spamalot, Wicked, Big, Footloose,* and *Ghostbusters* are all adaptations. Those who study adaptations would do well to more carefully and rigorously examine "intertextual" relationships in general. Poststructural theory seems an ideal place to begin this investigation, and we hope that this introduction, as well as the essays in this collection, will help readers consider what poststructural theory might offer the study of adaptation.

Both Brian McFarlane in his *Novel to Film* and James Naremore in *Film Adaptation* note that the field of adaptation studies has much to gain from a more sustained, more theoretically rigorous rethinking of various issues at work in film adaptations.[5] Not only does the field itself stand to gain a richer understanding of the materials in question, but such an understanding will contribute centrally to what Thomas Leitch terms "Textual Studies"—the general study of texts and media in disciplines such as cinema studies, literary studies, and cultural studies.[6] Naremore and Leitch emphasize that adaptation studies can offer exciting new insights into the ways texts shape each other and interact with cultural forces. So far, the burgeoning discipline of adaptation studies has largely been shaped by its institutional context. That is, adaptation is typically taught in an English department in which film is used only to supplement the study of literature. Thus, the recurring concern of adaptation scholars has been to consider film adaptations vis-à-vis their literary source texts, in a relationship of dependency that maintains a binary base positing literature against the cinema—as Naremore notes, thus solidifying "a series of binary oppositions that poststructuralist theory has taught us to deconstruct."[7] The fact that this rather narrow and simplistic approach has not been deconstructed is indicative of the field's range *and* standing: as a fringe discipline, "jejune" (in Naremore's frank assessment), clearly marginal to the larger interests of contemporary critical studies.[8]

In order to move from the fringe of critical studies and assume the more central role we believe adaptation studies can and should fulfill, a number of important ideas must be adopted. Perhaps the most significant of these is the notion that literature and cinema are radically different from each other. The idea that literature and film are different seems like an obvious assertion, but in both scholarly and popular ways we consistently fail to recognize those differences. We often say things like, "The film was *different* from the book." There would be no point in saying that unless we believed that the film should be, or at least could be, the *same* as the book. As readers, viewers, and scholars we have taught ourselves to ignore the differences that exist between novels and films. It should be no surprise that adaptation studies has often made it a point to focus on what novels and films have in common. Both novels and film, for instance, may be said to possess narrative structures, themes, point of view, and characters; both also adhere to similar notions of "realism" that postulate a perceived relation to the "real world." Moreover, adaptation studies scholarship consistently underscores similar investments in cultural capital: many film adaptations select their source literary texts from an Anglo-American literary tradition and many, if not the vast majority, of adaptation scholars are trained literature specialists whose typical aims in working with adaptations, at least in terms of pedagogy, consist of explicating film's investment in the traditional Western literary canon. In other words, scholars working in adaptation studies have had a vested interest in viewing adaptations as "branches" of literature with similar components and structures. For many of them, films are simply novels on the screen. As a result of such a conflation, the primary criterion of an adaptation's success or failure remains the marker of "fidelity."

Much that has been written about adaptation in the last fifty years has reinforced our willingness to ignore the *fundamental* differences between literature and the cinema and to look, instead, for *surface* differences. We might argue, for instance, that the narrative of the film differs slightly from that of the novel, or that an actor in an adaptation looks older than the age of the character in the source book. Looking for these surface differences between the film and the novel, however, is like looking for grass on a putting green, since any adaptation of a literary work consists of many more differences than similarities. Moreover, differences between media are likely to be much more fundamental than a narrative shift. William Arnold of the *Seattle Post Intelligencer*, for instance, writes in his review of Roman Polanski's *Oliver Twist* (2005), that "the most drastic of several liberties the film takes with the novel (and other film versions) is to completely delete the subplot of Oliver's mother and the matter of his parentage."[9] In selecting this difference as the most drastic, Arnold ignores, however, the fact that living people are portraying what were, in Dickens's novel, characters described by words on a page, or that explanatory chapter headings are not included in the film, as they are in the novel, or that the "voice" of Dickens's narrator, one of the most delightful features of the novel, is absent from the film, replaced by other features that are more distinctively "cinematic." Of course, he doesn't have to mention these more fundamental differences. As experienced film viewers we take them for granted. Like the background music in a department store, we have learned to internalize and thus ignore them. The problem with this attitude is that these kinds of differences are not incidental, but rather foundational. Ignoring these factors is exactly the way we may conflate literature and film.

Several years ago Andrey Tarkovsky declared that "Every art form
. . . is born and lives according to its particular laws. When people talk
about the specific norms of cinema, it is usually in juxtaposition with
literature. In our view it is all-important that the interaction between
cinema and literature should be explored and exposed as completely as
possible, so that the two can at last be separated, never to be confused
again."[10] To understand adaptation, for example, in the context of literature and film, we must begin by understanding that books and
movies are separate and should never be confused with each other. As
a somewhat Marxist starting point, it bears emphasizing that all works
of art are closely tied to particular relations of labor, production, and
capital. They were, in other words, made by real people, at a particular
historical moment. Moreover, most of these art works were expected
to make money. Accordingly, Jonathan Beller notes cinema's rise in
terms of its function as an industrial art, integrated into a system of
image-production. He writes that "all works of art are embedded in
certain material support structures; each art form has its corresponding social formation."[11] In his call for revisioning adaptation studies,
Naremore advocates "a broader definition of adaptation and a sociology that takes into account the commercial apparatus, the audience,
and the academic culture industry."[12] This understanding would contribute to adaptation studies by drawing productive analyses from historical differences, as well as differences between media, thus shifting
attention to the intertextual nature of all adaptations. Discovering difference then becomes not a quest to uncover the inevitable lack of fidelity, but rather an affirmative focus on how texts form and *in-form*
each other.

Many who have written about adaptation in the past, however, have
believed, either explicitly or implicitly, that works of literature ought
to be perfectly translated to the screen, so to speak. Geoffrey Wagner
expressed this idea in his 1975 book, *The Novel and the Cinema*, when
he suggested that there are "three types of transition of fiction into
film." For Wagner the first of these, and the simplest, was *"transposition*, in which a novel is directly given on the screen, with a minimum
of apparent interference."[13] The language Wagner uses here reveals a
great deal about his conflation of film and literature. How can a novel,
for instance, be "directly given on the screen"? In this paradigm, perceived changes to the *essence* of the novel are considered "interference," like the static on a radio, in the apparent attempt to transfer
the novel to the screen. The second of Wagner's categories he calls
"commentary. This is where an original is taken and either purposefully or inadvertently altered in some respect" as it is adapted. Wagner
suggests that these "commentaries" might be valuable as nothing

more than "so many cinematic footnotes to the original."[14] He believes that the best that can be expected of this kind of film is that it "may actually fortify the values of its original on the printed page."[15] The subjugation of film to literature is clear in these statements. The best a "commentary" adaptation can hope for is to supplement the original written text. Wagner's final type of adaptation is the "analogy," which "must represent a fairly considerable departure (from the original) for the sake of making *another* work of art."[16] Wagner struggles somewhat to define this kind of adaptation because the distinction he makes here is based not in a difference in *kind*, but rather in the assumed intentions of the filmmakers. Analogies differ from and rise above transpositions and commentaries in that they at least *aspire* to be art. Once again, Wagner's condescending tone toward film makes this definition highly problematic. And while we would not dispute that some filmmakers do seem to employ different aspirations, we would be hesitant to propose a system of classification based on our assumptions about those desires.

Adapters cannot "transpose" or transfer a novel, or even another film, to the screen. They must interpret, re-working the precursor text and choosing the various meanings and sensations they find most compelling (or most cost effective), then imagine scenes, characters, plot elements, etc., that match their interpretation. These very relationships are the subject matter adaptation theory seeks to explore. By declaring some films "transpositions," adaptation theorists have simultaneously declared themselves useless. There is no need to interpret a film or a novel if the two are "essentially" the same thing and if that "essence" is equally available to every reader. To be sure, most theorists, like Wagner, also note the existence of other, more complex kinds of adaptations, but each of these "higher" forms is built upon the foundation of a transposable essence that lies at the heart of any text. In this model any more complex adaptation is more or less a deformation of the original work and a mutation of the possible perfect transposition. This approach may be theoretically problematic, but it is also wrongheaded. It makes the study of adaptation an exercise in negativity, a quest to discover where the film maker deviated from the perfect original. The truth is that all adaptations are complex analogies. More importantly, adaptations, rather than being handicapped by their movements away from the earlier text, are often enabled by those differences.

In that light, the operative assumption in adaptation studies should be "difference," rather than the usually invoked "sameness." This new focus is ironic, since fidelity criticism is often an effort to discover what is different when a novel is adapted to the screen. The distinction between that and what we are suggesting is that a fidelity critic usually starts from the assumption that "sameness" is possible (and usually preferable), but that the filmmakers somehow just missed achieving this goal. We would suggest not only that sameness is impossible, but that difference, in fact, makes art possible. With Philippe Met, we want to argue that the "seemingly negative connotations (defeat, un-doing, defect) are somehow apt to define the ways literature and film tend to un-do or un-pack each other, rather than adapt (to) each other."[17] In other words, "adaptation" as the key term might be a mis-nomer altogether because it assumes that sameness forms its operative lens. However, as poststructural theory suggests, the making of texts as well as their reception are both destabilizing processes. Bakhtin makes the point even more succinctly: "Understanding," Bakhtin sug-gests, "comes to fruition only in the response."[18] Adaptations should be seen as responses to other texts that form a necessary step in the process of understanding. Rather than seeing adaptations as taking one thing (a novel's imagined "essence") and placing it into another context, we should recognize that the "essence" is neither knowable, nor directly representable. A novel's imagined essence remains elusive and ambiguous; what one does achieve in reading, or in adapting a text, is thus always more, less, or other than what the novel or the author wanted to express.

This complex notion of reading (and understanding) is explored by Derrida, who suggests that one never knows in advance just what a piece of art, or a text, might hold in its trace when it is being read or viewed. Referring to Rousseau's *Confessions*, Derrida notes that one of Rousseau's sentences "might always say, through using the 'supple-ment,' more, less, or something other than what he *would mean*."[19] That is to say, a text does not simply recreate reality or presence be-cause it uses representation—understood broadly as textual, pictorial, or aural language. A text cannot simply evoke the "real thing," but rather creates a *represented* thing. That representation, by not being the thing itself, must be *something else*—more, less, or something other than what the artist meant. Derrida thus invokes a wide range of possi-bilities, suggesting that a work of art (which would include adapta-tions) offers signs and symbols that have always already "missed" reality. "Re-presentation" takes the form of various artistic endeavors to name, describe, and construct *a sense of* "presence." However, rather than seeing this missed sense of presence as a failure, we want to argue that it forms the condition of art. As André Bazin notes, "Re-alism can only be achieved in one way—through artifice."[20] The un-mistakable lesson here is the poststructural injunction that texts inform other texts in vampiric, unexpected, and quite indeterminate ways. It is this sense of indeterminacy that we want to bring into the study of adaptation.

In *Of Grammatology* Derrida suggests in reading "we traverse a certain path within" a text. And yet, he urges, "are other paths not possible? And as long as the totality of paths is not effectively exhausted, how shall we justify this one?"[21] In this context "adaptations" may be understood as "readings," paths the filmmakers take through source text(s) that themselves are paths through other texts. This line of argumentation opens the door to some of the more important questions to which adaptation theory could and perhaps should address itself. What, for instance, is the particular path taken by this film adaptation? Why has *this* film taken *this* particular path through *this* particular novel? Are other paths possible? Why does this path make the most (economic, cultural, interpretive) sense? Why was this path chosen at a particular historical moment? What are some other paths other adaptations of this text have taken?

This notion of different paths through a text is another way of saying that adaptations are always interpretations—and interpretations are always adaptations. The story, so to speak, is never separate from the telling. There is no such thing as an abstractable (or extractable) "essence" in a novel or film that can be adapted to a new medium so that one may say, "It's the same story, it's just told in a different way." Any "retelling" of a story is a new story because the text has been interpreted by the "reteller." Bakhtin suggests that the "authors creating the text, the performers of the text (if they exist) and finally the listeners or readers who recreate and in so doing renew the text—participate equally in the creation of the represented world in the text."[22] This step of interpretation is both a key point and one that is often ignored in the case of very well known texts in which a certain interpretation has become part of our cultural background. *Frankenstein*, for instance, is so well known that a potential adapter/interpreter does not need even to have read the novel, since a particular interpretation of the novel, that of James Whale, has become part of our language, our cultural inheritance, if you will. Thus, many of the basic plot elements for a book like Betsy Haynes' *Frankenturkey* (1994) are predictable for most Americans.[23]

Nevertheless, any text, even a relatively simple one, arguably exists on many different levels at the same time in a reader's mind. That is, a particular event, character, or setting might have a meaning based on the plot or action of the story. But at the same time, a character could also have one or more metaphorical meanings, as well as political meanings, cultural meanings, and personal meanings. Thus Shelley's *Frankenstein* might be interpreted primarily as a frightening adventure story, a social commentary, a critique of science, etc., depending on the interpretation of the reader/adaptor. Someone working on yet another adaptation of Frankenstein may choose one of these less traveled paths to create a new and fresh reading, and thus a new and fresh adaptation of the novel.

We feel that adaptation studies must adopt this richer notion of intertextuality in which the interpretive roles of writers, directors, screenwriters, producers, etc., play a more significant part. Adaptation theory must, in other words, address *intentionality*. Despite the fact that poststructural theory has debunked an exclusive reliance on authorial intent, even labeling it a "fallacy," Bakhtin called for the study of texts that included a consideration of "intentional" factors, what he called "the impulse that reaches out beyond," noting "if we detach ourselves completely from this impulse all we have left is the naked corpse of the word, from which we can learn nothing at all about the social situation or the fate of a given word in life."[24] Texts are always inter-texts, and borrow, rework, and adapt each other in complex ways, but at the same time, we can discern specific forces (social, economic, historical, and authorial) at work in particular texts and inter-texts—that is to say, in specific "adaptations." To use Leitch's words, this "field of intertextual energy" needs to be put to theoretical and analytical work in thinking about adaptations.[25]

As adaptation studies adopts a poststructuralist lens and defines this richer notion of intertextuality, some of its key assumptions will change. Adaptation scholars will recognize that all film adaptations are intertextual by definition, multivocal by necessity, and adaptive by their nature. If you imagine a script or a treatment as a primary text, and if you imagine writers, directors, lighting specialists, and actors as collaborators, then all films are dialogic, heteroglossic adaptations. Adaptations are dialogues with other texts, including the texts upon which they are based, and those texts are in dialogue with adaptations. For example, Margaret Mitchell's novel *Gone With the Wind* can only be understood by contemporary readers in the context of the 1939 film, because the film has engendered a reception life of its own, so to speak, that a reader of the novel cannot escape.

Recognizing this reciprocal, intertextual quality of adaptations allows us to see some adaptations as critiques, parodies, homages, etc., of earlier texts. The contemporary notion of translation offers a powerful trope for adaptation. In contradistinction to Bluestone's understanding, "translation," as we use it here, emphasizes the differences between texts rather than their similarities. To that end, Mikhail Bakhtin suggests in the essay, "Discourse on the Novel," that "the element of translation and reworking is foregrounded" in early prose novels, and he argues that it may "even be said that European novel prose is born and shaped in the process of a free (that is, reformulating) translation of others' works."[26] Translation in the sense of reworking, in short, is one of the very sources of literature itself. For Bakhtin, literature was not properly conceptualized until it was "translated." Bakhtin's brand of poststructural thought seems potentially productive and empowering for adaptation theory, since adaptations are, in effect, free translations or reworkings of texts into new "languages."

Adaptation studies ought to focus on the space of disjunction between texts and media to ask what that space, that necessary difference, enables. One is reminded of Derrida's concept of the "aporia" of texts. According to Derrida, a text's promise can never be fulfilled because it poses a "promise [that] is impossible but inevitable."[27] For "a promise is always excessive,"[28] in that a text remains divorced from an essential reference to reality. Because of that same disjunction, however, the text remains open to a multitude of effects/affects. If "understanding" a text always implies that some part of it remains ineffable, then adaptations, rather than "adapting," in the simple sense, a prior text, actually create a new text with its own manifold relationships to source text(s). The crucial move here is the suggestion that, in their intersection, novels and films (and many other forms of adaptations across media) inhabit a sort of cross-fertilization that is both artistically productive and affirmative of difference.

"Creation" and "reaction," then, are both fundamentally indeterminate activities that cannot be grounded in an irreducible or universal "reality." In terms of "representation," art is a doomed project from the beginning—at least if one attempts to locate in art "the real" and "presence." Likewise, if one expects an adaptation to be the book, then he or she will always be disappointed. Art becomes a fecund and productive project, however, if one gives up the hunt for the real and instead focuses on what art actually accomplishes in that *huge* space in-between absolute presence and total absence. This focus would move adaptation studies away from concepts that keep repeating the binary of absence/presence—concepts such as the "fidelity" of a movie to its "source text" (does the movie version contain, possess in its presence, the essence of the novel?). As Met asserts, the goal of new directions in adaptation studies would be to offer a "viable theoretical alternative to the allegedly unilateral, 'translational' process of screen adaptation, which tends to postulate a predatory, quasi-vampiric or phagocytic bond between literature and film."[29] An approach to adaptation studies that takes into account poststructural notions of intertextuality might probe into the as yet mostly uncharted terrain of intertextuality in which adaptations happen.

As a final note, we argue that in approaching adaptations we need to avoid reductionist approaches to the texts in question. In *The World Viewed*, Stanley Cavell suggests that both films and literary texts are art, and, he argues, the only legitimate response to art is more art.[30] We have begun to feel that the analysis of adaptations is more of an art that a repeatable process, than is, it rather stubbornly refuses to be broken down into bite-sized steps. Auguste Renoir once noted of art critics, "nowadays they want to explain everything. But if they could explain a picture, it wouldn't be art."[31] The approach to adaptation we have outlined above suggests more of an art than a step-by-step program. Nevertheless, by suggesting principles that we believe should govern the study of adaptation, we hope to suggest an art form that may be taught. In other words, we are arguing for a revised approach to adaptation studies that takes into account the ways in which different media contain structures and constraints unique to a particular medium, while recognizing that these differences remain indeterminate and flexible relative to surrounding environments. Thus, an analytical model may be suggested here that offers on the one hand a heuristic that could be used in teaching adaptation, for instance; but at the same time one that might remain open to further developments and inevitable changes that affect our intertextual media landscapes. We hope that the essays in this volume walk that tightrope.

NOTES

1. J. Hillis Miller, *On Literature* (New York: Routledge, 2002), 8–9.

2. This does not include films like *Frost/Nixon* (2008) that were adapted from non-literary sources.

3. George Bluestone, *Novels into Film: The Metamorphosis of Fiction into Cinema* (Baltimore: Johns Hopkins University Press, 1957), 6.

4. Ibid., viii.

5. Brian McFarlane, *Novel to Film: An Introduction to the Theory of Adaptation* (New York: Oxford University Press, 1996); James Naremore, "Film and Reign of Adaptation," in *Film Adaptation*, ed. James Naremore (New Brunswick, NJ: Rutgers University Press, 2000), 1–18.

6. Thomas Leitch, "Twelve Fallacies in Contemporary Adaptation Theory," *Criticism* 45, no. 2 (2003): 170.

7. Naremore, "Film and Reign of Adaptation," 2.

8. Ibid., 1.

9. William Arnold, "*Pianist* Team Puts its Own Twist on the Newest *Oliver*," *Seattle Post-Intelligencer*, September 30, 2005, http://seattlepi.nwsource.com/movies/242776_oliver30q.html. To give Arnold credit, this point is not the focus of his well-written review.

    10. Andrey Tarkovsky, *Sculpting in Time*, trans. Kitty Hunter-Blair (Boston: Faber and Faber, 1986), 60.
    11. Jonathan L. Beller, "Capital/Cinema," in *Deleuze and Guattari: New Mappings in Politics, Philosophy, and Culture*, ed. Eleanor Kaufman and Kevin Jon Heller (Minneapolis: University of Minnesota Press, 1998), 89.
    12. Naremore, "Film and Reign of Adaptation," 10.
    13. Geoffrey Wagner, *The Novel and the Cinema* (Cranbury, NJ: Associated University Presses, 1975), 222.
    14. Ibid., 223.
    15. Ibid., 224.
    16. Ibid., 227.
    17. Philippe Met, "The Filmic Ghost in the Literary Machine," *Contemporary French and Francophone Studies* 9, no. 3 (2005): 249.
    18. Mikhail Bakhtin, *The Dialogic Imagination* (Austin: University of Texas Press, 1984), 282.
    19. Jacques Derrida, *Of Grammatology*, trans. Gayatri Spivak (Baltimore: Johns Hopkins University Press, 1976), 157–58.
    20. André Bazin, *What Is Cinema? Vol. I*, trans. Hugh Gray (Berkeley: University of California Press, 1967), 26.
    21. Derrida, *Of Grammatology*, 161.
    22. Bakhtin, *The Dialogic Imagination*, 253.
    23. Dennis was able to impress his preteen son a few years ago with his knowledge of this book he had not read.
    24. Ibid., 292.
    25. Leitch, "Everything You Always Wanted to Know about Adaptation Especially if You're Looking Forwards rather than Backwards," *Literature Film Quarterly* 33, no. 3 (2005): 239.
    26. Bakhtin, *The Dialogic Imagination*, 376–78.
    27. Jacques Derrida, *Memoirs for Paul de Man* (New York: Columbia University Press, 1986), 98.
    28. Ibid., 93.
    29. Met, "The Filmic Ghost," 245.
    30. Stanley Cavell, *The World Viewed: Reflections on the Ontology of Film* (Cambridge: Harvard University Press, 1979).
    31. Auguste Renoir, quoted in Hereward Lester Cooke, *Painting Techniques of the Masters* (New York: Watson Guptill Publications, 1978), 59.

I
Fidelity, Ethics, and Intertextuality

Being Adaptation:
The Resistance to Theory

Brett Westbrook

As CHRISTA ALBRECHT-CRANE AND DENNIS CUTCHINS POINT OUT IN their introduction to this volume, "adaptation theory has progressed very little since the 1950s."[1] Thomas Leitch agrees, claiming that "most general studies of adaptation are shaped by the case studies they seem designed mainly to illuminate."[2] This lack of theory about adaptation studies stands in direct contrast to the rise of theory in and of itself, at least in the academic academy, where it has become a field in its own right. John Crowe Ransom's famous "New Criticism" article appeared over sixty-five years ago; Jacques Derrida's *Of Grammatology*, spawning a multitude of schools of thought, is forty years old. Similarly, the lack of a firm theoretical grounding for film adaptation studies stands in contrast to film studies in general, a field underpinned by a solid body of theoretical work. Sergei Eisenstein began to theorize about cinema eight decades ago; the *Cahiers du Cinema* has passed the half-century mark. Certainly film critics write about adaptations, have written about them all along, and yet, as Leitch points out, "this flood of study of individual adaptations proceeds on the whole without the support of any more general theoretical account of what actually happens, or what ought to happen, when a group of filmmakers set out to adapt a literary text."[3] Given the receptivity in the academy to both theory and film studies as academic fields, and given the openness of film studies to theory, why then does film adaptation studies resist theory? Attempting to answer this question seems necessary if film adaptation studies is to incorporate theory and theorizing into the field of study.

TEXTS, PLURAL

The absolute given of all adaptations studies is comparison. No one writing about a film adaptation *as adaptation* writes about only the

movie or only about the novel (or short story, or television show, etc.).
Part of the resistance to theory may involve this reliance on not just
one, but two texts, despite the fact that the notion of "text," of "a"
text as monad, has been thoroughly, excruciatingly, exploded by critics
from across the academy. Terry Eagleton's explanation of the Derridean notion of text is that "there is nothing in the world that is not
'textual,' in the sense of being made up of a complex weave of elements
which prevents it from being cleanly demarcated from something else.
'Textual' means that nothing stands gloriously alone."[4] And yet, the
fundamental notion of an adaptation presupposes not just one, but two
identifiable texts: a precursor text and then the film based on that precursor text. In the academy, and certainly in most English departments, the older, earlier, text—usually a canonized novel—is always
already superior to the film. The highly problematized notion of text
in general, whether novel or film or some other "text," inhibits theorizing about a field the basis for which is composed of (at least) two
texts as they stand in relationship to each other. Leitch asks this question for adaptation studies explicitly: "given the myriad differences,
not only between literary and cinematic texts, but between successive
cinematic adaptations of a given literary text, or for that matter between different versions of a given story in the same medium, what
exactly is it that film adaptations adapt, or are supposed to adapt?"[5] In
other words, if "nothing stands gloriously alone" as an identifiable
text, how do critics even start to theorize about a field that is text-
dependent? An answer to this question, even a complicated or thoroughly interrogated answer, seems necessary to the formation of a
theory (or theories) for film adaptation studies.

In order to begin answering the question about which "texts" comprise the adaptation, another question must be answered first: what
"counts" as an adaptation in the first place? One complicating factor
in trying to answer such a question is that, to a degree, all films are
adaptations; or at least all Hollywood films are adaptations. Hollywood movies, even those not based on known (or acknowledged)
sources, generally begin as an idea being pitched, which gets written
down in a highly abbreviated form as a treatment. Eventually (budget
permitting), a rehearsal script emerges, then a shooting script, then
revisions. Directors have their scripts; actors and cinematographers
have theirs. Scripts are revised, sometimes over and over, while the
film is being shot, as the dailies reveal issues with acting, the set, etc.
Scripts of some movies are even published for a variety of reasons,
most often to prolong the commercial income from the movie, though
sometimes as an antidote to the film. Playwright and screenplay writer
Lillian Hellman, for example, had the script to *The North Star* (1943)

published as a corrective to the final print of the film, from which she disassociated herself entirely, paying MGM $30,000 to get out of her contract. The Academy of Motion Picture Arts and Sciences awards two Oscars for writing, making a distinction between "original" and "adapted" screenplays. The 2007 Oscar for original screenplay went to Michael Arndt for *Little Miss Sunshine*. In his acceptance speech, Arndt noted that "when I was a kid, my family drove 600 miles in a VW bus with a broken clutch."[6] Did he "adapt" that part of his childhood into a script, which directors Jonathan Dayton and Valerie Faris adapted from screenplay to screen? As Robert Stam and Alessandra Raengo note, the "point is that virtually all films, not only adaptations, remakes, and sequels are mediated through intertextuality and writing."[7]

The sorting out of what "counts" as an adaptation might be helped along by definitions. Constantine Verevis makes a distinction, for example, between a remake and an adaptation, the former being a film based on a previous film, while an adaptation points to a literary source. He asks a question of taxonomy: "how does film remaking differ from other types of repetition, such as quotations, allusion, and adaptation?"[8] This particular definition means that the field of adaptation studies must cede film remakes to another branch of the cinematic tree. Verevis, however, does not address how this degree of separation functions when the remake is based on an earlier film that is based on a literary or other more standard source. For example, *Dracula* (1992), luxuriously directed by Francis Ford Coppola and starring Gary Oldman, might count as a remake according to Verevis. There are plenty of prior vampire movies, starting with F. W. Murnau's *Nosferatu* (1922), silent and inexorably grim, starring Max Schreck (whose last name means, incidentally, "fright" in German). Over half a century later, in a sound remake, Klaus Kinski infused the vampire role with an incandescent and unnerving appetite. Frank Langella (1979) and Oldman (also an apt surname) reinvigorated the part with sex. In between Murnau and Coppola there are literally dozens of movies, some serious, some satires, many of them from Hammer Studios starring Peter Cushing and Christopher Lee (seen most recently as Saruman in *Lord of the Rings*, perhaps another version of embodied evil). Coppola's *Dracula* is a remake according to Verevis's definition, and yet it seems reasonable to assert that all versions of the vampire story answer to, or at least gesture toward, Bram Stoker's novel.

Trying to define an adaptation is a tricky enterprise, often raising more questions than it answers. Verevis, for example, does not address whether movies based on other filmic sources count as remakes, such as the host of movies based on television shows, e.g., *McHale's Navy*

(1964), *The Muppet Movie* (1979), *Dragnet* (1987) and *The Untouchables* (1987), the *Star Trek* movies (based on the original and the *Next Generation* series), the *Mission: Impossible* movies (1996, 2000, 2006), *The Addams Family* (1991, itself based on the Charles Addams print cartoons), *The Beverly Hillbillies* (1993), *The Fugitive* (1993), *The Flintstones* (1994), *The Brady Bunch* (1995), *The Avengers* (1998) and *The Wild, Wild West* (1998), *The Mod Squad* (1999), *Charlie's Angels* (2000), *Josie and the Pussycats* (2001), *Bewitched* (2005), *Starsky and Hutch* (2004), *Dukes of Hazzard* (2005), *Speed Racer* (2008) and many more. One might even argue that the critically acclaimed movie *Good Night, and Good Luck* (2005), co-written and directed by George Clooney (who also had a small role), is based on Edward R. Murrow's television show, *See It Now*. If so, then perhaps it is an adaptation as defined by Verevis. Perhaps it is more accurate to assert that it is based on Murrow's life (even a brief moment in his life), in which case it is a bio-pic and so falls out of Verevis's purview. Perhaps the movie "adapts" the *zeitgeist* of the McCarthy era, making it a particularly timely film because of the parallels with today's state of hyper-polarized politics. George Clooney and co-writer Grant Heslov were Oscar-nominated for best original screenplay. If it is original, adapting nothing, then it does not fall into the category of adaptation at all, regardless of the definition. Perhaps it makes sense, though, that the Academy does not count as adaptation a film based on history. Hollywood's take on historical events is quite often as "original" as fiction.

"Adapted films," Leitch argues, "are by definition irradiated with the traces of other texts they acknowledge in a mind-boggling variety of ways."[9] This state of affairs considerably complicates the task of sorting out the texts and constructing a definition. Take, for example, the 1964 film *My Fair Lady* directed by George Cukor. This film musical was based on the stage musical with lyrics and music by Alan Jay Lerner and Frederick Loewe, based on the straight (i.e., non-musical) play by George Bernard Shaw, based on Ovid's *Metamorphoses*, based on a Greek legend. Out of all of these "texts," which is the pre-cursor text for the screenplay writer, for the director, for the performers, for the audience? Given the general studio preference for pre-sold movies, the most likely precursor text is the stage musical. Certainly the original trailer emphasizes the musical (along with the five million dollars Jack Warner paid for the movie rights). And yet, that stage musical was itself based on a straight play, which had been filmed before in 1938. George Bernard Shaw won the Oscar in 1939 for Best Writing, Screenplay (though the Adapted Screenplay award was an option in 1939).

Even though the term "adaptation" absolutely presupposes a minimum of two texts (with all the difficulties encountered by that term), those who write about adaptations seem quite willing to cast a wide net into the cinema sea without answering this fundamental question about *which* texts. As a result, critics in the field generally take an overly simplistic, often reductionist stance, positing as givens the novel (standing gloriously alone) and then the resulting film as if the two exist in relationship to each other, yet curiously set apart from the rest of the nexus of production. Leitch argues that such a position promotes a conservative formalism, inevitably concluding that the novel is somehow "better" than any film. That there is a politics of the scholarly academy in play here seems reasonable to assert, though it is insufficient as an explanation. The slipperiness of terms so central to the field seems to be the locus of a significant point of resistance to theory. Perhaps that is the starting point as well.

What's Being Adapted?

Given that the field of adaptation studies is built on a comparison, another question that must be hashed out is, "what's being adapted?" This question must be answered if critics are to have a firm grip on what it is they are comparing. All films, even the most original, un-scripted, Warhol-esque art film, are created within a nexus of production, which brings to bear on the film a whole host of influences: money, the director, the cast (George Raft or Humphrey Bogart in *Casablanca*), sometimes even the weather. For adaptation studies, how-ever, the existence, the requirement of some sort of pre-cursor text, the act of comparison, pulls certain aspects of filmmaking into the foreground and may explain at least some of the resistance to theory. For example, in the case of *My Fair Lady*, in addition to the backwards trajectory from George Cukor to Ovid, a host of other factors went into the making of the movie version that any theorizing about the field must take into account. Shaw's play is set contemporaneously in pre-World War I London. As Leitch points out, "Hollywood adapta-tions of foreign novels invariably foreground their particular national-ities and historical moments in ways their source novels rarely do."[10] Which aspects of "Britishness" are not only adapted, but adapted for an audience of Yanks half a century after the play was written? Freddy, whom Eliza marries in the play, is a member of the impoverished gen-tility, a particular point in the history of the English aristocracy, laden with the foreshadowing of the sun setting on the British empire that would not seem to resonate with an American audience. The discus-sion of dialect and the ways in which it classes a speaker are not entirely foreign to Americans, though the actual rigidity of the English caste system might be. In the play, Eliza's opening dialogue includes the following line: "Ow, eez ye-ooa san, is e?" which means, "Oh, he's your son, is he?" After three lines, Shaw abandons this level of dialect as "unintelligible outside of London" and proceeds to write Eliza's lines in Queen's English. If Eliza's actual dialect was unintelligible outside of London, it is reasonable to assume it would have been equally unintelligible on the other side of the Atlantic and that the lines in the film—delivered in a Hollywood version of Cockney—were intended to be understood across the nation.

In addition to all things British, there are Cecil Beaton's astounding costumes, culminating in the black-and-white cupcake confection of a dress for Eliza at Ascot opening day. Are those part of the adaptation from stage to screen? The costumes are most certainly an important part of the overall feel of the movie. That one dress in particular is instantly recognizable and is endlessly repeated, especially in gay male drag shows. Beaton took home two Oscars for the film version: one for Best Art Direction–Set Direction, Color (along with Gene Allen and George James Hopkins) and one for Best Costume Design, Color. Did Beaton adapt Beaton? For that matter, did Lerner adapt Lerner? He won a Tony in 1957 for Author–Musical and was nominated for an Oscar for Best Writing, Screenplay Based on Material from Another Medium, while André Previn won an Oscar for Best Music, Scoring of Music, Adaptation or Treatment. Even if the discussion is limited to the movement from stage musical to screen musical, pinpointing exactly which elements comprise the adaptation proves difficult, even (or especially) for the Academy.

At least as complicated as sorting out Greek legend to Ovid to Shaw to Lerner and Loewe to Cukor is sorting out adaptations based on non-fiction sources, which may seem less complicated than fiction, at first. After all, this is fact, not fiction. History itself, however, is a complicated weave of narratives, about which absolutely everyone has an opinion and in which cultures and societies are heavily invested. And, as United States film-making is a for-profit industry, adapting an historical event to the big screen means that the adaptation must respond to those cultural expectations if the film is to make any money. Writing about Cecil B. DeMille's 1926 *The King of Kings*, Richard Maltby points out that there "had been at least thirty-nine earlier versions of the Christ story, of which the most commercially notable was probably Kalem's *From the Manger to the Cross* of 1912. Biblical epics, including DeMille's *Ten Commandments* and MGM's *Ben Hur*, had taken large grosses over the previous three production seasons."[11] Ostensibly, the source DeMille adapted was the New Testament; however, as

Maltby ably shows, the "film's doctrinal starting point was the religious doctrine of American cultural hegemony," and specifically a best-seller by Bruce Barton, *The Man Nobody Knows*. The novel "puts Jesus in the company of Benjamin Franklin, Abraham Lincoln, and other American 'success stories' in the Horatio Alger mode."[12] De-Mille also had a whole host of religious advisors, according to Maltby—Protestant, Catholic, Jewish, and Islamic. The resulting film clearly adapts so much more than the story of Jesus of Nazareth: a post-WWI, pre-Crash economic sensibility as related to religion; the United States response to Modernism and the apparent weakening of institutions such as the Church; the shifting role of women in United States culture, particularly after suffrage. In order to ensure that his film was commercially viable, DeMille had to respond to these cultural expectations.

Making a film about religious figures suggests another entry in the category "what gets adapted": audience expectation. No movie about Jesus of Nazareth, intending to be commercially successful, from De-Mille's *The King of Kings* to Mel Gibson's *The Passion of the Christ* (2004) can depict the central character as, for example, a womanizer, a drunk, or a lout. Such a constraint does not stem from the industry's pursuit of historical accuracy or any particular sensitivity. It would seem that comedies receive a certain dispensation, as Alanis Morisette can play God in *Dogma* (1999). In *Switch* (1991), God is embodied in both a male and a female form (the Devil is only male). The portrayal of a philandering, cocaine-addled messiah, however, would call down upon the hapless filmmaker the wrath of the entire Christian nation, along with that of the Islamic community and probably most other religious communities in solidarity, likely subjecting the industry to congressional oversight, a fate it has staved off for the last seventy-five years. The major complaint about the most recent, big-budget Christ film was that Gibson was obsessed with the physical trials of Jesus to the point of there being too much gore, and perhaps some anti-Semitism, too. Despite the gore, James Caviezel's Jesus of Nazareth was suitably Christ-like in terms of public expectations: calm, pious, doubtful, though not overly-doubtful, white, and handsome. Gibson did have Caviezel's blue eyes digitized brown, however.

Fictional sources, too, sometimes carry with them a similar level of audience engagement that figures into the adaptation. An early example is Margaret Mitchell's *Gone With the Wind*. The novel was published in 1936, winning a Pulitzer Prize the following year. David O. Selznick bought the movie rights to the novel for $50,000, the largest such sum ever paid out at the time. According to the *Gone with the Wind* Web site,[13] the novel has sold more copies than any other publication, except, of course, the Bible. Regardless, it developed an early, almost rabid, following of fans, who parsed its every word. Daimler-Benz has restored the Margaret Mitchell House and Museum in Atlanta, a spacious abode, though Mitchell herself wrote the novel in a cramped one-room apartment. The museum sponsors lectures, adult and children's creative writing classes, tours, and other cultural events.

To be sure, the frenzied preproduction period was a symbiotic relationship between the filmmakers and the readership. Selznick stoked the publicity machine, while understanding the expectation that the movie was obliged to replicate the novel, or at least, as Jan Cronin argues, the novel of the public's imagination. According to Cronin, Selznick hired a number of consultants, experts on the South, (as if it were some sort of identifiable monolith), one of whom was Susan Myrick, writer and friend of the reclusive Margaret Mitchell. Myrick chronicled the making of the movie in columns published in several Georgia newspapers. As Cronin argues, Myrick "ultimately is privileging not the textual reality of *Gone With the Wind,* but the space the book occupies in the public consciousness."[14] Cronin cites Mitchell's lament about this audience-driven expectation for the book and the film, that "the mythical Old South has too strong a hold on their imaginations to be altered by the mere reading of a 1,037 page book."[15] For Cronin, the "notion of the mythology of the South as the sum of individual imaginings lies at the basis of the processes surrounding the translation of the novel to film."[16] Theorizing those "individual imaginings," however, is problematic at best. To begin with, the imaginings have to be shown to exist at all. Cronin does a remarkable job, making excellent use of primary sources (diaries, letters, contemporary newspaper columns, etc.) to establish exactly what she means by the term. Then the critic has to show that these imaginings did indeed influence the adaptation and, again, Cronin succeeds remarkably well. Her article is an example of the academic rigor Leitch calls for in the field. It is no exaggeration to claim that the novel's fan base shaped the adaptation, and any theorizing about adaptation studies needs to include a way to bring this sort of influence into the discussion. Developing theory that will help the critic account for such a nebulous aspect of the adaptation process, however, is another point of resistance.

More recently, available technology has increased the level of expectation for what certain precursor texts will look like, notably fantasy novels and graphic novels. *The Lord of the Rings* trilogy, written by J. R. R. Tolkien between 1937 and 1949 was published in the mid-1950s. In order to produce an authentic-looking, live-action film a half century later (2001, 2002, 2003), director Peter Jackson tapped well-

known Tolkien illustrators John Howe and Alan Lee to help craft the
look of the film, from Hobbit feet to the Shire, Ents, Orcs, and wraiths
(Lee took home an Oscar for art direction on the third of the films)
all realized through computer-generated effects. Similarly, the Harry
Potter series has been meticulously articulated on screen in such a way
as to satisfy the mostly youthful, though exacting, fans of the J. K.
Rowling books. More recently, Zack Snyder has adapted *300*, a
graphic novel by Frank Miller and Lynn Varley, almost entirely
through computer-generated images. Solaceincinema, a user at flickr-
.com, has posted a comic-to-screen slideshow comparison.[17] The
match is unmistakable. Trickier to reproduce will be *Teenage Mutant
Ninja Turtles* (TMNT), which started out as a comic book, written by
Peter Laird and Kevin Eastman, but which quickly morphed into
video games, an animated television series, and eventually a live-action
film (1990). The new TMNT film, however, is all CGI. According to
a *Washington Post* interview, this was something that concerned director Kevin Munroe: "As soon as people heard CGI, they thought it was
going to be 'Over the Hedge' with ninja turtles. I realized that was the
biggest thing we had to overcome."[18] To assuage concerns that the
crime-fighting quartet would be reduced to bumbling, cutesy, comic-
strip stature, "Munroe said he hopes the script he wrote will ease any
doubts harbored by hard-core turtle fans about the presentation."[19]
When graphic novels are adapted for the big screen, what gets
adapted? The "look," the "feel," the audience's nostalgia? How does
a theory of adaptation account not only for audience expectation, but
also account for an expectation that seems to differ from the author's
expressed intent? Given the apparent impact that audience expectation
has on a film, adaptation studies must find a way to account for this
particular locus of control, which, though not in the control of writer
or director, still shapes how they proceed.

At least the New Testament, or J. K. Rowling's books, or graphic
novels are identifiable texts. One can buy copies at the book store or
borrow them from friends even as one discusses the decentered nature
of the text. Adaptation theory, however, must also wrestle with precursor "texts" that are even more nebulous than books and graphic
novels. Betty Comden and Adolph Green are credited with writing an
original screenplay for *Singin' in the Rain* (1952); however, as Carol
Clover points out, "the plot was famously invented to accommodate
the pre-existing songs of Nacio Herb Brown and Arthur Freed."[20] In
one sense, then, the screenplay is original and yet there is a catalogue
of precursor texts that effectively shaped the narrative line taken by
the film. More recently, the most successful pirate movie in almost five
decades is based on a ride at Disneyland. Clearly, none of the anima-

tronics seen by millions of visitors to the Happiest Place on Earth have eye-liner painted on them nor are their movements programmed for something along the lines of swishing or perhaps sashaying. (At least this was true before the release of the movie.) And yet the ride, Pirates of the Caribbean, is a "text" that has a definite bearing on *Pirates of the Caribbean: The Curse of the Black Pearl* (2003). If items like *"zeitgeist"* and a theme park ride fall into the category of what's being adapted, theorizing as a project seems severely taxed. That audience expectation (even demand) is a critical factor in adaptation seems reasonable. Getting one's hands on it in an unambiguous, rigorous way, however, complete with citations and "textual" support, seems dicey at best.

WHO DOES THE ADAPTING?

Along with *what's* being adapted, a concomitant point of resistance to theorizing film adaptation studies is *who* does the adapting. The obvious answer, the one pressed by auteur theory, for example, is the director. And yet, referring back to the "complex weave of elements" described by Eagleton, there can be no one-to-one correspondence between the precursor text and resulting film; the trajectory is not that simple. Here again audience becomes part of the equation and yet is no more stable an entity than the text itself. Janet Staiger argues that "immanent meaning in a text is denied," along with "free readers." In place of these discarded notions, she offers "contexts of social formation and constructed identities of the self in relation to historical conditions" in order to "explain the interpretation strategies and affective responses of the readers." This means for Staiger, that "receptions need to be related to specific historical conditions as *events.*"[21] And those events involve, for instance, the space of the exhibition itself. Robert F. Arnold argues that "film spectatorship (not to be confused with the individual spectator) is subject to a general set of historically determined conditions that typify film viewing (i.e., projection in a theater space rather than other possible modes of exhibition such as the Kinetoscope), and that a historical analysis of these conditions is a necessary component of a theory of film reception."[22] According to Arnold, the "social interaction of stage and audience is gone," having been "replaced by a new function: consumption," which means that "the spectator's place is not his or her real seat in the cinema but inside the imaginary space of the screen, shifting with every cut."[23] Part of that event includes *where* a movie is screened, which generates a time-bound and/or culturally determined reception. *The Wizard of Oz* shown at The Castro Theatre in the heart of the San Francisco gay neighborhood, for example, is a decidedly queer event, with the audience responding to the gay icon-ness of Judy Garland, perhaps knowledge or even memory of the 1969 Stonewall Riots in New York City on the night of her death lingering somewhere in the background. It would be not unreasonable to assume that audience members at that theater had dressed up as any one of the characters, though probably Glinda. The lines that get laughs and the lines that get groans are specific to that collective audience in that theater in that city at that time. In a sense, then, the audience adapts a movie for itself, across time and experience, both individually and collectively. *Brokeback Mountain* (2005), for example, plays differently in Los Angeles, San Francisco, New York City, Omaha, Salt Lake City, and Ceres, California, former hotbed of Ku Klux Klan activity, if it shows there at all.

Ultimately, audiences respond to a performance, which is at the center of the experience. According to Leitch, "movies depend on prescribed, unalterable visual and verbal *performances* in a way literary texts don't."[24] These performances, then, are part of the adaptation process. Of course, casting also has a bearing on the previous question, "what's being adapted." As Stam and Raengo argue, "like the filmmakers, performers too become, in their way, the adapters and interpreters of the novel, or at least of the screenplay, as they mold characters through gestural details, ways of walking or talking or smoking."[25] The trailers for the film version of Lillian Hellman's *The Little Foxes* (1941) announce, "The First Lady of the Screen"; cut to a close-up of Bette Davis, as Regina Giddens, in a hat with a veil and only her name on the title card. She dominates most of the shots in the preview and her name ends the trailer as well, which never mentions the character's name. The fact of Bette Davis-ness is an important part of the movie version of the play. Bette Davis does more than simply perform the role. She is Bette Davis while she performs, hence the emphasis in the trailer. No matter how Hellman wrote the part of Regina Giddens for the film version, it was still Bette Davis *as* Regina Giddens.

Just as films are performative in ways that printed source materials are not, films have a soundtrack, which print does not. Characters like Regina Giddens are not only embodied, they are voiced. When the voice is distinctive, like Davis's, that quality becomes a part of the adaptation. Bette Davis, her star quality and her renown along with her clipped intonation, wrist slinging gestures, and style all sell the picture and determine its tone and feel. The question, then, is how to account for those qualities, distinct from the actor's performance, yet no less an aspect of the resulting film.

In addition to audience reception and actor performance (and, of course, director, screenplay writer, etc.) a number of other factors shape the movie adaptation. As Thomas Schatz argues, "if recent studies of classical Hollywood have taught us anything, it is that we cannot consider either the filmmaking process or films themselves in isolation from their economic, technological, and industrial context."[26] Jack Warner made the decision to cast Audrey Hepburn instead of Julie Andrews in *My Fair Lady* solely on the basis of marketability. By the time she played Eliza Doolittle, Hepburn had already starred in such films as *The Children's Hour, Breakfast at Tiffany's* (both 1961), *Funny Face* (1957), *Sabrina* (1954) and *Roman Holiday* (1953), for which she won an Oscar for Best Actress. She had been directed by the likes of Billy Wilder and John Huston and played opposite leading men like Fred Astaire, Humphrey Bogart, and Mel Ferrer, and, even though she could not sing a note, she could still sell a musical film better than Andrews, known principally in London and New York

Directors, screenplay writers, and performers are all known (or at least credited). A more shadowy, though still powerful factor in film adaptation, is less easy to locate. Film adaptation studies has a tendency to discuss censorship almost exclusively in terms of blaming the Production Code for bowdlerizing works of art, which almost always means removing references to sex. Just about anything having to do with sex was right out under the Code. In the play version of *The Little Foxes*, 20-year old Leo has a mistress in Mobile, Alabama. His father Oscar has no particular objection, but only if Leo manages the affair properly: "You're young and I haven't got no objections to outside women. That is, I haven't got no objections so long as they don't interfere with serious things. Outside women are all right in their place, but *now* isn't their place. You got to realize that."[27] Of course, the Hays Office does have objections to even the mention of "outside women," and even more so that a father might instruct his young son on the timing of such affairs. This speech never appears in the movie. In fact, Leo is presented as rather dull and stupid. In the play, he is brutal as well as libidinous.

In addition to the sex, the overt racism in the play has been apparently wiped clean from the movie. The Code, too, is responsible for this "whitewashing," so to speak. The Hays Office was as determined to present a racially united America as it was to present a sexually chaste America, and both were equally unrealistic. For example, in the play, Ben describes the accoutrements of the Old South to the wealthy Northern industrialist, Mr. Marshall: "They had the best of everything. Cloth from Paris, trips to Europe, horses you can't raise anymore, niggers to lift their fingers."[28] He tells Marshall that

Southerners take pride in their work, promising, "That's every bit as true for the nigger picking cotton for a silver quarter, as it is for you and me."[29] Regina finds no comfort in the comfortably middle-class, as she tells her sister-in-law, Birdie: "I said I think you should either be a nigger or a millionaire. In between, like us, what for?"[30] Horace Giddens proposes to leave money to Addie, a black servant. She abjures, "Don't you do that, Mr. Horace. A nigger woman in a white man's will! I'd never get it nohow."[31] The "n-word" is used casually in the play as part of standard Southern-speak, used by white and black characters alike. This language is absolutely forbidden by the Code because it was considered inflammatory, not because it was demeaning. This push for an imagined unity shaped the ways in which Hellman and Wyler could bring the play to the screen even *before* filming began.

The Code is more relaxed now, replaced by a ratings system. But censorship is not dead. Movies rated NC-17 and X are frequently not advertised in daily newspapers, and Blockbuster, for example, refuses to carry them. Directors, then, must get that "R" rating for a film to be commercially viable. That X-rating seems to loom largest when the issue at hand is sex, while violence in Hollywood films seems more tolerable, attested to by Gibson's *The Passion of the Christ*. Film reviewer Roger Ebert said flatly: "This is the most violent movie I have ever seen." He even adds a note at the end of the review: "The MPAA's R rating is definitive proof that the organization either will never give the NC-17 rating for violence alone, or was intimidated by the subject matter. If it had been anyone other than Jesus up on that cross, I have a feeling that NC-17 would have been automatic."[32] Ebert's comment illustrates that censorship is a semi-permeable membrane: some items never penetrate the barrier, while others slip right on through. There are likely a number of properties that will simply never be made in the first place due to censorship concerns, at least not by Hollywood. According to Vito Russo, Samuel Goldwyn wanted to make a movie out of *The Well of Loneliness*. Russo reports that Goldwyn was "informed by a producer that he could not because the leading character was a lesbian. 'So what?' Goldwyn retorted. 'We'll make her an American.'"[33] If the ratings system shapes the movies that are made and, perhaps, prevents certain movies from even being attempted, then that level of control must somehow be accounted for in a theory or theories of adaptation.

FIDELITY

The facets of adaptation discussed up to this point—texts, reception, audience expectation, performance, leads who sing, leads who do

not sing, censorship, etc.—all provide fertile ground for the comparison that lies at the heart of adaptation studies. After all, why discuss
two texts unless it is to examine the differences between those texts?
Perhaps the greatest point of resistance to theory resides in fidelity,
which is also, maybe, the greatest source of pleasure, too. Lately,
though, the usual outcome of such a comparison, "the movie is not
like the book and clearly the book is better," has been jettisoned as
a legitimate critical point. Stuart McDougal insists that "any ideal of
complete fidelity to a source should be dismissed."[34] Thus, Stam and
Raengo rightly comment that the "ideal of a single, definitive, faithful
adaptation does not hold sway in other media,"[35] such as theater for
example, which tolerates the modernization of even Shakespeare's
plays. So common is this call for the rejection of fidelity in adaptation
studies, that Helena Goscilo, for one, is tired of it: "Proponents and
detractors alike keep this threadbare issue [fidelity] alive, despite its
manifest irrelevance to some of the screen's best recreations of literary
works."[36] Despite such calls for an end to fidelity as a legitimate touchstone for critical discussion of an adaptation, fidelity lingers on, perhaps at times on life-support, but it never goes away entirely.

    Given its persistence, and that comparisons seem irresistible when
discussing two texts, film adaptation studies as a whole must examine
why the fidelity issue recurs and then theorize a way to account for
this impulse to not just compare, but to prefer one "text" over the
other. As Leitch argues, "there is no reason why an adaptation's nominal source text should not provide one of many potentially illuminat-
ing frames for its interpretation; the fallacy lies in assuming that it
provides privileged criteria for its success."[37] Motive for the compari-
son-to-prove-superiority strategy, too, has been interrogated. Leitch,
Stam, McDougal, and a host of others have chronicled the way in
which Bluestone, et al. have used film adaptations as a means to solid-
ify the importance of the novel, to teach an aspect of the novel, to
denigrate film as a medium, etc.

    Such fidelity-driven evaluations fail in other ways, as well. John Paul
Athanasourelis, in his discussion of the relationship between Hollywood and Raymond Chandler's novels, points out how censorship
sapped the vitality of Chandler's vigorous narratives. For Athanasourelis, "Chandler resisted the idea that any one set of moral rules
could apply to all people; his position, both in his fiction and in commentary, was that differing, even conflicting, systems of ethics could
and must coexist."[38] The bowdlerization occurs when the movies
made by Hollywood out of Chandler's novels "are consciously constructed so as to depict a black-and-white moral universe and to pla-
cate civic and religious groups who dictated this sanitized and

simplified world-view to studio owners."[39] The result of this comparison is ahistorical as it seems to blame "Hollywood" as an entity for the debasement of Chandler's work. The Code did produce sanitized movies, and yet skillful filmmakers still made movies that challenge that status quo (*Citizen Kane*, 1941), that explore justice and the law (*The Oxbow Incident*, 1943), that generate sexual tension (*The Postman Always Rings Twice*, 1946, or anything with Lana Turner in it), that generate dramatic tension (*The Treasure of the Sierra Madre*, 1948). More productive than blaming "Hollywood" is to ask why studios would want to make movies based on Chandler's novels knowing before the cameras even roll that the best parts of those stories could never be put onto celluloid?

In addition to privileging novels and lending itself to ahistorical criticism, comparisons that rely on fidelity as an evaluative point also seem limited to certain precursor texts. Some sources, usually novels, apparently count more than others. This preference ties into the criticism of fidelity issues as partly a product of the academy. As James Naremore points out, "a great many film programs in the academy are attached to literature departments, where the theme of adaptation is often used as a way of teaching celebrated literature by another means."[40] Naremore points to *Mrs. Dalloway* (1998) as an example. Authors that claim critical attention are Austen, Shakespeare, Lawrence, Hemingway, Fitzgerald, the Brontës, Saroyan, Hawthorne, and others regularly found on literature survey syllabi.

In addition to authors who receive attention when their texts are adapted to film, a certain class of remake comes in for particular scrutiny: American remakes of French films. Examples include *À bout de souffle* (1960)/*Breathless* (1983), *La Cage aux folles* (1978)/*The Birdcage* (1996), *La Femme Nikita* (1990)/*Point of No Return* (1993) and the TV series, *La Femme Nikita* (1997–2001) among many, many others. In fact, Carolyn A. Durham in *Double Takes: Culture and Gender in French Films and Their American Remakes*, laments that "Hollywood's passion for remaking French films seems, if anything to be growing. Indeed it is somewhat discouraging to realize that the American film industry can apparently produce remakes faster than I, at least, and perhaps any single individual, can hope to analyze them."[41] The focus on American remakes of French films seems to have less to do with some intrinsic quality of either set of films as it does with a long-running feud between the two countries. Laura Grindstaff makes this point explicitly in explaining her choice of films to study:

> My main focus will be the circuit of exchange between France and the US, not because the Hong Kong versions [of *La Femme Nikita*] are any less

interesting or any less worthy of analysis, but because France and the US stand in a particular historical relation to one another regarding the matter of original and copy. This relationship looms large in the condemnation of Hollywood remakes by certain French critics who see in Hollywood's appropriation of foreign films not only economic exploitation and cultural imperialism but confirmation of the United States's derivative cultural status. [42]

Bemoaning Hollywood's gross exploitation of the French culture seems disingenuous, since the French moviemakers are not obliged to sell the rights to their films and given that they, too, profit from the arrangement. Still, this apparent feud drives the selection of films to study, not which ones are "worthy of analysis." And so the whole complaint may be an academic's version of Freedom Fries.

While almost all films are adaptations of a sort, not all adaptations are discussed in those terms. Classroom discussions of *Gentlemen Prefer Blondes* (1953) most likely do not linger over the Anita Loos collection of stories, *Gentlemen Prefer Blondes: The Intimate Diary of a Professional Lady* (1925). *The Wizard of Oz* (1930) is an adaptation of a long, complicated novel, one in a series of more than a dozen long, complicated, rather fantastical novels set in Oz, with titles like *The Scarecrow of Oz* and *Rinkitink in Oz*. A very important difference between the novel, *Dorothy and the Wizard of Oz*, and the well-known film version with Judy Garland is that there is a place better than home. In the book, Oz is a *much* better place to live than Kansas, which is boring and dreary, and everyone works too hard. Dorothy does go home, but only long enough to collect her family and friends. Everyone heads straight back to Oz where they are very happy. Certainly there is plenty of material to fuel study of *The Wizard of Oz* as an adaptation as it moves from novel (1900) to silent film (1925, Baum receives co-credit for writing) to film musical (1939) to stage musical (*The Wiz*, 1975), to film musical (*The Wiz*, 1978) back to novel (*Wicked: The Life and Times of the Wicked Witch of the West* by Gregory Maguire, 1996) to stage musical (*Wicked*, 2003—can the film version be far behind?). Implicit in the selection of which adaptations to study and which adaptations are not discussed in those terms reveals the need to theorize why some adaptations are studied as adaptations and some films are not, even when they also have a literary precursor.

What Does Theory Do?

Attempting to establish a theory of film adaptation studies begs one important question: What does theory do? The academy has privileged theory to the point of orthodoxy, but why do we need theory? This is not merely a rhetorical question. Understanding what critics hope to get out of theory will drive its formation. In the sciences, theory is predictive. In the early 1930s, for example, theoretical physicist Wolfgang Pauli was able to postulate the existence of a particle called the neutrino based on theories of how matter functions, though the technology to detect neutrinos would not be developed for another quarter century. Theories in economics predict and explain the ups and downs of money flow, patterns of savings and spending, and whether The Fed will adjust interest rates yet again. A theory argues for a certain understanding of how the matter at hand works, whether that matter is anti-matter, money, or consumer habits. In the humanities, that means understanding how the (ever-so-problematized) text functions in the way that it does. When theory serves critical thought well, it defines the scope of the project itself. Theory also limns the project, acknowledging that which cannot be seen through a particular lens, knowing there will always be outliers on the edges of any system of thought.

In addition to making an argument, theory also promotes an ideology, perhaps easiest to see in debunked approaches, such as the Great Man/Great Events approach to history. A Great Man was always white, some variety of Protestant (with the occasional Catholic allowed in), straight, middle-class, educated, etc. Great Events, comprising the canon of history, were wars, elections, and general exercises in the public realm of power. Those groups of people and types of events marginalized by such a take on history are now obvious, and much important work has been done to recover those histories and bring them to the fore. Theories about culture are no less ideological. Paul Schrader's theoretical position privileges aesthetics, for example. For this reason he can make the following argument about *Triumph of the Will* (1935): "most everyone would agree it's evil, but that's beside the point."[43] On the other hand, Janet Staiger's theoretical position does not hand canonized filmmakers a get-out-of-jail-free card: "Griffith's films may be claimed to transcend their time and place and to indicate a personal and coherent vision, but their racist, misogynist, and reactionary vision can be neatly eliminated from the discussion when historical, social, gender, and political effects are removed from the agenda."[44] Scientific theory, too, is limited by what it is willing to see. Feminist criticism points out the politics, for example, of women's biology as it is practiced—pathologizing menses, birth, sexuality, and concluding that a woman's smaller brain size results in diminished capacity. It is important to note that the Great Man approach to history was so entrenched in the academy that it was thought neutral, just as science presents itself as neutral. All theories, though, bear out an ideology. The best critics can do is practice a rigorous intentional fallacy on themselves, questioning motive, examining strategies, above all acknowledging limits so that theory does not turn into dogma.

What are the possibilities for film adaptation studies theory? Baetens suggests that "the starting point of a reflection on the relations between film and literature today should be the observation that the strict separation between these domains has been corroded."[45] This means that "the focus is no longer on the work but the relations obtaining between different works."[46] Leitch advocates for a kind of synthesis, "that might well be called Textual Studies—a discipline incorporating adaptation study, cinema studies in general, and literary studies."[47] Naremore proposes a similar tack: "I would suggest that what we need instead is a broader definition of adaptation and a sociology that takes into account the commercial apparatus, the audience, and the academic culture industry." He wants to "move the discussion of adaptation slightly away from the Great-Novels-Into-Great-Films theme," paying more attention to "economic, cultural, and political issues."[48] According to Naremore, adaptation studies as a field "needs to be joined with the study of recycling, remaking, and every other form of retelling in the age of mechanical reproduction and electronic communication. By this means, adaptation study will move from the margins to the center of contemporary media studies."[49] Jim Collins, et al., hope that *Film Theory Goes to the Movies* advocates a new emphasis, "on how films *work*, not according to some abstract set of principles, but rather in response to the divergent exigencies that arise when industry, audience, and aesthetic practice are all defined by their relative fragmentation, dispersion, and heterogeneity."[50] What these and other models have in common is that the boundaries of the project are vast. There is simply no way to account for all of the factors all of the time. Werner Heisenberg's uncertainty principle (1927) asserts that the act of observation changes that which is being observed. A scientist can observe the velocity of a particle, but by doing so loses the ability to fix its position. Similarly, once the particle's position is fixed, its velocity cannot be determined. Adapting Heisenberg's principle to adaptation studies means recognizing that any given study "fixes" the position of two (often swirling, nebulous) texts, thereby losing the ability to account for other, no less important factors.

My argument, finally, is that a grand unifying theory for adaptation studies is not, in fact, possible; the sheer volume of everything involved in a discussion of film adaptation is virtually immeasurable, which means that no one single theory has the capacity to encompass

every aspect of an adaptation. This is not to discourage the act of theorizing. Done well, it keeps the critic honest. Despite all the difficulties
presented by the idea of the texts involved, the core of adaptation studies lies in a comparison of texts. This comparison seems to promote a
longing for fidelity that must be recognized and understood as part of
the pleasure of consuming the adaptation. Rather than simply reject-
ing fidelity altogether, an approach likely to yield insights (assuming
that this is the critical enterprise), would be to ask what that comparison reveals? What can we learn from what Baetens calls "the ruptures
every adaptation necessarily supposes"[51] Pamela Demory's article on
Heart of Darkness and *Apocalypse Now Redux* suggests that "readings
change because readers change, are influenced by other texts, by history, by experience. *Heart of Darkness* today is in some ways not the
same text as *Heart of Darkness* twenty or fifty or one-hundred years
ago. By studying changing interpretations of *Heart of Darkness* we can
begin to chart our developing cultural understanding of the imperial
process."[52] Understanding that process, however, is possible as well
with a single text; no need for two. However, the intertextual apparatus of adaptation studies lends itself well to the complexities of colonial politics. As Demory argues, "*Apocalypse Now Redux*, especially if
read intertextually with *Heart of Darkness*, can thus be read as yet another chapter in the ongoing story of the dangers of wielding 'imperial
mastery and will' in foreign countries, and this as one of the cultural
documents [Edward] Said argues we ought to understand in order to
achieve 'a harmonious world order.' "[53] Similarly, Jan Cronin uses the
paratexts surrounding the making of, publicity for, and premier of
Gone With the Wind to argue "that Mitchell's novel, the film, and the
production of the film were conscripted into one apparently seamless
cultural narrative."[54]

Though Demory and Cronin make powerful arguments for their
various points and demonstrate the capacity of adaptation studies to
illuminate difficult topics, neither article is able to "describe the multiplicity of meanings that movies generate,"[55] nor should they try to.
Criticism, no matter the theory, fixes the text(s) in that moment for
examination. Not exactly pinning the butterfly to the board, but still
unable to account for all things all of the time. Since comparison lies
at the very heart of the field, the best question film adaptation studies
can ask itself is, "What can we learn *through* a comparison that cannot
be learned via a single text?" Critics then choose from a candy store
of available approaches: semiotics, feminist criticism, Russian Formalism, media studies—the whole menu. The resistance to theory does
not have to define the field. Instead the vastness of the boundaries proposed by Leitch and others can lead to a plurality of theories being

pressed into the service of examining a particular point of the intersection between two texts, in all their glorious plurality. This is no small feat, and articles such as those by Demory and Cronin reveal not only the theoretical rigor called for by Leitch, but the dazzling possibilities as well.

NOTES

1. Christa Albrecht-Crane and Dennis Cutchins, introduction to *Film Adaptation Theory*, ed. Christa Albrecht-Crane and Dennis Cutchins, 11.

2. Thomas Leitch, "Twelve Fallacies in Contemporary Adaptation Theory," *Criticism* 45, no. 2 (Spring 2003): 150.

3. Ibid., 149.

4. Terry Eagleton, "Jacques Derrida," *New Statesman* 14 (July 2003): 31.

5. Leitch, "Twelve Fallacies," 150.

6. "Winner Original Screenplay," *Academy of Motion Pictures Arts and Sciences*, 2008, http://www.oscars.org/79academyawards/winners/24_original_screenplay.html.

7. Robert Stam and Alessandra Raengo, *Literature and Film: A Guide to the Theory and Practice of Film Adaptation* (Malden, MA: Blackwell, 2005), 45.

8. Constantine Verevis, *Film Remakes* (Edinburgh: Edinburgh University Press, 2006), 1.

9. Thomas Leitch, "Everything You Always Wanted to Know About Adaptation Especially if You're Looking Forward Rather Than Back," *Literature Film Quarterly* 33, no. 3 (2005): 233.

10. Leitch, "Twelve Fallacies," 165.

11. Richard Maltby, "*The King of Kings* and the Czar of All the Rushes: The Propriety of the Christ Story," in *Controlling Hollywood: Censorship and Regulation in the Studio Era*, ed. Matthew Bernstein (New Brunswick, NJ: Rutgers University Press, 1999), 62.

12. Ibid., 63.

13. "The Story Behind *Gone With the Wind*," *Gone With the Wind*, 2008, http://gwtw.org/gonewiththewind.html.

14. Jan Cronin, "'The Book Belongs to All of Us': *Gone With the Wind* as Postcultural Product," *Literature Film Quarterly* 35, no. 1 (2007): 398.

15. Ibid., 396.

16. Ibid., 398.

17. Solaceincinema, "300 comic to screen comparison," posting on *flickr.com* http://www.flickr.com/photos/solaceincinema/sets/72157594312246529/detail/.

18. David Betancourt, "One Fan's Chance to Get Turtles Back in Fighting Form," *Washington Post*, Mar. 23, 2007, http://www.washingtonpost.com/wp-dyn/content/article/2007/03/22/AR2007032200568.html.

19. Ibid.

20. Carol J. Clover, "Dancin' in the Rain," *Critical Inquiry* 21, no. 4 (Summer 1995): 724.

21. Janet Staiger, "Taboos and Totems: Cultural Meanings of *The Silence of the Lambs*" in *Film Theory Goes to the Movies*, ed. Jim Collins, Hilary Radner, and Ava Preacher Collins (New York: Routledge, 1993), 143.

22. Robert F. Arnold, "Film Space/?Audience Space: Notes Toward a Theory of Spectatorship," *Velvet Light Trap* 25 (Spring 1990): 44.

23. Ibid., 51.

24. Leitch, "Twelve Fallacies," 154.

25. Stam and Raengo, *Literature and Film*, 22.

26. Thomas Schatz, "The New Hollywood" in *Film Theory Goes to the Movies*, ed. Jim Collins, Hilary Radner, and Ava Preacher Collins (New York: Routledge, 1993), 10.

27. Lillian Hellman, "The Little Foxes," *The Collected Plays: Lillian Hellman* (Boston, MA: Little, Brown, 1972), 158.

28. Ibid., 140.

29. Ibid., 141.

30. Ibid., 143.

31. Ibid., 184.

32. Roger Ebert, review of *The Passion of the Christ*, directed by Mel Gibson, *rogerebert.com*, Feb. 24, 2004, http://rogerebert.suntimes.com/apps/pbcs.dll/article?AID =/20040224/REVIEWS/402240301/1023.

33. Vito Russo, *The Celluloid Closet: Homosexuality in the Movies*, rev. ed. (New York: Harper & Row, 1987), 62.

34. Stuart Y. McDougal, *Made Into Movies: From Literature to Film* (New York: Holt, Rinehart, & Winston, 1985), 6.

35. Stam and Raengo, *Literature and Film*, 15.

36. Helena Goscilo, "Moving Images, Imagination, and Eye-deologies," *Russian Studies in Literature* 40, no. 2 (Spring 2004): 7.

37. Leitch, "Everything," 244.

38. John Paul Athanasourelis, "Film Adaptation and the Censors: 1940s Hollywood and Raymond Chandler," *Studies in the Novel* 35, no. 3 (Fall 2003): 327.

39. Ibid.

40. James Naremore, "Introduction: Film and the Reign of Adaptation" in *Film Adaptation*, ed. James Naremore (New Brunswick, NJ: Rutgers University Press, 2000), 1.

41. Carolyn A. Durham, *Double Takes: Culture and Gender in French Films and Their American Remakes*, (Hanover, NH: University Press of New England, 1998), 175.

42. Laura Grindstaff, "A Pygmalion Tale Retold: Remaking *La Femme Nikita*," *Camera Obscura* 16 no. 47 (May 2001): 135.

43. Paul Schrader, "Canon Fodder," *Film Comment* 42, no. 5 (2006): 46.

44. Janet Staiger, "The Politics of Film Canons." *Cinema Journal* 24, no. 3 (Spring 1985): 13.

45. Jan Baetens, "Novelization, A Contaminated Genre?" trans. Pieter Verrmeulen, *Critical Inquiry* 32, no. 1 (Fall 2005): 56.

46. Ibid.

47. Leitch, "Twelve Fallacies," 168.

48. Naremore, "Introduction," 10.

49. Ibid., 15.

50. Jim Collins, Hilary Radner, and Ava Preacher Collins, introduction to *Film Theory Goes to the Movies*, ed. Jim Collins, Hilary Radner, and Ava Preacher Collins (New York: Routledge, 1993), 5.

51. Baetens, "Novelization," 50.

52. Pamela Demory, "Apocalypse Now Redux: *Heart of Darkness* Moves into New Territory," *Literature Film Quarterly* 35, no. 1 (2007): 342.

53. Ibid., 349.

54. Cronin, " 'Book Belongs," 398.

55. Collins, Radner, and Collins, *Film Theory*, 2.

Turning Japanese: Translation, Adaptation, and the Ethics of Trans-National Exchange

Mark O'Thomas

Everyone around me is a total stranger
Everyone avoids me like a cyclone ranger
That's why I'm turning Japanese
I think I'm turning Japanese
I really think so . . .

—The Vapors, "Turning Japanese"

TURNING JAPANESE

IT'S 1980 AND IN "TURNING JAPANESE" THE POST-PUNK, NEW WAVE group *The Vapors* are singing about the isolation and pain of being in love, of being made to feel so culturally *different* that the singer's gaze becomes refracted into a myopic view of the world around him—a direct allusion to the physiogical narrowness (in comparative terms) of Japanese eyes. Some fans have claimed the song is about masturbation inside prison, others have made a bid for its latent homosexuality ("I have to kiss you when there's no-one else around") but whatever the impetus for "turning Japanese" back in 1980, the orientalist Vaporised *other* remained but a short hop from social exclusion albeit brought on by infatuation. Fast forward twenty-three years and Bill Murray and Scarlett Johansson are *Lost in Translation* in a shiny new twenty-first-century Japan, where Japan inevitably means Tokyo and Tokyo translates into a swanky hotel. Despite Murray and Johansson being the strangers in a strange land, the film portrays the Japanese locale as essentially foreign and quirkily different—the toilets are made for ridiculously small people, the Japanese eat bizarre food, talk odd and just don't *get* how funny Bill Murray really is. Thank God Bill and Scarlett find each other. Thank God for hotels, not sites of international exchange, but virtual drop-in centers of national mutual validation. Where "Turning Japanese" references a marginal other by stopping in the name of love, *Lost in Translation* references a majority other by positioning its ultimate *otherness* in relation to the comfort and kind-

46

ness shared by two American strangers. Cultural difference is something that both sets us apart and brings us together—it defines who we are in relation to who we are not. Thus what better place for lovers to be thrown together than in the discordant, glary maelstrom of otherness found in a culturally dystopian Tokyo where the East is all but a backdrop to a pantomime. The East of *Lost in Translation* is just as it was at the turn of the twentieth century in the theatrical fanciful follies of Oscar Asche and his long-running orientalist musical extravaganza *Chu Chin Chow*.

LOST IN TRANSLATION

Cultural difference has long been a central concern of translators whose bread and butter work is the business of striving to find sameness where none really exists. Ethically charged with the duty of importing a writer or director's work into a new cultural domain, translators are virtual gatekeepers in cross-national traffic. But their social, political, and cultural decisions remain concealed within the newly constructed target text. Fidelity to an original is the modus operandi for any translator whose mainstream mission remains to provide pathways into another culture through the soft landing of a domesticated textual whole. This "fidelity" is one based on a notion of equivalence, that two languages and cultures have direct correlations with each other—that *sayonara* simply means "goodbye" and what falls by the wayside, gets "lost" in the translation just as in the Murray/Johansson film what falls by the wayside is far greater than what is retained in any kind of cross-cultural understanding. Adaptation, like translation, similarly shares concerns of fidelity to an original text where the metalanguage of adaptation criticism has inevitably revolved around questions of "loyalty" and "betrayal." Here anteriority rules supreme—if you said it first, it's got to be better than someone else trying to say it later, and differently, because all they are really trying to do, after all, is say it again. From *Pride and Prejudice* (it's always Jane Austen in adaptation studies) to *Fight Club*, first is always best. However, recent poststructuralist turns in both translation and adaptation studies have begun to problematize the practice of both domestication in translation and fidelity in adaptation[2] where the work of Venuti (1998), Stam (2005), Stam and Raengo (2005), Leitch (2005) and others have sought to promote the role of the translator and adapter beyond its service provider/copier/second-hand understudy reputation to the elevated status of a creative artist in its own right.[3] But while adaptation studies has essentially concentrated on content in its cam-

paign against fidelity as an outmoded and ultimately conservative concept, within translation studies Venuti, in adopting a stance advocating
a translation strategy based on foreignizing, in some senses argues for
a practice of rewriting that foregrounds a fidelity of form. In this essay,
in considering the ethics of engaging in transnational adaptations with
particular reference to Western adaptations of Eastern sources and
vice versa, I will focus my discussion on both film and theatrical adaptations where the translative and intercultural practices of the latter
will be explored in order to contextualize and critique to some extent
those of the former. During this essay, the emphasis will not be so
much on what gets lost in translation, but on the challenges and po-
tentiality for artistic and dialogic engagement between cultures.

Adaptation Across Cultures

Most adaptations take place across *media* rather than cultures—
literature into film, diary extract into stage play, etc.—where the medium specificity of each particular form has historically played a
significant part and has been instrumental in its theoretical analysis.
While adaptations may be generated from a range of different media,
one adaptation mode has dominated academic study—something that
corresponds closely to its prominent position in economic terms
within a global cultural marketplace. The transformation of literature
into film, then, in terms of both its process and product, underlies an
unspoken definition of "adaptation" for many scholars working in the
field. George Bluestone's often invoked comment that "the end products of novel and film represent different aesthetic genera, as different
from each other as ballet is from architecture"[4] represents in itself a
reflection of the assumed primacy of cinematic adaptations of fiction,
that this mode of adaptation is privileged above and beyond all others.
In viewing adaptation as a cross-cultural process, however, the importance of considering different typologies, where the "translation" of
literature into film may form just one element of many, becomes clear.

Embracing translation theory's distinction between source and target language (a distinction that itself connects with the domestication/
foreignization binary), it might be possible to begin to engage with
adaptation in a way that promotes a kind of cultural ethics as well as
the particular specificity of each medium.

Adaptation, viewed in terms of target and source culture as well as
target and source text, can be classified into three broad groups (see
fig. 1). The first are those adaptations that do cross media but are
monocultural, such as Rob Marshall's film adaptation of the stage mu-

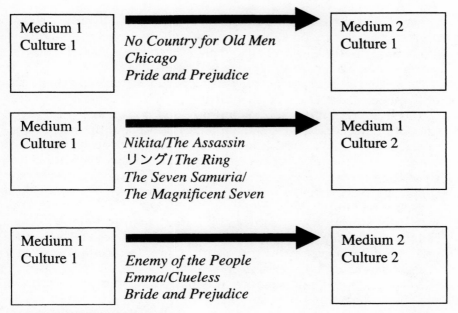

Adaptation: Text and Culture

sical *Chicago*. The adaptation remains firmly within its source culture and the rewriting that takes place is inevitably structured around fitting the narrative into its new medium.

The second grouping of adaptations are those that do not cross media but do cross culture (for example, NBC's remake of BBC Television's *The Office* or Hong Kong Cinema's *Infernal Affairs* in its United States incarnation *The Departed*). Here even when there is a high degree of equivalence between the original and target texts (to use the metalanguage of translation theory), the transfer process results in a range of cultural changes. Thirdly, there are those adaptations that cross both medium and culture, such as the multifarious stage adaptations of Ibsen's *An Enemy of the People* or Amy Heckerling's (far from) *Clueless* film adaptation of Jane Austen's *Emma*. In ethical terms, adaptations in the first category may well wish to jettison fidelity as an aim, based on what is now widely acknowledged as ill-founded assumptions about originality and medium specificity.

However, it is in the last two categories—where changes of culture take place—that the poststructuralist anti-fidelity project runs into trouble as, in seeking to justify the rewriting of anterior texts from other cultures just as it does for all adaptations, charges of colonialism or what Venuti has called "ethnocentric violence" to the original abound.[5] It seems too convenient to assume that all texts, be they source or target, are on an equal socio-economic footing, wherein in a relativistic postmodern world simply everything is available for rewriting, remaking, reinterpretation and renewal.

Although this is invariably schematic, what this form of categorization makes transparent is the intricate web of crossing cultures through different modes of cultural production. It seeks to highlight the political as well as the methodological aspects of the transformational process and has the potential to be developed further as a tool for analyzing the impact of such modes. Of course, adaptation like translation necessitates a degree of colonialism.[6] No text can ever be a simple norm-free copy of another, as Venuti concedes: "Not only does a translation constitute an interpretation of the foreign text, varying with different cultural situations at different historical moments, but canons of accuracy are articulated and applied in the domestic culture and therefore are basically ethnocentric, no matter how seemingly faithful, no matter how linguistically correct."[7]

Adaptations that cross cultures, too, inevitably offer interpretations of those cultures, but it is in the making of qualitative value judgements about those adaptations—how *good* they are as works—that a professional ethics enters the arena. Venuti, like Berman,[8] approaches ethical issues in translation through Schleiermacher's differentiating principle between domestication and foreignization in translation[9] where a domesticating translation drags the source culture to the target culture by eradicating as much of its original source as possible and making the rewritten text sound as natural as it can in its new language. Foreignization, however, seeks to do the opposite—the new text is positioned within the target language as one that indicates its source through perhaps the otherness of its lexical structuring, or even the anti-canonical choice of the text in the first place. For adaptation, as Robert Stam has noted, the cross-national enterprise is a form of *reaccentuation* where "a source work is reinterpreted through new grids and discourses,"[10] but the question of the power relations between source and target culture within those grids Stam neither defines nor explores. In talking of an ethics of cross-national adaptation, the ideological and historical relations between cultures cannot be simply ignored or factored out. It is not just a question of upholding an ethical base to fidelity where the original must be kept intact as far as possible in the adapted new work. What is needed is an ideological interrogation of the process and product that forges adaptations that eradicate the cultural integrity of the original in a narratological mission of crash and burn. And it goes deeper than just nationhood. Gender too can be seen as a loser in the cross-cultural transfer process where the whims of a culture's predilection for certain gendered practices can bear influence over an adaptation or translation in a censorious manner.[11]

The postcolonial theorist Tejaswini Niranjana has explored such power relations within translation practice, noting the existence of a clear hierarchy between source and target. Seeing this relationship in terms of colonised/colonizer, translation (and by inference cross-national adaptation) can be seen to serve hegemonic versions of the colonized, in Said's terms "objects without history."[12] Niranjana, then, like Venuti, favors a translation approach that seeks to be a site for resistance and transformation, where translation is an ideological act both of and for itself. Examples of such work within postcolonial literature are not in short supply,[13] but within the wider realms of adaptation it is theatre rather than film that appears in the vanguard of utilizing adaptation as a means of resistance. It was the French Canadian theater practitioner Robert Lepage who first coined the phrase "tradaptation" as a means of describing the annexing of old texts to new cultural meanings where the intentionality is not to censor or make palatable the original for the target culture but in a sense to force the target culture to confront itself through its exposure to the rewritten 'original.'"[14] Productions like the British Asian theatre company Tara Arts's reworking of a range of classic texts present real examples of this mode in practice where for example Sophocles's *Oedipus Rex* is "tradapted" into a tragic story of an immigrant's hubris. Might the capacity of a cross-cultural or trans-national adaptation to situate itself through these oppositional ways be one approach to making an ethical value judgement about its true worth? By foregrounding both its relation to its own culture as well as the culture and text of the original, the adaptation could provide a new, foreignized voice that speaks in a language other than, but paradoxically of, its own.

Adaptations that cross cultures inevitably deal with an *other*, whether their intention is to foreignize, domesticate, or annihilate. Ethics is itself no stranger to alterity. Indeed the French philosopher Emmanuel Levinas in his rejection of both philosophy and ontology created a new kind of ethics, an ethics beyond morality which placed alterity central to his analysis of ethical thinking where "the glimpse of the beyond as something sublime and elevating happens in the traumatic encounter with the Other."[15] Adaptation, then, might serve as a location for a meeting point between cultures—what theater practitioner and performance theorist Patrice Pavis has called a "crossroads," forming a dynamic base for cultures to engage in a benign process of exchange and transfer.[16]

Adaptations in Theater: West Looks East

Looking East, trans-national theater and film adaptations have developed in different ways and it is worth considering why and how such developments have taken place. The twentieth century saw an increased fascination on the part of European theater practitioners with the East. As Brecht looked to China and its theatrical traditions, the French theater director and theorist Antonin Artaud became fascinated with the dance theater of Bali—a fascination that informed his work and manifestos for the rest of his career.[17] These practitioners were the precursors to the intercultural performance training techniques of Jerzy Grotowski and Eugenio Barba, who developed a whole philosophy of actor training based on a kind of universalism in its syncretic approaches to thinking about the body[18] as a vessel for performance. This in turn informed the practices of theater directors like Peter Brook and his International Centre for Theatre Research in Paris. While Brook's adaptations of Eastern classics like *The Mahabharata* have endured some criticism,[19] their intention to thoroughly integrate different performance disciplines towards an end of creating a truly intercultural performance cannot be dismissed. Brook's choices of adaptation are wide-ranging and global—they do not represent a move to cull the texts of different cultures, but rather demonstrate a spirit of engagement with those texts in a variety of performative and syncretic ways. This "spirit" is in marked contrast to many of the Western cinematic adaptations of works from the East where concerns for any kind of syncretic universalism are few and far between.

Adaptations in Theater: East Looks West

For Antonin Artaud, the East offered the potential to call into question the very practice of theater itself and the opportunity to radically produce new dramatic forms. However, theater practice in the East at this time was far from being in a state of stasis, and had its own transnational encounters to confront and negotiate. In China, before the onset of the Cultural Revolution (1966–1976), a theatrical reform movement emerged which was charged with the idea of replacing traditional Chinese modes of performance with Western-inspired spoken forms.[20] In Japan, the Shing-geki movement of the early twentieth century was expressly focused on a modernization project of traditional theater where modernization inevitably meant Westernization as a range of plays were introduced by playwrights such as Chekhov and Ibsen.[21] However, jettisoning the tradition in favor of the foreign

proved to be a temporary reaction where ultimately, the kind of intercultural meeting points and process-driven practices of European the-
ater-makers such as Grotowski, Barba, and Brook were mirrored in
Japan by groups like the "Little Theatre Movements" which emerged
in the 1960s. Here a range of Western plays were adapted through a
use of traditional acting forms which were not simply rejected out of
a need for Westernised modernization, but explored within a contemporary Japanese context. In this sense, the practices of key Eastern and
Western theater practitioners moved away from a strategy of explicit
foreignization to one of partial domestication—a move towards the establishment of a bi-cultural syncretic underpinning to the work. Here
the very act of performance is a form of transcultural adaptation where
actors' bodies are themselves sites of Pavis's "crossroads of culture."[22]
Butoh remains as but one example of a whole theater/dance form—a
hybrid—that has emerged over the last forty years in direct response
to an intercultural meeting point between Western and Eastern forms.

ADAPTATIONS IN FILM: EAST LOOKS WEST

Film adaptations across cultures, and in particular from East to
West and West to East, proliferate, and in a globalized, technology-
driven world it is film rather than theater that has the greatest psychological, geographical and ideological reach. However, within cinematic adaptation, the story of cultures initially championing each
other and then moving towards a kind of synergetic resolution
through adaptation is not so well defined. With Oscar-winning adaptations like Martin Scorsese's *The Departed* (2006), the enormous box
office potential of rewritten classics from the Hong Kong cinema's
back catalogue is clear. Let us begin, however, by looking at film adaptation of Western sources in the East. Zhang Zhen's survey of an early
(1931) Chinese adaptation of Shakespeare's *The Two Gentlemen of Ve-
rona*[23] shows that trans-national film adaptations in the East got off
to a promising start. Zhang argues for the notion of "cosmopolitan
projections" as a model for looking at cinema that adapts across national boundaries—the creation of a virtual space in which "the original and the adaptation coexist with tension."[24] These projected acts do
not just "translate" from one culture in terms of another they also create a "surplus of meaning" that can never be subsumed: "Adaptations
of Western literature by non-Western filmmakers run the risk of mimetic identification yet also may seize opportunities to "reflect" on
that mimetic act and appropriate the source material by mobilizing the
aesthetic and expressive possibilities of cinema."[25] Zhang's proposition

of a Western adaptation seizing opportunities for reflection on the nature of its source comes close to Venuti's foreignizing proposition for
ethical translation, but how far does the reality come near to this optimistic view? Film theorist Brian David Phillips sees the Taiwanese film
Seven Wolves (1989) as a kind of composite adaptation of a number of
Western films, namely *The Goodbye Girl* (1977), *Flashdance* (1983), and
Streets of Fire (1984). Here the use of these sources is acknowledged
through a certain knowingness: a more than cursory nod and wink to
a knowing audience, who can recognize the intertexts as filmic quotations. Invoking literary theorist Harold Bloom's notion of "the anxiety
of influence" experienced by "strong poets" (i.e. those writers deserving of aesthetic value who suffer a concern that their new "original"
works might be tainted unwittingly by previous works they have read),
Phillips finds that a high degree of referencing of the source texts
within the film is matched with obliviousness where ". . . the Chinese
filmmaker seems to be either indifferent to his sources or experiencing
an anxiety for influence—he seems more willing for his audience to
know that he is imitating his precursors."[26] This kind of syncretism
can be seen to directly correspond to the intercultural practices of European theater makers cited above, so that Phillips's assertion that "a
tendency in Chinese society . . . to imitate directly from the West and
in the very imitative process to transform what is being imitated and
make it Chinese"[27] might take a more postmodern turn that reflects
back and questions both its sources and itself. Such a turn would bring
into play an ethical dimension to the adaptation in the sense that its
otherness is neither ignored nor wholly appropriated.[28]

Japanese cinema, too, has experienced its own adaptations of Western film, theater and literature, not least from the renowned filmmaker Akira Kurosawa, who has adapted *Macbeth* and *King Lear* from
Shakespeare and the Ed McBain American crime novel *King's Ransom*
(remade as *High and Low*). Kurosawa's adaptations are not founded on
principles of Westernization. Like Chu Yen-P'ing—the director of
Seven Wolves—his approach is rather to take aspects of the original and
blend certain elements into Japanese narratives and typographies. *Ran*,
for example, can be seen as a Japanese *response* to *King Lear* in its exchanging of the three sisters for three brothers, and its forging of the
Lear protagonist to the legend of the medieval warlord Moori Moto-
nari. His downfall is inevitably linked to his failed relationship as a
father to his sons where the film's stark visual imagery shows the personal turmoil literally projected on a national landscape. What is interesting and significant about these Eastern adaptations of Western
films is their ability to domesticate through a direct response to the
source work or works. Unlike the early twentieth century stage adap-

tations of Western plays, which sought to replicate Western acting styles and essentially naturalistic approaches to performance, these cinematic adaptations engage in a form of dialogism with their original works in new and interesting ways. In *Ran*, Kuwosara draws on a traditional Japanese style of acting known as *Noh* theater for two of his principle characters—Hidetora and Lady Kaede—where by mixing naturalism with tradition he demonstrates an ability to hone a new domestic meaning from an engagement with both foreign and home sources in a carnivalesque act of reformation, revelation, and resurrection.

Lastly, of course, the growing interest of Bollywood in adapting Western cinema for its home market cannot be ignored. Sitting in the second category of the adaptation/culture typology cited above, Bollywood continues to appropriate Hollywood in new and interesting ways. Christopher McQuarrie's landmark thriller *The Usual Suspects* (1995) tells a story of murder and intrigue when a group of crooks are arrested on suspicion of murder in San Pedro, California. Translocated to a snowy London on Christmas Eve, Vivik Agnihotri's *Chocolate* (2005) sees a gang of Asian men arrested following a jinxed heist that produced dead bodies rather than hard cash. Taking on aspects of post-9-11 Islamophobia, the adaptation forces viewers to question their own motives around apportioning guilt. Because London is located literally between India and the United States, it provides something more than just a geographical location, giving the original new life and new meanings in a "subsequent performance"[29] (to use Jonathan Miller's phrase) that allows the original to live on, to "adapt" in its biological sense, to its new cultural environment.

ADAPTATIONS IN FILM: WEST LOOKS EAST

Western cinematic adaptations of Eastern sources have largely occurred within the same form, i.e. from film to film where these "remakes" literally re-make the source within a new cultural framework. One of the most successful of these has been the horror movie *Ring* series,[30] which deals with a number of mysterious deaths related to the viewing of a video tape. Although the original film was in fact an adaptation of a Japanese novel, the American version is very much an adaptation of the Japanese film—an adaptation of an adaptation. Accepting that while it is not particularly appropriate to study adaptation through the mantle of loss and betrayal—an invidious exercise of compare and contrast—what is significant about the adaptation of *The Ring*, as it changes culture and moves from Tokyo to Seattle, is that it is amazingly (and ironically) so faithful to the source text. Fidelity and domestication, then, are not opposite ends of a binary scale, but can collude and collide in an act of cultural appropriation.

Moving from the horror genre to romantic comedy, *Shall We Dance?* (1996) was a popular box office success in Japan. It explored how the shy yet disciplined psyche of a happily married yet spiritually lonely man discovers the sheer joy of being alive through secretly taking after-work ballroom dancing lessons. The film might seem to pose problems for adaptation since the self-reflexive questioning of Japanese national character appears so endemic to its narrative drive and characterisation. The invoking of the otherness of the seaside northern United Kingdom town of Blackpool (of all places) where the annual championships are held as a kind of spiritual nirvana for the dancers, too, helps situate its own otherness even in the micro-world of ballroom dancing. However, with Richard Gere in the lead role in the United States adaptation, no problem is insurmountable, and the film is remade as Tokyo becomes Chicago. Even the opening voice-over of the film is retained, but rather than describing the potential conflict between ballroom dancing and Japanese shyness it is simply rewritten in the United States adaptation as a description of the history of ballroom dancing. The original themes of shyness, the need for a public respectability and the ridicule of ballroom dancers who keep their practices firmly in the closet are domesticated into the standard wholesome tale of an American family that almost crumbles until the husband realizes what he might lose—it's *Brief Encounter* meets *Stepping Out*.

What is evident from these West/East adaptations is that unlike either of their theatrical or their East/West counterparts, they are irretrievably ethnocentric. The original culture is there to provide a narratological template for the target culture to map onto—as if the meandering roads of Jakarta, say, might become New York if the city were razed to the ground and a replica New York City built in its place. It might still be Jakarta but it would always feel like New York. This is not to say that all Western cinematic adaptations of other cultures are fundamentally ethnocentric in a way that neither theatrical adaptations of Eastern works nor adaptations in the East of the West appear to be. American cinema is not a fixed medium and causes of optimism can be found in surprising places.

ETHICS AND ADAPTATION

In dealing with an ethics of trans-national adaptation, it is important to move away from notions of "sameness," despite the irrefutable dialectic between identity and what is "identical."[31] Emmanuel Lévinas, whose work went on to influence Derrida, moves ontology firmly into the realm of ethics with his preoccupation not with the ontological totality of being, but with what lies beyond this—the alterior, difference as opposed to sameness. The encounter with the other, then, is not about replication, mirroring, seeing yourself in the face of another, but

> A calling into question of the Same . . . which cannot occur within the egoistic spontaneity of the Same . . . is brought about by the Other. We name this calling into question of my spontaneity by the presence of the Other ethics. The strangeness of the Other, his irreducibility to the I, to my thoughts and my possessions, is precisely accomplished as a calling into question of my spontaneity as ethics. Metaphysics, transcendence, the welcoming of the Other by the Same, of the Other by Me, is concretely produced as the calling into question of the Same by the Other, that is, as the ethics that accomplishes the critical essence of knowledge.[32]

I began this essay by referring to a film, *Lost In Translation*, that is not an adaptation, but whose very title suggests a pessimistic encounter with the East and whose relationship and view of the other might well be considered in Said's terms orientalist. Another popular film which has been tagged with the same charge is the Quentin Tarantino saga *Kill Bill Volumes 1* and *2*. No stranger to adaptation (the films follow *Jackie Brown*, adapted from *Rum Punch* by Elmore Leonard), Tarantino's *Kill Bill* series can in some senses be viewed as adaptations, or at the very least palimpsestian uber-texts. These texts revisit a host of genres, characters and—in the case of the character Bill, played by David Carradine—even carry a physical intertext where the actor's presence is itself is a signifier of orientalism.[33] Treating the *Kill Bill* films as trans-national adaptations through our ethical frame offers up some interesting and surprising conclusions.

The *Kill Bill* films tell a story of revenge where "the Bride" sets out to hunt down and kill a group of people who themselves attempted to kill her (and her unborn child) during her wedding rehearsal. The group on her hit list are all either former or current assassins who have been trained in martial arts and are led by one man who is last on her list: Bill. The film flaunts its intertextual references in abundance, and chief among these are the Hong Kong action movies of the 1970s.[34] Far from faithfully reproducing these references in an American context by simply replicating narratives, the Other is referenced in a range of ways. The iconic yellow jump suit worn by the motorcycle-riding Bride is a two-piece adaptation of the suit worn by Bruce Lee in *Game of Death* (1973). Subtitles abound in this film where a foreign language is not seen as an impediment to a dumbed-down audience's understanding. Rather than mimic the poor dubbing that was used among such films in the 70s, Tarantino's Bride, and many of the other American characters in the film, speak fluent Japanese. Moreover, just as European directors like Almodóvar have taken the risk of implanting long sequences in their films, in radically anti-Aristotelian fashion, that take the plot into completely different genre[35]—a virtual film within a film—*Kill Bill's* Tarantino goes manga and takes an eight-minute sidebar into the Japanese cartoon genre in order to elucidate the back story of the half-Chinese half-Japanese American assassin O-Ren Ishii. These are all clear attempts at articulating a relationship with the foreign within a domestic frame, where the encounter with the East is both dialogic and coherent, intertextual and trashy. In Tarantino's world, turning Japanese is not about huddling together as a celebration of "me too" in a dystopian world of exotic craziness (*Lost in Translation*) or sticking masking tape on his Caucasian actors' eyes to give them a quizzical expression of confusion (as in the *Turning Japanese* music video); it's actually a site of cultural dialogue, albeit through the lens of the action movie genre.

These non-adaptations—*Lost In Translation* and *Turning Japanese*—demonstrate how the study of adaptation can be a convenient and useful trope for looking at cultural meeting points as well as an important ethical marker. In terms of a wider ethics of adaptation, Venuti's assertion for translation, that such an enterprise lies not simply in the choices made during the process (of translating), but in the choice of what to actually translate in the first place, is wholly appropriate to adaptation. Zhen Zhang's argument that Chinese cinema is now looking towards adapting work from the minority literatures of the Third World[36] suggests that globalization may be an aid to trans-national adaptation which need not necessarily produce texts that marginalize or consume the other, but might seek new, dialogic relations between texts. In this sense, translation and adaptation are allied pursuits which can lead rather than follow in an ethically framed artistic practice of rewriting across countries, continents, and cultures.

NOTES

1. The Vapors, "Turning Japanese," United Artists BP-334, and © 1980.

2. There is an irony here. An argument made for a foreignized rather than domesticated approach to translation is that it is more faithful to the original by reflecting its foreign-ness. See Lawrence Venuti, *The Scandals of Translation: Towards an Ethics of Difference*, London and New York: Routledge, 1998.

3. Robert Stam, *Literature through Film: Realism, Magic, and the Art of Adaptation*, (Malden, MA: Blackwell, 2005); Thomas Leitch, "Everything You Always Wanted to Know About Adaptation Especially If You're Looking Forward Rather Than Back," *Literature Film Quarterly* 33, no. 3 (2005): 233–45

4. George Bluestone, *Novels into Film* (Berkeley: University of California Press, 1961), 5.

5. Lawrence Venuti, *The Translator's Invisibility: A History of Translation* (London and New York: Routledge, 1995), 61.

6. See, for example, Susan Bassnett and Harish Trivedi, "Of Colonies, Cannibals and Vernaculars," in *Post-Colonial Translation: Theory and Practice*, ed. S. Bassnett and H. Trivedi (London: Routledge, 1999), 1–18.

7. Lawrence Venuti, *The Scandals of Translation: Towards an Ethics of Difference* (London and New York: Routledge, 1998), 82.

8. Antoine Berman, *Pour une critique des traductions: John Donne* (Paris: Gallimard, 1995).

9. Friedrich Schleiermacher, "On the Different Methods of Translating," in *Theories of Translation: An Anthology of Essays from Dryden to Derrida*, ed. John Biguenet and Rainer Schulte (1812; repr., Chicago: University of Chicago Press, 1992), 36–54.

10. Robert Stam and Alessandra Raengo, ed., *Literature and Film: A Guide to the Theory and Practice of Film Adaptation* (Malden, MA: Blackwell, 2005), 45.

11. Homosexuality, for example, was airbrushed out of Robert Graves's translation of Suetonius's *Twelve Caesars* (Venuti, *The Translator's Invisibility*) because of the sensibilities of the time.

12. Tejaswini Niranjana, *Siting Translation: History, Post-Structuralism, and the Colonial Context* (Berkeley: University of California Press, 1992), 3.

13. Else Ribeiro Pires Vieira, "A Postmodern Translational Aesthetics in Brazil," in *Translation Studies: An Interdiscipline*, ed. M. Snell-Hornby, F. Pöchhacker, and K. Kaindl (Amsterdam: John Benjamins, 1994), 65–72. See, for example, Vieira's work on an approach to translating poetry that privileges form over content by the Brazilian concrete poets Haroldo and Augusto de Campos. Here translation constitutes a cannibalistic act of reappropriation where there is an "acceptance of foreign nourishment but a denial of imitation and influence in the traditional sense."

14. Interview with Robert LePage, *The Guardian*, October 5, 1994. LePage refers to tradaptation as the means by which sources are forged onto and into new cultural contexts.

15. Fred Botting and Scott Wilson, "By Accident: The Tarantinian Ethics," *Theory, Culture & Society* 15, no. 2 (1998): 93.

16. Patrice Pavis, *Theatre at the Crossroads of Culture* (London: Routledge, 1992).

17. Russian acting gurus Michael Chekhov and Vsevolod Meyerhold were similarly enthralled by the theatre of the East and attempted to embed what they saw into their own theories of acting and performance.

18. It is interesting to note that while Grotowski proposes an idea of the actor's body as having an absolute presence which defies difference for the Levinas-inspired French philosopher Jacques Derrida, the play of difference is all there is.

19. See Rustom Bharucha, *Theatre and the World: Performance and the Politics of Culture* (London: Routledge, 1993); Rustom Bharucha, *Politics of Cultural Practice: Thinking Through Theatre in an Age of Globalization* (London: Athlone, 2000).

20. Yu Weijie, "Topicality and Typicality. The Acceptance of Shakespeare in China," in *The Dramatic Touch of Difference: Theatre, Own, and Foreign*, ed. E. Fischer-Lichte, M. Gissenwehrer, and J. Riley (Tübingen: G. Narr, 1990), 161–67.

21. Erika Fischer-Lichte, "Intercultural Aspects in Post-Modern Theatre: A Japa-

nese Version of Chekhov's *Three Sisters*," *The Play out of Context: Transferring Plays from Culture to Culture*, ed. H. Scolnicov and P. Holland (Cambridge: Cambridge University Press, 1989), 173–85.

22. Pavis, *Theatre at the Crossroads*.

23. Zhen Zhang, "Cosmopolitan Projections: World Literature on Chinese Screens," in *A Companion to Literature and Film*, ed. Robert Stam and Alessandra Raengo (Malden, MA: Blackwell, 2004), 144–62.

24. Ibid, 146.

25. Ibid., 147.

26. Brian David Phillips, "Cross-Cultural Appropriation: Seven Wolves and its American Sources (Levels of Imitation in Popular Chinese Cinema)," *The Journal of Popular Culture* 27, no. 4 (1994): 207.

27. Ibid., 197.

28. Popular Bollywood adaptations of Hollywood blockbusters such as *The Usual Suspects* and *Fatal Attraction* openly flaunt their appropriation of and their instrumental relation to their respective sources in this way.

29. Jonathan Miller, *Subsequent Performances* (New York: E. Sifton Books/Viking, 1986), 23.

30. *The Ring*, DVD, directed by Gore Verbinski (Universal City, CA: Dreamworks, 1998) and *The Ring 2*, DVD, directed by Hideo Nakata (Universal City, CA: Dreamworks, 2005).

31. Paul Ricoeur, *Oneself as Another* (Chicago: University of Chicago Press, 1992), 113–39.

32. Emmanuel Levinas, *Totality and Infinity; an Essay on Exteriority* (Pittsburgh, PA: Duquesne University Press, 1969), 33.

33. David Carradine starred in the hit television series *Kung Fu*, which explored the life of an American-Chinese Shaolin monk who was trained in martial arts.

34. Yuen Woo-Ping even used the fight choreographer in the movie.

35. *Hable Con Ella*, DVD, directed by Pedro Almodóvar (El Deseo S.A., 2002).

36. Zhang, "Cosmopolitan Projections," 161.

The Ethics of Infidelity
Thomas Leitch

SUPPOSE YOU DECIDE, AGAINST ALL ADVICE, TO HAVE ANOTHER crack at filming *Lolita*. In addition to all the problems facing the adapter of any literary work to the screen—the need to locate the holders of the adaptation rights and agree on a price, to raise funding for the rights and indeed the rest of the production, to agree how big Vladimir Nabokov's name should be on the credits compared to yours as screenwriter or director or producer—you face a host of other problems, many of them with specifically ethical dimensions. What sorts of people will you approach to get funding for a new film version of a story about a middle-aged émigré professor partial to pre-adolescent schoolgirls who first makes love and then falls in love with his own stepdaughter, and how will you pitch the project to your potential backers? Once you've secured funding, how will you advertise the film to entice the largest possible audience every investor will be seeking in order to maximize the return on their good-faith investments? Should you aim for an R rather than an NC-17? How can you attract the target audience of 12-to-21-year-old boys without which your project will languish as a mere niche film? How old an actress will you cast in the title role—a character who is twelve in Nabokov's novel—and how much do you really want to cast the sort of young women who are likely to audition, presumably with the support of their families? Since you're very likely to be casting someone underage, someone who won't even be able to see the completed film without her parents, what exactly are you going to tell her about the story, and what will you ask her to do in the movie? Will she be allowed shorter working hours because of her age, and if those hours require a more extended filming schedule, how will you justify the additional budget for sound recordists and electricians to your backers? How will you treat your underage star while she's on the set, and how closely will you monitor her relationships with the other performers who may well be offscreen lotharios—especially the actor playing Humbert Humbert, who's going to be playing her onscreen lover? If your Lolita's mother wants to be on the set throughout filming, how will you handle her request? Since the film will carry obvious commercial risks, how completely will you want to insulate your backers from those risks by handling both the filming and the publicity in a way that curries favor with moral avatars like Michael Medved and the Catholic Church? If you try to maximize your potential audience by minimizing any suggestion of onscreen sex, how will you deal with the backlash that's bound to come from the sizable audience that came to see the film specifically because of its promise of sex with a consenting child? How will you open and tour the film, and what sort of preparation and supervision will you want to give your lead actress when she appears on Letterman and *Good Morning America?*

Luckily, you won't have to answer most of these questions on your own. For better or worse, you'll have help at every step of the way from your lead actress, her parents, your releasing studio's publicity department, the Screen Writers' Guild, and the Nabokov estate. Even though you'll be making many of these decisions in consultation with other collaborators, or indeed, in deference to them, however, that collaboration merely spreads the ethical burden around; it doesn't make the questions any less ethical. The road to any new adaptation of *Lolita* is paved with ethical dilemmas.

But of course not one of these questions, urgent though they would be in any attempt to remake *Lolita,* is treated as significant in contemporary adaptation studies, which reserve their ethical solicitude for exactly one question: Is the movie faithful to the book? An enduring but unexamined question in adaptation studies is why students of adaptation with a soft spot for ethical behavior ignore the problems that arise from dealing with backers, studios, stars, technicians, publicists, and stage mothers to focus their attention on exactly one party, the author of the original property, the one party to the whole transaction who has been contractually compensated in advance without having to put in any unforeseen additional work, whose reputation is least likely to be damaged and whose person least likely to be insulted by anything that happens in the course of the shoot or its attendant publicity, and who may well share with Nabokov the additional luxury of having been removed from the whole sphere of worldly cares by merciful death years before the film ever goes into production. Why does adaptation study insist on treating the adaptation's relationship to its source text as an ethical issue while overlooking so many more deserving subjects for ethical concern?

It might be tempting to answer this question by arguing that an adaptation's ethical concern for the original author is actually a concern for the adaptation's prospective audience. And indeed the argument has often been made in exactly these terms. When David O. Selznick memorably reacted to Alfred Hitchcock's free-wheeling first treatment of their most famous collaboration with the withering response, "We bought *Rebecca*, and we intend to make *Rebecca*," he continued: "The few million people who have read the book and who worship it would very properly attack us violently for the desecrations which are indicated by the treatment."[1] But in fact there's no record of any such attacks greeting the release of the 3-D feature *Black Lolita* (1975) or indeed of *Lolita 2000* (1997), *French Lolita* (1998), *Emanuele e Lolita* (1991), *Toccata y fuga de Lolita* (1974), *Itazura Lolita: Ushirokara virgin* (1986), or any of the television docudramas about Amy Fisher, the Long Island Lolita.[2] The strongest generalization along these lines that seems prudent is that fidelity in adaptation is more important to some filmgoers than others. Indeed, a whole fugitive genre of softcore exploitation films—*Lady Godiva Meets Tom Jones* (1968), *The Amorous Adventures of Don Quixote and Sancho Panza* (1976), *Lady Chatterley's Lover* (1981), and so on—has thrived on the promise of a narrowly circumscribed notion of fidelity to their originals with no sign of complaint from a target audience with a higher tolerance than Selznick for free adaptations.

Why, after all, should filmmakers make such a fetish of following their originals as closely as Selznick when many prospective viewers of the films have never read the books in the first place? Granted, the example of soft-core pornography's relation to whatever source a given video's title may evoke is so extreme in its invitation to licentiousness that it might seem merely an exception to the well-established rule of fidelity. But the argument for hard-core fidelity itself is just as extreme in the other direction. If the audience in question has already read the novel or story or seen the play on which the film is based, surely they expect a different experience; otherwise, they would not be watching the movie at all. And if they have not already read or seen the source text, they are in no position to evaluate any claim to fidelity.

One might well argue that if the film is going to serve as a substitute for the book—a kind of SparkNotes for a school-age audience that could never make it through the book itself—then it must be faithful in order to insure that they pass their Monday morning quizzes. But I'm not aware that anyone apart from disgruntled students has ever advanced such an argument. Fidelity in adapting bestsellers like *Rebecca* and *Harry Potter and the Sorcerer's Stone*, or cult classics like *Lord of the Rings*, is a goal pursued for very different reasons than fidelity in adapting forgotten novels like *Build My Gallows High* or the kind of unread classics like *Crime and Punishment* most likely to turn up on course syllabi because only bestsellers or cult classics are likely to bring out cinema audiences both large enough and devoted enough to the source text to threaten serious economic damage in the form of boycotts or badmouthing. Absent such an audience, it's hard to see why filmmakers shouldn't feel free to do whatever they like with their source material.

But Selznick has another argument in reserve: "I have never been able to understand why motion-picture people insist upon throwing away something of proven appeal to substitute things of their own creation. It is a form of ego which has very properly drawn upon Hollywood the wrath of the world for many years."[3] Here the sin is not against author or audience but against one's own decorum; it is a sin of hubris, a usurpation not so much of the author's function as of the author's prerogatives, committed by filmmakers who mistakenly think themselves authors. This time, however, Selznick is more frank in his pragmatic response to Hitchcock's proposed transgression. Addressing one of the biggest egos in the history of cinema, he acknowledges: "I have my own ego and I don't mind letting my own creative instincts run wild either on an original, as in the case of *A Star Is Born*, or in the adaptation of an unsuccessful work, as in *Made for Each Other*. But my ego is not so great that it cannot be held in check for the adaptation of a successful work."[4] So Selznick's ego is freed from any taint of hubris as long as it's not competing with the author's. Although Selznick contends that it is the success of an original property that determines the amount of license permitted an adapter, it would be more accurate to substitute the term *prestige* for *success*, since *A Star Is Born*, the film that allowed Selznick's own creative instincts to run wild, was in fact an unacknowledged remake of *What Price Hollywood?* (1932). Nor does Selznick follow the silent producer Thomas Ince in insisting that the film be faithful to its screenplay, even though, as William Horne has noted in a survey of several directors like Renoir, Casavettes, and Godard whose work may seem to have only a tenuous relation to their screenplays, "even many of those films which renounce conventional narrative structure make profound use of a prior written text."[5] The resulting formula, shorn of Selznick's ethically charged rhetoric of "properly" and "desecrations," would prescribe fidelity to a source only when fidelity is likely to be a selling point in order to presell a particular adaptation by association with a commercially successful property or to claim a culturally ennobling mission for a film industry threatened by calls for censorship, as Hollywood studio heads evidently felt around 1907 and again around 1934—in either case, a commercial calculation without any particular ethical dimension at all.

It might seem that given Selznick's consistent eye on the dollar, he earned no right to use such ethically charged language in talking about adaptation. But not only is his language an unremarkable example of the discourse of adaptation; it is positively prophetic in its ethical force. Ever since George Bluestone dismissed as hopelessly naïve such judgments as "The film is true to the spirit of the book,"[6] that discourse has been organized around the dualities of artistic fidelity and artistic license. Even Brian McFarlane's *Novel to Film* (1996), which ruefully notes that "[d]iscussion of adaptation has been bedeviled by the fidelity issue,"[7] never gets beyond that touchstone itself; he simply attacks it like a scientist instead of a moralist. The persistence of fidelity as a benchmark for adaptations is doubly remarkable in view of the fact that adaptation theorists, the longtime custodians of that benchmark, have none of the financial interests in the process of filmmaking that made Selznick so protective of the author's prerogatives and prestige. Unlike Selznick, they have no need to balance their solicitude for the author against their concern for the care and feeding of screenwriters, directors, stars, backers, and audiences. Yet until very recently the primary question with which most film scholars approached the adaptations they studied was how faithful they were to their source texts.

Adaptation scholars have uncritically adopted Selznick's ethical rhetoric without any of his underlying fiduciary concerns for several reasons, none of them uplifting. One is their reverence for literature as such, a quasi-ethical countercurrent to the anti-literary, anti-aesthetic, anti-ethical tenor that has prevailed in academic film studies from its beginnings. Another is the essentially middlebrow view of artistic creation they inherit from Selznick, in which adapters are allowed to change features of their source texts only if they improve them, and a canonical or bestselling imprimatur inhibits free adaptation by guaranteeing in advance that no improvement is possible. The academic study of adaptation continues to be driven by such a depressingly middlebrow view of cultural currency, which allows only one creator per project and dismisses other claimants as either the creators of so much raw material, in the case of Shakespeare's source texts, or servile imitators, as in Robert Benton's film *The Human Stain* (2003), which couldn't possibly be very good, because Philip Roth's novel, in the zero-sum thinking typical of film reviewers, had already used up all the goodness allotted the property. Of all the curious signs of ethical concern that remain lodged in the academic discourse on adaptation, however, the most curious of all is the very choice of *faithful* and *fidelity* as its foundational terms.

Apart from adaptations, the main things that have been enjoined historically in specifically ethical terms to be faithful are husbands and

wives, either because a woman's adultery betrays her husband's pecu-
niary investment in her under the Mosaic law, or because both spouses
have a duty to re-enact Christ's faithfulness to the church in an analogy expounded in Paul's Letter to the Ephesians.[8] Yet because "con-
tracts *create* transgressions," as Tony Tanner argued thirty years ago,
the possibility of adultery, arousing both the condemnation of a heroine like Emma Bovary who violates the marriage contract and an em-
pathetic understanding of her avid reaction against the stifling bonds
of marriage, provides both a basis for the bourgeois novel, which incorporates "a tension between law and sympathy," and the seeds of its
dissolution.[9] "As the contract between man and wife loses its sense of
necessity and binding power," Tanner observes, "so does the contract
between novelist and reader."[10] Yet the possibility of adultery, so
threatening to both the fabric of bourgeois society and the novel, is
also productive because it "effectively 'renarrativizes' a life that has
become devoid of story"[11] and provokes the development of new kinds
of novels—*Madame Bovary, The Golden Bowl, Ulysses, Lady Chatterley's
Lover*—that are not simply iterations of the old. In the same way, adaptation depends on infidelity not merely in a negative sense, as the
failure to adhere to a pledge of fealty, but in a positive sense, as a response to an injunction to be fruitful and multiply untrammeled by
repressive social laws and mores.

The terminology traditionally used for the relationship between adaptations and their sources replicates this tension between negative
and positive judgments with surprising precision. Film adaptations
like *Lord of the Rings* are routinely described as faithful or unfaithful,
stage adaptations like Shakespeare's *Comedy of Errors*, to reverse the
polarities, as either free, creative, and imaginative or plodding, literal,
and servile. But it is surprisingly difficult to find descriptions of the
relationship between adaptations and their sources that are free from
both sorts of value judgments. Either adaptations have a responsibility
to stick as close as possible to their sources, it seems, or they have an
equally strong responsibility to strike out on their own.

This symmetry between these two poles is more apparent than real,
for the ethical imperatives of adaptation, whenever they have been articulated, have all been on the side of fidelity (that is, of mere transcription or servile imitation). However nice it may be to be creative,
adaptations never have an ethical imperative to do anything new with
their source texts. Their ethical responsibilities are all toward the original texts, or to the authors or fans of those texts, with whom they are
presumably joined until death or a more faithful remake do them part.
The main reason for this asymmetry is that the discourse of mimetic
art that descends from Plato and Aristotle comes with a heavy charge

of ethics built in. The discourse of art as a creative or imaginative endeavor, by contrast, stems from a Romantic aesthetic not notable for
any ethical emphasis, despite Shelley's assertion in "A Defence of
Poetry" that "[t]he great secret of morals is love. . . . A man, to be
greatly good, must imagine intensely and comprehensively; he must
put himself in the place of another and of many others; the pains and
pleasures of his species must become his own. The great instrument
of moral good is the imagination; and poetry administers to the effect
by acting upon the cause."[12]

It may well be impossible to recast adaptation studies in a way that
severs its ties to ethically charged language. The goal of this essay is
more modest: to encourage a more judicious balance between negative
and positive assessments of infidelity by looking in closer detail at two
cases that considerably complicate the assumption that fidelity is ethically superior to infidelity.

According to its credits, Robert Shaye's time-travel fantasy *The Last
Mimzy* (2007) is based on a screenplay by Bruce Joel Rubin and Toby
Emmerich, which is based on a story by James V. Hart and Carol Skil-
ken, which is based in turn on "Mimsy Were the Borogoves," a short
story by Lewis Padgett, the pseudonym of husband-and-wife science-
fiction writers Henry Kuttner and C. L. Moore. When the film's release prompted a resurgence of interest in the story, which had been
posted on Wikipedia, one of Moore's heirs requested that it be removed from the site and, writing as yarner58, protested on the imdb
.com message board that "it is stealing" to download the story from
the site instead of purchasing one of the collections in which it appears.[13] Yarner58's position, which for obvious reasons resembles Selznick's, is that filmmakers who purchase adaptation rights to particular
properties are purchasing, for example, the right to change specific elements in those properties. *The Last Mimzy*, for example, changes the
names of the children who find the box of toys sent by a scientist far
in the future, so that Scott and Emma Paradine become Noah and
Emma Wilder. In the film, the futuristic sender is no longer merely
testing his time machine; he is now appealing for an uncorrupted
DNA sample that will save his civilization. Finally, the film changes
the tone of the story's ending. "Mimsy Were the Borogoves" ends
with Scott and Emma mastering, or being mastered by, the patterns
of thought encoded in the toys and leaving their family to vanish into
an uncertain distant future. Shaye's film, by contrast, moves toward a
conventional happy ending through a heartwarming climax: the moment when Noah and Emma, after undergoing a similar pattern of
subliminal re-education, return the box with a tear that contains the
precious DNA sample.[14]

Perhaps, as Selznick claims, the right to make changes to the literary property does not give filmmakers the right to change absolutely any feature. But the primary emphasis of yarner58's remarks falls elsewhere, on the reasonable claim that acquiring an appetite for reading the source text does not give moviegoers a right to free access to that text, and on the implicit claim that whetting such an appetite as a precondition to selling access to its satisfaction is a legitimate function of film adaptations. In other words, yarner58 prizes *The Last Mimzy* both because it renews an appetite for "Mimsy Were the Borogoves" and because its necessary departures from the story make it incapable of satisfying that appetite. Its very infidelity is the basis of its appeal as a marketing device, and readers seeking to short-circuit that marketing effort by reading the story, now available in *The Last Mimzy: And Other Stories Originally Published as The Best of Henry Kuttner*, without paying Padgett's estate a second time are engaged in immoral behavior. Indeed the very retitling of the story and the collection in which it appears show that the copyright holder and publisher of the story seeking to maximize its exposure to potentially interested purchasers have no ethical responsibility even to keep it textually faithful to itself; the ethical responsibilities in question are all those of the audience.

The ethical questions raised by this adaptation are complicated still further by a consideration of another intertextual relation indicated by the titles of the story and the film, which both allude to the third line of "Jabberwocky," the nonsense poem Alice, that prototypical explorer of other worlds, reads in the opening chapter of *Through the Looking-Glass* (1872). No one would call *The Last Mimzy* an adaptation of *Through the Looking-Glass*, or even of "Jabberwocky." Instead, the film borrows a central premise of "Mimsy Were the Borogoves": that the apparent nonsense of Carroll's poem conceals a sense deeper than conventional modes of thinking can grasp. The relation between the story and the film, on the one hand, and the poem, on the other, might seem too tenuous to consider in the context of adaptation if it did not follow in a long tradition of unusually licentious adaptations of the poem. Virtually all film adaptations of "Jabberwocky" are notably unfaithful, if only because the poem is customarily cherry-picked, along with other episodes and characters from *Through the Looking-Glass*, and folded into adaptations bearing the title and the general structure of *Alice in Wonderland* (1865). Indeed Terry Gilliam's *Jabberwocky* (1977), which borrows only Lewis Carroll's nonsensical tone, the tale of a quest to kill a predatory monster, and the look of John Tenniel's pen-and-ink drawing of the monster, is one of the least faithful of all Carroll adaptations[15]; it is no wonder that the very last person credited on the film is "the Rev. Charles Dodgson," the historical person hidden behind the pseudonym Lewis Carroll. The *Alice* books, however, raise still further ethical problems than the unfaithfulness of the films they have spawned.

Martin Gardner has pointed out that the opening stanza of Carroll's poem, including the line in question, had already appeared seventeen years earlier in *"Mischmasch*, the last of a series of private little 'periodicals' that young Carroll wrote, illustrated and hand-lettered for the amusement of his brothers and sisters."[16] There is no ethical reason why an author should not reprint or extend his own youthful work, especially work that has been restricted to a privately distributed collection. But more pressing ethical dimensions enter the equation in another of Carroll's borrowings from his own earlier productions. Most readers of *Alice in Wonderland* and *Through the Looking-Glass* in English know the pen-and-ink drawings of John Tenniel with which they were first published. And many of these readers know that a large number of Tenniel's drawings were based on the drawings Carroll himself produced for *Alice's Adventures Under Ground*, the hand-lettered volume he presented to Alice Liddell, the young girl who inspired both volumes, in 1864. But a subtly different pattern emerges in the two sets of illustrations. Alice herself appears in twenty-seven of Carroll's thirty-eight drawings but in only twenty-three of Tenniel's forty-two drawings. Although many of Tenniel's drawings are designed to illustrate figures and incidents that did not appear in *Alice's Adventures Under Ground*, which is only half as long as *Alice's Adventures in Wonderland*, virtually none of these new drawings include Alice herself, who is clearly more interesting visually to Carroll than to Tenniel. Moreover, fully ten of Carroll's drawings, versus six of Tenniel's, show Alice's body distorted by some kind of physical transformation, rendered magically large or small or given an elongated or serpentine neck. In adapting the illustrations in Carroll's handmade volume, Tenniel both placed less emphasis on the heroine and idealized her body more completely.

Why was Carroll so much more interested than his illustrator in depicting his heroine's physical transformations? The final illustration in *Alice's Adventures Under Ground* suggests one reason. It is a photograph of Alice Liddell, age seven, pasted over the only surviving sketch Charles Dodgson ever made of his young friend, a sketch whose subject looks neither like that of Tenniel's drawings, whose model was the pouting Mary Hilton Badcock, nor like that of Dodgson's other drawings.[17] For Dodgson, the photograph conceals a drawn likeness that is more personal, linking him and his subject more intimately even though it looks less like her. At the same time, Lewis Carroll's drawings of his heroine can readily be seen as displacements of the

idealized photographs Dodgson took of many of the children he be-
friended, most of which, as Nina Auerbach has observed, used "costumes, props, and the imaginative intensity of an improvised scene
caught at midpoint" to "suggest that the mobile self-definition of acting crystallized the potential power he found in the little girl."[18] Dodgson was deprived of the theatrical props that would release his sitters'
power through role-playing in the nude photographs he took with
their parents' consent. In his monograph on the four surviving nudes
Dodgson photographed, Morton N. Cohen, quoting several letters
from Dodgson to parents, notes Dodgson's sensitivity about his sitters' nervousness, which would make nude photography impossible:
"To be successful as art, the picture required a relaxed child."[19] In both
the words and pictures of *Alice's Adventures Under Ground*, by contrast,
he takes pains to show his enterprising heroine thrust increasingly into
roles she does not choose, and indeed as uncomfortable as possible
within her own body, which becomes through its vexing transformations as foreign to her as the land down the rabbit hole.

Looking back from Tenniel's drawings to Carroll's drawings to
Dodgson's photographs discloses a series of ever more conventional-
ized images with less and less resemblance to the girl who first inspired
them. Tenniel's revision of Carroll's illustrations extends Carroll's
own pattern of deliberate infidelity as he moves from idealized photographs to a single portrait drawing concealed beneath a photograph to
often distorted drawings of his heroine's body. Although Dodgson,
who concealed his own identity behind a pseudonym, kept Alice Liddell's first name for his heroine and hid her complete name in the
acrostic verse that ends *Through the Looking-Glass*, her image has been
changed and changed again to protect the innocent. Such visual transformations make a powerful case for the ethical propriety of infidelity.
Clearly, complete fidelity to Alice Liddell's likeness would have
amounted to a serious violation of her privacy, especially if she was
one of the nude sitters whose photographs by Dodgson have not survived.

Although Carroll and Tenniel's illustrations for the *Alice* books
show only how infidelity can be a more ethical choice than fidelity in
visual representations of a heroine of tender years, they obviously have
broader implications for the ethics of infidelity that become more explicit in every *roman à clef* that changes proper names, place names,
dates, and situations in order to provide a legal fig leaf for its real-life
models, even if those models are clearly meant to be recognized, even
if they provide the novel's principal selling point.

It is true, of course, that the relation between a *roman à clef* and the
historical or autobiographical material on which it is based is very dif-

ferent from the relation between a film adaptation and the fictional material to which the filmmaker has acquired the rights. Gus Van Sant's notorious remake of *Psycho* (1998) has still more far-reaching implications for the assumption that fidelity to one's source, whatever its nature, is an ethical norm. As commentators have universally agreed, the relation of Van Sant's film to the 1959 Robert Bloch novel on which is based is less important than its relation to Alfred Hitchcock's 1960 film adaptation of the novel, which Van Sant often follows line by line and sometimes shot by shot. So close is Van Sant's remake to Hitchcock's film, in fact, that Esther Anatolitis has concluded: "What Van Sant achieves is to force the viewer into looking for differences within a field of repetition, where other remakes have us desperately looking for similarities and elbowing our friends in the darkened cinema when we recognise the ever so oblique references."[20]

Months before his film's release, Van Sant was already being condemned for his temerity in remaking Hitchcock's film, and remaking it virtually shot for shot. The consensus was that although any remake would have been ill-advised, Van Sant's idea of fidelity to Hitchcock amounted to grave-robbing, trading as it did on the reputation of an established classic instead of reconsidering it scene by scene. In *Psycho Path*, a documentary distributed with the 1999 DVD release of his film, Van Sant himself compared it to a forgery, although filmmaker Andrei Konchalovsky responded immediately afterwards that forgers do not sign their works. Once the film was released, an amusingly contrary critical note emerged. Not only was Van Sant presuming to remake Hitchcock with unseemly fidelity; he actually had the nerve to change many of Hitchcock's most sacrosanct details.[21] Ethical propriety evidently forbade both excessive fidelity to Van Sant's model and any unfaithfulness within the convention of exact duplication.

Widely embraced as both these positions have continued to be, they both seem to me blind to what Van Sant is actually attempting to do and fundamentally mistaken about the ethics of fidelity and infidelity. But the combination of them both sheds considerable illumination on Van Sant's project and the ethical problems it evokes. Given Van Sant's avowed intention of following Hitchcock's film shot by shot, his every departure from Hitchcock—the opening helicopter shot that substitutes for Hitchcock's dissolves over the Phoenix cityscape, the restoration of the line "only playground'll beat Las Vegas" to describe Marion Crane's bed, the choice of a new brick façade for the Bates house, the cut-ins that interrupt the murders of Marion (Anne Heche) and detective Arbogast (William H. Macy), the long crane-out over the closing credit crawl—is gratuitous. But a few changes are doubly gratuitous because they are both unnecessary and virtually invisible.

When Marion, fearful that a police officer is following her, trades in her car for another even though she realizes the officer is watching her, Van Sant's direction of his actors is different from Hitchcock's—it's hard to imagine a performance less like John Anderson's clipped turn as the used-car dealer than James LeGros's affable glad-hander—but painstakingly follows Hitchcock's blocking, cutting, and camera placement, with one crucial difference: in the first half of the scene, from Marion's arrival at the car dealership to her request for the ladies' room (running from roughly 16:30 to 19:37 on the DVD release), every shot is reversed from left to right. Background buildings and objects are placed on opposite sides of the screen, and characters move from left to right instead of right to left, as if the sequence had been based on the Hitchcock film reflected in a mirror, even though the second half of the sequence, from Marion's entrance to the ladies' room to the moment she drives away, follows Hitchcock's blocking without the mirror effect. Van Sant follows the opposite pattern in a scene beginning exactly an hour later (beginning at 1:16:40) when Lila Crane (Julianne Moore) and Sam Loomis (Viggo Mortenson) report Arbogast's disappearance to Sheriff Chambers (Philip Baker Hall). The dialogue is virtually unaltered from that of the first film, but although the first half of the scene closely follows Hitchcock's blocking, every shot in the second half, beginning when Sheriff Chambers crosses the screen to take the telephone, is a faithful mirror image rather than a duplicate of Hitchcock's.

In addition, Van Sant introduces a peculiar complication into one of the pivotal moments of the film, when Marion, stopped at a traffic light on the way out of town with $400,000 the Texas oilman Tom Cassidy (Chad Everett) has left with her boss Lowery (Rance Howard) to purchase a home for his daughter, sees the two of them crossing the street ahead of her stopped car and, realizing that they have also seen her, first sees herself through their eyes as a thief. Although Van Sant stages this shot at a different intersection than Hitchcock and eliminates the Christmas decorations across the roadway, he follows Hitchcock in showing several other pedestrians from Marion's point of view crossing in front of her car, including, as in Hitchcock, a woman carrying a large box (tied with a red ribbon in the Van Sant) and a man carrying his jacket over his shoulder, both crossing from right to left behind Cassidy and Lowery, who are crossing from left to right. Unlike Hitchcock, however, Van Sant shows this woman and man twice, first directly ahead of Marion, then, when she looks to her right to follow Cassidy and Lowery, off to screen right at a point they had already passed in the previous shot. Any audience noticing this second appearance at all will be hard-pressed to explain it logically. It is as if the passersby, like the tell-tale cat Neo sees in *The Matrix*, were crossing the street twice.[22]

It would be easy to dismiss this last moment as a continuity error if it did not fit so neatly into a pattern established by the complementary mirror-images in the first and second halves of the two more extended sequences and a remark of Van Sant's in the Production Notes pamphlet distributed with the DVD release of his *Psycho* that has been widely quoted but little analyzed: "*Psycho* is perfect to refashion as a modern piece. Reflections are a major theme in the original, with mirrors everywhere, characters who reflect each other. This version holds up a mirror to the original film, it's sort of its schizophrenic twin."[23] Van Sant's *Psycho* is not an attempt to duplicate Hitchcock's; instead it poses as its double, its twin, its mirror image.[24]

What does it mean for a remake to assume the status of an earlier film's double or twin? The question is particularly relevant to Van Sant because so many of his other films allude so pointedly to earlier films by other filmmakers he admired. *My Own Private Idaho* (1991), to take the most obvious example, refers more or less explicitly to *The Wizard of Oz* (1939), *Easy Rider* (1969), and several of Andy Warhol's films, especially *Lonesome Cowboys* (1969), whose title is echoed in Van Sant's own *Drugstore Cowboy* (1989). Just as *Lonesome Cowboys* was originally conceived as a Western *Romeo and Juliet*, *My Own Private Idaho* incorporates elements of both Shakespeare's *1 Henry IV*, *2 Henry IV*, and *Henry V* as filtered through Orson Welles's *Chimes at Midnight* (1965). Here too, much more incongruously than in *Psycho*, Van Sant borrows Shakespeare's dialogue and Welles's blocking and camera setups for several key scenes that help tell the story of two drifters, Mike Waters (River Phoenix) and Scott Favor (Keanu Reeves), as Mike searches for his unknown mother and Scott struggles to come to terms with his father, the mayor of Portland, Oregon.[25]

In support of his contention that "the 1998 *Psycho* is more a 'Van Sant film' than a slavish imitation of the original," Steven Jay Schneider has identified several thematic patterns in Van Sant's films: "an interest in rendering the subjective experience of troubled youths and young adults"; "the romantic idea of leaving home and heading on the road in order to escape what are felt to be repressive norms and expectations; and the longing for, and struggle to develop, an intimate relationship (whether primarily sexual, parental, or therapeutic in nature) with another human being."[26] Hugh H. Davis offers a way to sharpen these suggestions further through his attempt to disentangle the "mixed/confused identities and pasts" in *My Own Private Idaho*: "Bob Pigeon, the so-called 'traditional' Falstaff, is both Scott's 'true father' and his former lover. Mike, the roustabout companion Falstaff,

is certainly more a brother than a father for Scott, yet again the relationship is displaced by the degrees of the pair's intimacy."[27] Van
Sant's major films have mostly been either coming-of-age stories that
chart the maturation of a young hero through a series of confusing
encounters with multiple or equivocal authority figures (*Good Will
Hunting*, 1997; *Finding Forrester*, 2000) or accounts of the catastrophic
failure of a young hero or heroine to establish a stable connection with
any such figures, leaving the hero marooned and helpless (*Mala Noche*,
1985; *Drugstore Cowboy; Even Cowgirls Get the Blues*, 1993; *Gerry*, 2002;
Elephant, 2003). In *To Die For* (1995), the three would-be teenage heroes are used and betrayed by small-town weathercaster Suzanne
Stone (Nicole Kidman), who attempts instead to become her own authority figure. *My Own Private Idaho* incorporates both patterns in
Scott's rejection of the Falstaffian Bob in favor of a rapprochement
with his detested father and Mike's ultimate failure, which on the
whole seems more authentic than Scott's success.

In his most characteristic films, Van Sant explores these patterns, as
Schneider points out, "at both the narrative and purely visual levels."[28]
In *My Own Private Idaho*, he adds an explicitly intertextual level by
creating a story (the screenplay is Van Sant's own) in which the complex and troubled interactions of his two heroes with authority figures
are echoed by Van Sant's own attempts to deal with two figures of
towering textual authority, the Falstaffian Welles and the kingly
Shakespeare. It is especially telling that Van Sant's reimagining of
Welles's reimagining of Shakespeare departs in obvious ways from
both the setting of the sources from which he borrows visuals and dialogue and in its autobiographical stance. As Paul Arthur notes in *Kings
of the Road*, Welles casts himself as Falstaff, the eternally playful old
trickster whose ultimate rejection by Prince Hal "is obviously a para-
ble of [Welles's] own betrayal" by his Hollywood friends and col-
leagues, whereas "Van Sant is at once Scott and Mike," the hustler
rebels who must choose between embracing (perhaps selling out to) a
system that demands social and sexual conformity and remaining on a
lonely and unending road until death.[29]

Van Sant's *Psycho*, like *My Own Private Idaho*, is an anatomy of the
filmmaker's relationship to an authoritative master. Here again the
anatomy is equally critical, for the film everywhere acknowledges that
Van Sant can no more become Alfred Hitchcock, not even by following him line by line and shot by shot, than Norman can become his
mother, the fearsome authority figure who rules his every action even
though she is dead. *Psycho*, widely perceived as Van Sant's futile attempt to duplicate Hitchcock's film, is rather a mirror image or
schizophrenic twin that reveals in pitiless detail the folly of attempting

to become your mother by submerging your agency in her authority. In his presentation of both Marion Crane and Norman Bates (Vince Vaughn), Van Sant follows Hitchcock in tracing the horrifying consequences of refusing to take responsibility for one's actions by ascribing responsibility for them to someone else. But unlike Hitchcock, who dismissed the novel he had adapted in a famous remark to François Truffaut as raw material worthy only of transmutation into a Hitchcock original,[30] Van Sant uses the story of Norman Bates to explore his own contradictory relationship to Hitchcock and the mainstream cinema he represents. In *Psycho Path*, he acknowledges that although Universal repeatedly approached him with a list of potential projects that included remakes of Universal properties like *Psycho*, the decision to remake the film so literally was entirely his own, and one for which the studio originally had little enthusiasm. In the remake, Van Sant literally doubles for Hitchcock by taking his place in the director's obligatory cameo outside Marion's real-estate office. Although Van Sant looks nothing like Hitchcock, his five-gallon cowboy hat and the fact that he is seen only in one-quarter view make him a close double for the older director—the only such physical double in Van Sant's film. *Psycho Path* complicates this obvious doubling by doubling Van Sant with Norman Bates, especially in a cut from Hitchcock's Norman (Anthony Perkins) telling Marion that his mother is "as harmless as one of those stuffed birds" to Van Sant, who looks a good deal more like Perkins (and still more like Vince Vaughn) than like Hitchcock, sitting in exactly the same position.[31]

Van Sant's *Psycho*, which Anatolitis describes as "a film essentially about the debilitating effects of an obsessional repetition,"[32] makes a powerful, if largely overlooked, case for fidelity as psychosis. Every remake, every adaptation, is a mirror image or double or schizophrenic twin of its progenitor rather than its duplicate, and the attempt at literal fidelity is as deeply misbegotten as Norman's attempt, in the psychiatrist's words, "to be his mother." Van Sant has been almost universally reviled for vainly attempting such a literal remake by commentators who overlook the most strikingly original feature of his film: its link between literal fidelity to progenitor texts and its hero/villain's murderous psychosis. This link is found nowhere in Hitchcock, who prefers to disavow his sources instead of assuming the burden of exploring his relation to them. Van Sant's emphasis on the psychotic nature of the quest for fidelity is a logical outgrowth of the number, range, and peculiar quality of the intertextual references in his other films, a web of allusions that is one of the most intriguing aspects of what Paul Arthur calls Van Sant's "ambivalence . . . this little dance of rebellion and submission" to the Hollywood system that has characterized his entire career as an alternately independent and mainstream filmmaker.[33]

In using *Alice in Wonderland* and Van Sant's *Psycho* to make a case for the ethics of infidelity, I am well aware that neither case is reducible to a simple instance of a single adaptation of a single source text. As I have argued elsewhere, however, the multiple layers and modes of adaptation they both imply suggest a model commentators might well take more seriously as they grapple more closely—though perhaps less closely than either Lewis Carroll or Gus Van Sant—with the ethics of adaptation.

NOTES

1. David O. Selznick, *Memo from David O. Selznick*, ed. Rudy Behlmer (New York: Viking, 1972), 266.

2. This observation may be out of line, since I was unable to find any reviews of most of these films. The anonymous online review of *Lolita 2000* on Cold Fusion Video is instructive in its complaint that "the most common two [alternative] titles for this movie [*Lolida 2000* and *O Lita 2000*] are . . . devices to try to avoid any of the backlash around the 1997 movie version of *Lolita*, which then makes one wonder why they intentionally invoked that association at all." Cold Fusion Video Reviews, "*Lolita 2000* (1997)," http://www.coldfusionvideo.com/archives/lolida-2000-1997/.

3. Selznick, *Memo from David O. Selznick*, 266.

4. Ibid., 267.

5. William Horne, "'See Shooting Script': Reflections on the Ontology of the Screenplay," *Literature/Film Quarterly* 20, no. 1 (1992): 51; Jack Boozer, ed., *Authorship in Film Adaptation* (Austin: University of Texas Press, 2008). Boozer's recent collection seeks to redress the neglect of the screenplay Horne deplores by largely focusing on the screenplay's pivotal status as the intermediary between a film adaptation and its nominal source.

6. George Bluestone, *Novels into Film: The Metamorphosis of Fiction into Cinema* (Baltimore: Johns Hopkins University Press, 1957), 5.

7. Brian McFarlane, *Novel to Film: An Introduction to the Theory of Adaptation* (Oxford: Clarendon, 1996), 8.

8. Ephesians 5:22–28 (King James Version).

9. Tony Tanner, *Adultery and the Novel: Contract and Transgression* (Baltimore: Johns Hopkins University Press, 1979), 11, 14.

10. Ibid., 15.

11. Ibid., 377.

12. Percy Bysshe Shelley, *The Complete Works*, eds. Roger Ingpen and Walter E. Peck (New York: Gordian, 1965), 7:118.

13. yarner58's asseveration, formerly archived on the Internet Movie Database Message Board under *The Last Mimzy* at http://www.imdb.com/title/tt0768212/board/nest/68651032, has since been deleted.

14. *The Last Mimzy*, DVD, directed by Robert Shaye (New York City: New Line Cinema, 2007).

15. *Jabberwocky*, VHS, directed by Terry Gilliam (Python Films, 1977).

16. Lewis Carroll, *The Annotated Alice: The Definitive Edition*, ed. Martin Gardner (New York: Norton, 2000), 148 n. 16.

17. Lewis Carroll, *Alice's Adventures Under Ground* (Ann Arbor: University Microfilms, 1964).

18. Nina Auerbach, *Romantic Imprisonment: Women and Other Glorified Outcasts* (New York: Columbia University Press, 1985), 156–57.

19. Morten N. Cohen, *Lewis Carroll's Photographs of Nude Children* (Philadelphia: Rosenbach Foundation, 1978), 7.

20. Esther Anatolitis, "Re-making the Remake: Gus Van Sant's *Psycho*," http://peteg.org/toto/psycho.htm

21. Thomas M. Leitch, "101 Ways to Tell Hitchcock's *Psycho* from Gus Van Sant's," *Literature/Film Quarterly* 28 (2000–2001): 269–73. See Leitch for a catalogue of Van Sant's principal departures from Hitchcock.

22. *Psycho*, DVD, directed by Alfred Hitchcock (1960; Paramount, 1999); *Psycho*, DVD, directed by Gus Van Sant (1998; Los Angeles: Universal Pictures, 1999); *Psycho Path*, DVD, directed by D-J, DVD release of *Psycho* (Los Angeles: Universal Studios Home Entertainment, 1999).

23. "Production Notes," *Psycho*, DVD, directed by Gus Van Sant (Universal Pictures, 1999).

24. Gregg Uhlin develops this insight along somewhat different lines in "Gus Van Sant's Mirror-Image of Hichcock: Reading *Psycho* Backwards," forthcoming in *Hitchcock Annual*, an invaluable essay I encountered as the present essay was going to press.

25. *My Own Private Idaho*, DVD, directed by Gus Van Sant (New York: New Line Cinema, 1991).

26. Steven Jay Schneider, "Van Sant the Provoca(u)teur," *Hitchcock Annual* 10 (2001–2002): 142–44.

27. Hugh H. Davis, "'Shakespeare, He's in the Alley': *My Own Private Idaho* and Shakespeare in the Streets," *Literature/Film Quarterly* 29, no. 2 (2001): 118.

28. Schneider, "Van Sant the Provoca(u)teur," 144.

29. Paul Arthur, *Kings of the Road*, Disc 2, *My Own Private Idaho*, DVD, produced by Debra McClutchy and Kate Elmore (1991; The Criterion Collection, 2005).

30. François Truffaut, *Hitchcock*, revised edition (New York: Simon & Schuster, 1984).When Truffaut asked, "What was it that attracted you to the novel?," Hitchcock replied, "I think the thing that appealed to me and made me decide to do the picture was the suddenness of the murder in the shower, coming, as it were, out of the blue. That was about all" (Truffaut 205).

31. *Psycho*, directed by Hitchcock.

32. Anatolitis, "Re-making the Remake."

33. Paul Arthur, *Kings of the Road.*

"We're off to See the Wizard" (Again): *Oz* Adaptations and the Matter of Fidelity

Kate Newell

FOR MORE THAN FIFTY YEARS, SCHOLARS IN ADAPTATION STUDIES have addressed the matter of fidelity. While most major works on adaptation have dismissed fidelity as a measure of evaluation, analogies between source texts and adaptations continue to direct the reading and interpretation of adaptations. Christa Albrecht-Crane and Dennis Cutchins explore this history in the introduction to this collection, noting that, despite many contemporary scholars' "claim[s] to reject 'fidelity' as a marker of an adaptation's success . . . they continue a dedication to the literary values" that make such rejections impossible.[1] Robert Stam offers one explanation for the endurance of fidelity discourse: " 'fidelity,' however discredited theoretically, does retain a grain of experiential truth. Fidelity discourse asks important questions about the filmic recreation of the setting, plot, characters, themes, and the style of the novel."[2] Thomas Leitch offers another explanation: "the valorization of fidelity amounts to a valorization of literature as such in the face of the insurgent challenge of cinema studies."[3] As Albrecht-Crane and Cutchins, Dudley Andrew, Imelda Whelehan, and others have noted, much of the writing on and teaching of film adaptations of literary texts has come out of college and university English departments; this trend may account for a disproportionate privileging of literature and the author over cinema and collaboration.[4] Stam and Leitch highlight two possible explanations for the persistence of fidelity: one rooted in issues of interpretation and readability and another rooted in issues of authorship and institutionally valuable intellectual property.

Much of what is understood as fidelity discourse has developed out of attempts to rationalize or diminish fidelity's influence on adaptation studies, but little attention has been paid to understanding just how varied this discourse can be. Although "fidelity" may appear to develop straightforwardly from the premise that the degree to which an

image text casts itself as a visual translation of a written source determines its success as an adaptation, it is not so monolithic. Each adaptation tends to generate a distinct fidelity discourse, and each discourse
is informed by any number of agendas. Most fidelity-based evaluations
assume that fidelity is the only goal of adaptation and neglect to consider that, while some adaptations are informed by an agenda of fidelity, others are informed by an agenda of *infidelity*. So pervasive is the
source/adaptation dyad, even adaptations that profess only the most
tangential relationship to a source text are evaluated in terms of that
source, as though fidelity were the intention. When an adaptation's
infidelities are celebrated, the argument is made defensively and pro-
tectively, as though the infidelities are beside the point rather than the
point itself.

The history of fidelity discourse has been marked, paradoxically, by
an attempt to move away from itself. Early studies of adaptation
tended to dismiss fidelity as irrelevant even as it informed many of
their arguments. George Bluestone maintained that fidelity-based
evaluations assume erroneously that a novel's content can be "de-
tached and reproduced" in visual media and ignores that "changes are
inevitable the moment one abandons the linguistic for the visual medium."[5] Focusing on the specific abilities and disabilities of film and
literature as media, Bluestone's *Novels into Film* popularized what have
come to be recognized as medium-specific approaches to adaptation.
Virtually every adaptation theorist since Bluestone has agreed with the
basic tenets of his argument: most media are too distinct to allow
faithful medium-to-medium transposition, and fidelity arguments are
based on value judgments that cannot be substantiated and, therefore,
are theoretically inconsequential.[6]

Other approaches rest more firmly on distinctions between form
and content, and argue that, while a novel cannot be reproduced in
film, aspects of its content can transcend its form and be transferred
faithfully to another form.[7] The most prevalent of these models address the transference of textual or authorial spirit; they account for
infidelities by making strict visual translation of written text unnecessary, even undesirable, as long as the "spirit" is evoked. Stam has suggested that when writers praise an adaptation for being faithful to the
spirit of a text, what they mean is that the adaptation is faithful to a
cumulative understanding of what that text means as a piece of literature and as a cultural object.[8] Yet variations in interpretations, interpretive communities, and textual meaning prevent the spirit from
becoming anything objective or tangible.

Fidelity has also been conceptualized as a category of adaptation, or

as one of many choices an artist makes in adaptating. Geoffrey
Wagner, for example, distinguishes between the very faithful, the
moderately faithful, and the barely faithful in his "transposition,"
"commentary," and "analogy," models of adaptation,[9] while Dudley
Andrew views fidelity as a particular mode of adaptation distinct from
other modes such as intersecting and borrowing,[10] and James Griffith
uses the Romantic concept of imitation that allows unfaithful adaptations to be recast as faithful representations simply articulated through
new techniques.[11] Likewise, Lindiwe Dovey distinguishes between
what she calls pro-creation adaptations and appropriational adaptations.[12] As McFarlane sees it, categorical approaches, though problematic, reframe the dialogue around adaptation "so that fidelity to the
original loses some of its privileged position."[13] So far, however, categorization has not completely deprivileged fidelity to an original because the categories are configured according to the degree to which
the adaptation corresponds or is faithful to its source. For example,
for Andrew's "borrowing" category, "the artist employs, more or less
extensively, the material, idea, or form of an earlier, generally successful text"; for his "intersecting" category, "the uniqueness of the original text is preserved to such an extent that it is intentionally left
unassimilated in adaptation."[14] These categories do not so much de-
privilege fidelity as rationalize infidelity or provide a way to conceptu-
alize so-called unfaithful adaptations as faithful (e.g., Almereyda's
Hamlet[15] isn't unfaithful—it's *intersecting*). Such approaches position
themselves less as alternatives to fidelity discourse than alternative
ways to speak within fidelity discourse.

Recently, adaptation theory has been moving toward more intertextual models prepared to account for the multiple textual and cultural
influences and circumstances of production that shape adaptations. Instead of reading the activity of adapting in terms of exchanges between
media or in terms of form and content, these approaches, drawn
largely from the theories of Bahktin and Genette, view adaptations as
sites of intersecting codes and signals, texts and intertexts.[16] The gov-
erning question here is not "is this adaptation faithful?" but "to what
is this adaptation faithful?" and "in what terms does this adaptation
conceive fidelity?" Because intertextual approaches open the discussion of fidelity to the possibility of fidel*ties*, they provide a more flexible base from which adaptations can be critically evaluated. Stam
explains that in moving beyond a "dyadic source/adaptation model,"
intertextuality may "help us transcend the aporias of 'fidelity.'"[17] Yet
recognizing that both novel and film adaptation are products of multiple sources, generic influences, and production decisions will not nec-

essarily deter evaluations based on exactly how faithful an adaptation is to this or that source or generic influence.[18]

The multifariousness of fidelity discourse can be illustrated notably by responses to the multiple incarnations of *The Wizard of Oz*. *Oz* adaptations are unique in that each assimilates the iconography of earlier adaptations in ways that signal fidelity to *either* L. Frank Baum's novel, *The Wonderful Wizard of Oz* (1900), *or* to the 1939 MGM musical, *The Wizard of Oz;*[19] at the same time, each manipulates that iconography in order to fulfill a particular cultural or creative agenda and to appeal to a particular countercultural audience. While the variations in plot, character, and narrative that invariably attend each permutation are generally of little consequence to its reception, what is of consequence is that the agenda of fidelity dominates the agenda of infidelity. In cases in which the agenda of infidelity threatens to dominate or overpower the familiar narrative, the presence of narrative and aesthetic consistencies can come to be regarded as inadequate for fidelity. Two literary adaptations of Baum's novel, Gregory Maguire's *Wicked: The Life and Times of the Wicked Witch of the West* (1995) and Geoff Ryman's *Was* (1992), while dramatically different from Baum's novel and the 1939 film in terms of character and narrative development, are considered faithful to the political energy of Baum's novel and the themes of home, self-reliance, and coming-of-age that audiences have come to associate with Oz. By contrast, *The Muppets' Wizard of Oz* (2005)[20] is similar to Baum's novel, the 1939 film, and Sidney Lumet's *The Wiz* (1978)[21] in terms of character, narrative pace, and plot development, yet its postmodern and largely consumerist agenda trumps that of the classic tale.[22]

Oz adaptations are also unique in the sense that the fidelity discourses they generate tend to valorize not the literary source, as is the case typically, but the most venerated of its adaptations: the 1939 MGM film. Douglass Street explains that the 1939 adaptation "has so saturated generations of Americans that what most people assume to be Baum's story of a little girl from Kansas has actually little in common with the original publication."[23] Similarly, as Mark Evan Swartz points out, "so influential is this film that it, and not the novel, is generally the source of people's familiarity with the Wizard of Oz story."[24] Much of the quintessential *Oz* iconography comes from the 1939 film. "Somewhere Over the Rainbow," the ruby slippers, and the green-skinned witch are all familiar *Oz* icons, yet they do not originate in Baum's novel; they mark inventions of the adaptation process. Most post-1939 *Oz* adaptations acknowledge both Baum's novel and the 1939 film as inspirations, but shy away from self-identifying as adaptations. *The Wiz*, for example, identifies as "less a remake than a rein-

vention,"[25] while *Wicked* identifies as "a story of another life";[26] critics
and reviewers, however, ignore these identifications and evaluate the
texts in terms of fidelity to Baum and, even more so, the MGM
film. Yet the different agendas conveyed through discussions of these
adaptations are at heart variations on the same. For example, while
Maguire's *Wicked* and Ryman's *Was* are basically the same type of adaptation, readers tend to evaluate the former as an extension of *Oz*
texts that offers back story or an insider's perspective and the latter as
a meditation on *Oz* themes. *The Wiz*, by contrast, arguably the most
faithful of more recent adaptations, tends to be evaluated less as an
adaptation than as a black articulation of one of white America's beloved icons, while *The Muppets' Wizard of Oz* tends to be evaluated
equally as an adaptation and as a Muppet property.

   Despite Gregory Maguire's assertion that his novel is neither a retelling of nor a prequel to other *Oz* texts, reviews of the novel and its
musical adaptation by and large compare the texts to the 1939 film.[27]
Daniel Handler, for example, uses *Oz*'s most marketable name as a
signpost and claims, "Maguire gives us a universe we're more likely to
associate with J. R. R. Tolkien than Judy Garland."[28] A *New York Times*
review of the novel begins, "The Wicked Witch of the West revealed
as an idealistic victim? The green-skinned harridan played by Margaret Hamilton unmasked as the dermatologically challenged product of
a dysfunctional family? The scourge of Oz depicted as a dissident, a
brave fighter against a totalitarian regime?"[29] A review in *The Boston
Herald* asks, "But was the Wicked Witch of the West—Dorothy's
complexion-challenged nemesis in Oz—really evil? Or was she a victim of bad press and a really terrible skin-care regimen?"[30] Cathy
Hainer's *USA Today* review begins "Oz purists beware," and cautions
readers that, while Maguire's Oz is "vividly imagined," his "characters
are barely recognizable from their movie counterparts." She concludes that "*Wicked* is an outstanding work of imagination, a completed work of fiction not incumbent upon the film for meaning."[31]

   Wicked charts the history of Elphaba, the green-skinned child born
to the daughter of a Munchkinland dignitary and a unionist minister.
Maguire amplifies a role that occupies fewer than twenty pages of
Baum's 259-page novel and about fifteen minutes of the MGM film,
and then recasts it into familiar *Oz* narratives and landscapes, integrating narrative and iconic aspects peculiar to Baum and to the MGM
adaptation to a degree that it becomes difficult to distinguish points at
which the novel is being faithful to Baum and points at which it is
being faithful to the 1939 film. For example, Maguire chooses to present the Tin Man's history in a way that is more faithful to Baum than
to MGM. Baum's Tin Woodman relates that he was once human and

in love with a Munchkin girl who promised to marry him, but the old woman for whom the girl worked "did not want her to marry anyone," so the old woman went to the wicked Witch of the East, offering her "two sheep and a cow, if she would prevent the marriage. Thereupon the wicked Witch enchanted my axe, and when I was chopping away at my best one day . . . the axe slipped all at once and cut off my leg."[32] The Woodman visits a tinsmith, who makes him a tin leg, but the Woodman's axe continues to chop off limbs, and the tinsmith continues to replace them, until he is composed entirely of tin.[33] A parallel scene occurs in *Wicked:* Elphaba witnesses a conversation in which an old woman complains to Elphaba's sister, Nessarose, that her maid has fallen in love with a woodcutter. The old woman offers two sheep and a cow to have the woodcutter's axe bewitched.[34] The MGM film, by contrast, presents the Tin Man as having always been a Tin Man, who was simply created without a heart, and thus avoids the nightmarish allusions to a beloved character systematically being hacked to pieces by his own axe.

In contrast, certain details in *Wicked* signal fidelity to the MGM adaptation rather than to Baum. The Witch's green complexion and dark clothing, for example, are derived from this film. Similarly, *Wicked* opts to have Glinda greet Dorothy in Munchkinland, whereas in Baum Dorothy is welcomed by the Witch of the North. The charmed shoes spur Elphaba's pursuit of Dorothy in *Wicked,* just as they provide the impetus for the Wicked Witch of the West's frequent torments of Dorothy and her friends in the 1939 film, whereas, in Baum, the Witch does not notice the shoes until Dorothy is brought to her castle by the winged monkeys.

Unlike *Wicked,* Ryman's *Was* is not specifically about Oz, but rather the cultural effect of the Oz narrative and the ways in which its iconography has permeated the psyches of various readers and viewers. *Was* interweaves several narratives and time periods: that of Jonathan, an actor dying of AIDS, who feels an affinity to Oz and who, as a child with autism, imagined that the Oz characters were his friends; that of Dorothy, a young girl who moves to Kansas with her dog Toto to live with her Aunt Emily and Uncle Henry after her mother dies of diphtheria; that of L. Frank Baum, the substitute teacher who sympathizes with Dorothy; that of Frances Gumm (later Judy Garland) and her mother Ethel; that of Millie Haugaard, make-up artist to Judy Garland on the set of *The Wizard of Oz;* and that of Bill Davison, who cared for Dorothy Gael in a state home for several months before her death and who later became Jonathan's psychiatrist.

If Maguire's novel is interested in amplifying and complicating the internal landscape, Ryman's novel is interested in complicating the external landscape, most impressively by tackling Baum's source text. *Was*, like *Wicked*, evokes fidelity to antecedent *Oz* texts through familiar iconography. Shortly after Dorothy's arrival in Kansas, Uncle Henry kills her dog, Toto, because he attacks the hens, and Dorothy's only friend, Wilbur, the son of a neighbor, commits suicide. As Dorothy matures, Uncle Henry begins molesting her.[35] Dorothy confesses these abuses to Frank Baum, a substitute teacher, but when Baum contacts the authorities, he is told that Dorothy is lying. Baum brings a composition Dorothy wrote about Toto with him when he leaves town, and the novel suggests that this composition provided the inspiration for *The Wonderful Wizard of Oz*: "He stared at the piece of paper and nearly let it drop. Then he folded it up and put it in his pocket with its names—Dorothy, Em, Henry, Toto. He picked up the red book of Osmanli, the language of Oz. Then he moved on."[36]

Early in Ryman's novel Dorothy arrives in a strange land (i.e., Kansas), feels an immediate sense of alienation, and meets Etta Parkerson, whose "height and manner" "confuse" Dorothy, who "was not entirely sure if [Etta] was a child or an adult."[37] Etta counsels the displaced Dorothy: "any place is what you make it. . . . You've got to make it home."[38] The next morning Aunt Em and Uncle Henry come to collect Dorothy. Etta kisses the child on the forehead, and "Dorothy could feel it, as if it glowed. For a moment she felt as though nothing could hurt her."[39] To readers familiar with *Oz* iconography, these events recall Baum's recounting of Dorothy's arrival in Oz and her encounter with the Munchkins and the Witch of the North, who tells Dorothy, "no one will dare injure a person who has been kissed by the Witch of the North." The Witch's kiss leaves "a round, shining mark."[40] And the "home is where you make it" sentiment is surely familiar to anyone who has read the books or watched the MGM adaptation.

The number of comparisons between *Wicked* and *Was*, both in newspaper and magazine reviews and in online postings, indicates that they belong to the same genre of adaptation, yet despite their frequent pairings, the terms according to which they are evaluated differ. *Wicked*, in both its novel and musical forms, is evaluated most often as a text that extends the diegesis of the 1939 film by offering additional, "insider" information. Speaking of the Broadway musical adaptation of *Wicked*, Idina Menzel, who played Elphaba in the original cast, claims, "We like to say that 'Wicked' is behind the scenes of what you saw in the movie. . . . The film is [the witches'] public persona; their real life is what you see in" *Wicked*.[41] Similarly, according to a *USA Today* review of Maguire's novel, Maguire "has done a fascinating job of expanding the story beyond the confines of the 1939 film. The reader begins to see that the film gave a limited view of Ozian events and a skewed point of view at that."[42] By contrast, Ryman's *Was* is praised as "an incredibly imaginative meditation on The Wizard of Oz,"[43] and comments tend to highlight the method by which Ryman achieves thematic fidelity to antecedent *Oz* texts, particularly in his characters' quests for home and belonging. One reviewer writes that Ryman's novel "refracts the story of Dorothy through a prism to isolate . . . many different strands and themes from the story we love."[44] Another reader explains that the "themes, images, the entirety of this book is magic in its artistry and imaginative power. This book explores the nature of fantasy as born of tragedy and the timeless truth of 'There's no place like home.'"[45] Other responses focus on Ryman's fidelity to cultural and historical artifacts. According to Laurel Graber's *New York Times* review, Ryman's *Was* is not "an attempt to tell the 'real, awful' story behind 'The Wizard of Oz.'" Rather, Ryman explains that he "was treating a series of cultural artifacts—the Baum book, the film and this television ritual of watching it—as historical facts within a historical novel."[46]

Of the post-1939 *Oz* adaptations, one might assume that *The Wiz* would be most likely to elicit commentary that evokes Baum or MGM for fidelity comparisons, as it tells the story of Dorothy's journey to Oz at much the same pace as the MGM film and maintains a stronger sense of the characters developed by Baum than many other adaptations, yet its fidelity to *Oz* precursors is rarely a factor in evaluating its success as a film. As one fan cautions, "Do not watch this movie and compare it to the Wizard of Oz, it is not a remake. This movie is an interpretation of the book. It puts a wonderfully imaginative black twist on a familiar story."[47] The *Wiz* urbanizes *The Wizard of Oz* and, like Ryman's and Maguire's novels, reframes central narrative aspects. As Ethan Mordden observes, whereas Baum's novel, the 1939 film, and even the Broadway incarnation of *The Wiz* "featured a little girl who wants to get home . . . the new film gives us an older Dorothy who needs to get out in the world."[48] Although *The Wiz* has been praised for its musical numbers and set design, it has garnered little critical attention as an adaptation. When the film is discussed, it is usually remembered as one of the first big budget films to boast an all black cast and regretted as a musical hampered by a slow narrative pace.[49] Bonnie Allen's *Essence* review praises the film's high-energy dance numbers, but warns that "when the film flattens out . . . one sits through long static scenes waiting for the next get-down number."[50] Donald Bogle adds that the film is hampered by excessive long-shots that create too much distance between the viewer and the performers.[51]

Like other adaptations of *Oz*, *The Wiz* evokes fidelity to earlier *Oz* texts through characters, narrative events, and iconography. Despite its alternative settings, *The Wiz* maintains striking structural fidelity both to MGM and to Baum and develops at roughly the same narrative pace. *The Wiz* begins with a scene at home, followed by a cyclone that brings Dorothy (Diana Ross) to Oz where she meets the Munchkins and Miss One (Thelma Carpenter), the good witch who directs her to follow the yellow brick road to the Wiz. Along the way she meets the Scarecrow (Michael Jackson), the Tinman (Nipsey Russell), and the Lion (Ted Ross). Their journey forces them to confront various environmental obstacles, among them an aggressive subway station and narcotic poppy alley. They arrive at the Emerald City and eventually meet the Wiz (Richard Pryor), who refuses to grant their requests until they have killed Evillene (Mabel King). Returning to the Emerald City after fulfilling their mission, they discover that the Wiz lacks magical powers and is incapable of granting their wishes. Instead, he draws their attention to the gifts they have had all along. When his attempt to return Dorothy to Harlem fails, the group seeks the help of Glinda the Good (Lena Horne), who returns Dorothy home.

Instead of being held to textual or thematic fidelity, or even fidelity to historical facts, *The Wiz* is criticized for what might be termed cultural infidelities. Bogle claims, "scriptwriter Joel Schumacher . . . knew nothing about black speech rhythms or colloquialisms or a black point of view."[52] Similarly, as Jack Kroll sees it, Lumet's *Wiz* "looks very much like white 'liberal' condescension" and the opening scene "looks exactly like those happy black family parties you see on TV commercials for Pepsi or Budweiser."[53] Kroll's criticism of Lumet's film contrasts sharply with his praise for *The Wiz* stage production, which "absorbs . . . Baum's classic into the black experience with good-humored cleverness," as it "expropriat[es] one of white America's most cherished fantasies and turn[s] it into a pop allegory of the blacks' journey down a booby-trapped Yellow Brick Road toward self-realization."[54] A few reviewers compare Lumet's *The Wiz* to earlier Oz texts, but these comparisons also suggest the film falls short of any impressive cultural representation. A review in *Ebony* reports, "She's not a little country girl from Kansas anymore, but for a Harlem schoolteacher she's not all that hip. And her encounters on the way to the Emerald City . . . would send the Judy Garland 'Dorothy' screaming right up a wall."[55]

Like *The Wiz*, *The Muppets' Wizard of Oz* casts African-American actors in lead roles—Ashanti (Dorothy), Queen Latifah (Auntie Em), David Alan Grier (Uncle Henry)—yet, unlike *The Wiz*, it is not evaluated in terms of fidelity to Black culture.[56] Whereas *The Wiz* appropriates signifiers of 1970s Harlem to create an adaptation reflective of an urban Black American experience, *The Muppets'* appropriates signifiers of American popular culture to create an adaptation reflective of a twenty-first-century postmodern experience. *The Muppets' Wizard of Oz* initiates a unique fidelity discourse in that it marks the meeting of two beloved cultural icons.[57] Instead of being evaluated in terms of its fidelity to this particular cultural experience, *The Muppets' Wizard of Oz* tends to be evaluated in terms of its fidelity to the 1939 film and to other Muppets' or Disney productions.[58] At the same time, "fidelity" becomes less a matter of establishing a deliberate relationship to a source text than of signaling the field of possible source texts. Fidelity becomes less an issue of adhering to the "letter" or even the "spirit" of a particular source and more an issue of evoking the range of potential fidelities and infidelities.

The Muppets' Wizard of Oz's Dorothy Gale dreams of becoming a famous pop singer and escaping the drudgery of her life in Kansas. The Muppets come to town to audition singers for their "Star Search," but Dorothy arrives too late to audition. Later that afternoon, a tornado moves through Kansas, taking with it the family's trailer, Dorothy, and her pet prawn, Toto. Dorothy wakes in Oz and emerges from the trailer into Munchkinland to discover that she's killed the Wicked Witch of the East (Miss Piggy). The Good Witch of the North (also Miss Piggy), hearing Dorothy's desire to become a famous pop singer, suggests she visit the Wizard of Oz. On their journey down "the yellow road made of brick," Dorothy and Pepe meet Scarecrow (Kermit), TIN Thing (Gonzo), and Lion (Fozzie). The group reaches Emerald City and The Wizard (Jeffrey Tambor) agrees to grant their wishes provided that they bring him the all-seeing eye of the Wicked Witch of the West (Miss Piggy). Once they have completed this task, the Wizard grants Dorothy's wish, but she realizes that she misses her family and asks to return home. Glinda, the Good Witch of the South (Miss Piggy), grants her wish. Dorothy returns to Kansas to discover that Kermit has been waiting for her to ask her to join the Muppets' tour.

The Muppets' Wizard of Oz evokes fidelity to Baum's *The Wonderful Wizard of Oz* iconically and narratively. Both texts share enchanted accoutrements, among them silver shoes, all-seeing eyes, protective green spectacles, and charmed caps (a Golden Cap in Baum; an Enchanted Biker Cap in *Muppets*). Both texts feature four witches, representing the four corners of Oz, a helpful rodent population, and threatening forest creatures (Kalidahs in Baum; Kalidah-critics in *Muppets*). Like Baum's Tin Man, the Muppets' TIN Thing has been made so by the Wicked Witch of the West. In both texts Dorothy and the Lion are rescued from the poppy fields by the rodent community (mice in Baum; rodent-like Munchkins in *The Muppets'*). In both texts, each character enters the Wizard's chambers individually and he appears to each under a different guise. While *The Muppets' Wizard of Oz*'s only credited source text is Baum's novel, it evokes fidelity to both the 1939 film and *The Wiz* in many ways, among them the inclusion of musical numbers and the amplification of the Kansas narrative.[59]

The Muppets' Wizard of Oz attempts to align itself, albeit briefly, with its literary and cinematic antecedents before relocating itself in a more contemporary, concise, and largely reflexive narrative medium: the music video. The film opens in the manner of a conventional adaptation of a classic literary text, with a close-up shot of the book *The Muppets' Wizard of Oz*. The book opens onto an illustration of a corn field, but, as the camera tracks in, the film reveals the image to be imprinted on the side of a cardboard box used for shipping corn. The next shot, in which Dorothy throws corn husks into a trough, recalls the scene from the 1939 film in which Dorothy falls into the pig pen. As *The Muppets'* Dorothy begins to sing, text on the screen indicates that viewers are watching a music video for Dorothy Gale's song, "Gotta Get Out of Kansas," from her *Wishful Thinking* album, produced by Impending Cyclone Records. The receptacle into which she'd been throwing corn husks is revealed to be the dumpster outside Auntie Em's Diner. In this way, the film immediately establishes itself as both conscious of and distinct from existing *Oz* adaptations.

Much of the film unfolds via a system of avowing and disavowing the established *Oz* narrative. Unlike antecedent *Oz* adaptations, which strive to preserve the illusion of Oz as a magical yet plausible otherworld, the *Muppets' Wizard of Oz* rejects the willing suspension of disbelief and nods continually in the direction of its illusion. For example, when Dorothy refuses Tattypoo's gift of the silver shoes on the grounds they had been worn by someone else, a frustrated Tattypoo reminds Dorothy that magical shoes are a basic part of "how things work in enchanted lands." Dorothy is unswayed. It is not until after hearing that the shoes are designed by Manolo Blahnik that she finally agrees to wear them. In this way, any narrative fissures generated by the moments of disavowal are bound by the proliferation of of-the-moment intertexts.

What distinguishes *The Muppets' Wizard of Oz* from its more celebrated predecessors is its overt use of pastiche. The made-for-television adaptation draws from the camera styles of its sibling genres, the music video and reality television; it contains dialogue references to the reality television show *Girls Gone Wild*, Pink Floyd's album *Dark*

Side of the Moon,[60] celebrity Jennifer Lopez's marriages, and *Oz For Dummies*; it includes appearances by Kelly Osbourne and Quentin Tarantino (as themselves); it features contemporary fetish objects like cell phones and Manolo Blahniks. While this adaptation has been described as a "version [that] replaces the original's hope with a cacophonous, clanging din,"[61] much of its seeming incongruousness has precedent in pre-1939 *Oz* adaptations. As Swartz explains, advertisements for a 1902 musical production "made it clear that the show was to be a loose amalgam of forms, including not only the extravaganza but also the comic opera, the spectacle, and the pantomime."[62] While *The Muppets'* uncanny transformation of Toto the terrier into a prawn may appear to destabilize *Oz* iconography, Dorothy's animal companion has taken various forms through the years, among them a bulldog and a cow named Imogen.[63] *The Muppets'* is not the first *Oz* production to play with these signifiers, nor with the technique of pastiche.

Given *The Muppets' Wizard of Oz's* myriad intertexts, how is it possible to evaluate this film in terms of fidelity? Should it be evaluated in terms of the novel it signals as a source? Should it be evaluated in terms of a loose history of performance and generic cross-breeding? Some reviewers evaluate the film in terms of its fidelity to the spirit of Baum's novel or to the spirit of the Muppets. *Business Wire* writes, "Based on the book 'The Wonderful Wizard of Oz' by L. Frank Baum, the Muppets version gives the story a couple of twists and tweaks without ever losing the central meaning of the classic story."[64] Richard Clune's *Sunday Telegraph* review urges audiences to "Join Kermit the Frog, Miss Piggy and the other Muppet characters as they transform everyone's favourite classic tale into a madcap musical adventure that shines brighter than the Emerald City."[65] Many reviewers opt to focus on the film's music. Andy Smith reports that "Probably the biggest disappointment in *The Muppets' Wizard of Oz* is the music, or lack of it." He notes that "Ashanti does a couple of pallid numbers, and that's about it. There's nothing close to "Over the Rainbow," "Off to See the Wizard" or any of the other songs that helped make the 1939 movie so memorable."[66] Similarly, David Hinckley writes, "this film doesn't use the songs from the original, and no matter how nicely Ashanti sings their replacements, 'The Wizard Of Oz' without 'Over the Rainbow' is like a theater without popcorn. Maybe worse."[67] Chase Squires complains that "the Muppets offer fewer songs, and none that viewers will recognize. "Somewhere Over the Rainbow," "We're Off to See the Wizard," "Ding-Dong the Witch Is Dead," "Follow the Yellow Brick Road," "If I Only Had a Brain—all gone."[68]

What is significant about reviews of the film is how few evaluate it on its own terms. Rather, they evaluate the effectiveness of its articulation of the "spirit" of the novel, or what might be termed a communal understanding of "Oz" as garnered from the 1939 film. When reviewers write of "fewer songs" and "replacement" songs, or refer to songs as "all gone," they imply a gauge against which to measure the film's musicality; the songs had been there at one point and were later removed. What they are really evaluating is how well *The Muppets'* music measures up to the music from the MGM film. That *The Muppets' Wizard of Oz* purports to adapt Baum's novel and not the 1939 film is of little consequence. Other reviews are more overt in the comparisons. *The Chicago Daily Herald'*s Ted Cox reports: "Certainly, there's room for revisionist versions of a classic, like 'Wicked.' Yet when something is done right the first time, like the 1939 movie musical 'The Wizard of Oz,' why do it again?" Cox adds, "Actually, the Muppets' take on 'The Wizard of Oz' isn't based on the movie, but on the original L. Frank Baum children's book. . . . Yet it's heavily indebted to the movie version in style and look, and there are new songs right where the old songs used to be. They just aren't near as good."[69] *The San Antonio Express News* warns, "Though devotees of the beloved 1939 motion picture may have a tough time with this one, it's a fun ride for people who don't take their Oz that seriously."[70] Similarly, *The Providence Journal* writes, "So *The Muppets' Wizard of Oz* isn't about to replace the original. But, if you like the Muppets, there are enough clever twists on the old story to make this worth a look."[71]

Each of these *Oz* adaptations has configured and signaled fidelity in a particular way and has experienced, as a result, particular fidelity-based responses. We might conclude from these examples simply that distinct adaptations invite distinct fidelity dialogues, but such a conclusion would be premature, as similarly varied responses often develop in response to a single adaptation. In the next section, I will take a broader look at some dominant trends in fidelity discourse, some of the ways in which fidelity is deployed in service of specific arguments, and fidelity's currency as a term in evaluation and analysis.

The emphasis placed on fidelity in adaptation discourse ranges from explicit to implicit. As Stam observes, "fidelity theory does not always name itself as such"; it is often brought into discourse covertly, embedded in interpretive models that purport to move beyond fidelity.[72] The most overtly evaluative fidelity assessments use the terms faithful and unfaithful as synonyms for good and bad, praiseworthy and dismissible. They appear to evaluate the adaptation in terms of fidelity to a source, but their assessments are often are based on aspects or circumstances external to the progenitor text. For example, a reviewer of *The Muppets' Wizard of Oz* writes, "Judging from its pedigree," the film "has the makings of a hit: Disney, MGM, Muppets, Ashanti. But sift through the corporate synergy, convergence and strategic partnerships, and nothing is left but color and sound. Dorothy sold her soul. This is not the Wizard of Oz story you remember, or will remember."[73] While the reviewer couches his critique in fidelity discourse, his argument—that the film fails because it is unfaithful to what we remember of *Oz*—has less to do with fidelity than with the bureaucracy surrounding production. In a similar vein, referring to Jane Campion's *The Portrait of a Lady* (1996),[74] one viewer comments, "Nicole Kidman IS Isabel Archer! . . . [Kidman] has never looked more beautiful than in this film."[75] Although the implication is that Campion's *Portrait* is faithful because Nicole Kidman is beautiful, what is really meant is, "If you like Nicole Kidman, you'll like this film because it showcases her acting *and* her beauty."

Sometimes "faithful" is used in place of "realistic" or "believable," as in the case of *The Passion of the Christ* (2004).[76] One viewer writes, "This movie is the most realistic, historically accurate version of Christ's Passion on film to date. . . . The film is faithful to and based primarily on the four Gospels."[77] The aim of these comments is not to participate in a critical dialogue as much as it is to encourage or discourage like-minded readers from seeing the film. Other discourse takes the line that the more faithful an adaptation is, the better it is as a film and tends to offer detailed discussions of both the adaptation and the source to point out the ways in which the adaptor has either misread or correctly read the source text. Anita Gates's *New York Times* review of *The Muppets' Wizard of Oz* claims, "But something essential has been tampered with here. Garland's Dorothy just longed to go home; Ashanti's wants fame, fortune, bright lights and adoration. . . . It's not just that Dorothy never sings 'Over the Rainbow' (which would be sacrilegious), but that a world where 'happy little bluebirds fly' and 'troubles melt like lemon drops' holds no appeal for her."[78]

Many critics justify alleged infidelities as made necessary by the larger agenda the adaptation serves. For example, one reader cautions that, although Ryman's *Was* may not offer a recognizable reflection of Oz (e.g., "It's not the Oz you remember or even the Oz you want it to be"), its infidelities result in an even more powerful text that exposes the "fallibility of the characters that were once infallible."[79] Often fidelity discourse is used to demonstrate the method by which an adaptation prioritizes aspects of a source text that may be downplayed by the source text itself. It is not uncommon for adaptations studies to demonstrate that an adaptation is unfaithful in order to make the case that the infidelities enable the adaptation to articulate aspects of a text better than strict fidelity would. For example, fidelity discourse is

often pressed into discussions of the ways in which an adaptation amplifies the social concerns or conflicts of gender, individualism, class,
and race differently. Porton explains that "the screen version of *The
House of Mirth*, despite a few inventive deviations from its source, is
much more faithful to the novel than its harshest critics care to acknowledge. Nevertheless, Davies's faithfulness to the spirit of Whar-
ton cannot be separated from its spirited dialogue with her text—a
salutary recasting of the novel that offers a prismatic view of both the
past's economic rapacity and current permutations of the consumer
society."[80] Often the language of fidelity is put into service of arguments that defend an adaptation's infidelities as invited by the medium. Nancy Bentley's essay on Campion's *Portrait of a Lady* argues
that Campion's film finds cinematic analogues for James's novelistic
devices and, in doing so, substitutes fidelity to the medium of film for
strict textual fidelity. As Bentley sees it, Campion's *Portrait* "still deserves to be called a faithful adaptation of James's novel, though to do
so may require us to suspend our assumptions about what it means to
translate novels into films."[81]

Given that each of these writers makes an argument that could be
articulated without using or borrowing from the language of fidelity,
the question becomes, what is sought or gained from positioning an
argument in terms of fidelity? For example, Bentley's essay makes a
compelling and nuanced argument about spectatorship, female
agency, and sexuality vis-à-vis Campion's film that could easily stand
on its own, independent of its contextualizing fidelity argument. Much
fidelity discourse is structured as a defense, clarification, or alternate
reading of an adaptation and neglects to fully consider that, in many
cases, this structure is determined by the adaptation itself. Campion
defines her *Portrait* in cinematic, as opposed to literary, terms and in
doing so lays the groundwork for evaluations that consider cinematic
substitutions for literary devices. It is likely that readers' tendency to
mention *Was*'s historical accuracy largely stems from Ryman's concluding epilogue entitled "Reality Check," which distinguishes between aspects of the novel that are derived from facts and those that
are interpretations of facts.[82] Likewise, *The Wiz* frames itself as an *Oz*
text reflective of black Americans' search for home and belonging and,
therefore, invites responses about how well or poorly it articulates that
experience.

Early adaptation studies suggested accurately that evaluations determined by fidelity-based value hierarchies are unproductive. But such
evaluations mark just one strain of fidelity discourse. Each text signals
fidelity to multiple texts in multiple ways. While adaptive texts signal
fidelity to a nominal source text, the resulting source/adaptation dis-

course is not the only available fidelity discourse, as adaptations signal fidelity to texts outside their sources as well. Fidelity discourse is shaped by the agendas of writers, filmmakers, audiences and commentators. Regardless of whether the aim is to recommend the adaptation or to highlight the method by which it articulates previously neglected aspects of a source text, fidelity discourse is agenda-driven and not based, as has been commonly maintained, solely on correspondences between the source and adaptation.

NOTES

1. Christa Albrecht-Crane and Dennis Cutchins, introduction to *New Approaches to Adaptation Studies*, 12.

2. Robert Stam, *Literature and Film: A Guide to the Theory and Practice of Film Adaptation* (Malden, MA: Blackwell Publishing, 2005), 14.

3. Thomas Leitch, "Twelve Fallacies in Contemporary Adaptation Theory," *Criticism* 45, no. 2 (2003): 162.

4. See Albrecht-Crane and Cutchins's introduction; Dudley Andrew, *Concepts in Film Theory* (Oxford: Oxford University Press, 1984), 6; Imelda Whelehan, "Adaptations: The Contemporary Dilemmas," in *Adaptations: From Text to Screen, Screen to Text* (London: Routledge, 1999), 17. Recent adaptation scholarship has begun to challenge this trend. See Linda Hutcheon, *A Theory of Adaptation* (New York: Routledge, 2006); Thomas Leitch, *Film Adaptation & Its Discontents: From* Gone with the Wind *to* The Passion of the Christ (Baltimore: The Johns Hopkins University Press, 2007); and *The Cambridge Companion to Literature on Screen*, ed. Deborah Cartmell and Imelda Whelehan (Cambridge: Cambridge University Press, 2007).

5. George Bluestone, *Novels into Film* (Berkeley: University of California Press, 1971), 5.

6. See Seymour Chapman, "What Novels Can Do That Films Can't (And Vice Versa)," in *Film Theory and Criticism: Introductory Readings*, 5th edition, ed. Leo Baudy and Marshall Cohen (New York: Oxford University Press, 1999), 435–51, and Brian McFarlane, *Novel to Film: An Introduction to the Theory of Adaptation* (Oxford: Clarendon, 1996). Chapman holds that, while narrative aspects of a work can translate from one medium to another, other aspects, like tone, cannot. Similarly, McFarlane outlines various literary aspects that can be translated into film and those that require cinematic substitutions.

7. For a more developed discussion of these arguments see Kamilla Elliott, *Rethinking the Novel/Film Debate* (Cambridge: Cambridge University Press, 2003), particularly Chapters 1 and 5, and Robert Stam, "Beyond Fidelity: The Dialogics of Adaptation," in *Film Adaptation*, ed. James Naremore (New Brunswick: Rutgers University Press, 2000), 54–76.

8. Stam, *Literature and Film*, 15.

9. Geoffrey Atheling Wagner, *The Novel and the Cinema* (Rutherford, NJ: Fairleigh Dickinson University Press, 1975).

10. Dudley Andrew, "Adaptation," in *Film Theory and Criticism*, 5th ed., ed. Leo Braudy and Marshall Cohen (New York: Oxford University Press, 1999), 452–60.

11. James John Griffith, *Adaptations as Imitations: Films from Novels* (Newark: University of Delaware Press, 1997).

94 KATE NEWELL

12. Lindiwe Dovey, "Towards an Art of Adaptation: Film and the New Criticism-as-Creation," *Iowa Journal of Cultural Studies* 2 (2002): 51–61.

13. Brian McFarlane, *Novel to Film: An Introduction to the Theory of Adaptation* (Oxford: Oxford University Press, 1996), 10.

14. Andrew, "Adaptation," 454.

15. *Hamlet*, DVD, directed by Michael Almereyda (Los Angeles: Miramax, 2001).

16. See M. M. Bakhtin, "Discourse In The Novel," *The Dialogic Imagination* (Austin: University of Texas Press, 1981), 259–422; Gérard Genette, *Palimpsests: Literature in the Second Degree* (Lincoln: University of Nebraska Press, 1997); Erica Sheen, "Introduction," *The Classic Novel: From Page to Screen* (Manchester, UK: Manchester University Press, 2000).

17. Stam, *Literature and Film*, 27.

18. As Thomas Leitch has pointed out, "no intertextual model, however careful, can be adequate to the study of adaptation if it limits each intertext to a single precursor" ("Twelve Fallacies," 165).

19. *The Wizard of Oz*, DVD, directed by Victor Fleming (1939; Turner Entertainment Co. and Warner Home Video, 1999).

20. *The Muppets' Wizard of Oz*, DVD, directed by Kirk R. Thatcher (Los Angeles: 20th Century Fox Television, 2005).

21. *The Wiz*, VHS, directed by Sidney Lumet (1978; Los Angeles: MCA Home Video, 1992).

22. *The Wonderful Wizard of Oz* has been adapted multiple times in various media—including theater, literature, music, film, animation, and illustration. While generic distinctions are important to the adaptation process and to discussions of fidelity, I will not be addressing such distinctions here in depth, as my purpose in considering these text cases is to chart the various markers adaptations deploy to signal fidelity or infidelity.

23. Douglass Street, "The Wonderful Wiz That Was: The Curious Transformation of *The Wizard of Oz*," *Kansas Quarterly* 16, no. 3 (1984): 91.

24. Mark Evan Swartz, *Oz Before the Rainbow: L. Frank Baum's* The Wonderful Wizard of Oz *on Stage and Screen to 1939* (Baltimore: The Johns Hopkins University Press, 2000), 1.

25. Robert Lane, "Product description," online review of *The Wiz*, directed by Sydney Lumet, www.amazon.ca/Wiz-Sdney-Lumet/dp/1558801235

26. Daniel Handler, "Hey, Watch Who You're Calling *Wicked*," review of *Wicked*, directed by Joe Mantello, *The New York Times* Late Edition, June 29, 2003, 2:5.

27. Maguire's book is not the first to tell a familiar story from an alternate perspective or from the perspective of an absent or underdeveloped character. Sena Jeter Naslund's *Ahab's Wife; or, The Star-Gazer* (1999), Alice Randall's *The Wind Done Gone* (2002), Valerie Martin's *Mary Reilly* (1999), John Gardner's *Grendel* (1989), and John Updike's *S.* (1988) are just a few novels that offer alternate tellings of existing narratives.

28. Handler, "*Watch Who You're Calling*."

29. Michiko Kakutani, "Let's Get This Straight: Glinda Was the Bad One?" review of *Wicked*, by Gregory Maguire, *The New York Times* Late Edition, October 24, 1995, C: 17. LexisNexis Academic.

30. Stephanie Schorow, "Wicked of [sic] just Misunderstood?" review of *Wicked*, by Gregory Maguire, *The Boston Herald*, Oct. 28, 1996: 33, http://bostonherald.com

31. Cathy Hainer, "Somewhere over the rainbow lies a 'Wicked' fable," review of *Wicked*, by Gregory Maguire, *USA Today*, October 23, 1995, 5D.

32. L. Frank Baum, *The Wonderful Wizard of Oz* (New York: Dover, 1960), 58–59.

33. Ibid., 59.

34. Gregory Maguire, *Wicked: The Life and Times of the Wicked Witch of the West* (New York: HarperCollins, 1995), 313.

35. Chadwick's 1925 *Wizard of Oz* also depicts Uncle Henry as abusive, although not sexually. See Mark Evan Swartz, *Oz Before the Rainbow*, 209–12.

36. Geoff Ryman, *Was* (New York: Penguin, 1992), 180.

37. Ibid., 10.

38. Ibid., 12.

39. Ibid., 15.

40. Baum, *Wonderful Wizard of Oz*, 27.

41. Iris Fanger, "A New Twist on the Land of Oz," review of *Wicked*, directed by Joe Mantello, *The Christian Science Monitor*, October 30, 2003, 11, http://www.csmonitor.com/2003/1030/p11s02-almp.html

42. Hainer, "Somewhere over the rainbow."

43. Chris Orcutt, review of *Was*, by Geoff Ryman, *2 Walls Webzine*, Nov. 6, 2004, http://www.2walls.com/REVIEWS/BOOKS/Was.asp.

44. M. G. Jackson, "Oz Explodes!" online review of *Was*, by Geoff Ryman, Sept. 28, 2004, www.amazon.com

45. Owen Keehnen, "Oz-o-Rama," online review of *Was*, by Geoff Ryman, Sept. 1, 2004, http://www.amazon.com/Was-Geoff-Ryman/dp/B000IOEP6I/ref=pd_bbs_1?ie=UTF8&s=books&qid=1236455808&sr=8-1

46. Ryman quoted in Laurel Graeber, "Oz Can Be Anywhere," review of *Was*, by Geoff Ryman, *New York Times*, July 5, 1992, Book Review, 7.

47. "everyonelovestheboots," "I love this movie!" online review of *The Wiz*, directed by Sidney Lumet, Apr. 15, 2004, http://www.amazon.ca/product-reviews/0783233493

48. Ethan Mordden, *The Hollywood Musical* (New York: St. Martin's Press, 1981), 213. See also Jack Kroll, "Under the Rainbow," *Newsweek*, October 30, 1978: 89.

49. Ethan Mordden claims, "What killed *The Wiz* was too many songs and Sidney Lumet's sluggish pacing" (*Hollywood Musical*, 213).

50. Bonnie Allen, "A Funked-Up Yellow Brick Road," *Essence*, January 1979, 27.

51. Donald Bogle, *Toms, Coons, Mulattoes, Mammies, and Bucks: An Interpretive History of Blacks in American Films*, 4th ed. (New York: Continuum, 2001), 265.

52. Ibid.

53. Jack Kroll, "Under the Rainbow," *Newsweek*, Oct. 30, 1978.

54. Jack Kroll, "Oz With Soul," review of *The Wiz*, directed by Sidney Lumet, *Newsweek*, January 20, 1975.

55. "Diana Ross in *The Wiz*," *Ebony* 34, November 1978, 115.

56. Grier played The Wiz in a 2006 La Jolla Playhouse production of *The Wiz*. See www.playbill.com/news/article/102569.html.

57. Of course *The Wonderful Wizard of Oz* is not the first literary text to be adapted and adopted as a Muppets vehicle. Others include *Muppet Treasure Island* (1996) and *The Muppet Christmas Carol* (1992).

58. Henson Company sold the rights to the Muppets to Disney in 2003.

59. Most of the pre-1939 stage and film adaptations of Oz include musical numbers, and many extend or complicate the Kansas material in interesting ways. For an in-depth examination of these early productions, see Swartz.

60. Popular lore speaks of a "Dark Side of the Rainbow" effect, a series of sonic and thematic correspondences produced by playing Pink Floyd's *Dark Side of the Moon* album and the 1939 *Wizard of Oz* film simultaneously.

61. Chase Squires, "No Place like This, no Place like This," review of *The Muppets' Wizard of Oz*, *St. Petersburg Times*, May 20, 2005, 2B.

62. Swartz, *Oz Before the Rainbow*, 36.

63. Ibid.

64. "Walt Disney Records to Release 'Best of the Muppets Featuring the Muppets' Wizard of Oz' from the Upcoming ABC Telefilm, 'The Muppets' Wizard of Oz,'" *Business Wire*, April 14, 2005, *LexisNexis Academic*, University of Delaware Library Networked Databases.

65. Richard Clune, "The Funday Telegraph," review of *The Muppets' Wizard of Oz*, *Sunday Telegraph*, Sept. 3, 2006, 13.

66. Andy Smith, "On the Cover: The Muppets meet Dorothy in an updated Oz," review of *The Muppets' Wizard of Oz*, directed by Kirk R. Thatcher, *The Providence Journal*, May 15, 2005, T3.

67. David Hinckley, "Muppets not so 'Oz'-some in 'Wiz,'" review of *The Muppets' Wizard of Oz*, *Daily News*, May 20, 2005, 130.

68. Squires, "No Place."

69. Ted Cox, "Oz-ification. For all its disarming charm, 'The Muppets' Wizard of Oz' seems calcified and conventional next to the movie musical," review of *The Muppets' Wizard of Oz*, *Chicago Daily Herald*, May 20, 2005, 35.

70. Jeanne Jakle, "Kermit, Piggy meet Ashanti," review of *The Muppets' Wizard of Oz.*, *San Antonio Express-News*, May 18, 2005, 1G.

71. Smith, "On the Cover."

72. Stam, *Literature and Film*, 18–19.

73. Squires, "No Place."

74. *The Portrait of a Lady*, DVD, directed by Jane Campion (Polygram Filmed Entertainment, 1996).

75. anna-joelle, "Beautiful!" online review of *The Portrait of a Lady*, directed by Jane Campion, July 4, 2004, http://www.amazon.ca/Portrait-Lady-Jane-Campion/dp/6304419708/ref=sr_1_1?ie=UTF8&s=video&qid=1236451767&sr=1–1

76. *The Passion of the Christ*, DVD, directed by Mel Gibson (Twentieth Century Fox, 2004).

77. Joshua Vargas, "The Most Realistic Depiction of Jesus of Nazareth, Ever!" online review of *The Passion of the Christ*, directed by Mel Gibson, Dec. 4, 2003, http://www.amazon.com

78. Anita Gates, "Muppets as Munchkins: We're Not in Kansas Anymore," review of *The Muppets' Wizard of Oz*, *The New York Times* Late Edition, May 20, 2005, E26.

79. Mandi Marie Frederick, "An Emotional Ringer," online review of *Was*, by Geoff Ryman, Aug. 7, 2000, http://www.amazon.com/Was-Geoff-Ryman/dp/B000IOEP6I/ref=pd_bbs_1?ie=UT F8&s=books&qid=1236455808&sr=8–1

80. Richard Porton, "The Discreet Charm of the Leisure Class: Terence Davies's *The House of Mirth*," in *Literature and Film: A Guide to the Theory and Practice of Film Adaptation*, ed. Robert Stam and Alessandra Raengo (Malden, MA: Blackwell, 2005), 87.

81. Nancy Bentley, "Conscious Observation: Jane Campion's *Portrait of a Lady*," in *Henry James Goes to the Movies*, ed. Susan M. Griffin (Lexington: University Press of Kentucky, 2002), 128.

82. Ryman, *Was*, 365.

II
Literature, Film Adaptations, and Beyond

Visualizing Metaphors in *Brokeback Mountain*
Andrea D. Fitzpatrick

FROM HOMOSOCIAL LOVE TO HOMOPHOBIC VIOLENCE, FROM MOUN-
tain euphoria to acute melancholy, and among gutted sheep and tire
irons, how can one navigate—and better appreciate—the imagery that
so powerfully resonates across different versions of *Brokeback Mountain?* Because adaptation studies are interdisciplinary fields negotiating
literature and film (as well as other disciplines), and because this volume is dedicated to intertextual approaches that seek to multiply the
possible ways of considering adapted works, I am interested in exploring what an intertextual methodology characteristic of art history can
bring to this discourse, in particular to *Brokeback Mountain*, one of the
most celebrated and discussed adaptations in recent film history. Traditionally, art history is a discipline that has been sensitive to metaphor, allegory, narratives, formal qualities, and visuality. One of art
history's goals is to synthesize a diverse array of information into a
cohesive analysis of art works, which in turn must be situated within
specific cultural contexts. A methodology common to contemporary
art history involves interdisciplinarity, intertextuality, and a concern
for the processes of transformation between ideas and "texts" (artistic
and theoretical) from one medium to another. Art history is, therefore, not only potentially useful to adaptation studies, but also, adaptation studies are informative to art history because of their focus on the
interconnection between visual and written imagery, and their interdisciplinary involvement in literature, film studies, and other cultural
areas. My goal here is to employ an intertextual approach to some
compelling imagery in the set of texts collectively known as *Brokeback
Mountain*, namely the short story by Annie Proulx, the screenplay by
Larry McMurtry and Diana Ossana, and the film directed by Ang
Lee.[1]

The adaptation of *Brokeback Mountain* merits the analysis of a
number of metaphors because they tend to dissolve the boundaries between the page and the visual image, almost—but not quite—
seamlessly. The point is not to approach *Brokeback Mountain* as a

random or endless stream of possible interpretations, but to focus on imagery whose significance deepens by reading the texts in tandem, in a dialogic way. The goal is to intensify areas of richness across the different versions of *Brokeback Mountain* so that their baroque complexity is exposed and situated within specific cultural and political histories. This study will focus on two metaphoric figures—the gutted sheep and the tire iron—talismanic, spectral, traumatic figures whose emergence is slightly different in each *Brokeback Mountain* text. These figures are infused with the subtext of violence and are expansive (even attractive) in their visual potential. Metaphor analysis offers a productive means of inquiry because metaphors resist closure. Being contingent upon cultural and historical contexts, metaphors are unstable and open to a range of interpretations. Further, there is a fluid metaphoricity to *Brokeback Mountain's* key figures—the gutted sheep and the tire iron—whose shifting qualities resist essentialist interpretations and whose fleshiness and phallicism express themes of wounded masculinity. In order to draw out these metaphors, attention must be paid to the politics of gender so central to *Brokeback Mountain*, with its antiheroic exposure of the brutal homophobia permeating the rural American patriarchy. I would like to show how the complex nuances of these metaphors convey a spectrum of emotions and embodied experiences from violence to passionate love, from the lustful carnality of life to harbingers of death.

To demonstrate the richness of the various metaphors in *Brokeback Mountain* and to point to some of the cultural contexts that inform them, a theoretical background regarding intertextuality as a methodology is useful. The notion of intertextuality is based upon the theories of (among others) Roland Barthes, who distinguishes between the artistic entity that can be considered a "work," which is closed, complete, centered, and authored by a seemingly original, singular, source, and the alternative he advocates, the "Text," which is likened to a woven fabric involving "stereographic plurality" and "a serial movement of disconnections, overlappings, variations."[2] As Barthes suggests, texts are never considered origins but always implicated by prior fields of knowledge, language, and usage. It is important to keep in mind that a Text can be considered any theoretical or artistic entity (visual, musical, theatrical, or literary), and this openness as to what counts as a Text fosters interdisciplinarity, as Barthes also notes.[3] In adaptation studies inspired by intertextuality, one is not looking for conflicts of meaning, failures, and originary form as much as threshold areas where contingencies occur. Moreover, the "Text" for Barthes, "is a methodological field" that "poses problems of classification," so the term is appropriate to refer to the many different versions of

Brokeback Mountain involved in the adaptation process (the story, the score, the screenplay, the film, etc. . . .), which are interconnected and intermediary.[4]

Intertextuality as an approach to adaptation studies has been proposed largely to overcome the problems associated with fidelity criticism. As James Naremore points out, fidelity criticism is founded upon a hierarchy whereby the work of literature is considered the more authentic, primary work and the film a secondary deviation from it, to be judged on its accuracy (as if such objective analysis between media were possible or desirable). To the existing paradigms of adaptation studies, which all generally involve issues of "textual fidelity," Naremore proposes to "augment the metaphors of translation and performance with the *metaphor of intertextuality*."[5] In brief, intertextuality can be used as a theoretical adrenaline to achieve a "more flexible" and expansive approach to writing on adaptation, an approach better able to take into account a wider, less hierarchical range of artistic and (pop) cultural sources.[6] Further, according to Peter Brooker, who writes about postmodern adaptations, "Academic study has tirelessly returned to the criterion of fidelity and its other associated binary distinctions of type and value to critique their inconsistencies and implications. Most convincingly they have been deconstructed in favor of a preferred emphasis upon relations of difference or dialogue, not of hierarchy, between texts and media."[7] Aligned with the editors' proposal for an adaptation studies revitalized by poststructuralism, my approach will involve liminal areas where texts collide, overlap, and shift. If one keeps in mind that adaptation studies are unique in focusing on the interstitial areas *between* literature and cinema (as well as other disciplines), Jacques Derrida's theorization of *différance*, an approach which espouses a "play" of meanings (which cannot be set into a binary opposition or structured in a teleological way) becomes useful.[8] His emphasis on the "interval" and "spacing," in other words, shifts in context, history, and linguistic usage that keep interpretive meanings open, is vitally important when attempting to negotiate a "translation" or "transformation" between texts.[9] Derrida's thinking is also inspirational to adaptation studies in that he eschews notions of origin (i.e., "the original" or "source" text), in contrast to types of fidelity criticism that posit a hierarchized relation between a film and its literary precursor: "For what is put into question is precisely the quest for a rightful beginning, an absolute point of departure, a principal responsibility."[10]

Clearly, when film criticism and adaptation studies are dealing with the vexing issue of the "auteur," the thinking of deconstructionists and poststructuralists[11] can be useful in addressing the adaptation process itself, which demonstrates the renunciation of claims to authorial mastery associated with the singular, solitary author function.[12] Such a view is supported by Brooker who, when commenting on Barthes's essay "From Work to Text," writes that, "[his] intention was to demote the godlike figure of the (usually male designated) 'Author' to the figure of the 'scriptor' working laterally across texts, and to activate the reader."[13] As Larry McMurtry, Diana Ossana, and Annie Proulx make clear in their essays describing the process of adapating *Brokeback Mountain*, collaboration and a number of compromises were made, all of which certainly involve relinquishing the solo "author" function, when launching the story from the page to the screen.[14] The inter-reliance of the texts in *Brokeback Mountain*'s adaptation in the domain of the reader/viewer also suggests that cross-reading its texts (rather than positioning the literary version as the source) is necessary for the most nuanced understanding of the narratives. Lacunae and questions about one version are answered by the study of another, which in turn, are informed by fields of cultural, historical, and political knowledge. Switching focus between the story, the screenplay, and the film, the path of this essay resists a linear, hierarchical interpretation that would position the literary text as the primary, originating source and the film as secondary.[15]

However, potential criticisms of this approach could arise from followers of Fredric Jameson because in his understanding of postmodernism, he describes intertextuality as "a conception of practices, discourses and textual play" that is also a signpost for superficiality or at least "surface" as opposed to the "various depth models" attributed to modernist film, art, literature and their criticism.[16] Although Jameson is not offering a value judgment, the connotation that intertextual methods will be limited to surface grazing is still evident in, for example, Brooker's essay when he describes the "scriptor" and "reader" as figures who, "cruised, antennae bristling, across this layered textuality, but did not pause to dig below or look behind this surface for a book's single authorized meaning."[17] Despite this view, my intention is to take an intertextual approach to *Brokeback Mountain* and to achieve interpretive depth. An intertextual approach to *Brokeback Mountain* can, moreover, provide a framework for analysis that neither overemphasizes nor ignores the literary at the expense of the cinematic. The primacy of the literary at the expense of the cinematic will be avoided by my emphasis on visuality, not only with the art historical references, but also with the focus on motifs from Proulx's story that are luminous in their visual potential. Keeping in mind Brian McFarlane's observation that, "[the] term 'reading' is still much used for film, both strengthening the tie to the earlier medium and implying its primacy,"[18] what follows is an attempt at "seeing" the *Brokeback Mountain* texts to draw out the visual power of their imagery. I will forage among the texts for *différances* (in the Derridean sense) and intensities rather than deficiencies, not superficially, but according to the demands of the subject matter, the medium, and their aesthetic dimensions. Despite my attempts to identify metaphoric imagery in the *Brokeback Mountain* texts, their symbolic cultural content will always, fortunately, exceed any given frame of reference, and resist the mastery of any one critic.

"UP ON BROKEBACK . . ."

Annie Proulx starts the story "Brokeback Mountain" at the "end" when one of the cowboy protagonists, Ennis del Mar (who is barely middle-aged but poverty-stricken financially and emotionally) experiences a moment of morning lust: "he is suffused with a sense of pleasure because Jack Twist was in his dream."[19] Proulx's opening paragraph, which also mentions "the shirts hanging on a nail," hints at the effects of this surprising love affair and the beautiful environment on Brokeback Mountain in Wyoming where it flourished one brief summer in 1963, two decades earlier.[20] Proulx's description of Ennis's reverie is also conveyed with temperature, a sensual element that courses through the story in a poetic way: "If he does not force his attention on it, it might *stoke* the day, *rewarm* that old, cold time on the mountain when they owned the world and nothing seemed wrong."[21] Proulx aptly describes the memory itself like a campfire flame in need of gentle attention, so as not to burn out. However, Proulx's phrase, "nothing seemed wrong" is an indication that the present state of Ennis's universe is indeed wrong. This comprises one of the many premonitions that love will be lost and tragedy will ensue. Proulx's opening scene is closely related to—if not a retelling of—the concluding scene in the story in which Ennis experiences erotic dreams of Jack in the same dusty trailer, and with tear-filled eyes creates the memorial to his dead lover composed of the nostalgia-inducing shirts. The temporal structure of Proulx's story involves a loop, a figure that holds its own significance because it alludes not only to the Western genre (to the lassos with which the protagonists work), but also indicates the repetition and regression of Ennis's life without Jack. The temporality of the loop suggests not linear progression, but rather how Ennis's life is structured by a treadmill circularity and flatness punctuated only by memories.[22]

The film's director Ang Lee and the screenwriters Larry McMurtry and Diana Ossana begin the story of the love affair more optimistically when Jack and Ennis, both still teenagers, meet outside the foreman's trailer to get their instructions about summer work herding sheep on Brokeback Mountain. Lee exploits all the visual potential of the film medium, in particular, the magnetism of the gaze (involving exhibitionism, voyeurism, and narcissism) and how it exemplifies not only a homoerotic potential in the stylized machismo of the two characters, but also their personality traits: Jack (compassionately performed by Jake Gyllenhaal) is affable and extroverted with wide-open blue eyes; Ennis (brilliantly interpreted by the late Heath Ledger) is restrained and introverted with brown eyes squinting from beneath the rim of his hat. In the remarkable opening sequence of virtuoso editing and a subtle choreography of the young men's bodies involving posturing and display, Jack and Ennis furtively size each other up without a single word spoken between them. The homoeroticism of the scene is implied not only between the two young men (whose stolen glances suggest a possible "love at first sight"), but also by the camera's lingering looks, which caress their handsome faces with Lee's signature whisper-close framing. Proulx's description of this encounter also conveys latent sexuality, and may be making an ironic reference to the writing process: "they came together on paper as herder and camp tender."[23] Proulx's "union" of the two coincides with the delivery of the foreman Joe Aguirre's "point of view" as he barks out orders.[24] This is followed by Proulx's detailed descriptions of the characters, as endearing in their humanity as in their flaws. Jack Twist, with his "quick laugh" and "buckteeth," is "fair enough" and "infatuated with the rodeo life"; while Ennis is "scruffy" with "caliper legs" and a "supple body made for the horse and for fighting."[25]

At least three of the *Brokeback Mountain* texts (the story, the screenplay, and the film) convey the sensual liberties explored by Ennis and Jack while alone on Brokeback Mountain. Proulx writes a line that breathlessly captures the delirious freedom: "There were only the two of them on the mountain flying in the euphoric, bitter air, looking down on the hawk's back and the crawling lights of vehicles on the plain below, suspended above ordinary affairs and distant from tame ranch dogs barking in the dark hours."[26] Despite the fact that Ennis and Jack momentarily enjoy a transcendental, sovereign outlook and the joy of solitude in the landscape, the unbridled pleasure of the friendship and sex between them is qualified in the story and film by their terse disavowals whereby Ennis's "You know I ain't queer" is met with Jack's "Me neither."[27] After this homophobic exchange, the stern foreman Aguirre's arrival on horseback interrupts Ennis's and Jack's exuberant shirtless wrestling in a verdant meadow. In both texts, the young men's carefree sexual foreplay is seen through Aguirre's binoculars, the prosthetic device he uses to spy on them before he announces his presence, as if this phallic tool, empowered by his surveilling gaze, symbolizes patriarchal censure itself.

Despite these intrusions into their burgeoning romance, the mountain figures similarly in both story and film: Brokeback Mountain is the idealized talisman of impossibly-sustained pleasures, a phantasmic memory of unbounded experiences of romantic plenitude and lofty scenery that, over the next two decades, Jack and Ennis attempt to recapture with their horse-packing trips to other ranges, but never can.[28] Brokeback Mountain is where the men (and the reader/viewer) subsequently want to return, but cannot: a suspended time of apparent safety and near-perfect happiness that, as a paradise lost, will come to an end. This happens literally when they "come down" from the mountain at the abrupt, premature conclusion to their summer's work, a movement that in Ennis's mind is, "a slow-motion, but headlong, irreversible fall."[29] Proulx's Biblical references are important because they are picked up by the screenwriters, and it is difficult to avoid comparison with the Fall of Man, although with a significantly queer twist.[30] This view is supported by Eric Patterson's excellent, detailed study of the *Brokeback Mountain* texts, with his sensitivity to the obstacles of "men who love men" in the context of rural American cultural history and its social prohibitions: "The word 'fall' reverberates with implications. [. . .] The 'fall' can be thought of as one away from nature, back to society with its corrupt and corrupting notions of sin, and its compulsory pretense of heterosexuality."[31] The relatively unadulterated Edenic experience of Brokeback Mountain is corrupted in different ways in the film and in the story because, placed like the ponderous notes of Gustavo Santaolalla's score (yet another text among *Brokeback Mountain*'s weave of textualities), are dramatic signs of disaster whose complex iconography is neither moralizing nor dogmatic.

EVISCERATION AND INTIMACY: THE GUTTED SHEEP

After the initial sexual contact between Jack and Ennis during the first tent scene, there is an image of evisceration made explicit in the film. The morning after their spontaneous, drunken coupling, Ennis rides away on horseback in a somber mood, hurried and wordless, to a pasture where he finds a bloody sheep, splayed on its back and disemboweled by a coyote in the night. Ennis abruptly stops his horse and the camera cuts to what he sees—the shocking splash of red blood soaking the prone carcass of the once-benign sheep. The image screams tragedy [Figs 1 and 2]. Initially, the gutted sheep suggests Ennis's feelings of guilt for neglecting his herding duties, but in more nuanced terms, it expresses Ennis's feelings of "shame" towards the new relationship with Jack.[32] The association of the bloodied sheep with Ennis's conflicted emotions reflects (but does not endorse) themes of a politically conservative Christian tone in keeping with En-

Ennis del Mar (Heath Ledger) finding the dead sheep. Film still from *Brokeback Mountain*, © 2005 Focus Features. Courtesy of Universal Studios Licensing LLLP.

The eviscerated sheep. Film still from *Brokeback Mountain*, © 2005 Focus Features. Courtesy of Universal Studios Licensing LLLP.

nis's social conservatism. This issue of Ennis's own homophobia is complex and inherently paradoxical, and something the screenwriters address with subtlety and sympathy. Ennis's unshakable, culturally instilled homophobia is the central and irresolvable predicament that shapes the course of his life.

The dead sheep also suggests Biblical iconography with an extensive history in Western visual culture. Since ancient times, the lamb has been, according to James Hall, a "symbol of Christ in his sacrificial role."[33] That the film image of the sheep's destruction is a device with intentional Biblical overtones is made clearer with reference to the screenplay. The image of, in McMurtry and Ossana's words, "a shredded sheep, clearly the victim of a coyote pack," suggests the sacrificial lamb that is the prefiguration of Christ's crucifixion, a point that needs elaboration.[34] The painterly technique of Lee (working with cinematographer Rodrigo Prietro) is arresting in its uncanny beauty. The virulent red of the gutted sheep is the first color to so dramatically mark (or *mar*, after Ennis's surname) the cool luminosity of the mountain atmosphere, whose palette of forest greens, cerulean blues, velvet browns, and slate greys predominates. Further, the dead sheep is shown as an image whose stillness, two-dimensionality, and silence make it resemble a painting—not just any painting—but a painting, iconic in the history of Western art, whose subject matter and symbolism relate to the *Brokeback Mountain* image as loudly as its expressive formal qualities. The drama of an eviscerated animal has important precedents in Rembrandt van Rijn's painting from the Dutch Golden Age, *The Slaughtered Ox* (1655, Musée du Louvre, Paris), an image to epitomize the vulnerabilities of the flesh and the frailties of the human spirit [Fig. 3]. Rembrandt's painting *The Slaughtered Ox* is a genre work (although difficult to categorize as an interior, a still life, or a philosophic meditation) that, despite its overtly secular content, has strong Biblical overtones referencing the Crucifixion.[35] The Rembrandt painting is a classical image whose paradigmatic Christological content, the sense of tortured humanity, represents the inevitable mortality of all humans.[36] The magnitude of the gutted, dead sheep image in the film (evoking a tragedy of Christ-like proportions) can be summarized as follows: it is an aesthetic, narrative, and metaphoric gesture that is not only humanistic and universalizing but also—if one accepts the link between the crucifixion of Christ and the unlawful death of a gay man—a contemporary political statement advocating compassion towards those who suffer senseless, identity-based hate crimes.

The death of the sheep can therefore be seen as a prefiguration of Jack's death twenty years later, not as the result of a roadside accident

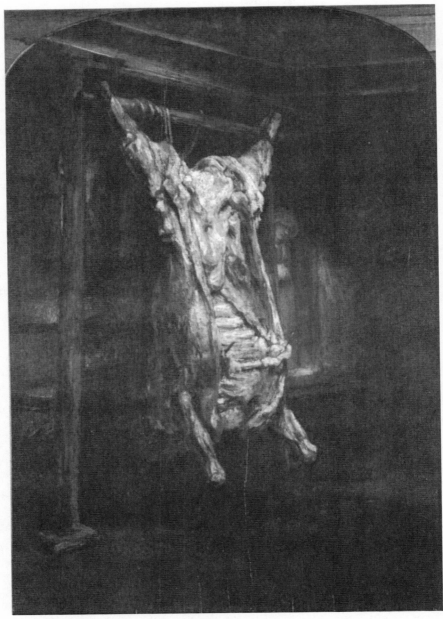

Rembrandt Harmensz van Rijn (1606–1669), *The Slaughtered Ox*, 1655, oil on panel, 37 × 26 ½ inches, Louvre, Paris. Photo credit: Scala/Art Resource, NY.

(as Jack's wife Lureen flatly claims) but a gay-bashing by a gang of Texan vigilantes (as Ennis believes). This interpretation of the gutted sheep as a direct allusion to the tragic murder of Jack is strengthened by the Biblical iconography of the lamb (like the sheep or ram), which according to James Hall is, "the attribute of the personifications of innocence, gentleness, patience, and humility."[37] In other words, Jack is an innocent victim, like the Biblical sacrificial lamb. Jim Kitses's sympathetic view of the "dead and scattered sheep" as metaphors of Jack's and Ennis's doomed situation substantiates this reading: "Yet if anything, paradoxically, such failures only serve to ennoble them in the innocence and depth of their love, and to dramatize the devastating scale of their—and everyone else's—*sacrifice and victimization*."[38] In contrast, D. A. Miller's reading of the scene takes issue with the sympathy it is meant to evoke by calling it "aversion therapy," which verges towards homophobia by the "corruption" that codes Jack's body in the next scene, where he is shown naked washing clothes by the stream: "His fresh nudity has already been 'spoiled,' assimilated to the carrion it will become."[39] Jack's nakedness, where the broad expanse of his pale shoulders visibly shudder in the mountain chill, could also suggest his vulnerability—that his "back was exposed"—and therefore could be seen as a prefiguration of his death, not as inevitable, but as the casualty of a society plagued by incendiary homophobia. To consider Jack blameless (a less literal or Biblical variation of "innocent") corresponds better to the queer-positive, liberal politics of the film and Proulx's story. This is articulated by a song on the movie soundtrack, *He Was a Friend of Mine* (written by Bob Dylan and sung by Willie Nelson), which evokes Jack's character from Ennis's point of view: "He died on the road. He never done no wrong. A thousand miles from home and he never harmed no one."[40]

In *Brokeback Mountain*, the eviscerated sheep (which appears to be still warm, wet, and buzzing with flies) conveys the primordial violence of predatory animals and the vulnerability of mortal bodies. In its glistening ruby color, the image also achieves a strange and painterly beauty.[41] Its saturated glow and jewel tones (the bloody carcass and the grey of the sheep's wool against the emerald grass) convey the dense pigmentation of oil paint. The crimson flesh offers itself angrily but voluptuously, unfolding its leaves to proffer its cavities like a trap for the eyes, a gift being unwrapped. The violence of the sheep's innards being unfurled (and as such, resembling the labial folds of drapery in Baroque paintings by Caravaggio, as described by Mieke Bal)[42] cause the stretched-out sheep to appear as much like a sacrificial figure as a spectacle of gleaming, visceral (dis)pleasure. Moreover, these effects do not necessarily cancel each other out. The sheep's borderline aesthetic between the gorgeous and the grotesque bring one into the realm of the abject according to Julia Kristeva, the specter of mortality that threatens and beckons the subject with its object–Other, that which must be kept at bay as both "me" and "not me," that which hovers at the defining limit of the body as refuse or the potential for death.[43] This primary ambivalence of the subject (Ennis) is conveyed by the film with this tightly-cropped image, the sheep's open cavities there to enfold if not devour him, yet simultaneously repulsing him with a threat of decay that is simultaneously moral and organic.

The dead sheep, whose appearance suggests a massive emotional wound *and* the deadly violence suffered by an innocent victim, is a relational figure between Ennis and Jack. The openness of the animal flesh in the film is a metaphor of transgression on some important levels, namely, the rupture of psychological cohesion and the violation of normative social boundaries. An essay about Rembrandt's painting by feminist theorist Hélène Cixous advances our understanding of the theme of emotional vulnerability and how it is linked to the eviscerated sheep in *Brokeback Mountain*. Cixous is known for a French theoretical style called *écriture féminine*, which espouses a non-linear strategy of poetic probing and affective relations between the writer and the object(s) under scrutiny. Cixous's writing heightens the metaphors of exposure made visual by Rembrandt's *The Slaughtered Ox*, and how the scrutinizing gaze of the artist (and, by extension, the viewer) opens up the flayed animal with such violating proximity that an intense relationship between subjects ensues: "You, as I see you when I see you as you really are: and to do this I have to draw the curtains aside, to slaughter you, to open you up—(with my gaze only). And then, naturally, it is me that I see, it is us, nude, it is our nuditude, magnificent, our power bound, our shining blindness. . . . Behold the portrait of our mortality."[44] The gaze Cixous describes in Rembrandt's work is a wounding contact, a painful manner of intimacy through revelation (literally, the unveiling of the animal's skin). In Cixous's writing, the carnal intimacy of Rembrandt's *The Slaughtered Ox* becomes a sign for human pathos and its ultimate exposure, an intimacy with the Other seen by way of mutual vulnerabilities and reciprocal openness. Lee's tight framing of the gutted sheep in the film, to the extent that the carcass is brought to the foreground with such airlessness, creates a psychological claustrophobia between the viewer and the sheep's innards, which are not only seen but also pornographically transgressed. The viewer instantly comprehends the potentially annihilating predicament that faces Ennis and the way it threatens him in an invasive way.

At this pivotal stage in the story and the film, while Ennis and Jack are still working on Brokeback Mountain, emotional, physical, and sexual barriers are dissolving in their tentative relationship. This is also suggested by the interior and exterior scenes near the erotically-charged pitched tent, with its hymen-like flaps (permeable membranes opening and closing to welcome and release Ennis by Jack) that are like the curtains of skin/fabric mentioned by Cixous. The premonition of Jack's mortality inherent to the image of the bloodied sheep is a rupture in the joy of the incipient love affair. Because the film image of the dead animal momentarily becomes an arresting painting (in its stillness and silence, at once seductive and sickening), the film medium also breaks from its flow. Captured in an instant with this foreboding image of violation are the emotional entanglements of Ennis and Jack involving feelings of desire, recrimination, and the terror (always experienced more by Ennis than Jack) of opening oneself to a forbidden pleasure whose consequences could be fatal.

The metaphor of evisceration is a relational figure between Jack and Ennis that also illustrates the suffering each will endure because of their illicit affair, a double-prefiguration of each lover's further ensuing pain. The conceptual link between Ennis and the gutted sheep (and therefore Jack) is clearer if one considers a line in the story in which Proulx describes Ennis's road-side reaction to parting ways with Jack (at the conclusion of their summer on Brokeback Mountain), a devastating separation both thought would be permanent: "Within a mile Ennis felt like someone was pulling his guts out hand over hand a yard at a time."[45] Ennis experiences the loss of Jack as gut-wrenching agony, an emotion of the most visceral sort because it cannot be clearly articulated. Rather than describing how Ennis feels through the metaphor of intestines being unwound (as Proulx does), Lee shows the drama of Ennis's incoherent suffering with a stark, back-lit scene of him breaking down—his composure coming undone—after Jack drives away. As soon as Jack's truck is out of eyeshot, Ennis starts to stagger down the road, then turns into a garage and collapses to his knees with dry heaves, and slams his fists into the wall in frustration [Fig. 4]. Through Ledger's phenomenal performance, Ennis's body convulses while he moans, gasps, and whimpers like a wounded animal, and then sputters to a hapless passing cowboy: "What the fuck you lookin' at?"[46] Ennis cannot openly admit his feelings for Jack because he is aware of the social abjection and horrific violence he might endure for these feelings. Nonetheless, the physicality of Ledger's performance conveys a graphic sense of wounded masculinity.

Ennis's double-bereavement (not only for the loss of Jack but also for his own inability to admit to it) is the sort that uniquely afflicts gays, according to gender theorist Judith Butler. In her Freud-inspired

Ennis del Mar (Heath Ledger) breaking down. Film still from *Brokeback Mountain*, © 2005 Focus Features. Courtesy of Universal Studios Licensing LLLP.

essay "Melancholy Gender/Refused Identifications," Butler describes the isolating experiences of silence for those who can't be "out" about their relationships, where one tragedy (the loss or death of a same-sex partner) is compounded by another (the necessity to disavow the loss due to social prohibitions against homosexuality). Butler brings attention to the pent-up sorrow that burdens gays who cannot openly express their losses; because the "successful" or "healthy" transition from melancholy to mourning never occurs, melancholy persists in the form of silenced grief.[47] In *Brokeback Mountain*, the dire social prohibitions of the West are the precondition for Ennis's love-sickness and the layered losses that wrack his body. Ennis's inadmissible grief is expressed by Proulx not by any dialogue, but by the evocative metaphor of intestines being unwound. In the film, Lee takes recourse to Ledger's emotive performance as Ennis, who slams his fists into a wall while his body crumbles to the ground.

All the *Brokeback Mountain* texts involve a complex politics towards homophobia, a politics that, in terms of narrative, metaphors, and stylistic devices, walks a tightrope between the reification of violence (psychic, social, and physical) and its critique. The consistent tone of the *Brokeback Mountain* texts hovers between the desire to make the reader/viewer acutely aware of the violence of homophobia in rural America without endorsing it. The rejection of sentimentality and facile melodrama in *Brokeback Mountain* should not be taken as ambivalence—or worse, moralizing censure. The strategy here is graphic realism, which is advanced by the correspondence of visceral imagery between the texts. In the film, the bloody, painterly image of the gutted sheep burns its metaphoric layers through the viewers' retinal and cultural memories by evoking a Biblical iconography of victimization, mortality, and the loss of innocence. Proulx's related metaphor of evisceration (involving intestines being unwound) speaks of how Ennis's stable sense of self is becoming undermined by feelings of love that are forbidden not only by society, but also by Ennis himself. Both the gutted sheep and the unraveling of intestines are violent metaphoric images that express the rupture of various boundaries, and the perils of emotional proximity involved in the transgression of a gay relationship within a homophobic society.

THE TIRE IRON AND WOUNDED MASCULINITY

In *Brokeback Mountain*, the tire iron is an object whose dense metaphoricity symbolizes the heteronormative imperatives of a patriarchal society that, in Proulx's American West, is especially brutal.[48] The tire iron, whose shape is direct, firm, and potentially-fatal, is for Proulx an object of the most extreme virulence and potency. The tire iron is a basic tool with the dual potential to fix things (like flat tires) when used as it is meant to, or to break things (like bones and bodies) when used by the menacing male figures that haunt Ennis's imagination. The simplicity of the tire iron's form belies the complexity of its meanings. For Ennis, the tire iron represents the prohibition to an openly gay relationship and the oppressive threat of homophobic violence he fears for himself and is convinced killed Jack. This fear is the result of his father's opinion that a violent death will and *should* befall any man who lives his life with another man.

The first mention of the tire iron occurs when Ennis tells Jack the story of his father forcing him, as a child, to see the abandoned corpse of a local rancher who was murdered for the audacity of living with another man: "[T]hey found Earl dead in a irrigation ditch. They'd took a tire iron to him, spurred him up, drug him around by his dick until it pulled off, just bloody pulp."[49] With nearly identical dialogue in the film and the story, Ennis's rendition of his traumatic childhood experience, being forced to see the dead man's tortured body, implicates Ennis's father as the primary source for the homophobic violence that permeates his worldview: "Dad made sure I seen it. Took me to see it. . . . Dad laughed about it. Hell, for all I know he done the job."[50] The sadistic father's "lesson" was so "effective" that it instilled in Ennis the causal connection between the idea of men cohabitating and "be[ing] dead."[51] This simple but non-negotiable equation is the foundation for Ennis's lifelong fear of entering such a life with Jack: "Two guys livin together? No."[52] One can read Proulx's scenario of homophobic fatherhood as patently symbolized or incarnated by the tire-iron, a prosthetic, phallic object whose threat imprisons Ennis in a life of missed opportunities. In the story, the tire iron's violence is so pervasive in Ennis's outlook that it almost becomes its own distinct character. In the detumescent hotel scene after Jack and Ennis have consummated their reunion after a four-year hiatus by "jouncing a bed," Ennis suggests that the reason he cannot start a life with Jack involves the lingering effect of his father's internecine homophobia: "If he was alive and was to put his head in that door right now you bet he'd go get his tire iron."[53] As if extending Ennis's dead father's reach from beyond the grave, the tire iron is the metaphor of homophobic wrath.

Not only does the tire iron signify the stringent prohibition against homosexuality, but also, according to the heteronormative mentality of the American West, it is the instrument this tradition would use to inflict such violence upon those who refuse to comply. This is explicit with the account of Jack's blood-soaked death, which happens towards the end of the story and the film when Ennis hears about the terrible "accident" from Jack's wife Lureen: "Jack was pumping up a flat on the truck out on a back road when the tire blew up. The bead was damaged somehow and the force of the explosion slammed the rim into his face, broke his nose and jaw and knocked him unconscious on his back. By the time someone came along he had drowned in his own blood."[54] Despite hearing Lureen's account of Jack's death, Ennis is convinced that Jack died at the hands of murderous homophobes: "No, he thought, they got him with the tire iron."[55] Ennis's counter-understanding of Jack's death as a murder is suggested in the film by a spectral image flashed for merely two or three blurry seconds, yet its brutality sears with intensity. Jack is shoved to the ground by a group of men who kick and beat him mercilessly with a tire iron so that, in an instant, his face (so gentle, open, and kind in all previous scenes) is slashed with a rapid series of blows, and erupts in crimson.

In both story and film versions of Jack's death, it is noteworthy that he is positioned like the gutted sheep: vulnerable, prone, and left to die drowning in his own blood on an uncaring cushion of grass while he faces the sky. While these visuals connecting the dead sheep to Jack exist explicitly in the film, there is a remarkable prefiguration of Jack's violent death that is tucked into the story that evokes an image of his face being slashed by a tire iron. On the final trip through the mountains Ennis and Jack will enjoy together, twenty years into their relationship, Proulx describes them traveling on horseback through the trails: "Going up, the day was fine but the trail deep-drifted and slopping wet at the margins. They left it to wind through a *slashy cut*, leading the horses through brittle branchwood. . . . Ennis, weather eyed, looked west for the heated cumulus that might come up on such a day but the boneless blue was so deep, said Jack, that he might *drown looking up*."[56] Proulx creates the image of Jack drowning while "looking up" at the cloudless sky. The phrase "slashy cut" is another virtuoso image that simultaneously conveys the pain of a hard metallic injury and the icy freshness of rushing mountain water. Proulx's recourse to an aestheticism that is nearly cancelled out by horrific violence—her multi-sensory images of sublime natural beauty lined with the threat of injury—is a prerogative she exploits through a unique turn of phrase and the play of opposites. Most importantly, Proulx's choice of words should be understood as a reference to Jack's face being slashed by the brutal cut of the tire rim/tire iron. Proulx's recourse to violent imagery is, however, meant neither to exacerbate the vulnerability of her fictional subjects, nor to exaggerate the homophobia that gays (as real individuals in the rural West) have historically experienced.[57] It is a tactic of unapologetically exposing a hostile social situation, which constitutes a significant protest. Proulx's intention is neither to wound her subjects nor to exploit their suffering. She does not suggest the inevitable tragedy of all gay relationships, but makes palpable, with unflinching articulation, the violence to which they have been and continue to be subject.

The menace of corporal violence that surrounds Jack is evident elsewhere in Proulx's provocative, phallic colloquialisms that speak of wounded masculinity and emasculation. The post-sex conversation between Jack and Ennis in the motel is animated by Jack's colorful language, which conveys how masculinity and vulnerability are inextricable for a bull-rider whose luck and money are running out: "Like I said, I'm gettin out a rodeo. I ain't no *broke-dick* rider but I don't got the *bucks* a ride out this slump I'm in and I don't got the *bones* a keep gettin wrecked."[58] "Broke-dick," "bucks," and "bones"—Proulx's delight with the hard-hitting, truncated sounds of the English language is not only for its alliterative potential (which brings to mind the fabled perversity of the name *Brokeback*), but also for its multiple meanings, which all suggest the loss of masculine pride.

In keeping with the transformations in *Brokeback Mountain*, the tire iron that haunts Ennis is not restricted to the realm of masculine violence, but morphs into an endearing symbol of cowboy domesticity, youthful happiness, and romantic love. The concluding paragraph in the story depicts Ennis (in a similar manner to the film) as a reclusive middle-aged man, solitary in his shabby trailer and reminiscing about his dead lover. What distinguishes Proulx's ending from the film's is the reference to the dreaded tire-iron so that the object achieves a surreal metaphoricity. Proulx writes how Ennis longingly remembers Jack as a young man, "curly-headed and smiling and bucktoothed," sitting on a log during their campfire dinners on Brokeback Mountain where, ". . . the can of beans with the spoon handle jutting out and balanced on the log was there as well, in a cartoon shape and lurid colors that gave the dreams a flavor of comic obscenity."[59] But Ennis's pleasurable dreams shift radically between desire and anxiety and are equally nightmarish: "The spoon handle was the kind that could be used as a tire iron. And he would wake sometimes in grief, sometimes with the old sense of joy and release; the pillow sometimes wet, sometimes the sheets."[60] Two important transformations are happening here. The first involves metaphoric objects that contort in shape *and* in meaning: the benign campfire spoon morphs into a virulent tire iron. Ennis's dream involves Jack's shifting attributes so that the spoon transforms from a symbol of campfire romance into the phallic object associated with pick up trucks, the open road, and the cruel retributions of the West. The second transformation involves the silent but nonetheless expressive way Ennis's body speaks (yet again) of emotions he cannot otherwise verbalize: tears of mourning and the erotic gush of ejaculation.

Not only do symbolic objects change dramatically in Ennis's mind, but his body's salty responses to bittersweet dreams of Jack shift poignantly. The alternation of Ennis's emotional "fluids" between stereotypes of femininity (with tears) and masculinity (with ejaculation) also shows metamorphosis. From the rustic whimsy of an old spoon to the murderous potential of a tire iron, these objects and body emanations convey radical shifts in morphology and meaning. The way the campfire spoon transforms into the tire iron alludes perhaps to Jack's surname Twist and may be a metaphor for the conflicting gendered identifications that Ennis undergoes as a result of his relationship with Jack, which pits homoerotic ("bent") desire in tension with heteronormative ("straight") masculinity.[61] For Ennis, the spoon ultimately involves memories of euphoria and the admission of heartbreak. It is a private icon of mourning and the haunting specter of Ennis's losses, a mixed metaphor of feelings that can neither be fully represented nor repressed.

CONCLUSION

What I hope to have accomplished here is a heightened awareness of the visuals conveyed by the *Brokeback Mountain* texts, their close reliance upon each other, and their multivalent symbolic content. Analyzing Proulx's short story along with the screenplay and the film (and other pertinent texts) augments their aesthetic choices, meanings, and areas of uniqueness. The chiasmic relationship between the texts also reflects the reciprocity of suffering experienced by the protagonists, the cowboy lovers Jack Twist and Ennis del Mar. The link between Jack's and Ennis's individual experiences of suffering is metaphorized by the eviscerated sheep, a catastrophic figure of wounded masculinity. Further, Proulx's recurring emphasis on hyper-phallic objects and adjectives comprises a symbolic language in which the performance of masculinity is fraught with failures, humiliations, and violence. Although expressed differently in the film and in the story, these images of violence and vulnerability (most explicitly with the gutted sheep and the tire iron) nevertheless echo each other when considered *across* the texts, not in a binaristic or hierarchical fashion, but in a complimentary way. Proulx's style in "Brokeback Mountain" (the contemporary poetry of her words, at once harsh, seductive, and portentous) gives a voice to horrific acts of violence in order to make clear the consequences of Ennis and Jack's courage to fall in love in such a hostile social environment. Lee, Prietro, McMurtry, and Ossana tell the story in ways that interpret and extend the richness of Proulx's metaphors with forceful images: the gutted sheep, Ennis's fists slamming into a wall, and Jack's face being slashed. An intertextual methodology provides an appreciation of the symbolic power of the metaphoric languages so evident on the page, the screen, and among the intermediary spaces of *Brokeback Mountain*. Collectively, these *Brokeback Mountain* texts create, but also rely upon, iconic images whose impact extends across and beyond the texts discussed here. The shifting connotations of the metaphors in *Brokeback Mountain* offer a series of lenses to perceive the transformative potential of desire and the vulnerability of bodies and emotions so urgently at stake.

NOTES

1. Annie Proulx, "Brokeback Mountain," in *Brokeback Mountain: Story to Screenplay* (1997; repr., New York: Scribner, 2005), 1–28; Larry McMurtry and Diana Ossana, *Brokeback Mountain: A Screenplay*, in *Brokeback Mountain: Story to Screenplay* (New York: Scribner, 2005), 29–128 [1–97]; *Brokeback Mountain*, feature film directed by Ang Lee (Alberta Film Entertainment, 2005).

2. Roland Barthes, "From Work to Text," *Image, Music, Text*, trans. Stephen Heath (London: Fontana, 1977), 159, 158.

3. Ibid., 155.

4. Ibid., 157.

5. James Naremore, "Introduction: Film and the Reign of Adaptation," in *Film Adaptation*, ed. James Naremore (London: Athlone Press, 2000), 12, emphasis added.

6. Ibid., 9.

7. Peter Brooker, "Postmodern Adaptation: Pastiche, Intertextuality and Re-Functioning," in *The Cambridge Companion to Literature on Screen*, ed. Deborah Cartmell and Imelda Whelehan (Cambridge: Cambridge University Press, 2007), 108.

8. Jacques Derrida, "Différance," *Margins of Philosophy*, trans. Alan Bass (Chicago: University of Chicago Press, 1982), 15.

9. Ibid., 13–14.

10. Ibid., 7.

11. Jacques Derrida, *Of Grammatology*, trans. Gayatri Chakravorty Spivak (Baltimore: Johns Hopkins University Press, 1974); Roland Barthes, "The Death of the Author," *Image, Music, Text*, trans. Stephen Heath (London: Fontana, 1977), 142–48; Michel Foucault, "What is an Author?" *The Foucault Reader*, ed. Paul Rabinow (London: Penguin, 1984), 107.

12. Craig Owens, "The Discourse of Others: Feminists and Postmodernism," in *The Anti-Aesthetic: Essays on Postmodern Culture*, ed. Hal Foster (Port Townsend, WA: Bay Press, 1983), 57–82. This reminds one that the "author function" has been, at least in much contemporary art and much critical theory, dismantled in favor of the discursive analysis of texts through fields of reference and citations. For example, Craig Owens, inspired by Jean-François Lyotard and Paul Ricoeur, brilliantly discusses the "master narratives" and "narratives of mastery" involving notions of originality and authenticity that have been so vehemently challenged by postmodern theory and the feminist, appropriation art of photo-based practitioners Cindy Sherman, Sherrie Levine, Barbara Kruger, and Martha Rosler.

13. Brooker, "Postmodern Adaptation," 107.

14. Annie Proulx, "Getting Movied," in *Brokeback Mountain: Story to Screenplay* (New York: Scribner, 2005), 129–38; Larry McMurtry, "Adapting Brokeback Mountain," in *Brokeback Mountain: Story to Screenplay* (New York: Scribner, 2005), 139–42; Diana Ossana, "Climbing Brokeback Mountain," in *Brokeback Mountain: Story to Screenplay* (New York: Scribner, 2005), 143–51.

15. Interestingly, with the film criticism of *Brokeback Mountain* the opposite tendency is evident, due perhaps to the greater media sensation made by the film. Much of the writing on *Brokeback Mountain* is by film critics who pay undue attention to "Lee's film" as if it were a singular monolithic unity, and at the expense of acknowledging Proulx's story or the screenplay, which contributed a substantial diegetic expansion of it. The special issue of *Film Quarterly* (60, no. 3, 2007) devoted to *Brokeback Mountain* is an example of this argument, as all of the half dozen essays focus primarily on gender politics or the genre issues at stake in the film, to the near complete occlusion of Proulx's story.

16. Frederic Jameson, "Postmodernism, or The Cultural Logic of Late Capitalism," *The New Left Review* 146 (1984): 62.

17. Brooker, "Postmodern Adaptation," 107.

18. Brian McFarlane, "Reading Film and Literature," in *The Cambridge Companion to Literature on Screen*, ed. Deborah Cartmell and Imelda Whelehan (Cambridge: Cambridge University Press, 2007), 18.

19. Proulx, "Brokeback Mountain," 1.

20. Ibid.

21. Ibid., emphasis added.

22. The loop also has Western genre associations that allude to the ranch work typical of Ennis's life as well as his comment to Jack explaining his own inability to change, "I'm stuck with what I got, caught in my own loop" (Proulx 14).

23. Proulx, "Brokeback Mountain," 2.

24. Ibid.

25. Ibid., 3.

26. Ibid., 7.

27. Larry McMurtry and Diana Ossana, *Brokeback Mountain: A Screenplay*, 20.

28. Proulx makes clear that, although they take many horse-packing trips together to other ranges, they never return to Brokeback Mountain (17). And recall Jack's resentful lamentation to Ennis in their final, parting argument about their lost opportunities for sharing a life together (the "I wish I knew how to quit you" scene), that twenty years into their relationship, what the intangible memories of Brokeback Mountain ultimately mean: "It's all we got, boy, fuckin all" (Proulx 21; McMurtry and Ossana 82).

29. Proulx, "Brokeback Mountain," 8.

30. Certainly Ennis and Jack's descent from Brokeback Mountain at Aguirre's behest to avoid a late summer storm rings of the Expulsion from the Garden of Eden after the Temptation (when Adam and Eve are seduced by the serpent to eat from the Tree of Knowledge). Recall some humorous dialogue in the film, Ennis's words to Jack while singing and talking about their respective families' religious persuasions (Ennis's Methodist; Jack's Pentecostal): "You may be a sinner, but I ain't yet had the opportunity" (McMurtry and Ossana, *Brokeback Mountain: A Screenplay*, 17). This conversation, notably, takes place during the drunken evening campfire that is the preamble to the tent scene that involves the first ravenous sexual encounter between the young men.

31. Eric Patterson, *On Brokeback Mountain: Meditations About Masculinity, Fear, and Love in the Story and the Film* (Lantham, MD: Lexington Books, 2008), 161.

32. McMurtry and Ossana, *Brokeback Mountain: A Screenplay*, 20.

33. James Hall, *Dictionary of Subjects & Symbols in Art* (New York: Harper & Row, 1974), 185.

34. McMurtry and Ossana, *Brokeback Mountain: A Screenplay*, 20.

35. This is an art history commonplace supported by Rembrandt's many drawings, etchings, and engravings of more explicit Biblical subject matter, including his numerous versions of the crucifixion entitled *The Three Crosses* (begun in 1625). Moreover, the obliqueness of alluding to the crucifixion with such mundane, secular subject matter is in keeping with the Calvinism of majority Dutch culture in the seventeenth century which, reflecting the legacy of the Reformation, abhorred the melodramatic excesses of narrative religious imagery characteristic of the art of the Southern Baroque churches in Italy during the Catholic Counter-Reformation.

36. Acknowledging Dennis Cutchin's comment that the eviscerated sheep carcass in the film has female overtones, I'd like to point out that a comparison could be made with the Cuban-American artist Anna Mendieta's *Silhueta* series of performative interventions in the Mexican landscape in the 1970s, where she dug shallow holes in the ground in the shape of her silhouette, and then covered them with bright red pigment to suggest the invagination of the earth's surface.

37. Hall, *Dictionary*, 185–86.

38. Jim Kitses, "All that Brokeback Allows," *Film Quarterly* 60, no. 3 (2007): 24, emphasis added.

39. D. A. Miller, "On the Universality of *Brokeback Mountain*," *Film Quarterly* 60, no. 3 (2007): 60.

40. Willie Nelson, "He Was a Friend of Mine," by Bob Dylan, *Brokeback Mountain Soundtrack*, compact disc, ©2005 Focus Features and The Verge Music Group.

41. Later in the film, we constantly see shades of red (or fuchsia) associated with

Jack, in his or Lureen's clothing, his pick-up truck, or in the furniture of his Texas home.

42. Mieke Bal, "Enfolding Feminism," in *Feminist Consequences: Theory for the New Century*, ed. Elisabeth Bronfen and Misha Kavka (New York: Columbia University Press, 2001), 321–52.

43. Julia Kristeva, *Powers of Horror: An Essay on Abjection*, trans. Leon S. Roudiez (New York: Columbia University Press, 1982).

44. Hélène Cixous, "Bathsheba or the Interior of the Bible," in *The Feminism and Visual Culture Reader*, ed. Amelia Jones (London: Routledge, 2003), 265.

45. Proulx, "Brokeback Mountain," 9.

46. McMurtry and Ossana, *Brokeback Mountain: A Screenplay*, 28.

47. Judith Butler, "Melancholy Gender/Refused Identification," in *The Psychic Life of Power: Theories in Subjection* (Stanford: Stanford University Press, 1997), 132–66.

48. This blunt symbolic object is also in keeping with Proulx's style in *Close Range: Brokeback Mountain and Other Stories* (1999; repr., London: Harper Perennial, 2006) in which the story lines are permeated by threats of physical violence and trauma. Consider, for example, the bull-rider Diamond Felts in "The Mud Below" (clearly a study for Jack Twist's trials), whose losing streak in the rodeo leaves him with bones broken and dislocated from their sockets. For a compelling detailing of the corrosive effects of homophobia on men who love men in rural American environments and in *Brokeback Mountain*, see Eric Patterson's chapter "'We Do That in the Wrong Place We'll Be Dead': Hatred and Fear," in his *On Brokeback Mountain*.

49. Proulx, "Brokeback Mountain," 14–15.

50. Ibid., 15.

51. Ibid., 14.

52. Ibid., 15.

53. Ibid., 11, 15.

54. Ibid., 23.

55. Ibid.

56. Proulx, "Brokeback Mountain," 18, emphasis added.

57. That the homophobia conveyed by Proulx's story is meant to reflect a contemporary social reality in Wyoming is made clear in her essay "Getting Movied," and by Diana Ossana in her reflections on the adaptation process in her essay "Climbing Brokeback Mountain," both in *Brokeback Mountain: Story to Screenplay*, where they both note the 1998 murder of Matthew Shepard in Laramie, Wyoming (Proulx, 130; Ossana, 146).

58. Proulx, "Brokeback Mountain," 14, emphasis added.

59. Ibid., 27.

60. Ibid., 27–28.

61. The allusions inherent to Jack's last name Twist are also apparent in Proulx's description of Ennis's and Jack's "contortionistic grappling," the wrestling match where Jack accidentally gives Ennis the bloody nose that stains their shirts on the last afternoon on Brokeback Mountain (26).

Jane Austen and the Chick Flick in the Twenty-first Century

Pamela Demory

SCENE: OPENING OF *PRIDE AND PREJUDICE* (1995):[1]

Close-up of a length of cream-colored fabric, embroidered with flowers and leaves in greens and browns. At the edge of the frame we see scissors, buttons, and a pincushion. A hand inserts a needle, pulls the thread through. The camera tracks across the cloth, the focus blurs. A series of dissolves follows, each shot a new piece of richly textured fabric revolving behind the titles: cream-colored satin with pink highlights, becoming increasingly elaborate in texture and decoration. Fade to black.

In the summer of 2005 I was talking with two female students in my film adaptation course about what texts/films I might teach the next summer, and together we realized that it would be possible to design my entire course around *Pride and Prejudice*. My students were extremely enthusiastic about this idea, although we also concluded that such a course would probably draw only women, because—as we knew without being able to define quite why—adaptations of Jane Austen's novels are definitely chick flicks. In a written survey, another female student urged me *not* to do any Austen films in my course—that she would "feel sorry for any guys" forced to study such films. I did not, as it happens, design my course around *Pride and Prejudice*, but the conversation has stuck with me: why are there so many film adaptations of Jane Austen novels—and of *Pride and Prejudice* specifically? And why, when the novels of Austen are routinely taught in college literature courses and considered perfectly appropriate for both men and women to read, should adaptations of her novels be seen as suitable only for women?

For more than a century, Austen's novels have been read seriously and enjoyed by both men and women, and, in fact, it seems that it is her male readers and fans who are responsible for her place in the canon. In Bruce Stovel's bibliography of key critical studies of Austen, male-authored studies outnumber those by women by about twenty to three,[2] And Claudia Johnson, in her study of Austen readership patterns, explains that whereas we now associate "literature written by women [as] literature for women . . . the Janeitism of the early twentieth century was . . . principally a male enthusiasm."[3] After 1970, with the rise of feminist literary theory and vastly greater numbers of women in the academy, the gender balance is more even—Stovel lists approximately thirty-eight male- to thirty-one female-authored studies—but still the majority of studies are by men.[4]

Scholarly and popular responses to the film adaptations, on the other hand, tend to be written mostly by women. Of the essays (aside from the editor introductions) in the three most recent collections of scholarship on Austen film adaptations, for example—Troost and Greenfield, eds., *Jane Austen in Hollywood* (2nd ed. 2001),[5] Pucci and Thompson, eds., *Jane Austen and Co.* (2003),[6] and MacDonald and MacDonald, *Jane Austen on Screen* (2003)[7]—thirty-one are written by women and four by men. And at the Republic of Pemberley website, where the vast majority of the 1200 + members have female-sounding names, a recent search for "film adaptation" on the *Pride and Prejudice* discussion board resulted in 378 individual postings from December 2006 through June 2007 by 143 people—133 of them women and 10 men.[8]

The term "chick flick" denotes not just gender, but quality as well. While Austen's novels are Great Books, the film adaptations are often seen by scholars as sentimental and frivolous. So the paradox is that on the one hand we have a classic work of literature—*Pride and Prejudice* by Jane Austen—an unassailable Great Book of the Western literary canon. And on the other hand, we have (for example) Joe Wright's 2005 *Pride and Prejudice*—a "chick flick"—a product of mass culture, lightweight, sentimental—apparently the opposite of "serious literature." So how is it that these two so different texts have the same title and are apparently telling the "same" story?

In order to answer this question, we need to look at how the adaptations of Jane Austen novels function in the twenty-first century. The traditional approach to studying adaptation—comparing the adaptation with the novel—will be insufficient. A new approach is needed. Robert Stam, Thomas Leitch, and James Naremore all suggest that studies in adaptation need to move away from questions about fidelity and evaluation, toward questions about function. Such an approach, Leitch suggests, would "turn the classical canon . . . into a field of intertextual energy past, present, and future."[9] *Pride and Prejudice* provides an excellent case study for such an approach, not least because of the sheer number of adaptations it has spawned in just the first years of the twenty-first century: *Bridget Jones's Diary* in 2001[10] (and the sequel, *Bridget Jones: The Edge of Reason*, 2004), Andrew Black's "Latter Day" *Pride & Prejudice* in 2003,[11] Gurinder Chadha's Bollywood *Bride and Prejudice* in 2004,[12] Joe Wright's *Pride and Prejudice* in 2005,[13] and *Jane Austen Handheld* (forthcoming in 2010).[14] The new millennium has also seen a burgeoning meta-Austen filmography, with *Becoming Jane* and *The Jane Austen Book Club* in 2007, and *Miss Austen Regrets*, the BBC television movie (part of *The Complete Jane Austen* series aired on PBS), in 2008. The 21st century has also seen a proliferation of criticism and commentary on the adaptations, ranging from the 2003 *Jane Austen on Screen* to the 2005 *Flirting with Pride and Prejudice: Fresh Perspectives on the Original Chick-Lit Masterpiece*, edited by romance novelist Jennifer Crusie. (The twenty-first century has also seen a dizzying array of Jane Austen-themed books, including, just to name a few, *The Jane Austen Book Club*, *Jane Austen's Guide to Dating*, *The Jane Austen Cookbook*, *Jane Austen in Scarsdale*, a Jane Austen mystery series, and two new Austen zombie books: *Jane Bites Back* and *Pride and Prejudice and Zombies*.) If, as Robert Stam argues, "the diverse prior adaptations of a novel can come to form a larger, cumulative hypotext available to the filmmaker who comes relatively 'late' in the series,"[15] a twenty-first-century *Pride and Prejudice* must necessarily be in some kind of intertextual relationship with the prior versions—hypertexts of the novel—and with other associated cultural phenomena. "Filmic adaptations," as Stam argues, "are caught up in the ongoing whirl of intertextual reference and transformation, of texts generating other texts in an endless process of recycling, transformation, and transmutation, with no clear point of origin."[16] For the twenty-first-century reader and filmgoer, then, even Austen's text is no longer *only* Austen's text.

Noting James Naremore's call for "a broader definition of adaptation and a sociology that takes into account the commercial apparatus, the audience, and the academic culture industry,"[17] I argue that *Pride and Prejudice* in the twenty-first century is a thick tapestry, comprising not just Austen's novel, but numerous other filmic and literary texts, and colored by various genre conventions, reader and viewer expectations, and market forces. In using the metaphor of the tapestry (instead of the more abstract terms "hypotext"—Stam—or "field of intertextual energy"—Leitch), I imagine not a fixed length of cloth hanging on a wall, but a piece of woven art continually in the process of being made—altered, embroidered, enlarged—with new threads sewn in and around the old, continually making new patterns and enlivening and changing the old images. I even imagine it animated, moving—a continual weaving and unweaving of differently colored threads—not unlike the swirling, overlapping images of embroidered fabrics that open the 1995 BBC *Pride and Prejudice*. This metaphor works particularly well for my subject, as textiles and weaving are associated with women's work (I think of the *Odyssey*'s Penelope continuously weaving and unweaving her length of cloth—keeping those suitors at bay), and thus it supports the gendered implications of my analysis.

In this paper, I tease out three strands of this tapestry: Strand 1: the literary tradition, which is itself made up of two distinct threads: academic scholars and devoted fans (the self-named "Janeites"); Strand 2: the popular romance, again composed of two threads: the conventional romance novel and "chick lit," and Strand 3: popular film, including the "chick flick," generally, and the Austen film adaptations of the 1990s, more specifically. A notable absence in my analysis is any discussion of Jane Austen's novel itself. My purpose here is *not* to study the relation between the films and the "original" novel, but to look at the intertextual relations among various current iterations of *Pride and Prejudice*. Primarily, I will be focusing my attention on the two most well-known twenty-first-century versions: *Pride and Prejudice* (2005), directed by Joe Wright, and *Bride and Prejudice* (2004), directed by Gurinder Chadha. This analysis helps to explain not only why Jane Austen adaptations are seen as "chick flicks," but also how these adaptations reflect twenty-first-century attitudes about gender and women's roles in society. It also exemplifies the way texts become transformed and informed by myriad textual and cultural transformations. "Jane Austen" is a complex interweaving of associated texts—literary, filmic, and electronic—as well as less tangible forces of convention, reader reception, and production.

STRAND 1: BOOK PEOPLE—AUSTEN SCHOLARSHIP AND THE ENGLISH LITERARY TRADITION

Scene: Opening of *Pride and Prejudice* (2005):[18]
A blackbird sings. Fade-in to a widescreen landscape shot of the English countryside at dawn. Everything is green: the field in the foreground, the woods in the mid and background. As the sun rises behind the trees, we see more clearly the lush dewy verdure. The piano theme begins and titles begin to appear, as the sunlight fills the frame, turning the scene from green to yellow. Cut to a midshot of a young woman walking in the same landscape, reading a book. Cut to a reverse shot of the book itself: it's the last page; we can just make out the words at the end of the text: "The End." She closes the book, smiles.
"In a way," comments director Joe Wright on the DVD commentary track, *"what she's doing there is reading the story that's about to happen to her."*

One of the reasons—perhaps the most significant reason—that so many Austen adaptations are produced is that so many readers are passionate about Austen's books. Lindsay Doran, for example (producer of *Sense and Sensibility*), reports in the introduction to the published screenplay that she became a Jane Austen fan in her twenties, when she spent several months rehabilitating from an automobile accident by reading all the Austen novels, chronologically, in the local public library, and deciding that *Sense and Sensibility* was her favorite, "not only of Jane Austen's novels, but of all the novels I had ever read. . . . I decided right there, in the reading room of the Brompton Road Library, that if I ever went into the movie business, . . . I would try to make *Sense and Sensibility* into a film."[19] Generations of readers—both scholars and fans—have loved her novels and/or found them intellectually stimulating, and have written hundreds, maybe thousands, of volumes testifying to this love. This body of work—so many words devoted to explaining, explicating, analyzing, or just plain gushing—has become just as much a part of the Jane Austen tapestry as the novels themselves.

Because filmmaking is a commercial enterprise, and filmmakers must appeal to their audience, and because any filmmaker attempting an adaptation of an Austen novel will undoubtedly anticipate that a large portion of the audience will be Austen fans, adaptations in the late twentieth and early twenty-first centuries are marked by their attempts to be faithful to the "spirit" of Jane Austen—a desire that, if it does anything, speaks to a need to satisfy both scholars and fans of her work. This is a challenge, for the two groups, though similar, have somewhat different agendas.

The scholarly thread of the Austen tapestry has its academic origins, according to Bruce Stovel, in A. C. Bradley's 1911 essay, in which he identifies Austen's key literary qualities: "she is a moralist and a humorist."[20] F. R. Leavis continues in this vein in his classic 1948 tome, *The Great Tradition*, in which he defines the canon of the English novel. The first line of this book reads: "The great English novelists are Jane Austen, George Eliot, Henry James, and Joseph Conrad."[21] (Later he adds one more: D. H. Lawrence.) Austen is the first of the great novelists, he argues, because her novels are formally perfect, because she creates "delightful" characters,[22] and because her formal perfection is based in "an intense moral interest" in life.[23] The dominant strain of Austen criticism until the 1970s continued along the lines established by Bradley and brought to such great heights by Leavis: scholars focused on her wit, her moral incisiveness, her careful attention to the particulars of domestic life, and her style. In the 1970s a dramatic shift occurred in Austen, as in other literary scholarship:

more and more her novels were seen as "products of a specific culture,"[24] and the rise of feminist scholarship and postcolonial criticism shifted critical focus even more dramatically.[25]

The Austen film adaptations are all informed by this tradition of literary scholarship—to some degree. *Mansfield Park*[26] is perhaps the most scholarly of the adaptations, referring (at least implicitly) to recent criticism by feminist and postcolonial scholars. Patricia Rozema (director and screenwriter) has stated that she read widely in Austen criticism and biography when writing the script, and in the DVD commentary she cites Claudia Johnson in particular as a literary critic whose work she found useful, particularly her notion that *Mansfield Park* is "saturated by an unwholesome sexuality."[27] And the film's explicit references to the Bertrams as slaveholders are clearly grounded in the postcolonial critique of *Mansfield Park* epitomized by Edward Said in his *Culture and Imperialism*.[28]

Similarly, Emma Thompson's conception of Austen's work is certainly influenced by the feminist scholarship she read as a student at Newnham College, Cambridge. According to the college's website, "Emma studied English at Cambridge, and much of the reading she did shaped her thinking about women. 'I'm not by nature an academic, but I am very enthusiastic about literature. Some of the forms of literary criticism I found very prescriptive and reductive, but as soon as I found women writing about literature my mind just kind of opened up. Feminist criticism was a great discovery for me. And the nineteenth century women authors influenced me profoundly, the Brontës, for example, Austen, and Eliot.' "[29] Even the adaptations that set Austen's stories in different times and places (*Clueless*,[30] *Bride and Prejudice*, *Bridget Jones's Diary*) take pains to draw explicit parallels between the movie characters and plot points and the novel characters and plot, thus implicitly appealing to readers of the novels (see synopses in Appendix).

In the twenty-first century, adaptations of *Pride and Prejudice* have not seemed (so far) to rise to the serious scholarly ambitions of *Sense and Sensibility*[31] or *Mansfield Park*, although a case might be made for *Bride and Prejudice* as an example of a post-colonial Writing Back (Filming Back?) to the Center (director Gurinder Chadha does make a couple of subtle digs at the British Raj). But these adaptations do seem designed to appeal to the Janeite reader. This second thread of the literary strand is even more populous and possibly more devoted to Austen's work than that of the scholars. Whereas the scholars treat the novels as texts whose elements can be analyzed, illuminated, and explained, the fans simply love the world that the novels create. They're interested in the characters, in the plot, in the details of the historical setting, the houses, games, dances, all the social interactions. These devoted fans read her novels over and over and enjoy parsing details of dialogue, motivation, and intention.

"Janeitism," according to Claudia L. Johnson, emerged in the latter part of the nineteenth century; the early twentieth-century Janeites were mostly men (illustrated in a Rudyard Kipling story entitled "The Janeites"), and their interest was not so much in the plots of the novels as in the details of characterization and setting—the world of Austen that (especially for the men in the story: shell-shocked World War I veterans) provides a soothing and ideal contrast to the "modern" world.[32]

The modern Janeite is epitomized by the very civilized Republic of Pemberley website[33] (www.pemberley.com), and is—unlike her early twentieth-century counterpart—mostly female. Although men occasionally post comments, the member list comprises about 92% women. And while Austen scholars undoubtedly contribute to the site, the postings do not delve into territory—literary theory or criticism— that the scholar might broach. The Pemberley Janeites are characterized by their insistence on civilized discussion. No one is allowed to be rude. In fact, comparisons among the film versions of any Austen novel are discouraged, as apparently comparisons between the 1995 and 2005 versions of *Pride and Prejudice* led to "somewhat heated arguments and unfriendliness."[34] The Janeite is most interested in the nuances of "correct" behavior—as expressed in Austen's novels—and is devoted to an idea of the author as wise, witty, and incisive—and definitely not sentimental. These Janeites are obsessive about Austen's novels *and* about the film adaptations (I found an entire thread devoted self-reflexively to discussing their obsessiveness). And they are intimately familiar with Austen's stories, having read the books and seen the films over and over.

Admirers of Austen's work tend to be highly ambivalent about the film adaptations. They put Austen on a pedestal and measure each film adaptation against the assumed superiority of the novel. As Linda Troost and Sayre Greenfield point out in their introduction to *Jane Austen in Hollywood*, "Both fans of Jane Austen ('Janeites') and literary critics are primarily book people," and they tend to value "the experience of reading" over that of watching.[35] Much of the scholarship on the Austen adaptations privileges the books explicitly;[36] on the Austen fan sites, adaptations are criticized if a line of dialogue seems to misrepresent the Austen character or to be delivered in a tone that doesn't reflect the novel's meaning (as understood by the person posting), or if a character's clothing or hairstyle seems wrong for the period.

Yet at the same time, these readers also make up a significant portion of the movie audience (as illustrated by the copious amount of published criticism and online discussion of the Austen adaptations). Readers, even if they are "book people," seem to desire the cinematic experience—a visceral engagement with Austen's world that the books, being words on the page, cannot offer. At the Republic of Pemberley website, the participants seem to be obsessed with the materiality of the film's representations, and especially with the physicality of the actors. A great deal of attention has been paid, for example, to whether or not Matthew Mcfadyen (in the 2005 *Pride and Prejudice*) is appealing to look at, aside from his effectiveness in portraying the character of Mr. Darcy.

And, on the whole, the Janeites at the Republic of Pemberley site see the adaptations as complementary to Austen's novels, part of what I'm calling the Austen hypotext. But they do want their adaptations to be "faithful." On the whole, what people seem to mean by this is a film that is set in an historically "accurate" time and place, that follows the novel's plots and subplots without deviating from Austen's narrative ordering, employs Austen's dialogue precisely, and refrains from cutting scenes and minor characters. Fans acknowledge that no adaptation can fully live up to these expectations, but those that adhere more closely are viewed with more favor. Emma Thompson's *Sense and Sensibility* screenplay is held in high esteem by the fans at the Republic of Pemberley, because, even though it "takes a lot of liberties, . . . [using] a surprisingly small number (5?) of lines directly from the book. . . . it's done so wittily, entertainingly and unobtrusively, and with such a sure hand, that it still feels faithful in spirit to the original, in a way that some other adaptations of the other novels are not."[37]

The response to Patricia Rozema's *Mansfield Park* was much less positive—especially among Janeite readers, who tended to object to the changes Rozema made in the novel's plot and characters, and to her graphic depictions of sex and slavery. According to one posting on the Republic of Pemberley website, "several Pemberleans were at a screening of MP2 [*Mansfield Park*, 1999] and Patricia Rozema herself was there for an interview and Q&A afterwards. Several people walked out during the movie. Several others walked out before the Q&A. Those of us who stayed heard Ms. Rozema say point-blank that she didn't like Fanny Price, that she didn't like MP [Austen's *Mansfield Park*] and that she thought she could improve upon Jane Austen. I don't know what you call that, but I call it hubris."[38]

For this reader, typical of the attitude among Janeites, the film failed due to Rozema's apparent lack of respect for Austen's work and the persona of Jane Austen herself. Some scholars have also been unpersuaded by Rozema's interpretation. While Claudia Johnson hailed it in the *Times Literary Supplement* as a "stunning revisionist reading of Austen's darkest novel . . . more of an intervention than an adaptation,"[39] Jan Fergus—a self-described "purist" in her views on adapting Austen—argues that Rozema's postmodern approach is ineffective and the film as a whole reductive.[40]

Interestingly, the adaptations that take *more* liberties with time and place tend to fare better amongst readers. *Bride and Prejudice* was screened for the United Kingdom Austen Society (according to Gurinder Chadha and Paul Mayeda Berges, on the DVD commentary), and despite its radically different setting and updating of Austen's story, it received hearty approval, with one member coming up to the director afterward and asserting (according to Chadha): "My dear, I do believe that if Jane were amongst us now, she would have thoroughly enjoyed this movie." This approval stands in marked contrast to the reception given Rozema's *Mansfield Park*. The more positive reception is likely because these films seem to appeal to both scholars and fans—perhaps because they're analogous rather than "faithful" in intent. The point is that these films adhere to the generally accepted sense of what Austen's work means to *readers* of Austen in the late twentieth and early twenty-first centuries. That is, they're about morals and manners, about wit and satire, about understanding the human condition.

Thus the BBC versions of the novels tend to come closest to fulfilling readers' requirements, largely because they run longer, as miniseries, than do two-hour features, and they have a reputation for more strict attention to historical detail. Screenwriter Andrew Davies is a particular favorite—his *Pride and Prejudice* (1995) is, according to one fan, "a model of how a novel ought to be transcribed for the screen."[41] These films adopt a scholarly, educational tone (they are productions of the "Masterpiece Theatre," after all), appealing to the knowledgeable Austen reader.

Of the BBC films, Davies' *Pride and Prejudice*, with Colin Firth and Jennifer Ehle (referred to on the site as PP2) is the fan favorite, so much so that the 2005 *Pride and Prejudice* (referred to in the lists as PP3) was at first viewed with some skepticism by fans. A comment from a posting on IMDb.com exemplifies this attitude: "The problem with attempting to produce a film version of this legendary book, just 10 years after the iconic TV series, is that the film must first of all justify its own existence, and then rise above its predecessors in glorious triumph. Sadly, any adaptation of *Pride and Prejudice* that reduces itself to 2 hours of screening time will never achieve this feat."[42] In addition to the film's telescoping of the plot, fans were also unhappy with casting choices. But some viewers applauded Wright for what

they saw as a more accurate, because more earthy, portrayal of the
Bennet family home. This perception of this film is particularly intriguing, as the film is *not* historically accurate. Wright says in the director's commentary that he deliberately set the story a few years later
than Austen's book, because he thought the period dresses "unflat-
tering." And other commentators have pointed out numerous anachronisms: the young women do not always wear bonnets (as they would
have in Austen's time), the house is too rustic for the Bennet's social
class (reviewers have referred to it as "Dickensian"), the mountain
scenes are Gothic in their dramatic excess. And yet the film is indubi-
tably "historical"; the costumes and sets are meant to invoke the feeling of a "period piece," and it's that feeling that Wright has
successfully evoked in the film, drawing in these otherwise notoriously
nitpicky fans.

The two traditions of Austen readers—the academic and the popular—seem at times antithetical to one another. After all, scholars are
often interested in the films because they prove useful in teaching
Austen to university students, or because they offer insight into the
changing reception of Austen's work over time; Janeites tend to be interested in the films because they bring the stories they love so much
to life. But there is evidence that these two camps are converging—or
at least finding some common ground. I found, for example, two articles that are structured as dialogues, devoted to the question of
whether or not a "popular" approach to Austen can be reconciled with
a "critical" approach. Even more interesting is that one of these dialogues appears in a recent work of scholarly criticism by Roger Gard
from Yale University Press,[43] a book very much a contemporary example of the F. R. Leavis tradition, while the other appears in *Flirting
with Pride and Prejudice*, the collection of essays edited by and with
contributions largely from romance novelists.[44] While the romance
essay begins with the premise that the Austen fan has true insight into
Pride and Prejudice whereas the literary critic is merely talking gibber-
ish, and the Yale University Press book begins with the premise that
the literary critic is the obvious arbiter of aesthetic truth regarding
Austen, both essays end up moving toward the middle—arguing that
perhaps *Pride and Prejudice* can be both popular *and* art, that both the
literary critic *and* the fan have something important to contribute to
the ongoing conversation about the novel.

The literary tradition—both scholarly and popular—contributes
significantly to the Austen tapestry. The early and mid-twentieth-cen-
tury readings of Austen that emphasized her moral incisiveness, wit,
and clear-eyed examination of social and male/female relationships is

clearly still important to readers—and this is reflected in recent adaptations. But the shift in gender balance among both scholars and fans,
with a large majority now being women, and the corresponding shift
in critical attention toward feminist scholarship is also now (somewhat
belatedly) reflected in the adaptations, which from 1995 on are much
more clearly geared toward a female audience. This shift, in turn, may
explain the general notion (expressed by my students) that Austen
speaks more to women than to men.

Strand 2: The Popular Romance

Scene: Near the end of *Pride and Prejudice* (2005):[45]
*The English countryside just before dawn. We can just make out a dark field
and a fence in the foreground, and in the upper half of the frame the lightening
sky: strands of pale pink and blue. The camera tracks forward slightly, the focus
becomes shallow, and Elizabeth moves into the frame bottom right. The camera
slows, then stops, but Elizabeth wanders on, from frame right to frame left and
then on into the landscape, becoming smaller, as the scene gradually lightens.*

*Cut to reverse mid-shot of Elizabeth, hugging herself against the pre-dawn
chill—she seems to have wrapped a dark cloak around her white nightgown. She
glances to screen right and we see that she is caught by some vision off-screen—the
camera moves to a close-up of her face. Cut to her point of view: Darcy, in sweeping dark cloak, white shirt, open at the collar, striding forward through the dewy
landscape. The cut emphasizes the contrast in lighting: Elizabeth in the dark;
Darcy in a misty pale light. The shot holds for a full 45 seconds, as we watch
Darcy striding towards us—eventually he fills the right side of the frame and the
focus has become shallow. Cut to Elizabeth in a matching shot—half turned away,
just her face at first, then turning to face forward.*

*A close-up, shot/reverse-shot sequence follows, as the daylight continues to in-
crease. Elizabeth's face glows against the green backdrop of the field, Darcy's
against the pale light of the sky. He professes his love for her in a halting, "I
love—I love—I love you, body and soul." Cut to a two-shot, Elizabeth moving
into the frame with Darcy, and as they join hands, the sun comes up behind them.
She kisses his hand, and the sun shines out yellow between them as they touch
foreheads.*

Director's Commentary: *"This was a magical morning. We all got up at 3
a.m. or something and went out and prepared in the dark and then waited for
first light and then we had about 50 minutes to shoot this scene . . . And as soon
as the light came we jumped into action. It felt really special doing it. I think it's
probably—I don't know, I really battled with myself over this scene, because I
think it's probably a bit over the top and a bit over-romantic and a bit slushy,
but— . . . One of the makeup artists stood beside me while we were shooting this,
and she whispered very quietly: 'I wish that was my life.'"*

One of the ways that Austen readers have found the adaptations disappointing is in the way they tend to conform to the conventions of the romance novel. From the perspective of the literary critic (and possibly the Janeite as well), the adaptations tend to "Harlequinize" Jane Austen: that is, adaptations turn Austen novels into formulaic romances, downplaying or cutting the subplots and constructing the narrative and style to shift the focus away from the novels' concern with moral behavior and irony and toward the central marriage plot. Harriet Margolis sums up what critics say is wrong with romance novels:

> Romance novels are bad because they are mass-produced, formulaic, limited in scope, accepting of a patriarchal status quo, overly concerned with sex, almost exclusively concerned with heterosexual sex, and appealing only to an unintelligent readership incapable of appreciating better writing.[46]

Certainly, the romance novel is another of the significant strands forming the present-day Austen tapestry. Both *Pride and Prejudice* (2005) and *Bride and Prejudice* draw on romance conventions—perhaps even more so than earlier adaptations: the 2005 film ratchets up the romanticism with sweeping widescreen shots of lush English countryside, brooding Darcy in long black coat, Elizabeth in flowing gown standing at the edge of a dramatic cliff—images that seem more Emily Brontë than Jane Austen. *Bride and Prejudice*, in its frank appropriation of Bollywood romance conventions of song and dance, longing looks in close-up, is sentimental to the extreme.

The romance novel formula has historically been viewed with disdain, especially by male readers and critics who considered the concerns and activities of women's lives trivial. Andreas Huyssen argues that the negative association of women with mass culture began in the nineteenth century: women were associated with inferior reading habits—popular novels, serials, and family magazines, while men were associated with authentic culture—high art. He cites as the central image of this dichotomy Flaubert's assertion of identification with his fictional creation Madame Bovary: "Madame Bovary, c'est moi." Huyssen proceeds to deconstruct that statement, pointing out that "woman (Madame Bovary) is positioned as reader of inferior literature—subjective, emotional and passive—while man (Flaubert) emerges as writer of genuine, authentic literature—objective, ironic, and in control of his aesthetic means."[47] He goes on to show how this gendered reading of mass culture became entrenched in western culture.[48] And, I argue, the traces of this bias are evident now in attitudes toward the romance novel, in all its various permutations. And it's not only male readers who take this position. Feminist critics wanting to distance themselves from works that seem to reaffirm women's roles as subservient in an oppressive patriarchy have claimed an intellectual and political distance between "literary" women's writing and the romance novel.

But not everyone reads the romance novel intertext as negative. Harriet Margolis points out a number of positive similarities between Austen's plots and those of the traditional romance novel: both focus on a female protagonist and her relationship with others, and protagonists base their decisions on similar moral criteria of behavior: "the good characters value people's happiness and well-being and often base decisions on how other people will be affected, while the bad characters evaluate people and objects in materialistic terms, selfishly preferring potential personal gain over communal benefit or consideration for other individuals."[49] Margolis goes so far as to argue that not only are characterizations and plots similar in outline, but they share similar ideological values: they both oppose the "effects of capitalism on human interaction." There is, therefore, "neither contradiction nor dishonor in arguing for similarities between Austen's novels and contemporary romance novels."[50]

Another thread entwined with the conventional romance novel is "chick lit." The term was coined by Cris Mazza in 1995 as an ironic appellation to describe new writing by women that was most decidedly *not* in the Harlequin mode, but it was later picked up in the popular press and applied to a trend in contemporary fiction of novels by, about, and for young single women coping with the challenges of careers and love in the modern world.[51] Although the genre distances itself from the Harlequin-style romance in several ways—it tends to include more sex, more emphasis on work, on living and enjoying being single, and more shopping—the genre retains the basic elements of a focus on women's lives, their relationships with other women and with family, their emotions and desires, and their search for love. The genre has received its share of criticism as a frothy waste of time. Doris Lessing is quoted in Suzanne Ferriss and Mallory Young's collection of critical essays on chick lit as suggesting that women novelists ought to write "books about their lives as they really saw them, and not these helpless girls, drunken, worrying about their weight."[52]

Both the Harlequin-style romance (particularly the Regency Romance) and chick lit claim Austen as a progenitor. Helen Fielding's *Bridget Jones's Diary*—the "ur-text" of chick lit—borrows heavily from *Pride and Prejudice*, so the Austen connection there is very direct. Shanna Swendson (one of the contributers to *Flirting with Pride and*

Prejudice), in her essay "The Original Chick-Lit Masterpiece," goes so far as to suggest that there really is no difference between an Austen novel and the standard chick lit book: "A smart publisher would put a cartoon cover on *Pride and Prejudice* and reissue it in a trade paperback edition, where it would fit in perfectly with all those other chick-lit novels on the "new in paperback" table at the bookstore. All that's really changed since then are the fashions, a few social mores and the technology that facilitates communication (and miscommunication) between men and women."[53] Both the popular romance and chick lit have their scholarly supporters. Janice Radway, in her ground-breaking *Reading the Romance*, takes a sociological or ethnographic approach to the romance rather than an aesthetic/textual approach.[54] She points out that, for the women who read romance novels, their appeal is that they focus their attention on recognizable everyday concerns of women and their relationships, and they offer—in the view of these readers—positive role models: they're strong, independent, steadfast, and in control of their own destinies (to the extent anyone can be). Further, it's through these positive qualities that these protagonists are able to find their true companion in love and marriage.[55]

Suzanne Ferriss and Mallory Young, in their collection of critical essays, *Chick Lit: The New Woman's Fiction*, published by Routledge, follow Radway's lead, arguing that the "astounding popularity [of chick lit] as a cultural phenomenon calls for a more considered response."[56] They point to the issues raised in chick lit: identity, race, class, femininity and feminism, consumerism, self-image, and they argue that chick lit's characteristic confessional narrative style—in diaries, letters, e-mails, or first-person narration—links the genre to a long tradition of women's fiction.[57] The Austen adaptations bear the traces of this tradition—as well as that of the traditional romance. In the 2005 *Pride and Prejudice* the connection to chick lit is subtle: the clothes and hairstyles are altered from what would have been historically accurate to make them more attractive to a contemporary audience, and I would argue that Keira Knightley's giggly Lizzy and the sisterly chats under the bedclothes have more to do with attracting the attention of the young women viewers who will see this film than with any reliance on Austen, or even on conventional romance. The chick lit connection is more evident in the updated *Bride and Prejudice*, with the heroine's insistence early on in the story that she intends to have a career and has no interest in being married off, in the foregrounding of race and class issues, and in the emphasis on travel, clothes, and parties.

Popular romance has traditionally been seen as low art, on the opposite end of the literary spectrum from classic literature (such as the work of Jane Austen). And yet it is an undeniably popular and influential form. Recent scholarship suggests that some of the disdain for the form may be due to longstanding cultural biases against the perceived inferiority of literature aimed at and written by women, and that the differences between the two may not be as great as critics have assumed. Clearly, the Austen adaptations mix high art and low art, appealing to readers of both classic fiction and light romance—and hinting that perhaps those two groups of readers overlap.

STRAND 3: JANE AUSTEN ON SCREEN

When you've been travlin'
And your nerves are unravlin'
You can cool off in a
Wet Shirt!
Walk through the weeds and
Take a dive through the reeds
To get your very own
Wet Shirt!
A cooler mind and body can
Resist Miss Lizzy's power.
It's the nearist [sic] cousin to a
Regency cold shower.
(Don't mind the scum)
The ladies will faint and blush
'Cause when we see you all soggy
Our brains turn to mush!
We love
Wet Shirt! Clinging to manly pecs!
Wet Shirt! Making us think of sex!
Wet Shirt! Cools you off while you look hot!
—from "Wet Shirt" (sung to the tune of "Downtown")[58]

The "chick flick" has not so far received the kind of scholarly scrutiny that chick lit has received,[59] and the term's exact meaning seems to depend on who is using it and in what context. But generally it seems to denote much the same idea as the traditional romance—with some of the more contemporary chick lit features thrown in. According to the *Online Slang Dictionary*, a chick flick is "a movie primarily of interest to females, often due to content (love, friendship, emotional scenes) or cast (primarily females)."[60] Like the popular romance, it is viewed with disdain by many people; note the following definitions at *UrbanDictionary.com:* "A film that indulges in the hopes and dreams of women and/or girls. A film that has a happy, fuzzy, ridiculously unrealistic ending";[61] "A movie that embodies all that is wrong with the world; a movie which displays a gross over-indulgence into [*sic*], and exploration of, the workings of the female psyche and the accompanying [*sic*] emotional tendencies."[62]

I would hazard a guess that these definitions were written by young men. In my circle of friends, the term "chick flick" is used with much more generous, and frequently ironic, connotations. In a similar way, Ferriss and Young, in the introduction to their collection of essays on the chick flick, acknowledge the "derogatory" popular definition, "a sappy movie for women that men don't like," but point out that the term has been re-appropriated. They define chick flicks broadly as "commercial films that appeal to a female audience."[63] But of course that neutral phrase belies the contradictory responses that the term engenders. For some, the chick flick represents a retreat to pre-feminist values that reinforce traditional gender roles and encourage passive acceptance by its female audience members; for others, the chick flick represents female empowerment, with its focus on female friendship, celebration of femininity, and frank recognition of female sexual desire.

The re-emergence of female-oriented film in the 1990s—after the largely male-oriented popular films of the 1960s, 70s, and 80s—harks back to the woman's film of the 1930s, 40s, and 50s,[64] and coincides (not coincidentally) with the revival of Austen adaptations. All the Austen adaptations, by virtue of their emphasis on women's lives and concerns, their central marriage plots, and their happy endings, *are* necessarily chick flicks, broadly defined. But the romance, and correspondingly, the Austen adaptation, appears in a great many forms[65]— some with the grand sweep of the romantic epic (*Sense and Sensibility* and *Pride and Prejudice* [2005]), some with the "cultural" cachet of literary romance (the BBC films, *Persuasion, Mansfield Park*), some light and sentimental romances (Douglas McGrath's *Emma* and *Bride and Prejudice*), some teen romance (*Clueless*). Both *Pride and Prejudice* (2005) and *Bride and Prejudice* draw on other sub-genres of romance as well—*Bride* on the highly sentimental (and musical) Bollywood romance tradition, and *Pride and Prejudice* (2005) on a Brontë-esque gothic romanticism (illustrating an intriguing intertextual prolepsis that might be an insightful postmodern blending of multiple traditions, or merely anachronistic, depending on one's point of view). And in their directors' commentaries, both Gurinder Chadha and Joe Wright, oddly enough, say that they were inspired by 1980s teen musicals—specifically *Grease*. Roberta Garrett argues that this genre-mixing—what she calls "metagenericity (the playful, self-reflexive mixing of well-known generic formulas)"—and cinematic allusions (direct or indirect) are characteristic of the chick flick, and mark it as inherently postmodern.[66]

The twenty-first-century *Pride and Prejudice* films are, of course, in an intertextual relationship with the previous Austen adaptations, particularly the slew of productions made in the 1990s. In general, *Bride and Prejudice* parallels Amy Heckerling's *Clueless* and the film version of *Bridget Jones's Diary* in setting the story in a new time and place—and it also embodies some of *Mansfield Park's* postcolonial critique. *Pride and Prejudice* (2005) parallels the visual style and scope of Ang Lee's *Sense and Sensibility* in its gorgeous widescreen English landscapes and country mansions, and of McGrath's *Emma* in its occasional picturesque prettiness and its gorgeous people, beautifully dressed.

But the really interesting intertextual relationships occur with *Pride and Prejudice* (1995). Jennifer Crusie, in her introduction to *Flirting with Pride and Prejudice*, indicates the influence of this production when she notes that Austen's *Pride and Prejudice* remains the same "except that Darcy now looks like Colin Firth."[67] Both *Bride and Prejudice* and the 2005 *Pride and Prejudice seem* quite different from the 1995 *Pride and Prejudice*—*Bride and Prejudice* because of its setting and *Pride and Prejudice* because it seems at pains to distance itself (as it *must*) from the BBC version: its lead actors are physically quite different from Jennifer Ehle and Colin Firth, it makes dramatic use of its widescreen cinematography, and it sets significant scenes in dramatically different locations. Nevertheless, some patterns of imagery have little to no relationship to the novel but are common to all three films. These patterns illustrate how the hypotext of *Pride and Prejudice* is being transformed with each new iteration. Two of these patterns, having to do with *mountains* and *water*, illustrate developments in Elizabeth's character and in the representation of sexuality.

Mountain Montage:
    (1) from *Pride and Prejudice* (1995):[68]
    Close-up of Elizabeth's feet, clad in black boots and long white dress, hiking across a boulder-strewn ground. She steps firmly on each rock, moving across and up over a particularly large granite boulder. Cut to long shot of Elizabeth, center frame next to a massive boulder (perhaps "Salt Cellar" on Derwent Edge in the Peak District), the misty landscape of fields, forest, and river far below her. She is, with the exception of the boulder, far above the rest of the world. From offscreen we hear Aunt Gardiner call out "Elizabeth! Be careful!" Cut to point-of-view shot of the other three travelers center screen, dwarfed by distance and the massive boulders around them. "How could I face your father if you took a fall?" continues her aunt. Cut to Elizabeth, medium shot, smiling at this, and then looking out across the landscape. In this shot, she's framed in the center—taller now than the

bulky boulder beside her—and dressed in a pale teal-colored top that blends into the hazy greenish-blue background of sky and faraway hillside. She's one with the landscape. "Beautiful!" she breathes. Cut to reverse shot, the landscape with Elizabeth's figure facing away and out to the same green vista we see.

(2) from *Pride and Prejudice* (2005):[69]

Extreme close-up of Elizabeth's closed eyes—light and shadow flickering across her face. Cut to extreme wide shot of Peak District landscape—Elizabeth in the center, a tiny figure standing at the edge of a high cliff. The camera moves left across the landscape, out over the edge, so we see the cliff falling away at Elizabeth's feet, the wind blowing her cloak back. Cut to low-angle close-up of Elizabeth—hair blowing in the breeze, against a cloud-spattered blue sky, looking quite satisfied.

(3) from *Bride and Prejudice* (2004):[70]

A series of close-up, low-angle two-shots of Lalita and Will Darcy in a helicopter—she's looking out the window, he's looking at her—intercut with point-of-view, sweeping helicopter shots of the Grand Canyon. Cut to a shot of Lalita standing at the edge of the cliff, wrapping her shawl around her, and looking, not at the view, but back at Darcy, who is walking up to join her. Cut to another two-shot of the couple—and then back at the view.

The mountain scenery is prompted by Elizabeth's effusive comment in the novel: "What are men to rocks and mountains?"[71] when the Gardiners invite her to travel to the Lake District with them. In the novel, that comment is all we get of "the celebrated beauties of Matlock, Chatsworth, Dovedale, or the Peak";[72] the action remains resolutely on lower ground. But the film adaptations *show* us the mountains. In the BBC *Pride and Prejudice*, we see Elizabeth climbing mountains—alone—giving us a visual analogue for her intrepid spirit, her rising to heights that others (her family) fear to follow. In the 2005 *Pride and Prejudice*, in what I believe to be a conscious re-interpretation of the shot in the earlier film, we get not just a rock on a hill, but Elizabeth—even more alone—on the highest point of a vast, wild landscape, the land falling steeply away at her feet—calling to mind *Wuthering Heights* more than any Austen novel. The exhilaration of the scene is enhanced by the circling helicopter shot. The sequence takes the concept from the earlier film and enhances it—Elizabeth is completely independent here and, if the exterior landscape is meant to reflect the character's inner state, then this Elizabeth is faced with an even more dangerous and thrilling prospect.

In *Bride and Prejudice* (which also seems to have the 1995 *Pride and Prejudice* scene in mind), the mountain shots are perhaps even more dramatic, with Lalita and Darcy *in* the helicopter, surveying the Grand Canyon. Again, the film seems to borrow and then enhance the earlier imagery, but *Bride and Prejudice*'s Elizabeth is noticeably less independent. Lalita is no adventurous loner, but part of a two-some—evident in the framing of the close-ups, and in the directions of the characters' gazes; the two are more interested in each other than in the scenery. So while the scale of the landscape is impressive, suggesting great heights and depths, the images seem to be emphasizing not Elizabeth's independence and strength, but the potential depth and grandeur of the love relationship.

In both cases, then, the twenty-first-century films take a concept from a late twentieth-century film and move it in more romantic (and Romantic) directions. And in so doing they illustrate one of the contradictory elements of the chick flick. We can easily see a feminist stance in the 1995 image of Elizabeth conquering mountaintops, but the others are more ambivalent. Is Elizabeth standing alone in a vast landscape a sign of her independence? Or in its lack of realism is it a regression to popular romantic fantasy? Is *Bride*'s presentation of Lalita and Darcy together in the helicopter a welcome sign of post-feminist acceptance of male/female partnerships—the woman no longer required to distance herself in order to be an individual? Or is this also a regression to traditional gender roles?

Probably the most influential—and most controversial—extra-textual element of the 1995 BBC *Pride and Prejudice* has to do with water, which has, as far as I can tell, no source in Austen's novel. There are three distinct "wet" scenes in the film. In the first, a shock cut takes us from a formal group shot in a Netherfield sitting room to a medium-close profile of Darcy soaping up in his bath. His valet pours a full pitcher of water over his head; Darcy leans back for a moment, and then stands—his valet decorously holding up his robe—and walks to the window to admire Elizabeth, who is outside playing with his dog.[73] Later, another sharp cut takes us from a long shot of Netherfield (where Darcy has just finished writing his letter to Elizabeth explaining Wickham's disreputable past) to a close-up of a washbasin: Darcy bends down, plunges his hands into the water and splashes his face—his shirt open, baring his throat and chest.[74] Still later we see him—determined to cool off after a hard ride following a fencing lesson where he has apparently been trying to exercise Elizabeth and her "fine eyes" out of his mind—disrobe down to breeches and a thin white shirt, and dive into a pond on his estate. After a brief swim he emerges, continues on his way to his house, only to come across Elizabeth, much to his surprise and discomfort, as he stands there, dripping, his shirt sticking to his chest, trying to make light conversation.[76]

Seemingly aware of the audience's potential familiarity with the wet shirt scene in the 1995 *Pride and Prejudice*, Joe Wright takes care to set the surprise Netherfield meeting scene indoors, where Darcy is fully dressed and engaged in the highly cultural pursuit of listening to his sister practice the piano. But the film more than makes up for that clothed and formal encounter by setting the proposal scene (which in the 1995 *Pride and Prejudice* takes place in a small sitting room) outdoors in a downpour.

The 2005 proposal scene begins with an extreme long shot of the landscape: we see the dark edges of the forest and the small figure of Lizzie running across a stone bridge that curves over the narrow end of a lake. Rain streams down. Cut to a medium close-up of a large stone monument, where Elizabeth stands, catching her breath, her wet coat flapping around her legs. Darcy appears, also drenched from the rain, professes his love, and asks her to marry him. She's surprised and affronted. They argue. Both of them are wet, with disheveled dark hair sticking to their faces, the rain pouring steadily, visibly, all around them. Darcy moves toward her, and the camera moves forward as well; now close-up shots of their faces as they almost kiss. Darcy's eyes move across her face to her mouth, he leans toward her, stops. The sexual tension is palpable.[76]

Bride makes full use of the water as sexual symbolism. Johnny Wickham first appears like some sort of mythical merman, emerging out of the ocean—his dripping torso, nicely muscled, accentuating his sexuality, in marked contrast to the carefully coifed and fully dressed Will Darcy sitting decorously on the beach.[77] Shortly thereafter, Darcy first appears as a sexual being in a dream sequence. Lalita is dreaming of marrying Wickham, but the dream shifts suddenly: Wickham transforms into Darcy, day turns to night, sunshine turns to thunder and pouring rain. Darcy takes her in his arms, bending her back, his face, wet with rain, moving over hers, closer and closer . . . and she wakes up.[78] Later, when they've realized their love for one another, we're treated to a dance number in an urban fountain: Darcy and Lalita dance across a plaza where dozens of fountains shoot water up all around them, in a clearly orgasmic display.[79]

Water of course denotes many symbolic associations,[80] but in all three of these films water seems mostly to have to do with sex. In the 1995 film's surprise meeting scene, in the 2005 film's proposal scene, and in *Bride and Prejudice*'s dream sequence, the images of dripping faces and wet clothes correlate with narrative moments of heightened sexual tension. The wetness has the effect of "making us think of sex" (in the words of the "Wet Shirt" song quoted earlier), in narratives in which convention precludes the literal depiction of sexual activity.

The allusions to the BBC *Pride and Prejudice* may not be deliberate, but for the Austen aficionado, the images in the more recent films cannot help but call to mind the parallel images in the earlier film, which we then hold in our minds simultaneously: Matthew Mcfadyen doesn't have to take his clothes off because Colin Firth already did.

This emphasis on sexuality and on the recognition of female desire is another of the hallmarks of the chick flick. Austen adaptations tend generally, according to Martine Voiret, to "cater to female desires and to the female gaze," to "allow the female viewer the pleasures of agency and looking usually reserved for the male viewer."[81] In the 1995 version the viewer's pleasure is enhanced by the vulnerability of Darcy in his wet clothes and bared neck and chest—a vulnerability that is more characteristic of women in Hollywood film, and which confers on the (female) spectator a power that other Hollywood films cannot offer. The gaze operates in a traditional way—just with the roles reversed. In many ways the twenty-first-century films follow suit—see, for example, the voyeuristic shots of Johnny Wickham in *Bride*, and the 45-second take of Darcy striding toward Elizabeth at the end of *Pride and Prejudice* 2005. But with the water imagery, there's an interesting shift in the twenty-first-century films toward what might be called "equality." In *Pride and Prejudice* (2005) both Elizabeth and Darcy are wet; they're sharing in the sexuality that the water implies. Likewise, in *Bride and Prejudice*, although Lalita doesn't get wet, by the last water scene, with the shooting fountains, she's a full participant in the metaphorical action. In these scenes, Darcy is no longer isolated in the frame, displayed alone for the viewer's pleasure.

The 1995 version of *Pride and Prejudice* is a key precursor to the twenty-first-century Austen adaptations, an integral strand of the Austen tapestry. Furthermore, tied as it is to the origins of "chick" culture,[82] it might be said to mark the historical moment when Austen adaptations became "chick flicks." But a close look at the differences between the 1995 and the twenty-first-century adaptations *as* chick flicks reveals a subtle shift in emphasis. The twenty-first-century filmmakers seem less interested in reversing male/female stereotypes; their female protagonists seem more at ease in the world and more confident in their sexuality. They are just as likely to exhibit sexual desire (metaphorically, of course) as their male counterparts. This shift suggests a move away from the feminist concerns characteristic of many of the 1990s Austen adaptations toward a more postfeminist sensibility, making these films more thoroughly representative of "chick" culture than their famous predecessor.

What I've tried to do in this analysis is to illustrate the value of looking at an adaptation as more than simply the relation between a film and its source text. A "traditional" approach to analyzing the adaptation might examine the controversy over whether Joe Wright's *Pride and Prejudice* is "faithful" to Austen's novel, or examine the nature of its difference from the novel, but I argue that such an approach cannot effectively reveal how Austen adaptations work, or what they signify in the 21st century. And while I cannot claim to have untangled all the myriad threads of the Austen tapestry, my analysis has demonstrated how three influential strands of literary/cultural/cinematic influence have shaped the 21st-century Austen "hypotext." By drawing on a classic literary text, the films borrow cultural capital, their romanticism authorized and validated by being connected to a literary masterpiece, and by drawing on the work of a great woman writer, they become associated with a female literary tradition. By drawing on the popular romance tradition and on elements of "chick" culture, they appeal specifically to female viewers, and by constructing a female gaze, they both provide that viewer with pleasures she may not find in more mainstream fare *and* draw attention to the issue of gender representation and the gaze in Hollywood film. And by blurring the boundaries between high art and popular culture, these films evince a postmodern aesthetic.[83]

These films also illustrate a large-scale shift in film and literary criticism toward female-oriented texts, and a corresponding shift in media attention to female audiences. Historically, popular genres associated with women readers and viewers—melodrama, popular romance, chick culture generally—have suffered critical neglect. Genre critics have valorized male-oriented genres such as science fiction and crime;[84] postmodern theorists have valorized male-oriented, violent films such as those by Quentin Tarantino (*Pulp Fiction*) and David Fincher (*Fight Club*).[85] Both have tended to ignore female-oriented films, privileging emotional distance and violent action over emotional engagement and interpersonal relationships. But this privileging of male-oriented genres is starting to change. The success of the Austen adaptations (and other literary chick flicks) indicates a heightened level of interest in and cultivation of a female audience by both critics and filmmakers.

Finally, the twenty-first-century Austen adaptations reflect—even more than the 1990s films—the ambivalence of our post-feminist age. Suzanne Ferriss asks about chick lit: Is it "advancing the cause of feminism by appealing to female audiences and featuring empowered, professional women? Or does it rehearse the same patriarchal narrative of romance and performance of femininity that feminists once rejected?"[86] Martine Voiret argues that part of the appeal of these films is that they allow us to live out a vicarious fantasy wherein the strong, sassy, independent heroine (us) is matched with her ideal partner: a strong, handsome, rich, yet sensitive man. For many women, this is a transgressive fantasy; the movies "remain attractive because while addressing our repressed desires, contradictions, and anxieties concerning masculinity and gender, they also suggest happy resolutions to those difficulties."[87] For some critics, that move toward happy resolution is unrealistic and dangerous, lulling the viewer into passive acceptance of the status quo. Others argue that such a reading gives too little credit to the female viewer, who is perfectly capable of recognizing the happy resolution as fantasy and of enjoying it as such. Either way, it seems to me that one of the most interesting features of the Austen adaptations is their embodiment of this ambivalence.

APPENDIX: SYNOPSES OF AUSTEN ADAPTATIONS DISCUSSED (ARRANGED IN REVERSE CHRONOLOGICAL ORDER)

PRIDE AND PREJUDICE (2005): This lavish production aims to be a "faithful"—if somewhat streamlined—representation of Austen's novel. Its primary difference from previous filmed versions is its more earthy portrayal of the Bennet family home—complete with pigs, chickens, and mud. (Running Time: 129 minutes)

BRIDE AND PREJUDICE (2004): This Bollywood version of *Pride and Prejudice* is remarkably parallel to the characters and plot of Austen's novel, especially given that the film is set in present-day India (with excursions to California and London). The narrative centers on a family of four sisters in Amritsar, India, all of whom are looking for husbands. The film opens when Balraj *Bingley* and his sister, along with good friend William *Darcy* arrive in Amritsar for a wedding. Bingley is immediately taken with the oldest daughter, Jaya, while Darcy finds himself unwillingly attracted to the second oldest daughter, Lalita, who finds him insufferably uptight. On a side trip to the sea town of Goa, the group meets Johnny *Wickham*, a dangerously attractive young man, whom Darcy knows and despises for reasons he's unwilling to state. But both Lalita and younger sister Lakhi find him appealing. A Mr. Kohli (Collins) arrives to find himself a good wife to take back with him to the United States. He first chooses Lalita, who is appalled. Her mother is horrified at her daughter's behavior, but Papa understands his girl. Mr. Kohli eventually settles for family friend Chandra. The family travels to California for the wedding, stopping on their way in London, where Jaya and Lalita visit Bingley's rather unwelcoming sister at the fabulous family mansion, and Lakhi meets up and attempts to run away with Wickham. Darcy saves the girl (unknown at first to the family), and they head off for California, where Lalita sees his grand home and meets his forbidding mother and sweet sister. As in *Pride and Prejudice*, Darcy first proposes to Lalita in a way that insults her and her family. But eventually the truth about Wickham and Darcy's sister comes out, and Lalita learns that Darcy's affections for her are genuine. (Running Time: 107 minutes)

PRIDE AND PREJUDICE: A LATTER-DAY COMEDY (2003): Set in present-day Provo, Utah, Elizabeth is a college student at a Mormon University, trying to balance the claims of her faith—to marry well, have children, and be a good Mormon—with her intellectual and career goals. The film has analogues for all the main characters of the novel, and for the main plot lines of the novel. (Running Time: 104 min.)

BRIDGET JONES'S DIARY (2001): Set in present-day London, the film loosely parallels *Pride and Prejudice*. Bridget and her circle of "singleton" friends (instead of sisters) are all looking for love—the one right match. As in *Pride and Prejudice*, Bridget meets Mark *Darcy* at a party, and finds him insufferable; he finds her and her family embarrassing. Again, as in *Pride and Prejudice*, he's from a very good family, is highly influential and respected—in this case as a well-respected and somewhat famous human rights lawyer—but also somewhat stiff and off-putting. Darcy states his interest in our heroine, but she doesn't trust him, mostly because of misinformation she hears from handsome playboy Daniel Cleaver (Hugh Grant), playing the Wickham character, with whom she has a fling. As in *Pride and Prejudice*, the truth about Darcy eventually comes out: the Wickham character is shown to be a jerk, and she realizes she loves Darcy after all. (The fact that Colin Firth plays Darcy in both the BBC version of *Pride and Prejudice* AND the film version of *Bridget Jones* only emphasizes the intertextual relationship among all these "Austen" texts.) (Running Time: 97 minutes)

MANSFIELD PARK (1999): This film is a combination of adaptation and imagination. It adapts the primary plot lines of Austen's *Mansfield Park*, but merges the character of Fanny with that of Austen herself. Drawing on Austen's juvenilia, Rozema re-imagines Fanny as a writer, endowing her with a personality and imagination much more in keeping with what we know of Austen than of the written character of Fanny. Rozema also creates new scenes to make explicit comments on sexuality and slavery that the novel only hints at. (Running Time: 112 minutes)

CLUELESS (1995): The film sets Austen's *Emma* in a late twentieth-century high school in Los Angeles. Like Emma, Cher (the protagonist) is an inveterate matchmaker, who learns through the course of the narrative that a person's social set does not determine character. Austen's Emma has been transformed from spoiled daughter of a wealthy country gentleman to spoiled daughter of a wealthy city lawyer; Mr. Knightley from a gentleman brother-in-law to hardworking law student; Harriet from a poor orphan to new girl at school; Mr. Elton from bachelor clergyman to high school party boy; and Frank Churchill from handsome young suitor who turns out to be secretly engaged, to cute new boy who turns out to be secretly gay. (Running Time: 97 minutes)

SENSE AND SENSIBILITY (1995): This celebrated adaptation aims to be a "faithful" rendition of Austen's novel. (Running Time: 136 minutes)

PRIDE AND PREJUDICE (1995): This mini-series is, still, the gold standard of Austen adaptations for many viewers. It is lauded for its careful attention to period detail and its long running time, which means that it has been able to include much more of the novel's plot than any of the shorter film versions. It is also well known for introducing a smoldering sexuality, quite new to BBC Austen adaptations, evident not in passionate embraces, but in the famous "wet shirt" scene and in the heated looks exchanged between the two leads. (Running Time: 300 minutes)

NOTES

This article is an expanded version of a paper I presented at the 2006 Popular Culture Association/American Culture Association national conference in Atlanta, Georgia. I have many people to thank for ideas, support, and editorial advice: The students in my English 160 (Film as Narrative) classes—especially Lauren Carroll and Amy Banham, whose conversation sparked the initial concept for this paper; the University of California at Davis, for funding to attend the PCA/ACA conference—specifically, awards from the Teaching Resources Center's University Instructional Improvement Program and from the University Writing Program's Clark Kerr fund; the attendees and presenters at the PCA/ACA conference who offered such helpful suggestions and comments; Brett Westbrook, who read and commented on an earlier rough draft; and Christa Albrecht-Crane and Dennis Cutchins, who provided wise editorial direction and apparently unlimited patience.

1. "A Man of Good Fortune," *Pride and Prejudice*, DVD, directed by Simon Langton (New York: A&E Home Video, 1995).

2. Bruce Stovel, "Further reading," in *The Cambridge Companion to Jane Austen*, ed. Edward Copeland and Juliet McMaster (Cambridge: Cambridge University Press, 1997), 227–43.

3. Claudia L. Johnson, "Austen Cults and Cultures," in *The Cambridge Companion to Jane Austen*, ed. Edward Copeland and Juliet McMaster (Cambridge: Cambridge University Press, 1997), 213.

4. Stovel, "Further reading," 240–43.

5. Linda Troost and Sayre Greenfield, ed., *Jane Austen in Hollywood*, 2nd edition (Lexington: University Press of Kentucky, 2001).

6. Suzanne R. Pucci and James Thompson, ed., *Jane Austen and Co.: Remaking the Past in Contemporary Culture* (Albany: State University of New York Press, 2003).

7. Gina Macdonald and Andrew F. Macdonald, *Jane Austen on Screen* (Cambridge: Cambridge University Press, 2003).

8. *The Republic of Pemberley*, 2007, http://www.pemberley.com.

9. Thomas Leitch, "Everything You Always Wanted to Know About Adaptation: Especially if You're Looking Forwards Rather Than Back," *Literature/Film Quarterly* 33, no. 3 (2005): 239.

10. *Bridget Jones's Diary*, DVD, directed by Sharon Maguire (Little Bird, 2001).

11. *Pride and Prejudice: A Latter-Day Comedy*, DVD, directed by Andrew Black (Salt Lake City, UT: Excel Entertainment Group, 2004).

12. *Bride and Prejudice*, DVD, directed by Gurinder Chadha (New York: Miramax, 2004).

13. *Pride and Prejudice*, DVD, directed by Joe Wright (Universal City: Focus Features, 2005).

14. According to IMDb.com, this film will re-tell "the story of Jane Austen's *Pride and Prejudice* through the lens of a fly-on-the-wall documentary crew."

15. Robert Stam, "Introduction: The Theory and Practice of Adaptation," in *Literature and Film*, ed. Robert Stam and Alessandro Raengo (Malden: Blackwell, 2003), 31.

16. Ibid.

17. James Naremore, "Introduction: Film and the Reign of Adaptation," in *Film Adaptation* (New Brunswick: Rutgers University Press, 2000), 10.

18. "Chapter 1," *Pride and Prejudice*, 2005.

19. Lindsay Doran, introduction to Emma Thompson, *The Sense and Sensibility Screenplay and Diaries: Bringing Jane Austen's Novel to Film* (New York: Newmarket Press, 1996), 11.

20. A. C. Bradley, "Jane Austen: A Lecture," *Essays and Studies by Members of the English Association* 2 (1911): 7–36, quoted in Stovel, "Further Reading," 233.

21. F. R. Leavis, *The Great Tradition* (New York: G. W. Stewart, 1948), 1.

22. Ibid., 5.

23. Ibid., 7.

24. Stovel, "Further reading," 234.

25. I'm relying primarily on Bruce Stovel's bibliography of Jane Austen criticism in the *Cambridge Companion to Jane Austen*. Isobel Grundy's and Claudia L. Johnson's essays in the same volume also provide useful information on the history of readers' relationships with Jane Austen's work (Isobel Grundy, "Jane Austen and Literary Traditions," 189–210; Claudia L. Johnson, "Austen Cults and Cultures," 211–26) as does Johnson's article "The Divine Miss Jane." (Claudia L. Johnson, "The Divine Miss Jane: Jane Austen, Janeites, and the Discipline of Novel Studies," *boundary 2* 23, no. 3 (1996): 150–54.)

26. *Mansfield Park*, DVD, directed by Patricia Rozema (New York City: Miramax, 1999).

27. Ibid., Director's commentary, "Horsing Around" and "Updating Susie."

28. Edward Said, *Culture and Imperialism* (New York: Vintage, 1994), 80–97.

29. "Will You Be Interested in Taking Part in the Dramaticals, Miss Thompson?" Newnham College Undergraduate Admissions, University of Cambridge, http:// www.newn.cam.ac.uk/admissions/emma.shtml

30. *Clueless*, DVD, directed by Amy Heckerling (Los Angeles: Paramount Pictures, 1995).

31. *Sense and Sensibility*, DVD, directed by Ang Lee (Culver City: Columbia Pictures, 1995).

32. Claudia L. Johnson, "The Divine Miss Jane: Jane Austen, Janeites, and the Discipline of Novel Studies," *boundary 2* 23, no. 3 (1996): 150–54.

33. The AUSTEN-L listserv also hosts a prominent gathering of Janeites, though on the whole they seem uninterested in the film adaptations, so I'm not discussing them here.

34. JulieW., comment on *The Republic of Pemberley*, December 30, 2006, http:// www.pemberley.com

35. Troost and Greenfield, *Jane Austen in Hollywood*, 8.

36. Troost and Greenfield end their introduction by saying that film adaptations "can supplement the text . . . in a most appealing way," but that they "have more to tell us about our own moment in time than about Austen's writing" (11), the implication being that Austen's writing remains superior. Gina Macdonald and Andrew F. Macdonald, editors of *Jane Austen on Screen*, include the view of both "film people" and "literary people," but at the end of their introduction they state their belief that "a good adaptation should take us back to the original work" (7). John Wiltshire is, like I am, interested in what the idea of "Jane Austen" signifies in the present moment, though, like Macdonald and Macdonald, his aim is to examine the idea of "Jane Austen" now as a way of understanding and coming closer to the historical Jane Austen (12); John Wiltshire, *Recreating Jane Austen* (Cambridge: Cambridge University Press, 2001).

37. Divya, *Republic of Pemberley*, December 9, 2006.

38. Julie P., *Republic of Pemberley*, January 7, 2006.

39. Claudia L. Johnson, Review of *Mansfield Park*, *The Times Literary Supplement* (December 31, 1999), 16–17, quoted in Jan Fergus, "Two *Mansfield Parks*: Purist and Postmodern," in *Jane Austen on Screen*, ed. Gina Macdonald and Andrew F. Macdonald (Cambridge: Cambridge University Press, 2003), 70.

40. Jan Fergus, "Two *Mansfield Parks*," 70.

41. Reiner, *Republic of Pemberley*, December 30, 2006.

42. Alison McFarland, comment on *The Internet Movie Database*, September 13, 2005, http://www.IMDb.com

43. Roger Gard, *Jane Austen's Novels: The Art of Clarity* (New Haven: Yale University Press, 1992).

44. Jennifer Crusie, ed., *Flirting with Pride and Prejudice: Fresh Perspectives on the Original Chick-Lit Masterpiece* (Dallas: Benbella Books, 2005).

45. "Chapter 15," *Pride and Prejudice*, 2005.

46. Harriet Margolis, "Janeite Culture: What Does the Name 'Jane Austen' Authorize?" in *Jane Austen on Screen*, ed. Gina Macdonald and Andrew F. Macdonald (Cambridge: Cambridge University Press, 2003), 24.

47. Andreas Huyssen, "Mass Culture as Woman: Modernism's Other," in *Studies in Entertainment: Critical Approaches to Mass Culture*, ed. Tania Modleski (Bloomington: Indiana University Press: 1986), 190.

48. Huyssen, however, in a very interesting move at the end of his article, argues that feminism has ended "the gendering of mass culture as feminine and inferior." The article was published in 1986—I wonder if he would now revise that optimistic stance?

49. Margolis, "Janeite Culture," 24.

50. Ibid., 25.

51. Cris Mazza, "What is Postfeminist Fiction?" in *Chick-Lit: Postfeminist Fiction*, ed. Cris Mazza and Jeffrey DeShell (Normal, IL: Fiction Collective 2, 1995).

52. Doris Lessing, "Bainbridge Denounces Chick-Lit as 'Froth,'" *Guardian Unlimited*, August 23, 2001, http://books.guardian.co.uk/bookerprize2001/story/0,1090, 541335,00.html, quoted in *Chick Lit: The New Woman's Fiction*, ed. Suzanne Ferriss and Mallory Young (New York: Routledge, 2006), 2.

53. Shanna Swendson, "The Original Chick-Lit Masterpiece," in *Flirting with Pride and Prejudice: Fresh Perspectives on the Original Chick-Lit Masterpiece*, ed. Jennifer Crusie (Dallas: Benbella Books, 2005), 69.

54. Radway's work has since been criticized by more recent scholars (and by romance novelists), who find her research methods inadequate (she bases her conclusions on a rather small set of readers who she argues is typical) and her attitude patronizing. I am indebted to the PCA/ACA 2006 romance panel (which included Jennifer Crusie Smith) for first alerting me to this re-assessment of Radway's work. I don't think, however, that they would disagree with Radway's general premise as I've stated it here.

55. Janice Radway, *Reading the Romance: Women, Patriarchy, and Popular Literature* (Chapel Hill: University of North Carolina Press, 1984).

56. Ferriss and Young, *Chick Lit*, 2.

57. They also, however, make a point of saying that "although Austen's work, together with a long tradition of women's writing, precedes Fielding's novel, chick lit cannot justifiably make a claim to comparable literary status" (4). So they end up still privileging Austen.

58. Debra R., "Wet Shirt," *Republic of Pemberly*, quoted by Geri-Lynn, February 18, 2008.

59. The recently published *Chick Flicks: Contemporary Women at the Movies*, edited by Suzanne Ferriss and Mallory Young (New York: Routledge, 2008), and *Postmodern Chick Flicks: The Return of the Woman's Film*, by Roberta Garrett (New York: Palgrave Macmillan, 2007), are just two indications that this scholarly absence is being rectified.

60. *The Online Slang Dictionary*, s.v. "Chick Flick," www.onlineslangdictionary .com

61. biggtones, comment on *Urban Dictionary*, September 19, 2004, s.v. "Chick Flick," www.urbandictionary.com

62. B-rad, *Urban Dictionary*, January 24, 2005, s.v. "Chick Flick"

63. Suzanne Ferriss and Mallory Young, ed., *Chick Flicks: Contemporary Women at the Movies* (New York and London: Routledge, 2008), 2.

64. See, particularly, Roberta Garrett's introduction to *Postmodern Chick Flicks* for a fuller discussion of the chick flick's history and its relationship to the classic woman's film.

65. Ferriss and Young tie the chick flick not only to the classic woman's film and to the screwball comedy of the same era, but point out that it also "includes the gun-toting heroines in *Thelma and Louise*, the strange mix of cannibalism and humor in *Fried Green Tomatoes*, the Cinderella story of *Pretty Woman*, the old-world elegance of *Pride and Prejudice* (2005)—and possibly the leather-clad futuristic revenge fantasy of Lara Croft" (*Chick Flicks*, 17).

66. Roberta Garrett, *Postmodern Chick Flicks: The Return of the Woman's Film* (New York: Palgrave Macmillan, 2007), 4–5.

67. Crusie, *Flirting*, 3. Apparently, Helen Fielding was writing *Bridget Jones's Diary*

in 1995 when *Pride and Prejudice* was causing a frenzy in Britain, suggesting that her novel is based more on the BBC film than it is on Austen's novel, and explaining why her characters are so infatuated with Colin Firth. Firth's association with Darcy was of course further enhanced when the actor was then cast *as* Mark Darcy in the two Bridget Jones films (not coincidentally, Andrew Davies, who wrote the BBC screenplay, was also a co-writer of the film version of *Bridget Jones's Diary*).

68. "Summer Travels," *Pride and Prejudice*, 1995.

69. "Chapter 11," *Pride and Prejudice*, 2005.

70. "Show Me To Love," *Bride and Prejudice*, 2004.

71. Jane Austen, *Pride and Prejudice* (London: Penguin, 1996), 152.

72. Ibid., 231.

73. "A Man Without Fault," *Pride and Prejudice*, 1995.

74. "Mr. Darcy's Letter," *Pride and Prejudice*, 1995.

75. "A Chance Encounter," *Pride and Prejudice*, 1995.

76. "Chapter 9," *Pride and Prejudice*, 2005.

77. "Indian Theme Park," *Bride and Prejudice*, 2004.

78. "No Life Without Wife," *Bride and Prejudice*, 2004.

79. "Show Me To Love," *Bride and Prejudice*, 2004.

80. For example, the washing scenes in the 1995 *Pride and Prejudice*—particularly with the valet pouring the water over Darcy's head—suggest a baptismal element that seems absent in the later films.

81. Martine Voiret, "Gender and Desire in Jane Austen's Adaptations," in *Jane Austen and Co.: Remaking the Past in Contemporary Culture*, ed. Suzanne R. Pucci and James Thompson (Albany: State University of New York Press, 2003), 230–31.

82. Ferris and Young argue that the chick flick is part of a larger cultural phenomenon: "chick," which includes chick lit, chick TV, and assorted other media and products created for a youthful female market. And they locate Helen Fielding's *Bridget Jones's Diary* as "a fairly clear starting point for the chick cultural explosion" (2).

83. See Roberta Garrett, who argues that chick flicks are inherently postmodern. The 2005 film is less obviously postmodern, but *Bride and Prejudice*, and all the more recent Austen films—*The Jane Austen Book Club*, *Becoming Jane*, and the forthcoming *Jane Austen Handheld*—all of which emphasize the meta-literary and cinematic— suggest an increasingly postmodern trend in Austen adaptations.

84. See Richard Maltby, *Hollywood Cinema*, 2nd ed. (Malden, MA: Blackwell, 2003), 101–6.

85. See Garrett, *Postmodern Chick Flicks*, 7.

86. Ferris and Young, *Chick Lit*, 9.

87. Voiret, "Gender and Desire," 242.

Converting the Controversial: Regulation as "Source Text" in Adaptation

Richard Berger

IT IS A TRUISM THAT WHILE OUR VISUAL MEDIA IS GENERALLY HEAVILY regulated, both in the United States and in the United Kingdom, literature is not. This paper is an attempt to broaden the range of adaptation studies to include the institutional influences that can affect an adaptation. This paper will explore the relationship between adaptation and the censorship and regulatory regimes of both the US and the UK. I will suggest here that the history of adaptation and the history of censorship are closely intertwined. Indeed, many controversial "taboo busting' films—as I shall show—have been adapted from literary sources. So, this examination of adaptation and censorship also throws a light on the elitism that surrounds perceived "high art" forms, as opposed to lower ones. Furthermore, this paper explores the history of adapting controversial novels for both film and television, and examines the ways in which adaptors have treated the most transgressive elements of their source texts. In this way, these adaptations can therefore be read both as a commentary on, and a response to, the novels they are based on.

Adaptation studies have largely been concerned with the relationship between texts (both source and target) and notions of authors. Adaptation theorists have deployed an array of comparative, and latterly medium specific, approaches to understand the relationship between source and target texts. However, current adaptation theorists, notably Sarah Cardwell, Julie Sanders, and Linda Hutcheon,[1] are recognizing the impact an adaptation can have on its source materials. Both Hutcheon and Sanders recognize that an adaptation can "oscillate" with its source material, and that adaptations are dependent on their source material. Both propose a relationship of dependency between an adaptation and its source, and both argue that adaptations should be viewed (and studied) as adaptations.

Similarly, Cardwell argues that an adaptation can "reconfigure" the source material.[2] These studies move us beyond binary notions of source and target texts, and it's this argument I want to build on here, by adding an institutional framework to this sphere of influence between texts and their adaptations. I want to combine industry analysis with an approach that recognizes the interplay and relationship of exchange between adaptations and their sources.

Any such study also serves to illustrate the hierarchy that often exists between cinema and literature. As I have pointed out, literature is not classified or rated, and I want to suggest that if a text is considered "classic literature," as opposed to "popular fiction," then more can be "got away with" it seems. Attempts have been made to ban literature, most notably with the trial regarding D. H. Lawrence's novel, *Lady Chatterley's Lover*, for obscenity in the UK in 1959. The trial judge famously asked the members of the jury if this was a novel that they would be happy for their servants to read. The author himself, D. H. Lawrence, described the censors as "morons." J. D. Salinger's 1951 novel, *The Catcher in the Rye*, was also marked as being controversial, and was singled out as being an influence on Mark Chapman's murder of John Lennon in 1980. So, there is an implicit elitism inherent in how different texts, from different media are treated by regulators.

The introduction of the Production Code (often called the "Hays Code" in the US) is probably the most significant date in the history of film censorship. This code was established by the then Motion Pictures Association, overseen by former postmaster, Will Hays. The MPA became known as the Hays Office, as it was run very much in line with Hays's own moral conservativism. In the UK, the British Board of Film Censorship (now Classification) was established in 1913, but it was the Hays Code and the Hays Office that dominated cinema regulation on both sides of the Atlantic, from 1924, right up until the 1960s. Tom Dewe Mathews describes the Hays Office as being "largely moral" and the BBFC as "political."[3]

The Hays Code stipulated that no thigh of a female body may be shown "between the garter and the knickers"; intimate relationships between black and white races was forbidden; if two people were seen on a bed, both must have at least one foot on the floor; no double-beds were to be shown, ever; and forty-three words including "Broad," "Tom-cat," and "Cripes" were banned outright.[4]

The Hays Office was very powerful, and studios were pressured into dropping some stars, such as Mae West, because of her film, *She Done Him Wrong* (1933). (Notably, in that same year, the Catholic League of Decency was established, and had over ten million Americans signed up as members.) There had been street protests regarding *She Done Him Wrong*, and Hays vowed to "do better."[5] The Office went so far as to place observers on the set of Mae West's next film, *It Ain't No Sin* (1934).

The early 1930s also saw the emergence of a new genre of movie: horror films. Movies such as *Dracula* (1931) and *Dr Jekyll and Mr Hyde* and *Frankenstein* (1932) were all controversial, and all adaptations. The BBFC had banned *Nosferatu* in 1922, but that was because the widow of Bram Stoker, the author of the novel *Dracula*, threatened to sue for copyright.

In 1936, Will Hays travelled to London to visit the offices of the BBFC, and the collaborative relationship between the two censorship boards was further entrenched. After WWII, a steady liberalization began, but the Hays Office still kept a tight grip on regulation. So much so, that screenplays were often submitted to the Hays Office for approval before even a single frame of a movie had been shot. So, in a sense, the Hays office was predominantly censoring what was arguably a *literary* form—the screenplay—throughout the 1930s and 1940s. In the UK, 80 percent of film screenplays were being submitted to the BBFC for approval during this time.

Many novelists at this time adapted their own work for the big screen. Arguably, many writers were influenced by cinema, and their work framed the "utterance" of film in many respects. The novelist Franz Kafka claimed that he was more influenced by cinema than literature, for example. In a sense, these writers adapted many cinematic styles and techniques into their writing, but the cinema also seemed to adopt literary practices: Sergei Eisenstein claimed he got his ideas for *montage* straight from the pages of Charles Dickens.[6] Many have pointed out the "camera tricks" employed by Virginia Woolf.[7] Another very visual and cinematic writer was Graham Greene. He adapted his own novel *Brighton Rock* in 1947. The novel was based on newspaper reports of the "Battle of Lewes," when organized crime first came to the attention of the British public. The screenplay went through a number of revisions because of the Hays Office and the BBFC, before a frame was shot. However, scene cuts from the script were reinstated in the shooting scripts, and subsequently, the finished film was heavily criticised for its violence and its portrayal of gang culture on the UK's south coast.

Often, in the UK, the BBFC would quietly suppress a film until the public outrage had died down. Frank Rooney's short story, "The Cyclists' Raid," was adapted as *The Wild One* in 1954 (starring Marlon Brandon), but it didn't get a classification in the UK until 1967. So, adaptations often made for the most controversial of films. The script for Stanley Kubrick's adaptation of Vladimir Nabokov's *Lolita* (1962) was continually submitted to the BBFC for approval. The film was adapted by Vladimir Nabokov himself, and the character of Lolita had to be made older—in the novel she is twelve-and-a-half, and in the film she is played by the fourteen-year-old Sue Lyon. The film also dispensed with the "unreliable narrator" device used in the novel, making for a much starker and more "closed" text. Kubrick's adaptation was then rendered far more palatable for the mainstream cinema audiences of the early 1960s, which was the prime directive of the Hays Code. A controversial novel was now a more straightforward melodrama in this cinematic incarnation.

By the late 1950s, the impact of the 1948 anti-trust legislation had finally seen off the studio system, and the power of the Hays Office and the BBFC declined. However, adaptations were still breaking cinematic taboos, again perhaps highlighting the elitism inherent in the relationship between cinema and literature. The British censor John Trevelyan later regretted passing two adaptations of Ian Fleming's spy novels at this time, as the films were so misogynistic: *Dr No* (1962) and *From Russia with Love* (1963).

An adaptation of Julio Cortázar's short story, "The Droolings of the Devil," was the basis for Michelangelo Antonioni's *Blow-Up* in 1966, which contained full-frontal female nudity for the first time in mainstream cinema, and scenes of group sex. An adaptation of James Joyce's multi-layered novel, *Ulysses*, was passed uncut in 1967, so mainstream cinema audiences were exposed to the word "fuck" for the first time in movie theaters. It did seem that if the film was based on a prior work that had some prestige and cultural value, then it was allowed its moment of "safe" and "contained" transgression. Just as transgressive, but more mainstream fare, tended to be cut or banned altogether by the Hays Office and the BBFC; in the UK town of Beaconsfield, the local authority owned the cinema and banned The Beatles' film, *Yellow Submarine* (1968) because it was "rubbish."

Literary adaptations were not always given a free ride, and some directors spent their career fighting for the integrity of their work on both sides of the Atlantic. Ken Russell is a British filmmaker very much influenced by literature, and his adaptation of D. H. Lawrence's *Women in Love* proved problematic for censors in 1968. Full frontal male nudity was clearly a step too far, and Alan Bates and Oliver Reed's nude wrestling scene had to be darkened. A few years later, Russell loosely adapted Aldous Huxley's *The Devils of London* as *The Devils* (1971), and the BBFC insisted on a great many cuts; the scenes showing masturbating nuns and the administration of an enema to a nun on an altar were both considered unacceptable. The director himself was (then) a devout Catholic, and insisted that his film was about the way in which religion can be corrupted for selfish ends. The footage cut from the film has only recently been found and restored.

Frank Marcus's play, *The Killing of Sister George*, was adapted for film in 1969, and portrayed a lesbian relationship for the first time in mainstream cinema. This was just a year after homosexuality was decriminalized in the UK. In the same year, the US finally got its cinema regulator, the Motion Picture Association of America. The Hays Production Code that had existed before this was now largely ineffective due a spate of taboo-busting films, in particular Alfred Hitchcock's adaptation of Robert Bloch's pulp novel, *Psycho* (1960) and the aforementioned *Ulysses*. The MPAA quickly adopted a new series of classifications, mirroring the BBFC in the UK. Regulators, however, were not the only ones banning films. Stanley Kubrick ended up banning his own adaptation of Anthony Burgess's *A Clockwork Orange* (1971) after several incidences of so called "copycat" violence were reported in the UK media. This moment was probably the most effective incidence of censorship in film history.[8] The film remained banned in the UK until after Kubrick's death in 1999.

Banning films became more complex with the advent of the VCR. Nicholas Roeg's interpretation of a Daphne Du Maurier novella, *Don't Look Now*, in 1973, caused a stir when it was suggested by some reviewers that the sex scene between Julie Christie and Donald Sutherland was real. But new exhibition technologies had loosened censorship in both the UK and the US and put the reception of such controversial scenes in the home for the first time. The late 1970s saw the domestic video recorder (VCR) become the fastest-adopted media platform in history, and caused a new headache for both the MPAA and the BBFC. New legislation was introduced to combat the new "folk devil," the "video nasty."[9] Some films, which were previously released for cinema, were effectively banned on video, such as William Friedkin's adaptation of William Peter Blatty's novel, *The Exorcist* (1973).

At this point I want to suggest that a new generation of adaptors and filmmakers was moving away from adapting "classic" or highly regarded literature to more contemporary, and often more controversial (and therefore transgressive) novels. Cinema, at this time, largely due to the cultural cachet of the *Nouvelle Vague* and the New Hollywood movement in the US, had thrown off its attempts to gain some of the status of literature. In a celebrated essay published in the *Cahiers du Cinema* in 1954, François Truffaut had attacked cinema's reliance on adaptation.[10] So, throughout the 70s and 80s a new generation of filmmakers, influenced by the *Nouvelle Vague*, seized upon contemporary literature. For example, besides adapting Mario Puzo's *Godfather* novels, Francis Ford Coppola used two of S. E Hinton's tales of teen-age gang violence as source material for the underrated films, *The Out-siders* (1983) and *Rumble Fish* (1983). In a sense, contemporary fiction took its cue from cinema, and attempted to be *as* "taboo-busting" and genre defining.

So, in the next section of this essay I want to sketch out a framework where we can see the adaptation acting against the source material. These films seem to be not just "oscillating" alongside literature, as Linda Hutcheon and Julie Sanders both suggest, but reconfiguring the work in some way, as Cardwell argues. A novel then, is almost legiti-mized by virtue of having been adapted, and as Giddings and Selby highlight, many authors become "canonical" writers because their work has been adapted so often:[11] would Stephen King be as well-known or as admired if his novels and short stories hadn't been such rich source material for cinema? I'm proposing here that an adaptation of a controversial and contemporary novel can make that novel "safe" and "contained" within a sphere of influence that could include a whole range of texts.

Despite new regulation to control what audiences could watch at home on their VCRs, the 1980s was still a "taboo-busting" decade. In 1986, Adrian Lyne shocked audiences with his adaptation of Sarah Kernochan's memoir *Nine ½ Weeks*, starring Kim Basinger and Mickey Rourke. In 1988, Martin Scorsese directed the adaptation of Nikos Kazantzakis' 1951 novel, *The Last Temptation of Christ*. Many were critical of the film's portrayal of Christ imagining a life with Mary Magdalene. The film garnered widespread protests, particularly in the US. In the UK, the then-head of the Roman Catholic Church, Cardinal Basil Hume, stated that it would be a sin if any practicing Catholic viewed the film. The BBFC screened *Last Temptation* to twenty-eight priests before issuing their "18" certificate. However, cinemas were picketed by Christians anyway. These instances high-light how an adaptation can draw fire away from a source text and take the flak of its source material. The protestors wanted the film banned, not the novel. They blamed the adaptation, and not the source text, a novel that had been in print for over thirty years.

Canadian filmmaker David Cronenberg's adaptation of J. G. Bal-lard's novel, *Crash*, in 1996, caused huge problems for UK censors. The film was passed by the BBFC, but Alexander Walker of the *Lon-don Evening Standard*, called the film "pornography" and led a cam-paign to have it banned. The *London Evening Standard* and its sister publication, *The Daily Mail*, attacked the BBFC, and even published personal details of BBFC employees, implying that they weren't quali-fied to judge the suitability of films for public exhibition. Westminster

Council in London ignored the BBFC's classification, and *Crash*, to this day, remains the only film to have ever been banned in the West End of London. A year later, in 1997, Adrian Lyne directed another adaptation of Nabokov's *Lolita*. However, he came up against the same problems as Stanley Kubrick had in 1962. In the aftermath of the *Crash* Westminster ban, Lyne's eponymous heroine was played by the fifteen-year-old Dominique Swain, as a fourteen-year-old Lolita. The film was largely praised, though, for its successful treatment of Nabokov's acclaimed novel.

Sometimes, however, literature can shock, before the adaptive cycle had been completed, highlighting how close an adaptation can be to the publication of its source text. The adaptation of "classic literature" affords the distance of decades, even generations. Adaptation of contemporary fiction does not. So, transgressive texts have far more of a dialogical relationship to each other in this instance. For example, in 1991, Bret Easton Ellis's novel, *American Psycho*, shocked readers in the UK and the US. As a consequence, its distribution in Germany was heavily restricted and in Australia it was illegal to sell it to minors.

Any adaptation of Bret Easton Ellis's second novel was going to be controversial, and British filmmaker Mary Harron spent many years trying to get the project off the ground. The film was released in 2000, and was less controversial than the novel which is far more graphic—at one point the serial killer of the title, Patrick Bateman, murders a child at the zoo. Literature can convey some events that a film never would be capable of, and Harron's film was no different. However, the film acted against the novel, rendering it "safe" and "contained" within the adaptation. The film played on the idea that Bateman is mad or suffering from delusions. This is only suggested in the novel, notably in a scene where Bateman fears he is being followed by a park bench, but the film eschewed the violence in favour of portraying a deluded madman, much as both adaptations of *Lolita* had done with the viewpoint character, Humbert Humbert. In fact, both versions of *Lolita* and *American Psycho* are remarkably similar for their controversial content, taboo-busting nature, treatment of their respective source texts, and journeys to the big screen: any ambiguity and ambivalence is ironed out of the adaptation, making, to quote Roland Barthes, a "readerly" text out of a "writerly" one.[12] This, I would argue, in turn neuters the source material to an extent, almost defusing the controversial content, and "reconfiguring" the work, as Sarah Cardwell suggests.[13]

However, regulation which favors the source over the target text can cause problems when both the novel and the subsequent adaptation are considered to be "prestige" artifacts. Three quarters of Academy Awards for Best Picture have gone to adaptations and there is even a category for Best Adapted Screenplay.[14] Often, the adaptations that win these awards are based on prestigious source material, by prestigious "literary" writers. But what happens when both source and target texts contain elements that would be controversial to a mainstream audience?

Joe Wright's adaptation of Ian McEwan's 2002 novel, *Atonement*, is one such case. Ian McEwan is a Booker Prize-winning writer, whose work has been the subject of numerous adaptations, notably *The Cement Garden* (1993) and *Enduring Love* (2004). Joe Wright's version of *Atonement* is firmly set in the heritage vein, and the film garnered a host of award nominations. The novel centers on a tragic misunderstanding when a thirteen-year-old girl, Briony Tallis, reads and then delivers the wrong love letter to her sister, Cecilia. The letter contains an obscene phrase written half in jest by Cecilia's suitor, Robbie Turner. Briony's misunderstanding sets in motion a disastrous change of events, which catastrophically damages the lives of the two would-be-lovers. The novel, in a sense, is about *the novel*, as the viewpoint character, Briony, is an elderly and terminally ill novelist who is attempting to make up for her dreadful past mistake.

The problem for the filmmakers and the censors is that the obscene phrase in question contained two uses of the word "cunt," not something you would generally hear in a film aimed squarely at the sorts of audiences that enjoyed another adaptation of another Booker-Prize winning author's work, *The English Patient* (1996). However, the film again seeks to make "safe" and "contain" its own source material by appropriating the literary form entirely. In the novel we read the word twice, and it gains its power and shock value by its singular use in one short sentence, in a novel that has few expletives. In the novel, Briony is even described as spelling the word out loud, backwards, to her cousin Lola. In the film, Joe Wright makes us read the word too, as we see Robbie typing the letter. The word is never spoken, but we see it typed twice (in "Old Courier" font), the repetition reducing the word's shock value—in a sense, unhooking it from the narrative of the novel.

The "C-word" in the film is framed in a montage sequence where we cut between Robbie typing two aborted versions of his letter, before typing the one with the "C-word", and six scenes of Cecilia smoking, putting on her makeup and dressing for dinner. The last cut is from a sequence where Robbie laughs after typing the "C-word", before looking over his shoulder, "at" Cecilia—as the scene cuts there to Cecilia dressing.[15] It's as if the two lovers are sharing an intimate moment together. So, the film uses this romantic device, expressed through montage, to neuter one of the greatest taboos in the English language. This sequence in Joe Wright's *Atonement* is similar in construction to the controversial sex scene in Nicholas Roeg's *Don't Look Now*, where the scene cuts between the sex and the couple dressing afterwards. In the novel the word is central, but in the film, it is not. This may be a result of Wright's own background. Wright is famously dyslexic, and didn't, for instance, read Jane Austen's novel for his adaptation of *Pride and Prejudice* (2005). It's possible that a similar situation existed in this adaptation. "Reading" a word in a novel is different from "gazing" at a word on screen—the latter is very much a collective experience—and this serves to defuse any controversy in the adaptation, and therefore, I would argue, reflect a sort of normalcy back on the novel also.

Why are adaptors and filmmakers drawn to such transgressive source material, knowing that they could fall foul of the regulatory frameworks that exist in the UK and US? I would argue that part of the answer lies in the fact that they are ultimately fans of the material, and I would also suggest therefore that directors of adaptations can often have a different relationship with their source material as a consequence. Ken Russell, for example, has made several adaptations of D. H. Lawrence's novels for both film and television, an author described as his "literary soulmate."[16] We can also perhaps see two adaptive modes here: the first being that adaptations of "classic" literature are often attempted for heritage and nostalgic reasons, and the second is that adaptations of contemporary fiction are done precisely for transgressive reasons, as the adaptations and directors attempt to appropriate some of the cultural cachet of such works as *Last Exist to Brooklyn*, *Fight Club*, and *Brokeback Mountain*. Some filmmakers, such as Joe Wright (*Pride and Prejudice*, *Atonement*) and Ang Lee (*Sense and Sensibility*, *Brokeback Mountain*, and *Lust, Caution*) seem to oscillate between these two positions.

It is for these reasons that adaptation studies need to perhaps broaden in scope, from narrow confines of texts, notions of fidelity and medium specificity, to taking into account institutional frameworks that act on any adaptation. The regulatory frameworks in the UK and the US can also serve to enforce self-censorship on an adaptation, with the filmmakers of *Perfume: The Story of a Murderer* (2006) again taking their cue from Stanley Kubrick's *Lolita*, in increasing the age of the central character, Laure, from the age suggested in Patrick Suskind's novel. So, it is clear, then, that regulatory frameworks (which often begat self-censorship positions on adaptors and filmmakers) can be called "source texts" themselves.

The history of adaptation is the history of censorship and regulation, and vice versa, and broadening out adaptation studies to take into account these institutional and cultural factors does offer up a new framework for analysis. This analysis highlights the elitism inherent in the relationship between literature and film, and it also shows the impact an adaptation can have on the receptions of its source material.

NOTES

1. Sarah Cardwell, *Adaptation Revisited: Television and the Classic Novel* (Manchester: Manchester University Press, 2002); Julie Sanders, *Adaptation and Appropriation* (London: Routledge, 2006); Linda Hutcheon, *A Theory of Adaptation* (London: Routledge, 2006).

2. Cardwell, *Adaptation Revisited*, 205.

3. Tom Dewe Mathews, *Censored: The Story of Film Censorship in Britain* (London: Chatto & Windus, 1994), 57.

4. Ben Yagoda, "Hollywood Cleans Up Its Act: The Curious Career of the Hays Office," *American Heritage Magazine* 2 (February/March 1980), 12–21.

5. Mathews, *Censored*, 76.

6. Sergei Eisenstein, "Dickens, Griffith, and the Film Today," *Film and Literature: An Introduction and Reader*, ed. Timothy Corrigan (London: Prentice Hall, 1999).

7. Sharon Ouditt, "*Orlando:* Coming Across the Divide," *Adaptations: From Text to Screen, Screen to Text*, ed. Deboraha Cartmell and Imelda Whelehan (London: Routledge, 1999).

8. Mathews, *Censored*, 209.

9. Patricia Holland, "Living for Libido, or 'Child's Play IV': The Imagery of Childhood and the Call for Censorship," *Ill Effects: The Media/Violence Debate*, ed. Martin Barker and Julian Petley (London: Routledge, 2001).

10. François Truffaut, "A Certain Tendency of the French Cinema," *Movies and Methods: Volume 1*, ed. Bill Nichols (Los Angeles: University of California Press, 1976).

11. Robert Giddings and Keith Selby, *The Classic Serial on Television and Radio* (Basingstoke: Palgrave Macmillan, 2001).

12. Roland Barthes, *S/Z* (Oxford: Blackwell, 1974), 4.

13. Cardwell, *Adaptation Revisited*, 205.

14. Brian McFarlane, *Novel into Film: An Introduction to the Theory of Adaptation* (Oxford: Clarendon Press, 1996).

15. *Atonement*, DVD, directed by Joe Wright (London, UK: Working Title Films, 2007).

16. Boyd Tonkin, "Ken Russell: The Film-Maker Laid Bare," *The Independent*, January 5, 2007.

Sausage Smoke Leading to Mulligan's Breakfast: Film Adaptation and James Joyce's *Ulysses*

David A. Hatch and David C. Simmons

JAMES JOYCE'S *ULYSSES* PRESENTS A GOOD CASE FOR EXAMINING FILM adaptation, not only because several unrealized screenplays and two film adaptations provide diverse perspectives on the process, but also because Joyce's project suggests a new approach for adaptation studies. *Ulysses* is, by design, an adaptation itself. In the novel, Joyce creates a confluence of themes from the Greek epic and the Dublin he presents, or to use language from T. S. Eliot's outline of Joyce's mythic method, Joyce maintains a "continuous parallel" between the contemporary, everyday experiences of Leopold Bloom, Dubliner, (as Joyce envisions them) and the grand, mythic experiences of Odysseus, adventurer and Trojan War veteran (as Joyce interprets them).[1] Joyce adapts the epic. He translates the themes and events of Homer's *The Odyssey* into a new permutation—one in which the source does not have more authority than the events of the adaptation, but in which both maintain an equilibrium that facilitates reciprocal criticism.

Using traditional criteria for successful adaptation, the novel is unfilmable. Even if one ignores differences in medium, any adaptation will, by necessity, have to leave out too much material to be "faithful" to the novel. Joyce acknowledges the difficulty of adapting his novel in a 1932 letter in which he recognizes the "filming as irrealisable."[2] This comment may be informed by the size and complexity of the novel—by the monumental task of adapting the thirty-hour oral reading time of the text to a two-hour film. The difficult concepts and anachronisms of the novel are hard to translate to film as well. Margot Norris observes, for example, that "the discussion of Irish oratory in the newspaper room refers to numerous Irish journalists, barristers, and politicians familiar at the turn of the century but thoroughly arcane some sixty years later. Even such a dramatic event as the Phoenix

Park murders—already more than twenty years in the past at the time of the novel—could not possibly bear the kind of repeated discussion it receives in the novel."[3] While the type of references discussed above present difficulties when adapting most novels, Joyce's penchant for detailed, topical, even obscure references exacerbates this problem.

These difficulties aside, Joyce's interest in cinema[4] and his application of what we might call "filmic" techniques in his work (informed by an affinity for the work of and a personal correspondence with Sergei Eisenstein) suggest unique possibilities for adaptation. Despite this situation, however, scholars have neglected the ways that adaptations of the novel revision Joyce's characters and themes for the film medium, that is, how directors establish a dialogue not only with the novel, but with earlier film adaptations as well. Yet on fundamental formal levels, the film adaptations resemble the novel no more than Joyce's mammoth modernist experiment resembles Homeric epic poetry. Joseph Strick, who adapted the novel in 1967, recognizes this fact, commenting to Margot Norris that he was interested in the idea "that if Joyce had taken a liberty with over 2,000 years, I could take the same liberty with 60."[5] Strick's comment reflects his justification, perhaps, of the choices he made in his adaptation (which we will discuss shortly), but also suggests that such liberty is necessary when moving to a new form. The comment also suggests that despite Joyce's hesitation about adapting the novel for the screen, to prioritize the novel over the adaptations would seem contrary to Joyce's own project. This is especially true, in part, because *Ulysses* is not just an adaptation of the Homeric epic, but a novel which is experimental partly because of the author's attempts, as Philippe Met observes, in his discussion of modernism and film, to "methodically appropriate a filmic grammar."[6] Because of this situation, film presents opportunities to extend Joyce's formal experiments in new directions and our discussion of adaptations of the novel should reflect this sense of experimentation. Like Joyce, these filmmakers translate his tale for their audience; each re-vision of *Ulysses* creates a confluence of the novel and the social/aesthetic environment of the filmmakers. Thus, the filmmakers are in an intertextual dialogue with Joyce's sources and with one another as much as they are with Joyce's text. Mario Serandrei's unrealized treatment, originally published in Alessandro Blasetti's *Cinematografo* in 1930,[7] and the 1939 film script created by Louis Zukofsky and Jerry Reisman,[8] for example, both reflect the eclectic, experimental period of early European art cinema and the anxiety of pre-War II Europe. Each draws on German Expressionism and Surrealist aesthetics. In contrast, Joseph Strick's 1967 version (black and white, with a Steven Dedalus who looks more like one of the Beatles

than a West Bank art student)[9] speaks to the American youth movement and emergence of art house cinema. Finally, Sean Walsh's 2003
adaptation *Bloom*,[10] released near the centenary of Bloomsday in celebration of a writer who has become an Irish cultural icon instead of a
censored expatriate, is warm, almost sepia-toned and elegiac—nostalgic for a Dublin that never was.

Although many important episodes occur in the fictional events of
June 16, 1904, as depicted by James Joyce in *Ulysses*, a primary thrust
is toward the intellectual joining of Leopold Bloom and Stephen Dedalus. In fact, much of the action of "Bloomsday" is involved with the
converging spiritual trajectories of these two men, and with the careful
exploration of the void in each character that the other will fill. A similar meeting of minds took place on November 30, 1929, between two
innovative artists, James Joyce and Sergei Eisenstein, whose paths
seemed to intersect in a similar manner. Although each man expressed
his art through a different medium, the two were united by a similar
avant-garde aesthetic and by the pursuit of a direct artistic expression
of the thought patterns of the human mind. There are no records of
any subsequent meetings or correspondence, and Joyce never mentions the encounter in his writing. The only source for the events of
this meeting is Eisenstein, who commented about it in an essay entitled "A Course in Treatment" in October, 1932: "When Joyce and I
met in Paris, he was intensely interested in my plans for the inner film-
monologue, with a far broader scope than is afforded by literature.
Despite his almost total blindness Joyce wished to see those parts of
Potemkin and October which, with the expressive means of film culture, move along kindred lines [with his own work]."[11] Eisenstein was
quite familiar with Joyce's work, having read several of his novels prior
to their encounter. Although there is no evidence that Joyce had seen
any of Eisenstein's films, it is likely, due to Joyce's interest in cinema,
that he was at the time at least aware of the general style of Eisenstein's work as well. Indeed, the meeting was arranged because of
a mutual desire to get to know one another and to share similar ideas.
Eisenstein was impressed by their discourse and the deeper understanding of Joyce's work that he acquired from it, to the point that he
mentions Joyce often in subsequent essays. In addition, having established The Film School in Moscow in 1931, he often gave his students
passages from *Ulysses* "as prose exercises, to be turned into script
form."[12] Joyce seemed similarly impressed; he later commented to Eugene Jolas "that if *Ulysses* were ever made into a film, he thought that
the only man who could direct it would be either Walter Ruttman the
German or Sergei Eisenstein the Russian."[13]

We may never fully understand how one artist may have influenced the later work of the other, nor is that the purpose of this exploration. Perhaps, as R. Barton Palmer suggests, the relationship between the two men should be viewed as analogous; the approach of each reflects an interest in the "phenomenon of inner speech and a technique to represent it."[14] As Alan Speigel has argued, Joyce refers repeatedly to cinematography because "the new medium provides him with new words to describe certain things which are happening in his mind and in his writing."[15] Eisenstein remarks on the converging nature of the two media when he notes that "what Joyce does in literature is quite near to what we do and even closer to what we have intentions of doing with the new cinematography."[16] Thus, while crediting one artist with influencing the other may be inappropriate, it is certain that each man experienced an affirmation of his interpretive approach through the perspective provided by the other's method. Both artists sought to illustrate the flurry of thoughts within the human mind: Joyce through juxtaposition of an "interior monologue" with objective narration and dialogue, Eisenstein through juxtaposition of images, voice-over and sound into "montage" assemblies. This juxtaposition unites the two methods; the reconstruction of diverse elements results in a greater and more diverse meaning than the individual parts.

Joyce uses several literary elements in *Ulysses* that approach cinematic techniques. For instance, he seems to be utilizing what film theorist Erwin Panofsky indentifies as cinema's ability to use "dynamization of space" and "spatialization of time."[17] In other words, "in a movie things move, and you can be moved instantaneously from anywhere to anywhere, and you can witness successive events happening at the same time."[18] We observe this motion in *Ulysses*. During the "Sirens" episode, for example, Joyce writes:

Tap.
By Larry O'Rourke's, by Larry, bold Larry O', Boylan swayed and Boylan turned.
From the forsaken shell miss Mina glided to her tankards waiting. No, she was not lonely archly miss Douce's head let Mr Lidwell know.
Walks in the moonlight by the sea. No, not alone. With whom? She nobly answered: with a gentleman friend.
Bob Cowley's twinkling fingers in the treble played again. . . . That's joyful I can feel. Never have written on it. Why? My joy is other joy. But both are joys.[19]

Here the reader is moved quickly between four different spaces. First, we are with the blind piano tuner who is heading toward the bar in the Ormand Hotel. Next, we are traveling alongside Boylan as he walks toward Molly's house. Then, we are in the mind of one of the sirens, Miss Mina Kennedy. Last, we are in Bloom's thoughts as he ponders the music of the room and the letter he is writing to Martha. The novel, like a film, is able to quickly move a reader/spectator through space and time without giving clear signifiers of the location change.

Another cinematic technique Joyce simulates is the point-of-view shot which, in film, is used so that the spectator experiences the sensations of the character (e.g. seeing what the character sees, hearing what the character hears, etc.) As such, the POV shot is part of a larger system known as subjective space, where the spectator temporarily relinquishes his or her own subjectivity to become the character for a certain space of time. We observe this element of film in the "Circe" section. Here, the reader goes into Bloom's mind and begins to experience his inner thoughts/fears/wishes as if they were outward events. For example, first we experience the "real" outward event of the street urchins of Nighttown telling Bloom to "Mind out mister."[20] Bloom reminds himself to "Beware of pickpockets" and we "hear" it as though he were speaking outwardly.[21] But then we see Bloom's dead father, Rudolph, who chastises his son for his poor financial skills.[22] In response to this, we "see" Bloom dressed as a schoolboy.[23] Soon we see such sights as a "Moorish" Molly beside a camel[24] and a bar of soap that has a conversation with Bloom.[25] Although "Circe" may be written like a drama, such things as instant costume changes, talking inanimate objects, horns growing from Bloom's head,[26] beagles growing into men,[27] Mrs. Breen's fading into nothingness, and vast cities appearing[28] have an easier time being depicted in film with its dynamization of space and spatialization of time than the theater. Instead of seeing this section as a stage script, it should perhaps be conceived as a screenplay, where cinematic elements bring us into the subjective space of the characters.

Joyce also seeks to approximate the close-up shot. In film, according to theorist Béla Balázs, this shot has not only widened our vision of life, "it has also deepened it . . . [by] not only reveal[ing] new things, but show[ing] us the meaning of the old. . . . [A] close-up reveals the most hidden parts in our polyphonous life, and teaches us to see the intricate visual details of life."[29] Clearly Balázs believes that the close-up has the power to show us new meaning in what would be considered ordinary circumstances. But more importantly, this passage suggests that this type of close examination provides priority and insight amid a flurry of impressions. The close-up functions this way in *Ulysses*, wherein, due to its unusual "close" narrative style, the author shows us the unusual in the ordinary. We observe this prioritization, for example, in the passage from the "Lotus Eaters" section where

Bloom leaves the pharmacy: "He strolled out of the shop, the newspaper baton under his armpit, the coolwrapped soap in his left hand. At his armpit Bantam Lyons's voice and hand said: Hello, Bloom. What's the best news? Is that today's? Show us a minute. Shaved off his mustache again, by Jove! Long cold upper lip. To look younger. He does look balmy. Younger than I am. Bantam Lyons's yellow blacknailed fingers unrolled the baton. Wants a wash too. Take off the rough dirt. Good morning, have you used Peter's soap? Dandruff on his shoulder. Scalp wants oiling."[30] Such a scene could appear to be a quite meaningless barrage of images. But *Ulysses*, with its often unclear signifiers of who is speaking and where we are, demands that every word be given attention. A skimming reader comes away from the text unfulfilled, in large degree because part of the power of the novel lies in the close-ups.

In this passage, for example, an ordinary bar of soap and a rolled-up newspaper become the mythic, Homeric-like shield and sword of the modern man.[31] The seemingly unimportant throwaway comment will reach catastrophic, near epic proportions in the "Cyclops" section[32] when two suitors of Molly's (Boylan and Lenehan)[33] are vanquished by this misunderstood comment of Bloom's. It's foreshadowed here, as Bloom, armed with the cleansing soap, stands opposite Lyons, who is described as having "rough dirt" among his other hygienic ailments. Part of the power of *Ulysses* resides in its use of literary "close-ups" such as this one, where level upon level of meaning is given that revitalizes the ordinary.

Joyce also uses techniques that resemble the film concept known as suture—a film theory which explains how to "stitch the spectator into the filmic text."[34] According to this theory, as the spectator views a film, she is aware of the Other who is controlling her gaze, and tends to fall out of an identification with the film. The spectator is stitched back into the film through the use of shot/reverse shots (first seeing the character, then seeing what the character sees). This removes the Other from having a controlling influence, and allows the spectator to reach an even closer identification with the film. Because this happens at a subconscious level (the editing is generally invisible to the spectator) the ideology of the filmmaker is unknowingly assimilated by the viewer.[35]

Several examples of suture-like components exist in *Ulysses*. One takes place in the "Proteus" section, when Joyce writes that "Stephen closed his eyes to hear his boots crush crackling wrack and shells. You are walking through it howsomever. I am, a stride at a time."[36] The focalization is first from an external focalizor, and then from a character-bound focalizor.[37] Put another way, first we have the shot that is looking *at* Stephen, then we have the reverse shot which brings us into Stephen's subjective space. In this way, like filmic suture, we are both outside and inside Stephen at the same time. We see everything and thus reach a close identification with Stephen himself.

Joyce also uses narrative elements similar to the editing element known as crosscutting, developed by cinematic pioneer D. W. Griffith. Crosscutting occurs when the camera jumps back and forth between action in one location and action in a separate location which is occurring simultaneously.[38] Crosscutting can be used as more than a mere narrative device that can emphasize a shared relationship between separate events. In the "Nausicaa" section, for example, Joyce crosscuts between a Benediction service at a church and Gerty on the beach with her friends:

> Queen of angels, queen of patriarchs, queen of prophets, of all saints, they prayed, queen of the most holy rosary and then Father Conroy handed the thurible to Canon O' Hanlon and he put in the incense and censed the Blessed Sacrament and Cissy Caffrey caught the two twins and she was itching to give them a ringing good clip on the ear but she didn't because she thought he might be watching but she never made a bigger mistake in all her life because Gerty could see without looking that he never took his eyes off of her and then Canon O'Hanlon handed the thurible back to Father Conroy and knelt down looking up at the Blessed Sacrament and the choir began to sing the Tantum ergo and she just swung her foot in and out in time.[39]

In this short passage the narrative crosscuts between the church, the beach, the church, and back again to the beach. Joyce does this crosscutting without any sort of signifier (or even punctuation) to clearly alert the reader to the shift in location. In function, this technique is similar to cinematic crosscutting, where the images alone are enough to signal the change of space. As in cinema, the crosscutting in this example sets up several layers of parallel meaning. Canon O'Hanlon is looking up at the Sacrament just as Bloom is looking up at Gerty: both are objects (inanimate sacrament/Gerty subjected to the Male Gaze) which are being adored. The connection is also established between the Virgin Mary and Gerty (both of whom are comforters.) And there is the relationship between the events as a whole: both are types of communion whereby the wounded partakers (men of the temperance retreat/Bloom) have a sort of mystical healing experience.[40] The literary crosscutting emphasizes these parallels powerfully.

Finally, Joyce uses "stream of consciousness" and the "interior monologue," two linked but different approaches. While both techniques are used to display the thought process of a character, stream of consciousness is the more "primitive," less conscious of the two. This primarily preverbal expression makes use of association, symbols, and the alteration of normal syntax and punctuation to simulate the flow of thought. Interior monologue is more consciously controlled and verbal, approximating mental speech and reason. In both cases, Joyce uses a montage-like reconstruction of the rules of traditional linear narrative to allow for a more symbolic, associative style. This concept of montage (with images exploding against one another to create new ideas in the mind of the reader) is so prevalent in Joyce's novel that Craig Barrow insists that *Ulysses*, as a whole, is best read as a series of montages.[41] In the "Lestrygonians" section, for example, we read:

> A sombre Y. M. C. A. young man, watchful among the warm sweet fumes of Graham Lemons, placed a throwaway in the hand of Mr. Bloom. Heart to heart talks. Bloo . . . Me? No. Blood of the Lamb. His slow feet walked him riverward, reading. Are you saved? All are washed in the blood of the lamb. God wants a blood victim. Birth, hymen, martyr, war, foundation of a building, sacrifice, kidney burnt offering, druid's altars. Elijah is coming. Dr John Alexander Dowie restorer of the church in Zion is coming. Is coming! Is coming! Is coming!!! All heartily welcome.[42]

In this passage, image after image explodes (in Eisenstein's terms) against the others, creating multiple new levels and layers of mythic/ Christian meaning in Bloom's epic journey. A stronger, more potent Bloom (in the form of the young Y. M. C. A. man amid sweet savors) hands Bloom a significant pamphlet that foreshadows his triumph over his own "throwaway" status with Molly. "Bloo . . . Me? No. Blood of the Lamb" connects the victim, the sacrificial Bloom, with the Messiah figure or at least the salvation associated with the Paschal lamb. "Riverward" reinforces the theme of rejuvenation, as do "saved" and "washed." "Birth" and "hymen" connote images of female fertility, that will be "restore[d]," but not before some notion of a "martyr" and a "war" are experienced. Eventually, Bloom, like Elijah, will be "coming" with "all heartily welcome." Bloom cannot be tied down to one symbol but is complex, like a real human being. He is both the sacrifice and the saved. He is a Jewish/Old Testament, a Christian/ New Testament, a pagan ("druids altars"), and a mythic (Homeric) figure. These complexities are achieved in a montage-like explosion of images in the reader's mind.

Joyce not only consistently uses variations on the interior monologue to portray the inner mental world of his main characters, but he also creates additional situations which provide unique juxtapositions. Examples include the juxtaposition of the disparate travel scenes in

"The Wandering Rocks," the comparison between the headlines and the corresponding texts in "Aeolus," the juxtaposition of the various literary styles in "Oxen the Sun," and correlation between the narrative capsules created in response to the objective questions in "Ithaca." Montage techniques are at the core of *Ulysses* to the extent that the mythical framework upon which the entire novel is based sets up an initial and powerful juxtaposition between classical Greek culture and modern Dublin—which is, at its most basic level, montage.

In this section we have seen how the novel *Ulysses* has many elements of film language that are utilized in a literary context. Harry Levin agrees when he describes Bloom's mind as a "motion picture, which has been ingeniously cut and carefully edited to emphasize the close-ups and fade-outs of flickering emotion, the angles of observation and the flashbacks of reminiscence."[43] These characteristics are not, of course, unique to *Ulysses*, nor is this an exhaustive compilation, but we provide these examples to demonstrate how the form of *Ulysses* shares a commonality with certain properties of film language, and how these properties might be exploited in the adaptation process.

Due to the similarity between the cinema and many of Joyce's literary techniques, one might expect that, despite the Herculean effort involved, the novel would translate effectively into film. Early treatments, such as the Reisman–Zukofsky screenplay of *Ulysses*, reflect much of this experimental, cinematic nature of the novel. Jerry Reisman and Louis Zukofsky began work on their adaptation in 1932 and submitted a full treatment to Joyce for his consideration in June of 1935. Soon after, Joyce responded through Paul Leon, who writes that Joyce found the treatment to be "on the whole quite commendable."[44] He praises their innovations such as using Shakespearean quotations to replace the discussion of Shakespeare in the library which, "by its nature does not lend itself to cinematic utilization." He also observes that there are "some connections photographically well used (e.g. the frying of the sausages by Bloom and its smoke leading to Mulligan's breakfast)," but cautions that the proposal fails to make "a complete use either of the book or all of the device[s] offered by the cinema technique."[45] This response provides some significant insights into this study for several reasons. First, the passage displays a certain degree of approval from Joyce of the Reisman–Zukofsky approach. This approval is especially significant when one considers that Joyce had rejected previous proposals and when we remember his attitude toward the difficulty of filming of the novel. Next, the appreciation of the montage shift from Bloom's kitchen to Mulligan's meal displays Joyce's awareness of the cinematic process of exchanging the word for the image. Finally, the comment about the Shakespearean quotes, to-

gether with Joyce's admonition to use "all of the devices offered by
the cinema technique," displays not only a recognition of the limits of
the film medium on the part of the author, but also an understanding
of how the filmmaker uses images to overcome these limitations.

Reisman and Zukofsky employed additional inventive methods in
their adaptation of which Joyce seemed to approve. First, a small
amount of new material was added, such as a shot of a Cyclops prepar-
ing to throw a stone at Ulysses' ship, which, as Joseph Slate argues,
"sets up the epic parallels and the importance of the sea as an image,
both of which must give the film narrative a background that the
reader of the novel must work out for himself."[46] Next, they created
vibrant inter-shot movement through creative editing such as gradually eliminating the characters through an "iris in," only to have them
reappear in the same positions on the new frame. Finally, they utilized
a split screen, with the action in the center and images as commentary
on the two sides. In shot 439, for example, we are shown Bloom mend-
ing Steven's coat as they sit in the former's home. In the next shot, the
characters reappear in the same positions in frame, but the screen
forms a triptych. On the right side Steven appears as Hamlet to Molly-
as-Gertude's admonition to "cast thine nighted color off "; on the left
(Bloom's side) the moon is seen through a telescope. The scene then
changes to reveal Bloom and Steven still in Eccles Street, while on the
right we are shown Hamlet with his father's ghost and on the left
Bloom and Molly weeping over the coffin of their son Rudy.[47] This
layering of images allows the filmmaker to communicate many levels
of understanding simultaneously and to represent a more creative (although still rather conventional) use of the film medium.

Other early treatments make similar use of "all the devices" available to the filmmaker. Joseph Slate notes that Stuart Gilbert wrote a
treatment, for example, which unfortunately has not survived, but he
observes that the author's adaptation of "Anna Livia Plurabelle" from
Finnegans Wake, "clearly parallels Eisenstein's theories and strongly
suggests that Joyce had developed or was developing a full grasp of
cinema's potential as art."[48] In addition, Slate unearthed a fragmentary
script of *Ulysses* by Mario Serandrei, which was published in Blasetti's
Cinematagrafo in 1930. Like the Reisman–Zukofsky script, this treatment demonstrates how creative filmmaking can communicate some
of the more abstract and complex ideas Joyce layers into his text. Slate
notes that Serandrei prefers a "succession of short, quick shots," and
notes that "the filmmaker has broken down the scene and recon-
structed it artistically."[49] He also observes the filmmaker's tendency to
use extreme close-ups: "images so large in relation to the screen that
they leave little room for background, foreground, or any part of the

surrounding environment."[50] These close-up shots replicate Joyce's dwelling on details in the text and his accentuation of the "unusual in the ordinary" as discussed above. Finally, Slate observes that Serandrei tells the story with image more than dialogue, that he "treats the dialogue so casually that it might appear he was writing a silent film script."[51] As a part of this technique, Slate asserts, the filmmaker makes heavy use of lap dissolve to both join the shots smoothly and create meaning through juxtaposition, "because at the moment when one shot dissolves into the other, the two images are superimposed and thus identified with each other."[52]

We have no evidence that Joyce was even aware of the Serandrei script. Reisman and Zukofsky, however, continued to pursue their *Ulysses* project for several years, but in the end no film was produced and there is no clear evidence why Joyce lost interest in the script. Whatever the reason the movie was never produced, it is unfortunate that the only film versions have been produced after Joyce's death. For without a doubt, his collaboration would have greatly enhanced the filmed representation of the inner monologue and other Joycean trademarks.

In contrast, Sean Walsh's 2003 adaptation, *Bloom*, replicates almost none of the filmic innovations of the novel. This film is, above all, pretty, with design that conveys compellingly the decor of 1904 Dublin at the same time that it reflects the timing of this production to coincide with the centennial of Bloomsday. The film is a celebration. As such, it steps away from the revolutionary substance of Joyce's novel in order, perhaps, to reach a larger audience who would appreciate the artistic sentiment of the novel's plot, but not the challenging, experimental aesthetics of the text. Perhaps with this in mind, Margot Norris observes that "instead of restoring the novel's historical and political preoccupations and thereby giving it a revitalized ideology edge, Walsh's beautiful cinematography gives Bloom's turn-of-the-century world a mellow, nostalgic glow."[53] With this comment, Norris gently chastises the filmmaker for the missed opportunity of re-visioning the ideological message of the text to reflect the issues relevant to contemporary Ireland, and to thus put the film in dialogue not only with Joyce's novel, but with Strick's earlier adaptation, which, as we will see, attempts this type of re-visioning. In a similar vein, Richard Brown acknowledges Walsh's attempt to reach a broader audience, but suggests the filmmaker seeks to appeal to the Joyceophile as well, with the ultimate result, Brown argues, that the film "has the capacity to delight and animate and probably infuriate both these audiences."[54] Despite his opinion that Walsh misses the mark here, however, Brown recognizes current cultural relevance which Norris does not. "As much as anything," Brown writes, the film is "an adaptation that's about not being entrapped by too much reverence for the established, which sees the freshness of Joyce for a new Dublin, of cheap airline tickets, mobile phones, house-price inflation, and consumer debt-driven prosperity."[55] This comment suggests that the major cultural issues addressed in *Ulysses* have been eliminated, or at least replaced, in the lives of modern audiences; that colonialism, racism, gender relations, and the general isolation and trauma reflected in modernist literature no longer impact our lives.

Evidence of this disengagement from Joycean revolutionary ideas and the formal innovations which facilitate their development appears in the filmmaker's global choices. Walsh makes no attempt to develop the possibilities of the music in the "Sirens" episode, for example, which film could have enlightened. Similarly, the "Lestrogonians" section is eliminated almost entirely, except for a short shot of Bloom eating his cheese sandwich and retreating from the restaurant. In addition to these eliminated scenes, Walsh also neglects much of Stephen's intellectualism, including his poem in "Proteus" and the story in "Aeolus." His theory of Shakespeare's *Hamlet* is, out of necessity, severely truncated in a way that underscores the significance of the father/son theme Joyce develops between Bloom and Stephen, but it also seems simplistic and apolitical. The result of these choices, as Brown observes, is that "we don't really get enough to be engaged with him as an intellectual," and "subversive political anger is out of the frame for the most part."[56] This observation suggests that on some fundamental level Walsh has missed the point of the novel; although he largely follows the novel in his presentation of the characters and events, the substance and implications of these elements has been neglected.

Despite the overall conventional nature of the film, Walsh makes some stylistic choices that engage Joyce's themes and bring them to the foreground. The best example of what Brown labels "Joycean tricksyness" appears in the "Circe" episode. The style of this section departs so abruptly from the rest of the film that it seems to be another project entirely. In this episode, which at twenty-three minutes represents twenty percent of the film's 113 minutes, Walsh engages Joyce's experimental style more fully than elsewhere in the film.

In contrast to the easy pace the filmmaker develops elsewhere, for example, Bloom's Nighttown excursion is marked by fast cutting and a pronounced "shaky cam," as well as swift location and costuming changes. Steven Rea as Bloom, so mildly melancholy and endearingly docile in previous scenes, deliberately overdevelops his previous characterization with affectations such as rolling his eyes, panting, sticking his tongue out at people, and generally being the rakish rogue Bloom imagines himself to be in this scene. Walsh accents the comedic aspects of these scenes, having Bloom make his "New Bloomusalem" speech sitting on the jakes in full regalia while reading the "TitBits" magazine (updated for this scene from the "TidBits" publication from which he reads while making his visit to this lavatory in an earlier scene). In another instance, Walsh blares calliope music after the lid of Patty Dignam's casket falls off so that the corpse can provide an alibi for Bloom during the latter's trial. These scenes contrast with more disturbing and surreal scenes, such as when Steven imagines his mother's corpse, which is made up in similar fashion to Dignam's, screaming at him and pleading for his soul. Or when leather-clad Bella dominates Bloom in a harshly red-lit, shadowy dungeon. She pushes him off the bed and the camera focuses on him from below as, kicking, he falls a great distance. The camera then follows Bella in the same way as she falls menacingly after him with claw-like fingers extended. In a following shot we see a dress-wearing Bloom, framed between the dominatrix's legs as she (apparently) urinates into a chamber pot, which he subsequently drains. While these events appear in the novel, the amount of time the filmmaker devotes to them and the stylistic departure of this section from the rest of the film reveals the thematic importance Walsh places on this section.

Another example of Walsh's more innovative filmmaking occurs when he begins and ends the film with selections from Molly's soliloquy from the "Penelope" chapter. Not only does this device frame the story in a way that emphasizes the central relationships and heartache that inform the plot, but the filmmaker also moves the audience around in time and space in a way that approximates for us the wanderings of Molly's mind, and foreshadows the physical wanderings of the other characters during the day. Walsh accomplishes this by having Angeline Ball's Molly speak directly to the camera at times while sitting up in the Bloom's well-lit bedroom, instead of always lying half shadowed in bed with a sleeping Bloom beside her. While she talks to the audience in what can best be described as a reality-television confessional way, the film flashes to other scenes: of the Blooms on the cliff overlooking the sea, of her afternoon tryst with Boylan, of the day Rudy was conceived, of her speculations about Stephen, and of her planning for a future with Bloom. These scenes are so comprehensive, in fact, that they act almost as thesis and summary paragraphs for the film, establishing characters and underscoring the themes that are handled less substantially elsewhere in the film. Like the frame narrative of *1001 Arabian Nights*, the choice to split Molly's stream of consciousness musings provides structure and meaning for the rest of the narrative.

Ultimately, *Bloom* is a strikingly pretty film, but despite the above moments of insight and creativity, it lacks the experimental aspect of both the novel and earlier treatments to the point that it is almost a film *about* the novel instead of an adaptation of the text.

Joseph Strick's cinematic adaptation, *Ulysses*, results in a compromise between these two more radical approaches. Rudolph Von Abele asserts that Strick's goal was to make a film that would provide substance for the educated elite, but would also be entertaining and informative for other audiences.[57] Although the film adheres fairly faithfully to the events of the novel, the style and intellectual nature of the novel are lost. The major problem with the film is that the filmmaker eliminates many of the cinematic elements from Joyce's narrative and fails to fully utilize the medium of film. The bulk of the interior monologues are eliminated when the opportunity to translate these thoughts by using simple voice-over narration was readily available; both Bloom and Stephen spend considerable time walking through the physical action of the film in silence during scenes when Joyce provided the reader with access to their thoughts. Thus, the film is a mystery to those who are unfamiliar with Joyce and a halting effort for those familiar with it. This limitation may be a result of Strick's attempt to cater to two audiences, a vision which may have been driven as much by financial concerns as by artistic motivation, since an intellectual film would earn praise for him, but little else.

In addition to the artistic differences listed above, Rudolph Von Abele has explored what he believes to be the ten greatest incongruities between the film and the novel,[58] the most accurate of which are the lack of interior monologue, the monostylistic nature of the film, and the anti-intellectual bias. The impact of the seeming disregard for these three essential elements in the novel reflects an incomplete understanding of the novel, which is unfortunate, because these elements could have been translated effectively though a more creative use of the medium.

Despite the fact that there are some fundamentally negative artistic choices in the Joseph Strick film, however, the film is successful in many ways. Those scenes described above that are the most cinematic ("Proteus," "Circe," and "Penelope") translate most easily to the screen. Several of the other episodes, although severely truncated, display imagination and subtle power. In the "Lestrigonians," for example, Bloom's repulsion at the sight of the diners at the Burton restaurant is communicated through the overlay of loathsome barnyard sounds. This use of asynchronous sound communicating Bloom's repulsion is a creative method unique to film.

Strick gives nearly half of his film time to two sections of Joyce's novel: "Circe," where we explore the inner workings of Bloom's mind, and "Penelope," where we explore Molly's. For example: during the "Penelope" section, the spectator is taken into Molly's subjective space. This moment gives us a sense of the film's potential. An establishing shot shows us that we are in Molly's stream of consciousness, and we go, ironically, through the bed frame to get into her inner self. As she remembers a sexual moment with Blazes Boylan, we flash into the image of the two of them embracing. A match cut takes us to a parallel image, a carving of two lovers kissing as Molly thinks, "theres nothing like a kiss long and hot down to your soul almost paralyses you."[59] In the confessional with Father Corrigan, Molly recounts in the novel how the priest asked her to describe a sexual transgression: "whereabouts on your person my child on the leg behind high up was it yes rather high up was it where you sit down yes O Lord couldnt he say bottom right out and have done with it."[60] In the film version Strick captures Molly's hard question of confession to the church ("what did he want to know for when I already confessed it to God") by placing the voice-over sexual confession over stained glass religious images, which include sitting figures and nudity of the baby. The sacred and the secular are examined simultaneously. Molly asks herself "I wonder did he know me in the box" while Strick has Blazes Boylan exiting the confessional, dressed as Father Corrigan. The "I didnt like his slapping me behind going away" line of Molly's is match cut from Father Boylan slapping Molly's behind in front of the church to Lover Boylan slapping her behind in bed. Molly's sexual experiences are juxtaposed with a fish being gutted, as if to show that these sexual tristes are tearing out her insides. A fish is thrown down in a pail with other fish as the actress delivers her line, "I felt lovely and tired myself and fell asleep as sound as a top the moment I popped straight into bed."[61] Molly's remembering of the jingling of the bed is juxtaposed against an image of girls playing jump rope.

As demonstrated by this innovative scene, much potential exists to do remarkable things in a filmed version of *Ulysses*. Strick reaches this level in his "Circe" and "Penelope" sections. In these two sections, Strick has the time to be his most creative. It is here that he comes closest to tapping into the cinematic properties already at work in *Ulysses*. Unfortunately, his *Ulysses* is mostly a film about "Circe" and "Penelope." The other sections generally don't have the time devoted to them to develop their creative possibilities.

To give these two sections the time they deserve, Strick cuts a complete chapter ("Eumaeus"), almost all of another ("Sirens"), and spends anywhere from half to a quarter of the total percentage of time that Joyce does on many of the middle chapters of the novel ("Lotus

Eaters," "Aeolus," "Lestrygonians," "Scylla and Charybdis," "Wandering Rocks," and "Nausicaa"). The cuts make the film into a manageable two hour experience. However, we miss many of Bloom's inner monologues, including ponderings on the lemon soap, the Elijah pamphlet, and the letter from Martha. The Gerty incident and the bestial eating of the Lestrygonians are reduced to very brief incidents with no explanations. The "Wandering Rocks" chapter no longer shows the intricate, complex, interconnected nature of Dublin's citizens. The Hamlet discussion is cut from "Scylla and Charybdis," leaving that chapter almost entirely unexplored in Strick's film.

In addition, Joyce's tremendous literary innovations are largely unexplored in the film. There are no longer any headlines in "Aeolus." There is no music in "Sirens." There is no character-focalized narrator or an exploration of different styles of writing as used in "Cyclops." There is no delving into the way culture is assimilated as in Gerty's sentimental, romance novel style in "Nausicaa" (or even the crosscutting of the adoration in the church and on the beach). There is no exploration of the different modes of English throughout history as used in "Oxen of the Sun." Although this may be asking for the impossible (or perhaps a 20-hour film), the use of voice-over—which worked well in the catechism of "Ithaca" and Molly's thoughts in "Penelope"—could provide a more meaningful glimpse into some of these techniques.

As we have argued, Joyce's novel *Ulysses* contains many cinematic elements. Marshall McLuhan agrees, seeing Joyce's form as "the transfer of film technique to the printed page."[62] One of the reasons for the novel's difficulty may be due to what Craig Barrow calls the "juxtaposition of exterior and interior images without narrative comment."[63] In other words, the novel takes us from outward events to inward thoughts without verbal signifiers to alert the reader to the change in space.

Joseph Strick's film version of *Ulysses*, with visual images that clearly indicate changes in space, has replaced some of the novel's missing signifiers. The story's linear plot elements are thus easier to discern in the film. Unfortunately, Strick doesn't always utilize the many cinematic elements in Joyce's work to their full potential. Joyce's powerful crosscutting technique of "Nausicaa," for example, is completely disregarded. The intimacies of the "close-ups" (such as Bloom with his soap as a shield) are seldom utilized. The power of montage (such as Bloom being given the "throwaway") could be much greater. This is one of the ways this film version is hampered. Whereas Joyce opened up literature to new levels of subjective space (partially through the use of filmic devices), Strick presents a fairly closed film with occasionally under-utilized cinematic techniques.

How, then, do these several aborted and realized adaptations of *Ulysses* inform our understanding of the adaptation process? If we follow tradition and consider a successful adaptation in terms of fidelity to the text, novels of this scope invite criticism of the process since by necessity one has to cut large sections of the text to have the time to engage the others in depth (Strick's approach in some degree), or to include each scene faithfully but superficially (closer to Walsh's strategy). The length and complexity of Joyce's novel exacerbate this problem to the point that any adaptation of this text will draw fire from critics more often than other adaptations. This situation thus highlights the notion that we should consider an adaptation's success based on other criteria.

We could, for example, examine how well an adaptation conveys the larger thematic issues of the text—how well the filmmaker captures what we might call the mythopoetics of the original material. While this could easily slide into dangerous questions of how well a film maintains the author's intent, this approach could include discussion of not only how well the filmmaker selects and communicates the essentials of plot and character, but also how well she might address larger issues of theme, motif, or even formal innovation. In his assessment of Strick's adaptation, for example, Slate argues that the filmmaker seems "unwilling to follow Joyce in breaking new ground."[64] This comment not only reprimands the director for not making more of his medium, but it also suggests that adaptation should respect and reproduce not only the plot and characters of a work, but also the aesthetic theory and practice of the material's creator. The concept of mythopoetics suggests that the filmmaker seeks to capture both the thematic and formal elements of the original text at the same time that the use of a new medium demands that these two elements are presented in original fashion, using the best components and devices available in this medium. For this reason, perhaps, the earlier, unrealized adaptations of *Ulysses* seem more fulfilling; not because they are more accurate, but because they demonstrate an awareness of this situation and exploit it as they engage Joyce's experiment and permutate it for a new medium.

NOTES

1. Eliot makes this observation in "Ulysses, Order, and Myth," *The Dial* 75 (1923): 480–83.

2. Richard Ellman, ed., *Selected Letters of James Joyce* (New York: Viking Press, 1975), 262–63.

3. Margot Norris, "Updating *Ulysses:* Joseph Strick's 1967 Film," *James Joyce Quarterly* 41, no. 1–2 (2003): 82.

4. His interest in film is demonstrated by the time and effort expended in his attempt to open the first movie theater in Dublin. On December 20, 1909, his work was rewarded as this cinema, the Volta Cinematograph, opened for business (Ellman 192). Several of Joyce's personal letters reflect not only his exhaustive work but his feeling of triumph as the project was accomplished (see Ellman 187).

5. Quoted in Norris, "Updating *Ulysses*," 81.

6. Philippe Met, "The Filmic Ghost in the Literary Machine," *Contemporary French and Francophone Studies* 9, no. 3 (September 2005): 248.

7. Joseph Evans Slate, "The Reisman–Zukofsky Screenplay of *Ulysses*: Its Background and Significance," *The Library Chronicle of the University of Texas at Austin*, n. s., no. 20/21 (1982): 125.

8. "Reisman–Zukofsky Screenplay of *Ulysses*," Harry Ransom Humanities Research Center, University of Texas, Austin.

9. *Ulysses*, DVD, directed by Joseph Strick (Image Entertainment, 1967).

10. *Bloom*, DVD, directed by Sean Walsh (Odyssey Pictures, 2003).

11. Gosta Werner, "James Joyce and Sergej Eisenstein," *James Joyce Quarterly* 27 (Spring 1990): 495.

12. Slate, " Reisman–Zukofsky Screenplay," 110.

13. Ibid.

14. R. Barton Palmer, "Eisensteinian Montage and Joyce's *Ulysses:* The Analogy Reconsidered," *Mosaic* 18, no. 3 (Summer 1985): 74.

15. Alan Speigel, *Fiction and the Camera Eye* (Charlottesville: University Press of Virginia, 1976), 78–79.

16. Slate, "Reisman–Zukofsky Screenplay," 109.

17. Erwin Panofsky, "Style and Medium in the Motion Pictures," in *Film Theory and Criticism*, 4th ed., ed. Gerald Mast, Marshall Cohen, and Leo Braudy (New York: Oxford University Press, 1992), 235.

18. Stanley Cavell, "From The World Viewed" in *Film Theory and Criticism*, 4th ed., ed. Gerald Mast, Marshall Cohen, and Leo Braudy (New York: Oxford University Press, 1992), 295.

19. James Joyce, *Ulysses*, ed. Hans Walther Gabler (New York: Vintage Books, 1993), 231.

20. Ibid., 355.

21. Ibid., 357.

22. Ibid.

23. Ibid., 358.

24. Ibid., 359.

25. Ibid., 360.

26. Ibid., 384.

27. Ibid., 385.

28. Ibid., 391.

29. Béla Balázs, "From Theory of the Film," in *Film Theory and Criticism*, 4th ed., ed. Gerald Mast, Marshall Cohen, and Leo Braudy, (New York: Oxford University Press, 1992), 260–61.

30. Joyce, *Ulysses*, 70.

31. Harry Blamires, *The New Bloomsday Book: A Guide Through Ulysses*, 3rd ed. (New York: Routledge, 1997), 33.

32. Joyce, *Ulysses*, 267.

33. Ibid., 602.

34. Susan Hayward, *Key Concepts in Cinema Studies* (New York: Routledge, 1996), 371.

35. Daniel Dayan, "The Tutor Code of Classical Cinema," in *Film Theory and Criticism*, 4th ed., ed. Gerald Mast, Marshall Cohen, and Leo Braudy (New York: Oxford University Press, 1992), 188.

36. Joyce, *Ulysses*, 31.

37. Mieke Bal, *Narratology: Introduction to the Theory of Narrative* (Toronto: University of Toronto Press, 1985, 104). Focalization is a photographic term that literary theorist Mieke Bal applies to literature. It means "the relationship between the "vision," the agent that sees, and that which is seen" (104). She delineates a character-bound focalizor where the "seeing" is done by a character in the fabula internal story (104) and an external focalizor where the "seeing" comes from "an anonymous agent, situated outside the fabula" (105).

38. An example of crosscutting occurs near the end of *Return of the Jedi* (Richard Marquand, 1983) when the spectator is taken back and forth between (1) Luke Skywalker battling Darth Vader and the Emperor on the Death Star, (2) Han Solo and Leia Organa fighting the imperial troopers on the forest moon of Endor, and (3) Lando Calrissian in his ship attacking the Death Star from space. Within the narrative structure of the plot, all of these actions occur simultaneously.

39. Joyce, *Ulysses*, 295.

40. We are indebted, for some of the ideas in this paragraph, to Blamires (137–38).

41. Barrow, *Montage*, 199.

42. Joyce, *Ulysses*, 124.

43. Harry Levin, *James Joyce: A Critical Introduction*, rev. ed. (New York: New Directions, 1960), 88; quoted in Barrow, *Montage*, 12.

44. Slate, "Reisman–Zukofsky Screenplay," 119.

45. Ibid.

46. Ibid., 122.

47. Ibid., 130.

48. Ibid., 112.

49. Ibid., 128.

50. Ibid., 129.

51. Ibid.

52. Ibid. We see evidence of this fast-paced, image heavy montage style in the series of shots creating the scene where Bloom imagines himself walking in the orient. Slate illustrates in the following list:

36. Lap dissolve. Oriental landscape (photograph of an old engraving).
37. The gate of a Turkish city (photograph, tight shot).
38. A sentinel with long mustaches, leaning on a lance (tight shot).
39. The street in an oriental city, with the usual characteristics: men in turbans, rug vendors seated with crossed legs, who smoke long serpentine pipes (tight shot).
40. Oriental city at sunset (tight shot).
41. Oriental night. A girl who plays by the light of the moon (tight shot).
42. Lap dissolve. The camera continues to make a long pan of the street of shot thirty-four, until it approaches an Irish bar, stopping in front of it and framing, in the background, the old proprietor with a bald head, in shirt sleeves; he leans on a crate of sugar and watches his employee occupied with a pail of water and a rag cleaning the floor, then turns toward the door and speaks some words of greeting. The camera continues along the street and passes in front of the building of the municipal school, which has its windows open.

43. Upon a white background, large letters of the alphabet march rapidly.
44. Face of a child, spelling.
45. As in shot 43. The letters are superimposed, deformed . . .
46. The camera passes by the school and approaches a pork butcher's which has on display long rows of sausages.
47. Lap dissolve. On a white background swiftly rotate letters, numbers, arithmetic signs smaller than in shot 43.
48. Lap dissolve. Extreme close-up. Large shining sausage. (Slate, "Reisman–Zukofsky Screenplay," 128.)

In the novel, Bloom hears children reciting lessons through the open window to the above school as he walks past the pub on his way to buy his breakfast kidney. The succession of "oriental" shots does little more than establish the decor of Bloom's imagination. But the later juxtaposition of sausages suggests possible connections between school exercises and the butcher shop, or between masculinity and knowledge. The montage even evokes Swift's "A Modest Proposal" by suggesting that Irish children are, in some way, fuel for the sausage grinder of English imperialism, which reflects Stephen's rebellious tendencies. Above all, the above scene moves quickly and relies on a montage of images to communicate the narrative instead of dialogue. We observe almost no dialogue, in fact, and certainly none that we might identify as Joycean.

53. Norris, "Updating *Ulysses*," 86.
54. Richard Brown, "The New Faces of the Blooms," *James Joyce Broadsheet* 66 (October 2003): 1.
55. Ibid.
56. Ibid.
57. Rudolph Von Abele, "Film as Interpretation: A Case Study of *Ulysses*," *The Journal of Aesthetics and Art Criticism* 31, no. 4 (Summer 1973): 494.
58. Ibid. We have included Von Abele's complete list below:

1. The primary emphasis in the film Ulysses is on the last half of the novel.
2. The film dispenses with most of the novel's interior dialogue.
3. The film excludes virtually all the past history of its three protagonists.
4. The film radically simplifies the public environment in which the action takes place.
5. The film both blurs and accelerates the passage of fictive time.
6. The film is, comparatively speaking, quite abstract.
7. In the film, the human organism is presented in a relatively one-dimensional way.
8. The film has a distinct anti-intellectual bias.
9. The film is monostylistic where the novel is polystylistic.
10. The film wholly dispenses with *The Odyssey* skeleton on which the narrative of the novel is claimed to be built.

59. Joyce, *Ulysses*, 610.
60. Ibid.
61. Ibid., 611.
62. Marshall McLuhan, *Understanding Media* (New York: McGraw-Hill, 1966), 295.
63. Barrow, *Montage*, 5.
64. Slate, "Reisman–Zukofsky Screenplay," 114.

Shane and *Man on Fire:* George Stevens's Enduring Legacy of Spirituality and Violence

Dennis Cutchins

Aлтноисн Тому Scott's *Man on Fire* (2004) was a popular film, it was not received with open arms by the critics.[1] Guy Westfall, in his review in *Sight and Sound,* called *Man on Fire* "a revenge movie, plain and simple," and compared it to the *Death Wish* films for its "gratuitous violence, knee-jerk hostility to due process and deeply racist scenario," although he argued that these elements were "ciphered by the clever casting of Denzel Washington."[2] Andrea Toal offered a similar judgment when the film was released on video, adding that casting the blonde and fair-skinned Dakota Fanning "betrays the film's lamentable attitude to the developing world."[3] In his *Village Voice* review David Ng did suggest that the film was "viewable," but added that "high-grade weaponry and the bodies of dirty foreigners" qualified it as a "right-wing fever dream."[4] The main complaints against the film seemed to be complaints against its violence and its racism. Both are likely well-founded.

The A. J. Quinnell novel upon which the film was based has a somewhat similar reputation, at least here in the United States.[5] Although the racist elements may be toned down, it is, like the film, a bloody and violent story of revenge. In the novel, ex-soldier of fortune John Creasy is hired as a bodyguard for Pinta, the young daughter of wealthy parents living in Rome. A kind of father–daughter relationship develops between the two, helping to bring Creasy out of his war-induced depression. But soon the girl is kidnapped by the Mafia and held for ransom. Creasy is wounded during the kidnapping, and while recovering he discovers that Pinta has been killed by her kidnappers. Most of the rest of the novel focuses on Creasy's bloody revenge on anyone involved with the kidnapping. *Man on Fire* was the first novel of A. J. Quinnell, a pseudonym for Briton Phillip Nicholson, and the story was loosely based, according to the author, on the 1960s kidnapping of the eldest son of a rich businessman from Singapore.[6] According to Quinnell, the man "refused to pay the ransom and his son was

180

murdered. His refusal," Quinnell continues, "meant that his other children would never be targets. The will to make that sacrifice fascinated me."[7] Quinnell suggests that the hero of his novel, John Creasy, "was based on a mixture of characters that I knew in the sixties and seventies in Africa and Vietnam."[8]

Most viewers took the film's title and its claim to be directly based on Quinnell's novel at face value, despite the important differences that exist between the novel and the film.[9] The film distinguishes itself from the novel in some significant ways, and the source for many of these changes may be a surprising one. The 2004 film version of *Man on Fire* bears a distinct resemblance to George Stevens's 1953 film *Shane*,[10] as well as to a handful of other films. In the past we might have spoken of *Man on Fire* as an "unfaithful" adaptation, flawed in its refusal to follow its literary predecessor. But this adaptation, far from being handicapped by its movement away from the Quinnell text and closer to *Shane*, has become a much more interesting and complex film, particularly in terms of its treatment of spirituality and violence, *because* of its "infidelity."

Understanding the connections between *Man on Fire* and *Shane*, however, requires that we take a somewhat non-standard approach to the film as an adaptation. Certainly Scott's film is "based" on Quinnell's novel, but just as clearly it is an adaptation of other, earlier texts, although these texts are not named as sources. Thus, in order to comprehend *Man on Fire* as an adaptation, we must look beyond the film's obvious antecedents to discover these other, unacknowledged hypotexts. Moreover, we need to recognize that the conscious or unconscious choice to bend *Man on Fire* toward *Shane* may be the result of cultural pressures, even though it's quite possible that none of the film makers could have named these pressures at the time.

Biologists call this phenomenon convergent evolution, and note, for instance, that giraffes have long necks, and some dinosaurs had long necks, although the species are not related. Rather, long necks are the result of similar evolutionary pressures. The fact that both *Shane* and *Man on Fire* came out when American soldiers were returning, or had recently returned, from a war is probably no coincidence. Both films suggest that violence is justified and necessary in certain circumstances, and both films take pains to outline those circumstances. *Man on Fire* may "adapt" *Shane* along with Quinnell's novel, but likely both films are also the product of similar, though distinct cultural pressures.

Shane is an interesting and important film. It helped to redefine film Westerns in an age when Westerns were one of Hollywood's most popular genres. Many of the original viewers of this film were touched by it in ways that they might have had difficulty explaining. As evidence of this cultural impact, though it is certainly anecdotal evidence, I note the number of middle-aged men who are named "Shane." I have met at least ten or so, mostly from Wyoming and Idaho.[11] The film seemed to strike a chord in postwar America. Stevens certainly intended this film to be more than just another adventure-story Western. When asked why he made the film, he answered, "Film and T.V. were full of guys with guns. Everybody was bang-bang-banging with cap pistols. And I knew this story called *Shane*. It was a real put-down on the heroic aspects of the six-shooter and the Western legend, and that really started the motivation. I thought it was a good time to do that kind of a thing about this weapon. You know, not give it a sense of grace, but to show it for what it was: a destructive, violent instrument."[12] In other words, Stevens meant *Shane* to be a serious film, rather than a simple adventure story, and one that was less about the West, in some ways, than it was about postwar America.

Ex-soldiers trying to resume their old lives in the late 1940s and early 1950s had a unique perspective on Schaffer's 1949 novel and Stevens's film about a gunfighter who longs to live a normal life. Films like Nunnally Johnson's *The Man in the Gray Flannel Suit* (1956) addressed questions of the soldier's place in civilian life more straightforwardly, but *Shane*, in its metaphorical treatment of the struggles ex-soldiers faced in adapting to normal life, seemed to cut more deeply. In both the novel and the film Shane, a world-weary gunfighter, gives up his guns and attempts to live like a farmer with the Starrets, his new surrogate family. Joe and Marion Starrett seem sympathetic to his plight, and the family's only child, Bob (Joey in the film) treats Shane like a second father. Shane's plans to lead a normal life, however, are thwarted by the violence that quickly descends on the Starrett home. Fletcher, the owner of a nearby large ranch, attempts to push the Starretts and their neighbors off of their homesteads so that he can have the range to himself. He soon hires Stark Wilson, a gunfighter, and Wilson kills one of the homesteaders as a warning to the rest. Shane eventually finds it necessary to abandon his pastoral dream, strap on his guns, and resume the life of violence he has always known in order to save the Starrets and the other homesteaders.

In his film version, George Stevens made Schaefer's postwar allegory all the more evident by renaming Fletcher, the belligerent rancher, "Riker." The reference to the Third Reich is clear and unmistakable. It's also exactly the kind of weighty symbolism Stevens was prone to employ after the war. In fact, he never did return to making the kind of light comedies and adventure stories he had made earlier in his Hollywood career. He remained, to the end of his life, a thoughtful and a serious film maker. That seriousness was certainly noticed by his Hollywood peers. He was nominated for an Academy Award five times for his directing, and won the award twice; once in 1951 for *A Place in the Sun*, and again in 1957 for *Giant*. Although he never won a Best Picture award, four of his films, including *Shane*, were nominated. Despite these significant achievements, Stevens's awards may not reflect his most lasting influence: at least two generations of film makers were deeply influenced by his films, particularly by *Shane*.

This influence is evidenced by the fact that the plot and themes of *Shane* have been borrowed and adapted several times. Clint Eastwood's *Pale Rider*[13] certainly owes something (or perhaps everything) to *Shane*.[14] And the most recent *Shane*-influenced film may be Eastwood's *Gran Torino* (2008).[15] In that film, Eastwood plays an aging war veteran, a man still quite capable of violence, but one who has settled into a peaceful, solitary life. Once again this reluctant hero is placed in a position where he must sacrifice himself in order to save a boy from a life of crime and a small family from a gang of thugs. But Don Siegel's *The Shootist* (1976),[16] best known as John Wayne's last film, holds a particular interest to me because it is something of a special case of adaptation, one that appears to be a parallel to *Man on Fire*. Just as Tony Scott's film claims to be based on A. J. Quinnell's novel, so Siegel and his screenwriters, Miles Swarthout and Scott Hale, ostensibly based *The Shootist* on Glendon Swarthout's novel of the same name. Changes in the characters, plot, and even the central themes of the film, however, make it lean away from Swarthout's antiheroic and darkly violent novel, and towards the more hopeful *Shane*. Thus *The Shootist*, like *Man on Fire*, is definitely an adaptation, but the hypotext(s) are not simple and straightforward. The best example of this shift is reflected in the two "boys" of *Shane* and *The Shootist*, and in the trope of redemptive violence they exemplify.

It's worth taking a few moments to look at *The Shootist* in order to shed light on the adaptation of *Man on Fire*. In Swarthout's novel Gillom Rogers, like Bob Starrett in Schaefer's novel, is a young man who idolizes a gunfighter who is temporarily living in his home. In Gillom's case it's the aging, cancer-ridden, though still formidable, John Books. As Shane does with Bob/Joey, Books recognizes Gillom's misplaced hero worship and tries to steer the young man away from a gunfighter's life. In both Schaefer's novel and Stevens's film this attempt is apparently successful: Shane manages to save Bob/Joey's father from certain death and rid the valley of its dangerous men in a final violent act of service to Bob, his family, and the other homesteaders. In some of his final words to Bob in the novel, Shane explains that Bob's father will give him "the chance another kid never had."[17] He thus puts the boy on the path to a good, normal life. Recognizing Shane's sacrifice as an act of redemption, Michael Marsden calls Shane a "frontier Christ" and a "Savior in the saddle."[18]

Apparently looking for a similar outcome, Swarthout's John Books conceives a plan that will redeem both Gillom and the town of El Paso, and will likely cut short his own battle with cancer. Similar to Shane's rendezvous with Fletcher/Riker and his men, Books arranges to meet El Paso's three gunfighters at a downtown saloon on a given day. He sells his horse and belongings and leaves the proceeds, $532, to Bond Rogers, Gillom's mother, with a note that reads in part, "Use this money and send the boy away to school."[19] Immediately after doing this good deed, Books rides the streetcar into town and manages to kill El Paso's three most infamous gunhands, as well as a fourth who has shown up at the affray. As Shane had done, Books attempts to redeem both a boy and a community through an act of violence. But unlike Shane, Books fails miserably, at least in his effort to redeem the boy. As soon as Books leaves the house to meet his fate in the saloon, Gillom sneaks into his room and steals the money the gunfighter has left for his schooling. He then heads downtown just in time to steal the guns from the wounded Books. Gillom begins his life of violence by shooting his hero through the head.

At least, that's how it happens in the novel. This is not, however, the way Siegel's *The Shootist* ends. Apparently unwilling to accept Swarthout's sardonic irony, Siegel has his Gillom explicitly reject the gunfighter's life. As he had in the novel, the movie Gillom, played by the 22-year-old Ron Howard, finds the wounded Books after the gunfight seems to be over. But in the film Gillom then witnesses the bartender mortally wound Books in the back. Gillom takes Books's gun and quickly kills the bartender. The camera gives a quick reaction shot of a concerned Books as he lays on the floor. Gillom stares for a moment at the gun he has just used, then flings it across the room. The dying John Wayne,[20] as the dying John Books, gives an approving nod and peacefully passes away. This simple change, all by itself, makes Siegel's *The Shootist* resemble *Shane*, at least in tone and theme, much more than it resembles Swarthout's novel, since the film version of Books successfully saves both Gillom and El Paso with an act of redemptive violence.

In what should be a surprising parallel, Tony Scott's *Man on Fire*, although apparently based on both the 1980 A. J. Quinnell novel and the 1987 Elie Chouraqui film, also owes a great deal to George Stevens's *Shane*. Scott's film, in fact, follows a very similar trajectory to Siegel's *The Shootist*, turning a dark and violent novel into a story of redemption through violence. A number of important similarities between *Shane*, *The Shootist*, and *Man on Fire*, are worth noting because in the case of the later films these similarities are not included in the novels from which the films were adapted.[21] In all three films a man who has made a living through acts of violence leaves his former haunts and his former occupation seeking a new, more peaceful life. In each film this protagonist stumbles, more or less accidentally, onto a small family. In all of the films there is an almost immediate sexual tension between the wife/mother of the family and the protagonist, though this relationship is consummated in none of the films. In all of the films the child in the family begins to look to the protagonist as a kind of mentor and father figure. Each of the families is eventually placed in jeopardy by violent criminals, and in each of the films the protagonist sacrifices himself and his chance for a peaceful life, or in John Books's case, a peaceful death, in order to save at least one member of the family.

I might attribute these similarities to random chance or simple thievery, but, as I noted earlier, *Man on Fire* is an adaptation based on a novel. Nevertheless, each time Scott chooses to deviate from the A. J. Quinnell novel, he moves his film away from the book and closer to *Shane*, not simply in plot and characterization, but in theme and ultimate meaning. There are many examples of this movement, but I hope a few examples will illustrate the idea. For instance, in the novel the sexual tension mentioned earlier quickly becomes a meaningless sexual episode between the protagonist, Creasy, and the mean-spirited wife and mother of the family, Rika. In the film, on the other hand, this tension, as in *Shane*, is never resolved. Creasy and Lisa, the mother's name in the film, are clearly attracted to each other, just as Shane and Marion are, but that is the extent of their relationship. The fate of the young girl follows a similar pattern. In Quinnell's book the child, a girl named Pinta, is killed about a third of the way through the novel by her kidnappers, setting off Creasy's bloody 220-page quest for vengeance. In the film, Pita (the child's name in Scott's film) does not die, but is eventually saved, literally redeemed by Creasy. Perhaps the most important of the plot changes occurs towards the film's ending. In the novel Creasy assassinates the kidnappers and their associates, meets a beautiful Italian woman in the process, and at the end of the novel the couple move to a secluded island to live, we must assume, happily ever after. In the last ten minutes of Scott's film, on the other hand, Creasy discovers that Pita is alive, abandons his quest for revenge, and sacrifices himself in order to save the young girl. All of these changes would indicate that director Tony Scott and writer Brian Helgeland made at least an unconscious effort to bend Quinnell's story to fit the pattern that had been set fifty years earlier by *Shane*.

There is more to this adaptation, however, than the borrowing of plot elements from George Stevens. One of the most important aspects of this "bending" of *Man on Fire* toward *Shane* is the addition of what may be termed "spiritual" elements into the film. Creasy, for instance, prominently reads and displays a Bible in his small apartment. He even quotes from it more than once in the film. Indeed, the very premise of Scott's film rests on what must be understood as a spiritual question. In the second scene after the titles Creasy asks his ex-CIA buddy, Ray, played by Christopher Walken, "Do you think God will forgive us for what we have done?" Both men agree that He will not. Much of the rest of the film, however, seems to hinge on this central question. The most eye catching of Scott's spiritual additions to Quinnell's tale are what he, in the DVD commentary, calls his "baptism" scenes.[22] After each episode of Creasy's increasingly violent revenge against those who have kidnapped and, he believes at first, murdered Pita, Creasy submerges himself momentarily in water. Surrealistic underwater footage emphasizes the way Creasy's blood mixes with the water in an obvious Christian metaphor.

None of these religious or spiritual elements are found in the novel. If anything, Quinnell's novel is anti-religious. Quinnell's Creasy finds religion in general "a subject of massive contradiction."[23] His parents died when he was a boy and "that early experience, followed by a lifetime of war, had not brought him to God. He could not fathom a Supreme Being so disinterested as to allow millions of innocents to die in all the wars he had seen."[24] Quinnell goes on to describe Creasy's bitterness over "babies roasted in napalm," "a young girl, endlessly raped," and a priest tortured to death.[25] Quinnell's Creasy lives in a world devoid of God and bereft even of the guiding hand of fate. As Creasy imagines more than halfway through the novel, "nothing was fated. Every incident, every event involving people, was the result of actions by themselves or others."[26]

Scott's film, on the other hand, clearly rejects Quinnell's godless world, and the life of his Creasy is seemingly steered by what can only be called a beneficent fate. This fate is evidenced in the film's plot and imagery, but it is also manifest in the editing. In the first scenes of the film, for example, Scott inserts short clips from the last scene of the film. These visual cues imply that everything about to happen is somehow part of a plan, "fate," if you will. Creasy nearly spoils the "plan," however. Near the beginning of the film, soon after starting his job at the Ramos home, Creasy sits dejected in his apartment and contemplates suicide. A recording of the question he asked Ray earlier about God's forgiveness replays several times in a confusing soundtrack. In a drunken haze Creasy eventually places his automatic pistol to his head and pulls the trigger. When nothing happens, Creasy ejects the bullet to discover that it has been dimpled by the firing pin, but has somehow failed to fire. In a centerfire automatic this is a fairly rare occurrence. It is rare enough that in the middle of the night Creasy phones Ray to question him about it. In answer Ray repeats what is apparently an old saw between them, "the bullet always tells the truth." From this point on in the film Creasy seems to recognize the hand of fate in his life, and he begins to heal from the mental and emotional wounds his life as a CIA agent has caused. He drinks less, smiles more, and starts to form connections with the other characters around him. This failed suicide attempt has seemingly led him to believe that God does care about him and may, indeed, forgive him.

These spiritual episodes, so prominently absent from either Quinnell's novel or the earlier film, seem to suggest that the hypotexts for *Man on Fire* included a healthy dose of *Shane*. The source is a little more specific, though. The spiritual elements of *Shane* are much more evident in Stevens's film than they are Schaeffer's novel. Thus the way Stevens came to his own spirituality is an important part of this analysis. Let me take a moment here and confess that defining an idea like "spirituality" is difficult. What does it mean to be spiritual? Perhaps much of the definition of this word is implied, but let me make at least part of my definition explicit. Spirituality must include a belief that humans are more than simply complex animals or random products of evolution. Spirituality suggests that we are part of a larger, if unseen, world. Spirituality entails a faith in ultimate justice. It also implies that life is more than eating, drinking, and getting. In short, spirituality suggests that life is deeply meaningful, despite all evidence to the contrary.

Using this definition of "spirituality," the central spiritual theme of *Shane* may be summed up in a statement Stevens made in 1962 as he worked to complete *The Greatest Story Ever Told*, his version of the life of the Christ. Stevens explained that in making an adaptation of the Gospels he intended to show the world "a new vision of Christ, a powerful man without the nursery kindness which Sunday schools perhaps tell you that he had. If love wants to create justice, it can't be gentle, and I think that is the way of love this Christ really preached. Love is not sentimental."[27] The hard, realistic spirituality he aimed to create in *The Greatest Story Ever Told* is also clear in the earlier *Shane*. In fact, part of the power inherent in this western is the close connection Stevens manages to create between the violence that is and was common to westerns, and the powerful and unsentimental love that Shane and the Starrett family share.

Despite my suggestion that Shane is a "spiritual" film, Stevens was not a churchgoing man, and thus the roots of this quite conscious spirituality are debated by scholars. His experiences during the war certainly had something to do with the tone of his later films. Shortly after the United States entered World War II, the nearly 40-year-old Stevens volunteered for service in the signal corps and filmed much of the Allied war effort in Europe. Traveling with the troops Stevens saw a world of genuine evil. His crews filmed D-Day and some of the bloodiest battles of the war. He and his film crews also documented the liberation of Mittelbau labor camp, the place where Hitler's V-2 rockets were manufactured and where 25,000 prisoners died in forced labor. Later he shot the first allied film of Dachau prison camp with its starving inmates, gas chambers, ovens, and mass graves.[28] Stevens looked evil in the face and found that Sunday school softness was no match for it. Perhaps more importantly, Stevens saw thousands of young men die to combat this evil. Simply put, Stevens must have wondered, as thousands of Americans did, if these deaths were worth it. *Shane*, with its belligerent aggressor and reluctant savior, is one of the cinematic answers Stevens offered to that question. Certainly his films *The Diary of Anne Frank* and *The Greatest Story Ever Told* are other answers to the question, but it is *Shane* I am concerned with here.

In *Shane*, and in several of his later films, Stevens worked to create what I will call a space for spirituality. In post-war America spiritual space had become complex and problematic, particularly for those who had experienced the war firsthand. The place of the spiritual in everyday life became much more tenuous, something that had to be consciously created in the face of violence and evil. It probably should not be surprising that Stevens turned first to a Western to express this dilemma since one of the central features of Westerns has always been violence. In fact, the place of violence in Western films has rarely been questioned. In making *Shane*, Stevens took a film genre in which violence was casual and almost always laudatory—and in which spirituality was generally a sign of weakness—and turned it on its ear.

This mingling of spiritual elements with a Western setting and storyline was something of a strange combination. In *West of Everything*, Jane Tompkins argues that serious Westerns, as a genre, were spurred into being by spiritual novels like Charles M. Sheldon's *In His Steps*. In what Tompkins calls "far and away the most popular book of its time,"[29] a minister is brought to a sharp understanding of his own hypocrisy and commits himself to a life of asking, "what would Jesus do" before making any decision. Tompkins suggests that novels like this portrayed "men of the nineteenth century who have been enfeebled by the doctrines of a feminized Christianity."[30] According to Tompkins, Westerns, with their emphasis on quick action, vigilante justice, and hardy manhood, offered the antidote to the weakened, Christianized, feminized men portrayed in novels like Charles M. Sheldon's *In His Steps*.

In this light, the story of redemption that forms the basic structure of *Shane* seems somewhat out of place in a Western; yet there it is, alongside the violence that is always threatening the characters in both the film and the novel. Perhaps the best illustration of the film's violence is the death of Torrey, one of the homesteaders. In the novel the death of the homesteader[31] is only narrated secondhand, but in Stevens' film it is shockingly explicit. The violence portrayed here is so horrifying and repulsive that it seems almost out of place in this 1953 film. Torrey and another homesteader, Shipstead, ride into the muddy town and Torrey is almost immediately called out by Stark Wilson. As the two men walk toward the saloon, Torrey stays in the street while Wilson climbs the steps of the boardwalk. Eventually Wilson stands a full three feet above Torrey. Wilson taunts the smaller man who is eventually goaded into drawing his gun. Wilson has his revolver out and pointed, however, before Torrey's gun can clear leather. After smiling at Torrey and waiting for what seems like an eternity, Wilson shoots him in the chest. The force of the bullet drives Torrey several feet back and splashes him into the mud of the street.[32] Although, as Tompkins points out, violence is common to Westerns, the casual brutality of Wilson's actions and the pitiful death of Torrey are horrifying, even by today's standards.

I have come to believe, however, that this shocking and horrific vision of violence is integral to Stevens's idea of spirituality. The violence is, in fact, at least part of the source of what was to become his "new vision of Christ" as a powerful figure without nursery kindness, one who creates justice, but whose gentleness is mixed with strength. Stevens realized that in order to survive in the modern world, spirituality must be able to encompass the kind of violence epitomized by the death of Torrey, the same kind of appalling inhumanity he had witnessed in Europe. To deny the nature of violence is to deny the pain and the meaning of the sacrifice of the millions of men and women who died during the war, and the millions who survived the war and returned home. It is, then, Stevens's acceptance of violence, his refusal to turn the camera away from horror, that gives this film its spiritual power. This willingness to look evil in the eye allowed *Shane* to address the question on the tongues of millions of Americans in 1953: how can there be a place for the spiritual in the world after what I have seen?

Earlier I outlined several similarities between *Shane* and *Man on Fire*. Clearly these films are linked, despite outward differences in plot and setting. The films are set in vastly different times and places, for instance. One is set in the old West, Wyoming of the 1880s, and the other in contemporary Mexico City. This surface difference, however, only lightly covers a deeper similarity. If Wyoming of the 1880s, with its range wars and cattle barons, is the epitome of the old wild West, then Mexico is certainly perceived as the "new wild West" in the popular imagination. Films like *The Wild Bunch* (1969), *Rolling Thunder* (1977), *El Mariachi* (1992), and *The Mexican* (2001) exploit that popular perception. Cormac McCarthy, among other modern and contemporary American writers, has exposed this perception of Mexico in his novels. Certainly Scott's portrayal of Mexico City as a place where gun-toting gangsters and single-minded vigilantes are unhampered by police interference looks a great deal like the wild West of John Wayne, Clint Eastwood, and Alan Ladd.

The same may be said of the obvious casting differences. Stevens chose a short white man to play Shane, and Scott chose a tall black man to play Creasy. Surprisingly, though, both actors had recently played very similar parts. Alan Ladd was well know for his work in film noir, and had recently played a gun-running pilot of questionable morals in *Thunder in the East* (1952), and a vigilante ex-army officer in *Captain Carey, U.S.A.* (1950). Both of these characters served as context for his portrayal of Shane, a character who has lived a violent and questionable life, who seems now to seek a more peaceful existence, but who, in the course of the film, will be forced into an act of vigilante violence. Denzel Washington's career is probably more familiar to us. When he made *Man on Fire* he had recently starred in *Out of Time* (2003) and *Training Day* (2001), both films about a lawman who finds himself on the wrong side of the law. In *Training Day*, in fact, Washington plays the same kind of vigilante Ladd had played in *Captain Carey*. The casting in *Shane* and *Man on Fire*, like the plots and settings of the two films, seem more similar than different in the final measure.

Perhaps the most important link between these two films is the way the film makers themselves view *Man on Fire*. Although most of the critics who reviewed *Man on Fire* saw it as yet another revenge movie in the vein of *Death Wish*, both the screenwriter, Brian Helgeland, and the producer, Lucas Foster, deny that they made a revenge film. Helgeland suggests that perverse and obtuse critics purposefully misread the film, refusing to "let it be more than that."[33] They argue that they made a film about sacrifice and redemption, and that these elements of the story are what initially attracted both of them to the story. I would suggest, however, that it is not the critics, but rather Foster and Helgeland who have done the misreading. This *is* a revenge film. At least, it is a revenge film until its last ten minutes. It is only then that both Creasy and the audience members discover that Pita has not been killed, and that the kidnapper is willing to trade her life for Creasy's. At that point Creasy certainly sacrifices what is left of his life to save her. But Foster and Helgeland couldn't have been attracted to these elements in the original story because they are absent from the 1980 novel and the confusing 1987 adaptation altogether. If they are not to be found in these earlier texts, how then were Foster and Helgeland initially attracted to these story elements? The answer is probably suggested by the fact that Helgeland first read Quinnell's novel while he was employed by producer Alan Ladd Jr.[34] Yes, Alan Ladd Jr. is the son of Alan Ladd, the star of *Shane*. This odd little connection, small as it is, may be the smoking gun that connects *Man on Fire* with *Shane*. Certainly it seems that Helgeland's interpretation of Quinnell's novel was one in which Stevens's film played a significant role.

Several possible conclusions might be drawn from the particular path I have just traced through these texts. One, of course, is a reminder, if we need one, that directors are not the only *auteurs* involved in making films. As scholars we regularly, often to our chagrin, overlook the contributions of producers, writers, editors, and others. After listening to Tony Scott babble on the *Man on Fire* DVD commentary for hour and a half, I was pleasantly surprised to discover a second commentary track featuring Helgeland, Foster, and Fanning. Listening to that second track has led me to believe that much of the real thought behind the film came from Helgeland and Foster. Scott does create some stunning visual images, but the philosophical depth of the film seems to have come from sources other than the director.

The evidence this analysis offers for a non-linear, intertextual approach to *Man on Fire* suggests a second possible conclusion. As noted earlier, this film is an adaptation, but its hypotexts are not limited to Quinnell's novel and Chouraqui's film. It's tough to say exactly how elements of *Shane*, and particularly George Stevens's odd spiritual justification of violence, made their way into *Man on Fire*, but clearly they did. Suggesting that adaptations like this one are intertextual reminds us to look outside of the box, so to speak, when we are searching for connections. Helgeland, Foster, and Scott adapted plot and characters, but they also adapted *ideas*, what we used to call themes or tropes. In suggesting connections between *Shane* and *Man on Fire* I am not arguing for a skin-deep or surface similarity between the two films, but rather pointing out a kinship in their cinematic DNA—a genetic connection that may very well be a result of unrecognized cultural pressures.

With these cultural pressures in mind, the final conclusion I will propose has to do with the timing of the four films I have mentioned.

Freud's concept of "complexes" may be useful in understanding this timing. Freud argued that emotionally charged images, events, or ideas might be temporarily forgotten, submerged in one's subconscious. But in the junkyards of our minds these items tend to gather other memories, ideas, and images to them like psychic magnets, forming *complexes* that reemerge into conscious thought periodically, though often in unpredictable ways. I'm tempted to suggest that *Shane* may be the most readily identifiable expression of what we might call a cultural "Shane complex."[35] For evidence of the existence of this complex I would note the release dates of the films I have discussed. Dozens of individual decisions affect the release date of a film, but each of these movies may be easily associated with the end of a war. *Shane* was released eight years after WWII, and right at the end of the Korean War. *The Shootist* came out in the final days of the Vietnam War, and *Pale Rider* appeared in theaters in 1985, at about the same time that Mikhail Gorbachev and Ronald Regan began talks that would signal the beginning of the end of the Cold War. *Man on Fire* was released about a year after President George Bush famously declared the war in Iraq a "Mission accomplished!"[36] My guess is that each of these release dates, though they may not have been conscious decisions made by producers or studios, reflects one of the important cultural roles films play in our lives. Each of these films depicts an unjust world in which the innocent are often made to suffer, and each film offers this as a justification for righteous violence. Perhaps most surprisingly, all of these films hold out a hope that seems to fly in the face of common sense: that there can be such a thing as redemptive violence. For Stevens that hope was hard-earned on the battlefields and in the concentration camps of Europe. For Scott, Helgeland, and Foster the connection between spirituality and violence is simply part of the air they breathe, a Hollywood archetype.

Notes

1. A note on writing about adaptations: Essays on adaptations are often exercises in footnotes. That is true for what are, perhaps, obvious reasons. The intertextual nature of the adaptation process, and the fact that those who study adaptations are particularly focused on these intertextual elements means that as analysts we are constantly being sidetracked. To make matters more complicated, essays on adaptations often deal with two, three, or even more individual texts, each with its own contexts. As I have commenced writing this particular paper, I have been tempted to write a paper that consists of three or four pages of text, and twenty pages of footnotes. I have resisted the urge, but that is the nature of the game we have chosen to play. Thus, as the introductory essay in this volume suggests, I have chosen a particular path through this material, but clearly it is only one possibility among many.

2. Guy Westfall, review of *Man on Fire*, directed by Tony Scott, *Sight and Sound* ns14, no. 11 (Nov 2004): 59.

3. Andrea Toal, review of *Man on Fire*, directed by Tony Scott, *Sight and Sound* ns15, no. 3 (March 2005): 84.

4. David Ng, "He Got God: Denzel Gets Even in a Blitz of Christian Retribution," review of *Man on Fire*, directed by Tony Scott, *The Villiage Voice* 49, no. 17 (2004): 70.

5. Quinnell's novels do have a following in the United States, but apparently the Creasy books (there are five of them) are quite popular in Japan.

6. Quinnell also cites as inspiration the 1973 kidnapping of John Paul Getty III in Rome.

7. A. J. Quinnell fan Web site, http://web.singnet.com.sg/~tonym/quinnell.html

8. Ibid.

9. No doubt some will accuse me of being a "fidelity critic" based on my observation of differences. But recognizing the differences between two texts does not make one a fidelity critic any more than recognizing skin color makes one a racist. As we note in the introduction to this volume, "Discovering difference then becomes not a quest to uncover the inevitable lack of fidelity, but rather an affirmative focus on how texts form and *in-form* each other" (15).

10. *Shane*, VHS, directed by George Stevens (Hollywood, CA: Paramount Pictures, 1952).

11. "NameMapper," The Baby Name Wizard website, http://namemapper.baby namewizard.com. The "NameMapper" website suggests that "Shane" began to be a popular baby name in Utah, Idaho, Montana, and the Dakotas in the mid-nineteen-sixties, and hit its peak of popularity in Montana in 1972, about the time that those who had seen the film as youngsters would have been starting families.

12. *George Stevens: A Filmmaker's Journey*, VHS, directed by George Stevens, Jr. (Janus Films, 1985).

13. *Pale Rider*, VHS, directed by Clint Eastwood (Hollywood, CA: Warner Brothers, 1985).

14. Ann Ronald, "Shane's Pale Ghost," *New Orleans Review* 17, no. 3 (1990): 5–9. Ann Ronald cleverly labels *Pale Rider* "*Shane*'s Pale Ghost." Ronald suggests that Eastwood's film ultimately fails, however, because it puts "archetype before humanity," and because "the plot, the characters, even the mythic foundations, so appropriate for a hungrily romantic generation, are out of place now. Thus, *Pale Rider* creaks on the hinges of outmoded conception and present day execution" (5).

15. *Gran Torino*, DVD, directed by Clint Eastwood (Warner Brothers, 2008).

16. *The Shootist*, VHS, directed by Don Siegel (Hollywood, CA: Paramount Pictures, 1976). Gabriel Miller notes the parallels between *Shane* and *The Shootist* in his article "Shane Redux: The Shootist and the Western Dilemma," *Journal of Popular Film and Television* 11, no. 2 (1983): 66–77.

17. Jack Schaefer, *Shane: The Critical Edition*, ed. James C. Work (Lincoln: University of Nebraska Press, 1984), 263.

18. Michael T. Marsden, "Savior in the Saddle: The Sagebrush Testament," in *Shane: The Critical Edition*, ed. James C. Work (Lincoln: University of Nebraska Press, 1984), 398. Ron Large notes that any act of redemption requires help from the outside, a redeemer, because the people involved are "unable to save themselves." Thus, "redemption requires some form of intervention" (232).

19. Glendon Swarthout, *The Shootist* (New York: Berkley Books, 1975), 179.

20. Production notes for the film housed in the Don Seigel papers at the Brigham Young University Library in special collections suggest that Wayne's illness set the

production back weeks. Elizabeth G. Norton, Siegel's secretary, noted "Principle actor ill with the flu" on March 15 and made similar notes regularly throughout the shooting schedule. *The Shootist* was Wayne's last film. He would be dead within a few years of its completion.

21. Most of these elements also apply to *Pale Rider*.

22. *Man on Fire* with commentary, DVD, directed by Tony Scott (Los Angeles: Twentieth Century Fox, 2004).

23. A. J. Quinnell, *Man on Fire* (New York: Avon Books, 1980), 131.

24. Ibid.

25. Ibid., 131–32.

26. Ibid., 191.

27. "Forget the Incense," *Time*, December 28, 1962, 34.

28. For an account of Stevens's wartime activities see Marilyn Ann Moss, *Giant: George Stevens; A Life on Film* (Madison: University of Wisconsin Press, 2004), 115–26.

29. Jane Tompkins, *West of Everything: The Inner Life of Westerns* (New York: Oxford University Press, 1992), 30.

30. Ibid., 33.

31. In the novel the homesteader killed by Wilson is Ernie Wright.

32. Pete Martin, "The Man Who Made the Hit Called *Shane*," *Saturday Evening Post*, August 8, 1953, 32–33, 46, 48, 53. In his extended 1953 review of the film Pete Martin noted of this scene that "Stevens refused to settle for . . . mock violence. When a slug from a six-shooter is supposed to slam into an actor in Shane, the audience sees the impact. The actor is attached to a wire worked by a block and pulley. The wire, in turn, if fastened to a leather belt buckled around the actor's middle. When the imaginary slug plows into him, the wire jerks him backwards, just as he would jerk if real led hit him" (48).

33. *Man on Fire* with commentary, DVD, directed by Tony Scott (Los Angeles: Twentieth Century Fox, 2004).

34. Ibid.

35. In a 1992 article in the *Journal of Evolutionary Psychology* Ron Large identifies a similar pattern and calls it, "the most enduring and compelling of American myths, that of the redemptive hero" (232).

36. Jarrett Murphy, "Text of Bush Speech," May 1, 2003, CBS News Web site http://www.cbsnews.com/stories/2003/05/01/iraq/main551946.shtml

III
Adaptation as Departure

Talking Pictures: Language and Emotion in Lubitsch's *The Shop Around the Corner*

Nancy Steffen-Fluhr

Twenty-five of Ernst Lubitsch's twenty-seven Hollywood films are adaptations, but Lubitsch rarely receives more than a passing mention in adaptation studies, largely because his preferred hypotexts—boulevard comedies by "obscure Hungarians"—seem too frothy for scholarly consideration.[1] Emerging from college English departments, adaptation studies traditionally saw film *through* Serious Literature, as if the former were a mistranslated copy of the latter. In recent years, the field has moved toward a more complex and embracing understanding of intertextuality. Nevertheless, the tendency to conflate filmic adaptation as a whole with the adaptation of canonical novels has endured, as has the related tendency to discount the intimate connections between film and theatre. Both of these tendencies impoverish critical practice in adaptation studies, limiting our ability to explore the ways in which all art is dialogic and many-voiced.

The problematic opposition of literature and film implicit in much of adaptation studies not only privileges canonical texts; it privileges the word over the image. Film theorists who privilege the image (e.g., Metz and Stam) reverse the polarity, but they do not alter the binary nature of the game, which remains saturated in unacknowledged literary metaphor. In her 2003 book on adaptation studies (*Rethinking the Novel/Film Debate*), Kamilla Elliott calls down a plague on both houses, arguing that novels and films are hybrid forms in which words and images interpenetrate.[2] Elliott uses Ernst Lubitsch as an extreme example of the belief that films = images, citing a 1923 quotation in which Lubitsch seems to disavow words: "I try to exclude titles whenever possible. . . ."[3] In editing Lubitsch's quotation, Elliott has elided part of his point, however. Lubitsch is not opposed to title cards because they use words. What he dislikes is cutting away from action to "dead air." The salient binary system for Lubitsch is not words versus images, but the theatrical opposition of telling versus showing.[4]

Lubitsch came to film by way of the theatre and to directing by way of acting. He began his career in 1908 on the Berlin stage eventually playing bit parts for director Max Reinhardt, then moved on to German silent film, where he achieved stardom as a slapstick comedian. Lubitsch often played directly to the camera, holding up objects for the audience to see. His subsequent directorial obsession with metaphorical indirection—i.e. his tendency to tell (narrate) by showing—is a product of his early experience with pantomime. Lubitsch's choice of hypotexts flows from his theatrical background as well. Nearly all of his Hollywood films are adaptations of European plays. His camera re-stages these precursor texts, translating them from three dimensions to two in ways that increase the metaphorical free-play space they contain. His "actor's sense of business"[5] evolves into an idiosyncratic editing technique in which the prop-passes within the frame are matched by a kind of syntactical prop-passing from frame-to-frame. Emotionally charged objects are glued together diachronically to create new intratexts, an expressive mode that resembles collage, transcending the narrative line contained in the title cards, or, later, in the dialogue.

To describe this collage-making process—and to explore the neglected issue of intentionality in adaptation—I propose to track the choices that Lubitsch and his co-writer, Samson Raphaelson, make as they cannibalize Miklós László's 1937 play *Parfumerie* and a series of apparently unrelated intertexts in order to "assemble" the 1940 MGM film *The Shop Around the Corner*.[6] The trope of *assemblage*—"readymade" art composed of found objects—is especially appropriate for Lubitsch, who approached film-making as a spatial problematic, alert to the expressive possibilities in juxtaposition and contiguity. In order to map the distinctive shape of the Lubitsch "readymade," we need to read two ways at once, however—first identifying the idiosyncratic patterns of excess that appear when *Parfumerie* is transformed into *Shop*, and then noticing how these very excesses are erased when *Shop* is transformed into two Hollywood-normal genre pictures, *In the Good Old Summertime* (1949) and *You've Got Mail* (1998).

Shop itself is usually regarded as a Hollywood-normal genre picture, a "holiday film classic" that often double-bills at Christmastime with *It's a Wonderful Life.* James Harvey sees the film as straightforward, lacking Lubitsch's usual double entendres and "metaphoric values."[7] Raphaelson reinforces this view, insisting that *Shop* is dialogue-driven: "The scenes were explored in *language.* . . . There [are] no 'Lubitsch touches.'"[8] Raphaelson is wrong, however. And the critical consensus is wrong as well. The dialogue-driven film that Raphaelson thinks he and Lubitsch have written is not the film that Lubitsch has put up on the screen, a film in which the language of flowers, the language of music, the language of objects, the language of pictures, and, not least, the language of desire, compete with, and ultimately obliterate, everything that Raphaelson means by "language." The Capra-like simplicity of the film's surface is deliberately deceptive. *Shop* is a work of extraordinary semiotic complexity, the most passionate and heartbreakingly personal film in Lubitsch's canon; but it is also the most diffident. Like Jimmy Stewart's character ("Kralik"), the film does and does not want to disclose itself, and for good reason. In ninety-seven minutes of screen time, Lubitsch takes his characters through loneliness, adultery, pain, madness, suicide, and death, not to mention bouts of metaphoric copulation. Then he passes the film off to Joe Breen as a Goyishe Christmas movie!

Passing as a Dickensian *Christmas Carol* (genre "spoofing") is one thread in the web of intertextual gamesmanship that Lubitsch practices in *Shop*. Masquerading as social realism is another. Like *Parfumerie*, *Shop* appears to be a comic *Kammerspiel* that gently satirizes working-class pretensions. Indeed, William Paul argues that Lubitsch's "concern for realistic detail" marks a turn toward "naturalism."[9] This judgment misses the stylized, reflexive, and fundamentally metaphorical nature of Lubitsch's *mise-en-scène*, however. László's play is solidly grounded in prewar Budapest just as Nora Ephron's *Mail* is grounded in General X Manhattan. In contrast, Lubitsch's film is not really grounded at all. Studio-bound, subtly claustrophobic, it calls attention to its own diorama-like representation of a world that no longer exists.[10] Lubitsch refuses to Americanize László's setting, the obvious adaptive move; instead, he hybridizes it, juxtaposing the European inflections of Felix Bressart with Jimmy Stewart's iconic American face. We seem to be in two places at once, exiled between cultures, at a crossroads that sometimes looks like Andrassy and Balta Street and sometimes looks like Hollywood and Vine.

Raphaelson downplays the film's hybridity and discounts László's hypotextual influence as well. Raphaelson maintains that he never read the "base play"; instead, Lubitsch merely "doled out" bits of ur-plot to him as they talked their way through the script in front of a secretary. "Not one line of dialogue [in *Parfumerie*] coincides with the film!" Raphaelson insists.[11] This assertion is demonstrably untrue, of course. The *Shop* script actually follows *Parfumerie* very closely. However, Raphaelson is right to believe that the film is idiosyncratic. Even when the changes that Lubitsch/Raphaelson[12] make are quite small, they have a big effect on semiotic structure, which, in turn, has a big effect on meaning and emotion. The distinctive language that *Shop* speaks arises not from the film's dialogue but from its *intratexts*, the

web of diachronic connections among dialogue segments, props, business, and intertextual allusions. Unlike *Parfumerie*, which is full of
telegraphic explication, *Shop* never stops to tell us what it is about; but
it is unceasing it its efforts to *show* itself to us, right up to the final
moment in which a pair of naked legs reveals the hidden body of the
text.

There is nothing hidden in László's text. Structurally, *Parfumerie*
belongs to the same dramaturgical family as Ferenc Molnár's *The
Guardsman* (1910), a surrealistic comedy about an actor who finds
himself by getting lost in his part—the kind of wry exploration of
emotional knowledge to which Lubitsch was deeply attracted. *Parfumerie* is much less reflexive than *Guardsman*. There is no metaphoric
substrate, no "intertextual energy," as mentioned in the introduction
of this book.[13] Nevertheless, László's plot is relatively complex. Four
narrative strands are woven together into an ensemble piece that follows the employees of an upscale Budapest cosmetics store as they interact during the two weeks prior to Christmas: *Mr. Hammerschmidt*,
the store's owner, becomes suicidally jealous of his head salesman, *Mr.
Horvath*, whom he wrongly suspects of having an affair with his wife.
The culprit turns out to be another employee, *Mr. Kadar*, a ladies
man, who is simultaneously trying to seduce his former "fiancée," *Miss
Ritter*. Meanwhile, Horvath discovers that the female pen pal with
whom he has fallen in love ("Box 1347") is actually a fellow employee,
Miss Balash, with whom he constantly bickers. At the end, Hammerschmidt apologizes to Horvath, fires Kadar, and reconciles with his
wife; and Horvath, now on good terms with Balash, prepares to disclose his secret identity.

In 1948 when MGM producer Joe Pasternak and director Robert
Z. Leonard adapt the plot as a Judy Garland vehicle (*Summertime*),
he makes the obvious Hollywood moves: Americanizing the setting,
eliminating the adultery motif, and centering the story on the bickering lovers.[14] The shop owner is reduced to a supporting character, one
half of a musical comedy "second couple." In *Mail* (1998), writer-di-
rector Nora Ephron goes further, excising everything but the pen pal
love story. In contrast, Lubitsch/Raphaelson make adaptive choices
that go against the grain of 1940 genre norms. They eliminate the
Kadar/Ritter romance but *increase* the importance of the adultery plot,
fusing it with the love-by-mail story.[15] Why? To explore Lubitsch's
intention here, we need to go back to the beginning of *Shop* and pay
attention to the small changes that Lubitsch/Raphaelson make as they
adapt László's play, the swapping of intertexts, the addition of props
and business. We need to interrogate each of these transformations,
looking for patterns: Why *these* texts, *these* props? What do they have

in common? If these objects could speak, what would they say? For in Lubitsch's world, objects *do* speak, and God is always in the details.

The most articulate object in *Shop* is the shop itself. In László's play, the set is simply an open space defined by a series of doors. In the film, the shop is a metaphorical structure, the outermost container in a nest of Chinese Boxes. *Parfumerie* begins inside the shop, with Hammer-schmidt already serving a customer, the start of a tedious establishing sequence in which the characters tell us who they are and what they feel. In contrast, Lubitsch/Raphaelson position us outside, opening the film and opening the shop at the same time. The employees arrive one by one, as if they were stage players making an entrance. Each entrance is subtly "captioned" by a shtick that prompts us to make an inference. (In a Lubitsch film, narration is an audience participation game.) By the time the boss, *Mr. Matuschek*, arrives with the key to the shop door, we already have the key to the function and personality of all seven characters present—and to one character who is absent, Mrs. Matuschek. Or so we think. (More about her anon)

Some of the character shticks are verbal. For example, the film's vil-lain, *Mr. Vadas* (László's *Kadar*) hails the others with, "Friends, Ro-mans, countrymen, to tell you the truth," an allusion that defines Vadas as a man who does not say what he means. More often, the sh-ticks involve idiosyncratic bits of business, e.g., *Mr. Pirovitch* is defined by a single prop: the stub of a cheap cigar. A brief exchange in the opening minute of the film establishes that Pirovitch has cut down on his smoking in order to pay for a top-notch doctor for his ailing son. A large-hearted man, he makes himself small in relation to the bluster-ing Mr. Matuschek because he needs his job to take care of his family. The cigar stub *is* Pirovitch. It embodies his love and his helplessness. László's equivalent to Pirovitch (*Mr. Sipos*) smokes, too, but in *Par-fumerie*, a cigar is just a cigar; in *Shop*, it is a synecdoche—and an intra-text. That is, Lubitsch not only uses the prop to define Pirovitch; he uses Pirovitch to "charge" the prop. Saturated with his vulnerability, the cigar now has the power to transport that emotional state to other places in the text. This is exactly how Lubitsch employs it in Sequence B, when we see the autocratic Mr. Matuschek become suddenly sub-missive as he speaks to his wife on the phone. The cigar in his hand "reads" the tableau for us: Mr. Matuschek relates to Mrs. Matuschek the same way Pirovitch relates to him.

If Pirovitch is a cigar, then Kralik is a box. Closed and empty at the beginning of the film, his psychomachical task (his "character arc") is to open up and be filled up. This metaphorical equivalence of persons and objects is subtle but relentless, established by the accumulation of physical detail. Each detail has a naturalistic function; as details connect, mirroring each other, however, they create a semiotic excess that precipitates out of the narrative until Matuschek's shop glows with latent emotion. In this manner, while being technically faithful to the *Parfumerie* script, Lubitsch/Raphaelson quietly subvert László's dramaturgical point of view, transforming a comedy of observation into a series of visceral emotional embodiments. László stands outside his characters, at a distance from their comic angst; we look over his shoulder. In contrast, Lubitsch/Raphaelson take us *inside*, where the feelings are.

This metaphorical movement from outside to inside "the box" is announced in the film's opening sequence. Lubitsch positions his camera on the sidewalk, facing the shop's gated door. When Matuschek leads his employees through the door, the camera does not follow, however. Instead, Lubitsch discreetly jump cuts to a privileged point of view deep inside the showroom, the camera wedged under a balcony, looking out toward the front windows. In the next shot, the camera has moved further inside, behind a stack of boxes in the storeroom, the innermost of three nested spaces: shop, showroom, storeroom. Pirovitch enters, carrying seventeen identical boxes stacked atop each other. Kralik is already there, half-hidden behind other boxes and containers. In this protected position, he opens up to Pirovitch, letting him in on his secret correspondence with a woman he knows only as "Box 237." "Want to hear . . . a letter from a *girl?*" asks Kralik, eyeing Pirovitch intently. Speaking slowly, sensually, he reads a passage from the letter: "'My heart was trembling as I walked into the post office. And there you were, lying in box 237.'"

In *Parfumerie*, the postal box is simply a plot element. We never see it. In *Shop*, Box 237 is embodied, part of a semiotic system of physical boxes each of which "contains" the same desire: to be "opened up" and "filled up." Like the initial movement of Lubitsch's camera from outside the shop's façade to inside a "backstage" room, the letter that Kralik reads to Pirovitch describes the sequential penetration of four nested containers: the post office, inside of which is Box 237, inside of which is the envelope, inside of which is Kralik's letter, a letter that is synonymous with his male body ("you" "lying there"). Stewart's line-reading eroticizes the image—"I took you out of your envelope and read you, read you *right there*"—as if two metaphors were copulating on the cold granite floor of the Budapest central post office.

In her 1992 book on Lubitsch's German silents, Sabine Hake laments the loss of eroticism in Lubitsch's later Hollywood work, the disappearance of his polymorphous-perverse "world of objects."[16] It has not disappeared, however; it has merely been hidden where Joe Breen will never find it—in plain sight. In *Shop*, this tactic comes into play as the action shifts from the storeroom to the showroom. Here the commercial nature of the shop becomes important. László's decision to have Hammerschmidt sell cosmetics is essentially arbitrary. Thus in *Summertime* when Joe Pasternak and Leonard change the venue to a music store in order to set up Judy Garland's songs, nothing much changes in László's postal lovers plot; however, the switch obliterates the core of Lubitsch's film. Lubitsch/Raphaelson's decision to have Matuschek sell small leather goods is *not* arbitrary. It is a semiotic strategy. Unlike Mr. Hammerschmidt's cosmetics, Mr. Matuschek's goods are "goods to think with" (in Lévi-Strauss's phrase), *objets trouvées* from which Lubitsch/Raphaelson are assembling a ready-made. Luggage, purses, wallets, boxes—these containers not only share a set of physical possibilities (open/closed; full/empty); they share a "skin" (leather). Metaphorically, the shop in *Shop* is filled with empty bodies, waiting to be filled up. One metaphoric container in particular moves to center stage in the initial showroom scene between Kralik and Matuschek, a prop that has no equivalent in *Parfumerie:* a musical cigarette box that plays "Ochi Tchornya," a traditional Gypsy melody ("Dark eyes, talk to me").

At the beginning of the showroom scene, Matuschek passes the music box to Kralik: "What do you think of it? I think it's great!" Kralik looks at the box as "Ochi Tchornya" plays. "It's not for us," he says firmly, closing the box. Bristling, Matuschek turns for an "honest opinion" to Vadas, a consummate toady, who tells Matuschek exactly what he wants to hear: "It's sensational!" Matuschek subsequently orders dozens of boxes, but they don't sell, forcing him to periodically reduce the price. *Summertime* repeats this sequence verbatim, with one exception: the music box is replaced by a small harp, setting up a Garland song. Like Matuschek, the music store owner buys the harps against the advice of his head salesman. The "reduced price" sign in his shop window is thus a sign of his stubbornness, a trait that creates a comic subplot. The "Dark Eyes" box in *Shop* is not merely a character tag, however. It is a node that connects multiple, often contradictory readings to each other. It is a metaphorical container of desire, an intertext, a projective screen, and, not least, a metonymy for the blindness that cripples all of the principals—a blindness in which we are ultimately implicated as well.

In *Parfumerie*, vulnerabilities are expressed in dialogue. In *Shop*, they are embodied in the *mise-en-scène*, e.g., Lubitsch positions Vadas between Kralik and Matuschek as Kralik explains that the "leather" covering the music box is imitation. "I know that!" Matuschek bridles. It is clear he did *not* know it, however, just as he does not see that Vadas is a phony, something we have already deduced. The function of the music box here is clear as well: it is an authenticity test—a test of the relationship of words to feelings. What people *say* is not what people *are*. This is obviously true of Vadas; and it is true of Matuschek, who does not really want an "honest opinion" and whose bluster hides deep insecurity. Less obviously, it is true of Kralik as well.

Commenting on the cheap construction of the box, Kralik complains, "the whole thing will fall apart, and all you'll have left is 'Ochi Tchornya.'" The music means "nothing" to him; when he opens the box, all he hears is noise. When *Klara* (László's *Balash*, played by Margaret Sullavan) opens the shop door a few frames later, all Kralik sees is a commission. Turning on his sales pitch, he flatters her the way Vadas flatters Matuschek. When he discovers that Klara wants a job and not a purse, he rebuffs her, speaking *for* his boss. "I know Mr. Matuschek inside and out," he says, blind to the fact that Matuschek is standing behind him. He is blind to something else as well: Klara is "Box 237." Love has just walked through the door, and he does not see it. There is no irony here, except in retrospect, however. Unlike the remakes, in which we learn early on that the bickering shop clerks

The Shop Around the Corner (1940). Directed by Ernst Lubitsch. Shown from left: Margaret Sullavan (as Klara Novak), James Stewart (as Alfred Kralik), Frank Morgan (as Hugo Matuschek). Courtesy of MGM/Photofest © MGM.

are the postal lovers, the *Shop* script withholds Klara's secret identity from *us* as well as from Kralik.[17] We are as blind as he is.

The characters' manipulations of each other within the narrative mirror the film's manipulative relationship to its audience—a playful reflexivity that is wholly foreign to *Parfumerie* and *Summertime*. This playfulness surfaces in the second half of the showroom sequence when Matuschek asks Klara for her "honest opinion" of the Ochi Tchornya box. Unlike Kralik, Klara sees the box as "romantic" ("moonlight and . . . cigarettes and music")—a line that morphs the prop into a Silver Screen onto which we project our desires. A fat customer perks up her ears. "It's a candy box, isn't it?" she says, projecting *her* desire onto it. Klara concurs and opens the box, displaying the "food of love" it contains. But the fat woman agrees with Kralik. The music would drive her nuts. Desperate to demonstrate her sales skills, Klara transforms the box again. Filling it up with the desire to be attractive, she sells the box to the woman as a diet aid! (The maddening music is a lock that keeps the box closed.)

Lubitsch gets us to buy the film the same way Klara gets the fat

The Shop Around the Corner (1940). Directed by Ernst Lubitsch. Shown from left: Margaret Sullavan (as Klara Novak), Grace Hayle (as Plump Woman). Courtesy of MGM/Photofest © MGM.

lady to buy the box, using an adroit combination of textual passing and
flattery. The flattery involves recurring shticks that Lubitsch trains us
to anticipate, until we start to believe that we are co-directing the picture with him. Some of these repeats are rhythm jokes—e.g., Pirovitch
fleeing every time he hears Matuschek ask for an "honest opinion."
Other reprises are more fugue-like—e.g. the way the film keeps circling back on its structure. Thus Sequence B begins just as Sequence
A began: we are outside the shop waiting for Matuschek to open the
door. There is a Christmas tree in the window now, however, along
with thirty-three Ochi Tchornya boxes arranged around a sign: "Reduced from 5.50 to 2.29." The sign is a sign that Mr. Matuschek has
made a "bad judgment." It reifies all the other bad judgments in the
film, including our own condemnation of Mrs. Matuschek. There are
other signs in the *mise-en-scène* as well, small details we are challenged
to "read." If we connect the dots properly, will see what Kralik does
not see: that Klara, who is leaning against the Ochi Tchornya box display, reading a thick book, is the Girl in Box 237, who has promised
to meet him tonight in the Café Nizza carrying, as a sign of her identity, a red carnation inserted into a copy of *Anna Karenina*—a semiotic
move that transforms a text into a kind of box.

The metaphorical complexity here transcends any narrative requirement. Indeed, it endangers narration. (We can easily miss the
clues.) A more normal adaptive move is to disclose the lovers' double
identities early and clearly, maximizing audience pleasure in possess-
ing privileged knowledge. (Ephron does this in *Mail* before the credits
even finish rolling.) In *Shop*, privilege has to be earned, however.
There is a "reading requirement." That is, the text exhibits the same
reticence as the characters within it. Lubitsch signals Kralik's reticence by juxtaposing him with the closed music boxes in the shop window. Kralik's closed state is connected, in turn, to the "blindness" he
shares with Matuschek: e.g., speaking for Matuschek, Kralik instructs
Klara to never again wear "that yellow blouse with the light green
dots." Bristling, she corrects him: it is "a *green* blouse with light *yellow*
dots." The two motifs (see/open) come together at the end of the
scene when Kralik opens up to Pirovitch about his fear of opening Box
237—i.e., seeing his postal lover in the flesh. He compares his situation to an employee's reluctance to look inside an envelope that may
or may not contain a big bonus. The dialogue and the *mise-en-scène*
work together here to create a hybrid semiotic system in which words
generate invisible prop-play which acts out an emotional state. This
"signing" process is barely liminal, however. That is, Lubitsch's style
in *Shop* is expressive without being communicative. Like the multiple
frame masks and abstract crowd movements that Lubitsch plays with

The Shop Around the Corner (1940). Directed by Ernst Lubitsch. Shown from left: Margaret Sullavan (as Klara Novak), James Stewart (as Alfred Kralik). Courtesy of MGM/Photofest © MGM.

in his silent films, the repetitive patterns in *Shop* constitute a private textual music.

The structural changes that Lubitsch/Raphaelson make to László's play are part of this textual music. The sign-in-the-window scene has no equivalent in *Parfumerie*, nor does the Café Nizza scene that follows it. Even Matuschek's attempted suicide, which seems to have been taken directly from *Parfumerie*, is subtly different. László plays the incident for suspense, dropping the first act curtain on the gunshot. Lubitsch plays it for tragedy, setting up a crucial shift in focus. Matuschek waits in his deserted showroom, its display cases draped in white sheets, like a mortuary. The detective arrives and confirms Mrs. Matuschek's adultery, not with Kralik, whom Matuschek has just fired, but with Vadas. Matuschek is shattered, not simply because he has lost his wife, but because he has lost Kralik, his closest professional colleague. He goes into his office, closes the door, and blows his brains out. This is not what happens literally, of course, but it is what happens essentially. From this point on, *Shop* is no longer "the story of Mr. Matuschek," or of Mrs. Matuschek. It is the story of Kralik and

Klara, who have *replaced* the Matuscheks and are moving back in time
toward their first kiss.

In order to understand this subtle but important adaptive change
that Lubitsch/Raphaelson have made, we need to pair the visible intertext that Klara carries with her to the café (her copy of *Anna Karenina*)
with an invisible intertext from a very different source: Lubitsch's own
life. The anchor point is a small detail that surfaces when Matuschek
asks Kralik about "the little poem" he wrote in Mrs. Matuschek's
guest book. "Did you make that up yourself?" "It's . . . half Shakespeare and half me," Kralik replies modestly. If we have been paying
attention, we will recognize that Kralik's Shakespearean poem must
be a "sonnet." What we will probably not recognize is that "Sonnet"
is the surname of Lubitsch's first wife and that "Kralik" is a variant of
"Kraly," the surname of Lubitsch's first writing partner.[18] And therein
lies a tale.

For seventeen years, Hans Kraly was Ernst Lubitsch's closest pro-
fessional colleague. Kraly co-wrote virtually all of Lubitsch's German
silents and earned credits on seven of the eleven Hollywood films that
Lubitsch directed from 1923 through 1929. They were very close.[19]
Kraly was a frequent houseguest, playing tennis with Lubitsch's wife
Leni, née Sonnet, a widow with two young sons. (When he married
Leni in 1922, Lubitsch took her to his favorite place in the world,
Budapest, where they honeymooned to Gypsy violins, music he
adored.)[20] Then, in May 1930, Lubitsch discovered that there was
more going on between Kraly and Leni than a shared interest in out-
door sports. Lubitsch left home in a rage and obtained a quick inter-
locutory decree, but he remained obsessed. He began to stalk Kraly
and Leni, unable to forgive, unable to let go. On October 4, 1930, at
Hollywood's Embassy Ball, Lubitsch spotted Kraly, who was very tall,
dancing with Leni in a manner that seemed to mock his own short
stature. "They mimic me when I dance. They laugh at me."[21] Lubitsch grabbed Kraly and slapped him. Leni slapped Lubitsch. Friends
hauled Lubitsch away, but not before the press got wind of the brawl.[22]
For Lubitsch, who was very Germanic when it came to matters of
emotional display, the compound loss was devastating—the loss of his
wife, his family, his partner, and, not least, the loss of his self-control.
He was still brooding about it a year later.[23] By the time Leni remar-
ried (not to Kraly) in 1932, however, Lubitsch had closed the door and
locked it. He never again spoke to either Leni or Kraly. He ended all
contact with his beloved stepsons. His marriage and the appalling way
it had ended became unspeakable subjects. He did not, could not, talk
about them.[24]

Except in his films. The structured process of adaptation—the secure framework of the "base play" (in this case, *Parfumerie*)—freed the hyper-controlled Lubitsch to "act out" emotional states that he could not express directly. He did his acting out quite literally. As he and Raphaelson talked their way through a script, Lubitsch played all the parts, leaping about the room.[25] On the set, Lubitsch showed each actor exactly what to do, even the ingénue.[26] Once the shooting began, Lubitsch would lose himself in the scene, leaning forward in his director's chair "with his face expressing the same emotions as the actors."[27] In short, Lubitsch didn't simply direct his films; he *inhabited* them.

In transforming *Parfumerie* into *Shop*—which he shot in sequence— Lubitsch is acting out a private *Christmas Carol*, giving himself what Dickens gives Scrooge: a second chance. The appearance of his "ghosts" allows Scrooge to feel the love, and the loss, that he has locked away in his strongbox. And feeling releases him from a living death. For Lubitsch, the release comes from restructuration. In *Parfumerie*, the Hammerschmidt plot and the postal lovers plot play out separately, linked only by a "misunderstanding." There is no big clinch and no big loss. Hammerschmidt simply forgives his wife's adultery and goes home to Christmas dinner. In assembling *Shop* from the shards of László's text, Lubitsch simultaneously restores the loss— and erases it. He transforms the two love stories into reverse mirror images of each other, positioned back to back in time. Mr. and Mrs. Matuschek begin with love (twenty-two years ago) and move toward anger and estrangement. Kralik and Klara begin with anger and estrangement and move toward love. In his thwarted suicide attempt, Mr. Matuschek "puts out the light," metaphorically blinding himself for having been so blind. Kralik puts out the lights in the shop at the end of the film because a touch in the dark is all he desires. Thus the Klara/Kralik love story ends where the Matuscheks' (and the Lubitschs') love story began: with a honeymoon in Budapest.

Did Lubitsch intend to put himself into his film, as a kind of living intertext? Yes and no, I think. In adaptation studies, we need to distinguish intention-as-desire ("I want to do this rather than that . . .") from intention-as-analysis ("I want to do this *because* . . ."). The obsessional desire to do it *this* way drives all great filmmakers, including Lubitsch; but that drive is part of an intuitive creative process that operates largely outside of awareness. As Billy Wilder observed, "If I become analytical . . . I would only produce a dead thing."[28] When the writers of *Summertime* change László's "Horvath" to "Larkin," they intend to do so *because* they are Americanizing the text so it will play better. When Lubitsch changes "Horvath" to "Kralik," he intends to do so, but there is no obvious "because" at work. "Kralik" doesn't play any better in Dubuque than "Horvath" does. Lubitsch simply *wants* the name. Is he *aware* that "Kralik" is one consonant away from "Krali" (Kraly) or that he has made a joke about a "sonnet" or that **L**(ubitsch) is the missing "letter" between **K**(ralik) and **M**(atuschek)? Probably not. He does not need to be. All he needs to do is to put the dots in the right places, and the picture draws itself when he is not looking.

Lubitsch's silent films are full of such rebus-like pictures. In *Die Puppe* (1919), e.g., a paper heart falls out of a frightened man's trouser leg, literalizing the German idiom for "scared to death" ("Ihm fällt das Herz in die Hose"). In *Die Bergkatze* (1921), a grieving man literally "cries a river," a gusher of tears that cuts a channel in a mountainside. In both examples, Lubitsch transforms a verbal phrase into body language that acts out a feeling. When Lubitsch writes in 1925 that "Motion pictures are essentially words translated into human action," he means it quite literally.[29] This projective visualization of emotion goes underground as Lubitsch adapts his style to Hollywood sound-era norms, but it never entirely disappears. In *Shop*, camouflaged by the realistic *mise-en-scène*, actions still "speak."

In *Parfumerie*, big emotions come in big speeches. In *Shop*, emotion comes in little hand moves—one hand move in particular. Klara believes she has been deserted by her postal lover. In an equivalent moment in *Parfumerie*, László has Balash tell us about her pain. In *Shop*, Lubitsch *shows* us pain, using a shot from inside the box. We are suddenly in the back room of a post office. The camera dollies in rapidly on Box 237, its back side open, a move that makes us voyeurs. The little door at the far end of the box opens. A gloved hand reaches into the empty space, probing. It carefully strokes the sides of the box, then "slumps." Klara looks into the box, her eye and part of her mask-like face visible in the open door. Her eye closes. In the public world of the shop, she is resilient, well-defended; but here we see her backstage, without her makeup and her lines. Lubitsch holds on that image of vulnerability for a beat. Then the door closes, and the little scene is over. The nominal *big* scene in the film takes place later, in a psychiatric ward, where Matuschek, literally "driven mad" by jealousy, apologizes to Kralik. It takes up nearly three minutes of screen time and has forty-two lines of dialog, much of it drawn directly from *Parfumerie*; but there is little real emotion. Matuschek simply tells us what he once felt. It is all talk. In contrast, the Box 237 scene, which lasts barely twenty-six seconds and has no dialogue, is all emotion. The camera's lunge toward the open box is like a blow to the heart. We feel what Klara feels as she feels it: the "emptiness inside" has been "translated into human action."

The empty postal box is a pivot point for Klara, just as the detective's report is a pivot point for Matuschek earlier. Looking inside his marriage and finding empty space, the controlling Matuschek loses control, shattering like the light fixture on his office ceiling. The light does not go out, but Matuschek does, essentially disappearing from the film. When he returns much later, he is a Ghost of Christmas Past, looking through the shop window from the outside. Inside, Kralik has replaced him. Lubitsch/Raphaelson set up this replacement from the very beginning, quietly establishing Matuschek and Kralik as age-asymmetric doppelgangers. When Kralik first appears, he touches his stomach and sends the errand boy, Pepi, for some bicarb. He dined with the Matuscheks the night before and had "a little too much goose liver," Kralik explains. When Matuschek arrives a few frames later, he touches his stomach in the exact same way and sends Pepi for some bicarb. Later, when Kralik confronts Klara, he speaks *for* Matuschek, virtually impersonating him. Kralik's blindness in these moments mirrors Matuschek's blindness. In the second half of the film, the equation of Matuschek and Kralik is explicit. Kralik now has the key to the shop door; he inhabits Matuschek's office; he runs things. "I'm Mr. Matuschek," Kralik tells Klara. She faints "dead away," as if she had seen a ghost.

Kralik *is* Matuschek's ghost, a younger edition who serves a curative function similar to Dickens' ghosts. The transition between the twin narratives—Matuschek moving away from love, Kralik moving toward it—is marked by the gunshot. Lubitsch cuts from the shattered light in Matuschek's office to Kralik in the darkness, walking toward the light of the café. A man who prides himself on seeing clearly, Kralik has missed everything that is important, even the color of Klara's blouse. And he misses everything now when he looks through the window and sees Klara and *Anna Karenina* at the table. Disgusted, he leaves, abandoning them. . . . Then he comes back. We see him before Klara does, his face framed in the glass pane. He is giving himself a second look. He is giving "Mr. Matuschek" a second chance.

Klara gives Mrs. Matuschek a second chance—or rather, gives *us* a chance to reconsider our view of her. "[Mrs. Matuschek] is . . . almost the most important character in the picture," Lubitsch insisted.[30] And yet, like the proprietor's wife in *Parfumerie*, she never appears. For László, this choice is pragmatic: he has too many characters on the stage already. For Lubitsch/Raphaelson, the wife's absence is strategic; they use it to draw us into a circle of unreliable narration. The game starts with the goose liver. Vadas suggests that Mrs. M is a "bad" cook, but Vadas is untrustworthy. Perhaps Kralik and Matuschek have eaten too much of a *good* thing. This is not a trivial issue. Whether Mrs. M

The Shop Around the Corner (1940). Directed by Ernst Lubitsch. Shown from left: James Stewart (as Alfred Kralik), Margaret Sullavan (as Klara Novak). Courtesy of MGM/Photofest © MGM.

is "good" or "bad" is at the heart of the film. Over and over again, Lubitsch/Raphaelson lure us into judging Mrs. M based on second-hand reports of her behavior, tempting us to condemn her without ever knowing her. We buy into Pepi's mocking impersonations of her, denying her even the minimal humanity we grant to the foolish Mr. Vadas. Pepi—a teller of tales with an axe to grind—is even less reliable than Vadas, however. The judgments that Matuschek, Kralik, and Klara make about each other are false, based on inadequate knowledge. Perhaps our condemnation of Mrs. M is fallible, too. She is a foolish woman—because Vadas is a foolish man—but perhaps no more foolish than the fat lady who is seduced into buying the empty music box because she is starved for a little candy.

In *Parfumerie*, the foolish wife is simply "Mrs. Hammerschmidt"; in *Shop*, however, Mrs. Matuschek is also called "Emma," a name that tells a story. It is *that* story that Klara carries with her to the Café Nizza. "Emma M" is the text within the intertext. *Anna Karenina* "contains" her, the way Klara's book contains the red carnation or Box 237 contains a letter to an unknown woman. When Kralik and Klara sit back to back in the café bickering, they throw intertexts at each other—intertexts that share the theme of "crime and punishment." "Have you read Zola's *Madame Bovary?*" Kralik asks. "*Madame Bovary* is *not* by Zola," Klara replies tartly. Kralik's "mistake" dares us to see something the film does and does not want us to see: that Emma Matuschek is poor dumb adulterous Emma Bovary, a woman more sinned against than sinning.[31] And that Klara has taken her place in this poignant fable of second chances.

Both remakes retain the *Shop* café dialogue and business virtually verbatim . . . except for three apparently minor changes: the name of the book that the ingénue carries, the species of the flower within the book, and the Gypsy orchestra that plays "Dark Eyes" in the background. Unfortunately, these little changes change everything. László alludes to *War and Peace* simply to poke fun at Horvath's literary pretensions. When Lubitsch/Raphaelson swap Tolstoy novels and add Flaubert, they are doing more than merely alluding, however. They are assembling a readymade, an expressive subtext. The flower is part of that assemblage. It not only points to the intertext; it *is* an intertext. As the waiter in the Café Nizza points out, the Language of Flowers is a semiotic system. ("About three months ago, we had a very sad case with gardenias. . . .") In *Shop*, the flower and the book and the song ("Dark Eyes") work in synch, each changing the sign of the other. Together, they mark a place of desire that it also a place of loss. In *Summertime*, when Judy Garland carries a pink rose ("a woman's love") inside a book of Elizabeth Barrett Browning's poems instead of a red carnation ("my heart aches") inside *Anna Karenina*, those interconnections break, and *Shop*'s elaborate underwater engineering collapses and disappears.

In adapting *Shop* as *Mail*, Ephron makes more interesting choices initially. Her "Final White Script" riffs on Emma Bovary's "*coup de foudre*" and alludes playfully to *Anna Karenina* as well.[32] That is, *Mail* "reads" *Shop*, its structure and its intertexts. Unfortunately, Ephron later subjects her script to a Disney makeover that leaves Anna Karenina and Emma Bovary on the cutting room floor. Like Kralik and Klara, Ephron's "Joe Fox" (Tom Hanks) and "Kathleen Kelly" (Meg Ryan) still live intertextual lives; (two bookstore owners, they talk a lot about their product); but because Ephron is now using different intertexts than Lubitsch, the subtext generated by the Kelly–Fox conversation is very different from the *Shop* subtext, even when the dialogue and business are virtually identical. By replacing *Anna Karenina* with *Pride and Prejudice*, Ephron has erased adulterous crime and punishment as a central theme and substituted a Hollywood version of *Sleeping Beauty*. Joe Fox, whose signature intertext is Coppola's *The*

Godfather, is positioned as Kathleen's fairy godfather/Prince Charming, come to awaken her from excessive mourning for her mother and normalize her spinster sexuality.

In the first half of *Shop*, the spinster in the text is Kralik, a man who is afraid to "open the envelope." (He cannot hear the music in the music box.) In the second half of the film, however, Kralik and Klara switch positions, as the narrative moves toward an apparently normalizing clinch. The shift begins when Kralik takes a second look at Klara through the café window. A curtain splits the frame horizontally, shielding him, exposing her. She is the Object of his Gaze. At the end of the scene, Klara attacks Kralik, comparing him to various empty containers (a handbag, a suitcase). The Gypsy violins mirror the metaphor by launching into "Ochi Tchornya." Klara and Kralik almost get the joke; then another round of insults begins, culminating in Kralik calling her "an old maid." At the moment he says "old maid," Kralik ceases to be an old maid. He has been wounded, and pain brings him to life.

So does bondage. In the first half of *Shop*, Kralik commits a crime against Klara, analogous to Matuschek's crime against him (and our crime against Emma): he judges her without knowing her. He has failed to see her green blouse with the yellow dots correctly. In the second half of film, Kralik is appropriately punished, through his eyes, by being put into Sisyphus-like constraint. He can see Klara, but he cannot touch her. Like Molnar's Actor in *The Guardsman*—another silent intertext—Kralik has become trapped in his disguise. His "Guardsman's Dilemma" becomes apparent when Kralik visits Klara who, literally "sick at heart," has taken to her bed. As her postal lover ("Dear Friend"), he has rhetorically seduced her. She loves his mind. Now he wants her to love his body as well, but he cannot get out of the envelope. Then, just when the situation seems hopeless, Kralik makes the first of two Houdini-like escape moves. Significantly, he uses the same adaptation strategy that Lubitsch/Raphaelson have used to assemble the film: that is, he transforms one metaphoric object into another. The sequence begins when Klara, resurrected by a new letter, decides to buy an "Ochi Tchornya" box for her Dear Friend as a Christmas present. Kralik tries to talk her into buying a wallet instead: A wallet is practical. An empty box is impractical. For Klara, however, the box is full, of "romance." In order to win his point, thus Kralik must use legerdemain (not patter), selling Klara the wallet the way she sold the fat woman the music box, by filling it up with desire: "A wallet is quite romantic," he tells her. "On one side he has your last letter, on the other side, a picture of you. When he opens it, there you are. And that's all the music he wants." Magically, Kralik has fused the two containers (the wallet and the music box), a move that anticipates the Big Clinch to come. "Why, Mr. Kralik, you surprise me," says Klara, as if seeing him for the first time.

It is not enough to transform the wallet, however. To get the girl, Kralik has to transform *himself.* For Klara, "Kralik" and "Dear Friend" are villain and hero in a Romance she has created to fill up the empty places in her heart. ("Where you would say 'black,' he would say 'white.' ") In order to win her, Kralik needs to adapt Klara's text, reversing its black/white polarity, as Klara reversed his misperception of her green/yellow blouse. This process begins when Kralik opens a box, thus revising the moment earlier in the film when he closed the "Ochi Tchornya" box. In effect, Kralik (and through him, Lubitsch) is rewriting the past.

Lubitsch takes us to a closed space we have not seen before, the shop's locker room—the innermost box in the film's nest of boxes. Klara is inside, closing up a box that contains the wallet (itself, a container) and wrapping it in tissue paper and string. Kralik enters. "Want to see something?" (Here comes the final prop.) He takes a jewelry box out of his pocket, removes the tissue paper, opens it, and shows its contents to her, a lovely necklace. The original script italicizes the metaphoric nature of Kralik's gesture by specifying the necklace as a "locket," i.e., a hard, closed metal case that contains, and conceals, a tender sentiment. Kralik is that "hard case" and that concealed heart. In putting the locket around Klara's neck, next to her breast, he gives himself to her . . . but without touching her or being touched himself. And therein lies his conundrum. He can be protected or he can be loved, but he can't be both at the same time.

Kralik tries to have it both ways—that is, to take off his disguise without leaving himself naked. He does this by rewriting the script. "Dear Friend" suddenly acquires a name: "Popkin." Klara reacts as if she has been poleaxed. "Popkin?" Less than a half minute ago, she was ecstatic about getting engaged; now she is repelled. What is going on? The writers of *Summertime* recognize the problem and substitute "Newspickle," a silly-sounding name that explains Garland's reaction. Klara's reaction is unexplainable, except by anti-Semitism.[33] That is, Kralik's reverse make-over transforms Klara's Prince Charming into a frog by transforming him into a Jew. A fat, money-grubbing Jew, in fact. Using Lubitsch's own indirect style of narration—planting clues that set up inferences—Kralik pretends to have met "Popkin," portraying him as old, unattractive, and mercenary. As he talks, Kralik moves through the showroom, turning off the lights one by one. "Well, anyway, he has a fine mind," says Klara, desperately quoting from one of "Popkin's" letters: " 'True love is to be two, and yet one.'" Kralik joins her, completing the quote from memory ("A man and a woman blended as angels"). In *Parfumerie*, Balash reveals her identity by quoting a literary allusion from one of her postal lover's letters—an allusion that Horvath recognizes as his own. There is a crucial difference here, however. In *Parfumerie* intertextual allusion discloses identity, erasing the double. In *Shop*, the allusion creates a new double. "Popkin" and "Kralik" *are* one, and Kralik's recitation should disclose their equivalence; but Klara misses the point, focusing instead on Kralik's revelation that Popkin stole the line from "Hugo." In other words, "three are one": *Popkin, Kralik*, and *Hugo* are versions of the same person, connected by an intertext whose subject is interconnection. Moreover, "Hugo" itself is an intertext. It points outside *Shop* to Victor Hugo, but it also points inside to Hugo Matuschek. "Hugo" is a first name as well as a surname. ("Two are one.")

So, who's the thief? (Or maybe at this point, "Who's on first?") Popkin stole something (a "two-for-one") from the proprietor of the shop. In his ethnic guise, however, Popkin (the fat Jew) *is* the proprietor of *The Shop* (Lubitsch). Now Kralik is stealing a two-for-one from Popkin: Klara/Emma. (He is also stealing Popkin from Klara.) "Oh, and I thought he was so perfect," Klara says, already speaking in the past tense. She has been madly in love since the beginning of the picture; now, after only twenty-four lines of dialogue, she is going to dump the fat Jew and run off with this tall, handsome Aryan. But the Aryan Kralik *is* the Jew Popkin. They are both stealing from the proprietor of The Shop; but since everybody is everybody else, *there is no loss*. Scrooge does not lie under a neglected tombstone in a desolate cemetery, and Tiny Tim never died. As Kralik removes his Popkin disguise, the fat Jew simply puts on his inner goy, translating himself into someone who looks an awful lot like Jimmy Stewart. (The frog "était un prince" after all.) [34]

Klara still doesn't get it. Self-protectively blind, she is in the dark (literally), afraid to open the box, lest she find it empty. Averting her eyes, she heads for the door, clutching the tightly wrapped wallet. Kralik stops her, taking her in his arms. For the first time, he speaks his feelings directly, albeit still clutching his sexual metaphors. "I can't stand it any longer. Take your key and open post office Box 237, and take me out of my envelope and kiss me!" Lubitsch cuts to a close-up of Klara's face, her eyes wide open. The words in the Hugo quote meant nothing to her; but these embodied words (the box, the envelope) are a revelation. They disclose authentic emotional knowledge. Kralik has got her number.

If Lubitsch were playing by Hollywood rules, Stewart would pull Sullavan down into the Big Clinch right here; but he doesn't. Instead,

Lubitsch postpones his climax until he can get the girl back on top—his favorite position, cinematically speaking. Kralik has been doing all the talking; now suddenly it is Klara's turn. She remembers how she brutalized him in the café, calling him bowlegged. It looks as if she is going to apologize for having misjudged him; instead, she demands that he pull up his pants so she can *see* his body! Lubitsch cuts to an insert shot as Kralik meekly exposes his bare flesh. She inspects him, taking her time about it. Finally, she throws her arms around him and pulls *him* down into the kiss that ends the picture.

Samson Raphaelson was always embarrassed by the bow legged shtick at the end of *Shop*, regarding it as "absurd"; and he is right, of course.[35] In Hollywood, bow legged men don't get the girl. Fat Jews like Popkin don't get her either. Guys with goyishe names and bodies like Jimmy Stewart get the girl. Except in *this* fairy tale. As anybody knows who has seen him in Lederhosen in *Meyer Aus Berlin*, the proprietor of *The Shop Around the Corner* was bow legged. And *that* is why Stewart has to pull up his pants, so that Lubitsch can elbow the tall Goy out of the way and get into position for the big finish. The victory is ambiguous, of course. (The legs we see are *not* bowlegged.) And the happy ending is provisional as well. If Klara is a young version of Emma, then Mrs. Matuschek is what Klara will become, just as Mr. Matuschek is what Kralik will become. But in this heart-wrenching fable of imaginary second chances, the narrative line moves against the current, into the past, obliterating the Ghost of Christmas Yet to Come. In the end, the pathetic, greedy Mrs. M is re-embodied as a passionate young girl, and the lonely, hungry Mr. M becomes once more an eager young man, trembling with naked desire, as he opens himself to the woman he adores. There is a honeymoon coming, in Budapest.

Coda

"Every text, and every adaptation, 'points' in many directions, back, forward, and sideways," Robert Stam has observed.[36] In this essay, I have barely begun to map the labyrinth of forking paths that passes as *Shop Around the Corner*, a film that, by most accounts, is merely a *gemütlich* little Christmas movie. In addition to *Parfumerie*, *Shop* is promiscuously related to at least seventeen other texts and paratexts, each of which has also "slept around." This hidden complexity illustrates again that intertextuality is unbounded—an inconvenient truth that wreaks havoc with traditional source versus copy approaches to adaptation. Ironically, the postmodern dynamiting of textual borders has thrown "criticism" (including adaptation studies) back on its origins in "appreciation"; and it is in that spirit that I have approached *Shop* in "Talking Pictures," recognizing that the film is easy to love but "impossible to parse."[37] That is, my analysis is a "readymade." I have *assembled* the artifact I describe in "Talking Pictures," working in much the same manner as Lubitsch/Raphaelson, choosing attractive *objets trouvées* from among the vast array in the textual field. In this meta-adaptive process, I have been less interested in "meanings" than in capturing the film's distinctive connective patterns, its open/closed body rhythms, its *music.* As Cutchins and Albrecht-Crane stress in their introduction to this volume, if adaptation studies is to take a new direction, it needs a new discourse, grounded in a recognition of difference. We approach that goal when we move away from a concern about what films say and toward a heightened awareness of distinctively cinematic paralanguage, synesthesia, and metaphorical embodiment. In it only through the language of the body that we can begin to understand a visceral/visual artist such as Lubitsch and to hear the textual music in the Ochi Tchornya box. "Music was really organic to him. . . . [an] extension of his soul," Nicola Lubitsch has said of her father.[38] The labyrinthine interconnectivity of *Shop* flows from that soulfulness. It acts out what Flaubert means when he writes, in *Madame Bovary*, that: "language is like a cracked kettle on which we beat out tunes for bears to dance to, when what we long to do is make music that will move the stars to pity."[39]

NOTES

1. In addition to the twenty-seven Hollywood feature films he directed, Lubitsch also contributed segments to *Paramount on Parade* (1930) and *If I Had a Million* (1932). *That Lady in Ermine*, the film Lubitsch was working on at his death, was essentially directed by Otto Preminger, although Lubitsch received posthumous credit for it. Lubitsch is sometimes incorrectly credited as the director of *A Royal Scandal* (1945), a remake of his silent *Forbidden Paradise*, and he did work on the preproduction; however, after his heart attack, he was replaced by Preminger as director.

2. Kamilla Elliott, *Rethinking the Novel/Film Debate* (Cambridge: Cambridge University Press, 2003), 2, 124–25.

3. Ibid., 83.

4. Robert Stam, "Introduction: The Theory and Practice of Adaptation," in *Literature and Film: A Guide to the Theory and Practice of Film Adaptation*, ed. Robert Stam and Alessandra Raengo (Malden, MA: Blackwell, 2005), 35.

5. Leo Braudy, "The Double Detachment of Ernst Lubitsch," *MLN* 98, no. 5 (December 1983): 1078.

6. Miklós László, *Parfumerie: A Comedy in Three Acts* [Typescript with penciled annotations by Samson Raphaelson], Samson Raphaelson Collection, Box 20, (New York: Columbia University Rare Book and Manuscript Library). *Shop Around the Cor-*

ner, DVD, directed by Ernst Lubitsch (1940; Burbank, CA: Warner Home Video, 2002).

7. James Harvey, *Romantic Comedy in Hollywood, from Lubitsch to Sturges* (New York: Knopf, 1987), 396.

8. Samson Raphaelson, *Three Screen Comedies by Samson Raphaelson* (Madison: University of Wisconsin Press, 1983), 269. Although Lubitsch never took a writing credit, Raphaelson stresses that he and Lubitsch worked as a team: "We wrote it together, that's all. You couldn't trace it," he told Barry Sabath. Barry Sabath, *Ernst Lubitsch and Samson Raphaelson: A Study in Collaboration* (Ph.d. diss., New York University, 1979), 89.

9. William Paul, *Ernst Lubitsch's American Comedy* (New York: Columbia University Press, 1983), 169.

10. WWII began while Lubitsch was shooting *Shop*. By the time *Shop* was released, Budapest was part of the Third Reich.

11. Sabath, *Ernst Lubitsch*, 177.

12. Raphaelson uses "our" and "we" when he talks about the *Shop* script. I honor this practice by creating a composite auteur.

13. See Thomas Leitch, "Everything You Always Wanted to Know about Adaptation Especially if you're looking forwards rather than back," *Literature/Film Quarterly* 33, no. 3 (2005): 239.

14. László's battling lovers are a working class version of Shakespeare's Beatrice and Benedick.

15. Only the Broadway musical adaptation, *She Loves Me* (1963), retains the Kadar + Ritter subplot.

16. Sabine Hake, *Passions and Deceptions: The Early Films of Ernst Lubitsch* (Princeton: Princeton University Press, 1992), 74–75.

17. In *Parfumerie*, Horvath doesn't learn that Balash is his postal lover until Act II; however, László telegraphs the game early on.

18. "There are many variants of the name [including] . . . KIRALY . . . and KRALIK" <http://www.4crests.com/krall-coat-of-arms.html>

19. Scott Eyman, *Ernst Lubitsch: Laughter in Paradise* (1993; repr., Baltimore: Johns Hopkins University Press, 2000), 118–21.

20. Ibid., 83–84.

21. Ibid., 163.

22. Ibid., 162–63.

23. Ibid., 167.

24. Ibid., 165.

25. Sabath, *Ernst Lubitsch*, 89; Eyman, *Ernst Lubitsch*, 178.

26. Kristin Thompson, *Herr Lubitsch Goes to Hollywood: German and American Film After World War I* (Amsterdam: Amsterdam University Press, 2005), 97, 99, 102; Eyman, *Ernst Lubitsch*, 78, 102, 119, 122, 252, 285, 296; Harvey, *Romantic Comedy*, 369, 481; Neil D. Isaacs, "Lubitsch and the Filmed-Play Syndrome," *Literature/Film Quarterly* 3, no. 4 (1975): 307.

27. Eyman, *Ernst Lubitsch*, 78, 128.

28. Michel Ciment, "Apropos Avanti!" in *Billy Wilder Interviews*, ed. Robert Horton (Jackson: University Press of Mississippi, 2001), 71.

29. Charles Musser, "The Hidden and the Unspeakable: On Theatrical Culture, Oscar Wilde, and Ernst Lubitsch's *Lady Windermere's Fan*," *Film Studies* 12, no. 4 (Summer 2004): 15.

30. Sabath, *Ernst Lubitsch*, 203.

31. The literary allusions in *Shop* might seem to suggest the bookish Raphaelson

as their author, but this is not necessarily so. Lubitsch knew Shakespeare from his work with Reinhardt, and all the other allusions were available to Lubitsch through film adaptations. For example, he undoubtedly screened Garbo's two *Anna Karenina* films before he directed her for the first time in *Ninotschka*. A German version of *Madame Bovary* was released in the United States in 1937 starring Lubitsch's old screen partner, Pola Negri. Dickens's *A Christmas Carol* hit the theatres in 1938 while Lubitsch and Raphaelson were working on the *Shop* script, etc.

32. Nora Ephron and Delia Ephron, *You've Got Mail* . . . "2nd Final White revised Feb. 2, 1998", *The Internet Script Movie Database*, http://www.imsdb.com/scripts/You've-Got-Mail.html.

33. Although there is probably no such thing as a "Jewish name," the ethnic allusion is implicit. "Popkin" is not a stereotypical Jewish surname such as "Goldberg." However, "Popkin" and its many variants ("Pupkin," "Popken") appear frequently in Jewish genealogical databases, and there are many Popkins/Pupkins in the Yad Yashem archive of Jewish holocaust martyrs (e.g., "Yitzkhak Popkin," "Shlomo Popkin," "Ester Popkin," "Golda Popkin), most of them from Poland and Belorussua, from whence the Lubitsch family came as well. See *Avotaynu: Consolidated Jewish Surname Index*. http://www.avotaynu.com/cis/csi-result.html?page = next. See also The Central Database of Shoah Victims' Names, "Yad Vashem, The Holocaust Martyrs' and Heroes' Remembrance Authority. http://www.yadvashem.org/wps/portal/IY_HON_Welcome.

34. "Lubitsch etait un prince" is the title of Francois Truffaut's 1968 *Cahiers du cinema* tribute.

35. Sabath, *Ernst Lubitsch*, 208; Samson Raphaelson, "Freundschaft: How it Was with Lubitsch and Me," in *Three Screen Comedies*, ed. Samson Raphaelson, 25. The insult in *Parfumerie* is "flat-footed." Raphaelson knew Lubitsch was bow legged ("Freundschaft" 25); but he didn't understand why Lubitsch wanted to end with the apparently unsexy "pants up" bit.

36. Stam, "Introduction," 27.

37. "Raphaelson at MOMA." Samson Raphaelson interviewed by Richard Corliss at a 1977 Museum of Modern Art screening of *Heaven Can Wait*. ("*Heaven Can Wait*, DVD, directed by Ernst Lubitsch [1943; The Criterion Collection, 2005].)

38. Nicola Lubitsch, "Introduction to Ernst Lubitsch: A Musical Collage," *Heaven Can Wait*, DVD.

39. ". . . la parole humaine est comme un chaudron fêlé où nous battons des mélodies à faire danser les ours, quand on voudrait attendrir les étoiles." Gustave Flaubert, *Madame Bovary: Moeurs de province* (Paris: Michel Lévy frères, 1857), 270–71.

Quiet, Music at Work:
The Soundtrack and Adaptation
Glenn Jellenik

I think we are starting to think in soundtracks.

—Alan Rudolph

My greatest frustration as a novelist is that books don't get to have soundtracks.

—Christopher Bram

In "TWELVE FALLACIES IN CONTEMPORARY ADAPTATION THEORY," Thomas Leitch leads with the fallacy that "There is such a thing as contemporary adaptation theory."[1] Thus, among all the counter-productive notions that the adaptation critic must negotiate (the fidelity principle, the high/low culture divide, etc.), Leitch's prime-mover fallacy is the existence of a theoretical underpinning for the field of adaptation studies itself. The problem, then, is not the amount of critical attention paid to the subject of adaptation but, rather, that "this flood of study of individual adaptations proceeds on the whole without the support of any more general theoretical account of what actually happens, or what ought to happen, when a group of filmmakers set out to adapt a literary text."[2] In short, we face a crisis of quantity over quality. And that over-arching theoretical shortcoming goes on to serve as the context for many of the specific fallacies that follow.

Interestingly, Leitch's assertion also scratches the surface of a stunting paradox within the field of adaptation studies at the moment. On the one hand, as "Twelve Fallacies" posits, the lack of a systematic foundation of theoretical guidelines hampers the field and keeps it from moving forward. Yet on the other, the most fundamental systematic assumption of adaptation studies, as we know it, may also be its most crippling with regard to its ability to move in new directions: the assumption that the practice of adaptation represents the creation of a set of texts with a traceable set of correlations. In other words, the commonly held notion that a film adaptation's primary concern and

source is the novel on which it is based presents a false flattening of
the film text.[3] According to Mireia Aragay, such criticism " 'impoveris-
hes the film's intertextuality' by reducing it to a 'single pre-text' (i.e.
the literary source) while ignoring other pre-texts and codes (cinematic, cultural) that contribute to making 'the filmic text intelligible.' "[4] As the field exists, the mere labeling of a film as an
adaptation—an act implied by any and every adaptation study—at
least potentially tethers the film text to that which it adapts. And that,
naturally, tends to tether the critic's analysis to the interplay between
the film and that "source"—to the concept of adaptation as a sort of
generic translation. The problem enters that equation with the fact
that adaptation-as-translation is not a one-size-fits-all formula. Simply
put, it would seem that not all adaptations endeavor to be translations.
And indeed, translation itself is neither a transparent nor simply de-
finable process.

Still, in the textual chaos of the poststructural reading world, it is
easy to see why such a solid, if over-simplified, formula would be attractive. If we are to believe Roland Barthes, we lack the linguistic capacity to write even an original sentence, let alone an original story.
For Barthes, any and every text represents a web of intertexts, "a
multi-dimensional space in which a variety of writings, none of them
original, blend and clash . . . a tissue of quotations drawn from innu-
merable centres of culture."[5] In contrast to that muddied textual landscape, the idea that a novel functions as a definitive original and a film
as its copy could be seen as a refreshing, if deceptive, bit of clarity.
Indeed, within the field, those adaptation studies that have the most
solid grounding in a theoretical system avoid poststructural muddying
and focus on developing a structuralist framework within which to understand the practice of adaptation, a primary example being Brian
McFarlane's *Novel to Film* (1996). But in our particular cultural moment the blurring lens of poststructuralism is too wide to escape.
Thus, when McFarlane attempts to negotiate the obstacle of fidelity—a notion that represents the extreme exaggeration of the urge
to flatten the film text into a one-to-one relationship with its
"source"—he relies on the same concept touched on by Aragay: intertextuality. For McFarlane, "The stress on fidelity to the original un-
dervalues other aspects of the film's intertextuality. By this, I mean
those non-literary, non-novelistic influences at work on any film,
whether or not it is based on a novel. To say that a film is based on a
novel is to draw attention to one—and for many people, a crucial—
element of its intertextuality, but it can never be the only one."[6] In
short, the traditional view of adaptation imposes a constricting one-
dimensionality on its readings.

This essay endeavors to focus on alternate intertextual sources and draw attention to the work of a non-literary, non-novelistic aspect that, to this point in adaptation studies, has remained largely in the margins of the field. It explores the work performed by the soundtrack in adaptation; more importantly, it sets forth that work *as* adaptation.[7] That is, in certain texts, the soundtrack functions as an adaptive *mise en abime*, an adaptation embedded within an adaptation. Indeed, if we look and listen closely to certain films, we can trace the collective musical choices forming a parallel text—one that performs independently, in that it has the capacity not simply to highlight or underscore the meanings constructed by the visual and verbal narrative, but to generate an intertextual discourse in ways that image and dialogue cannot. Further, in certain films, the soundtrack can be read as the richest adaptive text—a parallel text that produces constructive readings for adaptations that, on the surface, seem to add little substance to our overall discussion. Such films have been good, mainly, for presenting another opportunity for the high-fidelity crowd to scream "Butcher!" when a film's attempt to adapt a complex novel seems to fall flat.

On a microscopic scale, then, this essay inspects the uses and possibilities of musical tracks within adaptation. On a macroscopic scale, it highlights the complex and layered intertextual nature of film adaptation and suggests the potentially productive practice of de-centering the film's perceived surface engagement with the novel.[8]

Understandably, that direct surface engagement between novel and film lies at the center of the academic study of film adaptation. George Bluestone begins his seminal work, *Novels into Film* (1957), with the idea that there are two ways of seeing: "One may . . . see visually through the eye or imaginatively through the mind."[9] And that visual distinction provides the foundation of Bluestone's study: "between the percept of the visual image and the concept of the mental image lies the root difference between the [novel and film]."[10] Thus Bluestone begins his definition of film adaptation by establishing difference— that is, by saying what the adaptation is not. And more specifically, that definition through negation positions the film as relative to the novel. Subsequent generations of adaptation critics have cleaved to that formula—novels are verbal, films visual—and built their readings around it. However, critics have recently begun to productively query that Bluestonian notion. While the first of Leitch's "Twelve Fallacies" treats the lack of theoretical groundwork in the field, he reserves the title of "most enduring and pernicious" fallacy for Bluestone's formula: "It is obviously untrue, not because literary texts are not verbal, but because films are not strictly speaking visual. . . . Films since the coming of synchronized sound, and perhaps even before, have been audio-visual, not visual, depending as they do on soundtracks as well as image tracks for their effects."[11] Indeed, the shift from novel to film does not represent simply the move from word to image. It also creates an audience, in the true sense of that term. Film literally transports that audience from an internal world of silence to an external world of sound. As Michel Chion points out, "Films, television and other audio-visual media do not just address the eye. They place their spectators—their audio-spectators—in a specific mode of reception which . . . I shall refer to as *audio-vision*."[12]

However, no sooner does Chion coin the terms "audio-vision" and "audio-spectator" than he goes on to point out that this expanded concept of reception continues to be obscured by the concept that film is a strictly visual medium: "In continuing to say that we 'see' a film or television program, we persist in ignoring how the soundtrack has modified perception."[13] Beyond acknowledging our visual preference, Chion views ocular dependence as a wall that blocks the audio-spectator from fully accessing the capacity of that audio-visual mode of reception. Music theorist Claudia Gorbman also points out the interpretive lacuna created by our inability/unwillingness to hear films: "We need to start listening to the cinema's uses of music in order to read films in a literate way."[14] Here Gorbman's ironic use of the word "literate" hints simultaneously at a shortcoming and productive possibility for film studies. To treat a film like a novel, to merely read it, is not sufficient. Film literacy requires listening. Arthur Knight and Pamela Robertson Wojcik are even more explicit in their "Overture" to *Soundtrack Available: Essays on Film and Popular Culture* (2001): "Most writing on film music has not adequately described popular music's role in film or people's experience of it (in the theater or outside). We believe, nonetheless, that serious thinking about soundtracks—in their many varied manifestations—is crucial to our understanding of film and music."[15] And those errors of omission by the audio-spectator—that inability to hear the work of sound—has been reproduced by the adaptation critic. For in largely ignoring the soundtrack, adaptation studies misses an opportunity to inspect a huge intertextual aspect of the move from novel to film.

In "The Dialogics of Adaptation," Robert Stam places film adaptations within the context of Barthes's notions of intertextuality and then shifts that theory into a potential practice: "Film adaptations can be seen as a kind of multileveled negotiation of intertexts. Therefore it is often productive to ask these questions: Precisely what generic intertexts are invoked by the source novel, and which by the film adaptation?"[16] A look at the intertextual engagements of the 2001 film

Shrek, with a particular focus on the work performed by the sound-track, offers a revealing illustration of Stam's concept at work.

At its most basic level, the movie earns entrance to our conversation by virtue of the fact that it adapts William Steig's 1990 children's book of the same name.[17] However, I would argue that the film's relationship with Steig's text represents, perhaps, the least productive adaptive ground over which to travel. Although Steig's *Shrek!* presents roughly the same upside-down fairy tale setting and plot as the film, there is very little in the book that anticipates what the film will become. Indeed, the fact that Steig's purposely un-polished illustrations completely lack depth works as an interesting contrast to the characters and *mise-en-scène* "fleshed out" by the film's multi-dimensional animation. But while a study of the film as a one-to-one adaptation of the book folds into a relatively flat and limited conversation, an investigation of its other intertextual engagements opens out into new and potentially productive directions.

Among other things, *Shrek* literally thematizes the generic play between book (in this case, fairy tale) and film. In other words, that idea that we see at least tacitly at work in any book-to-film adaptation—the interactive relationship (and tension) between written source and filmed adaptation—functions on the surface of the film in a series of meta-moments.[18] And within that intertextual theme, we also find the adaptation of the fairy tale as a genre—a shift from classic to neo-fairy tale. The film also engages with classic literary texts, such as Chaucer's "Miller's Tale" and Shakespeare's *Richard III*, and film texts, such as *Raiders of the Lost Arc* and *Crouching Tiger, Hidden Dragon*. Beyond that, the film functions as an adaptation of twin issues of cultural homogenization: gentrification and disneyfication. And directly attached to its play with the theme of disneyfication within its content, the form of the film engages in an intertextual generic dialogue with the dominant children's film of that time: the Disney-style children's musical.

By looking at the intertext of *Shrek*'s soundtrack and its uses of music, I argue that we can see the film as a generic adaptation of a children's film—a shift out of the Disney children's musical and into something more in line with a millennial romantic comedy. And while more than music goes into the achievement of that shift, a close inspection reveals that the film's soundtrack does much of the heavy lifting.

Again, the idea here is that, more than simply *reflect* the adaptive process, the music of a film *affects* it, and at times acts as one of its prime engines. A close look at—and listen to—*Shrek* bears that out from the start. The film opens with a heavenly light shining out of a starry sky and down onto a rich leather-bound text perched on an altar. The book opens, and a generic medieval fairy tale appears on the pages. A Scotsman's voice (Mike Myers) reads the words aloud as the viewer sees them spelled out on the screen. Thus we begin with a classic filmic engagement with a written text. The book is fetishized as an object, and literal words hold our gaze. But then, amid that unfolding story, at the very point of Prince Charming's day-saving entrance, Myers pops out of the moment and severs the narrative thread by laughing and saying, "Yeah, right! Like that's ever going to happen." Suddenly a green warty hand covers the page of the book, crumples it and tears it out. A flushing sound suggests that the gilded leaf of the fairy tale has been used as toilet paper. And indeed, the jump cut to the next shot visually introduces the ogre Shrek, as he emerges from his outhouse with a page of the book stuck to the bottom of his shoe. He looks down, notices it, and with a kick, shakes it loose.[19]

Clearly, the film begins with a coded set of visual elements that signal a generic rupture between fairy tale and film. However, while *Shrek* opens with the images I have described, the first thing the "viewer" experiences is actually music. Prior to the appearance of the heavenly light, we hear a harp and flute gently playing "Fairytale," a score composed by Harry Gregson-Williams and John Powell. The music may be described as a classic fairy tale song—one instantly recognizable to the point of cliché.[20] Thus, when the "source text" enters our view, it is bathed by both heavenly light and recognizable music. And the two combine to place the viewer in perfectly familiar territory. Further, a sudden stop to that harp music, complete with the aural icon of a needle scratching a record, accompanies Myers's narrative rupture. And finally, when Shrek bursts from the outhouse and shakes the discarded bit of fairy tale from his shoe, he does so with a parallel outburst from the film's soundtrack: Smash Mouth's "All Star" (1999). Needless to say, the boisterous pop song offers a tangy contrast to the honeyed tones of the happily-ever-after harp.

But the opening's use of music goes deeper than mere tonal contrast. "All Star" goes on to play over a montage of Shrek going about his typical day. The song's chorus, "Only shooting stars break the mold," is repeated throughout various scenes of the ogre clearly and humorously breaking the mold of accepted hygiene and decorum as well as heroic behavior. Thus we can read the song's message as integrating with and developing the character of Shrek. Both soundtrack and cinematic montage, audio text and visual text, signal the arrival of a new breed of hero and a break with the past. In that regard, the character of Shrek functions to represent the film that bears his name. The fairy tale formula will be broken (or at least have its binaries flipped for awhile). Neither the audio track nor the montage works alone to develop the character; they work together.

Yet despite our ability to interpret the song as neatly applicable to and furthering the concerns of the film, it first appeared on Smash Mouth's *Astro Lounge* (1999). That is, the piece of music has a prior existence to its appearance in the film and it functions in certain ways as a signifier that has nothing to do with Shrek. Thus the film adapts the song, pulls it out of its original context and puts it to its own use. By looking closely at the two pieces of music that open in the film, we comprehend the general strategy of the film as a whole—a constant play of tension derived from the juxtapositional mingling of traditional fairy tale tropes with a millennial pop culture and ethos. Not only does the soundtrack serve as an accompaniment to the film as a whole, it also has the capacity to exist as an adapted text within an adapted text.

The film goes on to employ its soundtrack for very specific thematic, character-development and plot-development purposes. For example, Joan Jett's pop/punk anthem "Bad Reputation" provides the aural background for an early fight scene. On the surface, the song's driving beat and wild vocals integrate with the on-screen action. But the song works on the viewer/listener on other levels as well—namely generic subversion. Jett's lyrics—"I don't give a damn about my reputation / Livin' in the past, it's a new generation"—suggest both a hero and a film consciously toying with and flouting the conventions, tropes and expectations of the fairy tale and the children's movie. Such moments earned the film a PG rating. In the end, the film simultaneously employs and exploits the rebellion of punk rock. It taps into its discordant theme of subversion against the establishment, but at the same time, *Shrek* commodifies that rebellion in a good-humored children's film, thus ultimately flipping the dynamic and subverting the subversion. Not at all coincidentally, that is the exact move made by the film as a whole in the end. Thus the adaptive work of the previously recorded soundtrack parallels and even drives the adaptive work of the whole. In his essay, "Rock 'n' Roll Sound Tracks and the Production of Nostalgia," David Shumway traces the possible effect of pop music in certain films: "The music . . . is meant to be not merely recognized but often to take the foreground and displace the image as the principle locus of attention."[21]

That use of previously recorded music also marks a shift away from the accepted trend in children's films through the late twentieth century. Disney "instant classics" such as *The Lion King* (1994) and *Tarzan* (1999) commissioned rock musicians (Elton John and Phil Collins, respectively) to write and perform songs for their specific stories. The result was that one measure of a children's film became directly linked to the prestige and originality of its soundtrack. Between 1989 and 2001 (the year of *Shrek*'s release), eight animated children's films won the Academy Award for Best Original Song.[22] Further, *Shrek*'s recycling of established songs from a specific period—the 70s and 80s—functions as a signal of departure within the genre and also offers an opportunity to appeal to adult viewers. For Shumway, such music does double work: "[It] secures a bond between consumer and product while arousing a feeling of generational belonging in the audience."[23] In other words, the music solicits an investment from the viewer. With regard to *Shrek*, it attempts to insure that adults will engage with an animated film.

But the songs that are included in the soundtrack do not represent the movie's only use of music. Indeed, we can productively consider the significance of the music that is specifically excluded by the movie. That is, *Shrek* engages in a consistent frustration of the musical number, and thus in a conscious omission that signals its adaptive shift away from the Disney model.

At two moments when the formula children's film of its time would launch into a musical number—when the main character and side-kick meet, and when the quest begins—*Shrek* abruptly interrupts the musical urge. In both cases, Donkey (Eddie Murphy) fulfills his traditional role and begins to sing. In the case of the initial meeting, he launches into "You Gotta Have Friends"[24] only to have Shrek refuse to play along and yell menacingly, "Stop singing!" And as the same two characters set out in search of Lord Farquad, Donkey lapses back into song, this time, "On the Road Again." Again, Shrek interrupts: "What did I say about singing!?" Finally, in a moment that actualizes Shrek's threatened violence against the musical urge, Princess Fiona (Cameron Diaz) interrupts Monsieur Hood's song and Riverdance number with a flying dropkick to his head. Indeed, throughout the film, all push and pull towards the sort of diegetic music that typified the period's children's movie is blatantly frustrated and denied.[25]

While *Shrek* stubbornly and significantly refuses to behave like a Disney musical, its music plays a huge role in multiple facets of its adaptive project. Indeed, its soundtrack functions as such a vital intertext that the entire film might be considered a non-diegetic musical. Far beyond merely integrating with the visual text in the film's multi-leveled adaptive engagements, there are moments and situations in which the soundtrack drives and carries those adaptations, and the musical tracks become, as Shumway posited they might, the central locus of both attention and adaptation.

Still, in some ways, this exercise in listening to *Shrek* amounts to begging the question. That is, the text is so consciously concerned with adaptation and building meaning through intertextual play that it naturally reads well in those contexts. In no way does that diminish the work done by music in the text. However, it might open this essay to the charge of cherry-picking a text bound to provide a fruitful analysis. Moreover, that text can be seen to avoid many of the typical pitfalls of the typical adaptation. In other words, *Shrek* is a clever and thoughtful film that adapts a low-stakes text, and Steig's book is unlikely to be defended by fidelity critics.[26] Further, that book is a short children's story rather than a novel. Again, such points in no way affect the analysis of the soundtrack's adaptive capacity. But they do call into question my claim that the soundtrack can represent a parallel text capable of producing constructive readings for those adaptations that would seem to prove the fidelity-claim that film cannot successfully adapt a complex novel.[27]

With those objections in mind, I will turn to a case study of Paul Robeson's *Big Fella*,[28] a 1937 musical comedy that presents a "loose adaptation" of Claude McKay's 1929 novel *Banjo*. If *Shrek* represents a dubious case study here because it endeavors to be more than its "source," *Big Fella* is our "ideal" text, in that it treats a complex and nuanced meditation on race, identity and culture (among other things) in a seemingly over-simplified and frivolous way. Indeed, on the surface, *Big Fella*'s adaptation of *Banjo* moves beyond over-simplified and into the realm of offensive.[29] And, with our focus primarily on the ways in which the film's visual text translates the novel, it is easy to imagine (and hard to argue with) the fidelity-critic who stands and shouts, "Butcher!" Yet a listen to the adaptation offers the possibility of a different picture.

Before going any further, however, I must return to the concept, touched on earlier, that not all adaptations endeavor to be translations. Several lines ago, I referred to *Big Fella* as a "loose adaptation" of *Banjo*. The scare-quotes are a nod to the fact that it is a vague term. It would seem to signify the text's engagement with fidelity: "Loose" adaptations take liberties with a source rather than remain "faithful." But as Stam points out, a term such as "fidelity" is equally vague: "The question of fidelity ignores the wider question: Fidelity to what? . . . plot? . . . author's intentions? . . . the style of a work? . . . its narrative point of view? . . . its artistic devices?"[30] Unless we are willing to grant a novel an essential nature, a move that runs counter to prevailing literary values, the term "loose adaptation" is relatively meaningless.

And that realization points towards another obstacle facing the adaptation critic: the absurdly large and diverse community of texts covered by the blanket-term "adaptation." Consider, *Harry Potter and the Sorcerer's Stone* (2001) and *Psycho* (1960) are both adaptations of novels.

Orson Welles's *Macbeth* (1948), Akira Kurosowa's *Throne of Blood* (1957), and Billy Morissette's *Scotland, PA* (2001) are all adaptations of the same text. In the end, the amount of ground the term covers renders it almost meaningless. Yet we depend upon it for specific significance. Numerous studies have endeavored to classify adaptations into types.[31] But none of these systems has succeeded in parsing the term for the field. With that in mind, Brian McFarlane offers a logical warning: "unless the kind of adaptation is identified, critical evaluation may well be wide of the mark."[32] In other words, filmmakers use "source" texts for various reasons and employ various levels of engagement. To assume that the goals of all adaptations are the same is to risk gross critical misinterpretation.

Thus, I will begin by typing *Big Fella*. By almost all fidelity-criteria, the film does demand to be called a "loose adaptation." That is, in the end, it has made wholesale changes to McKay's plot, characters and structure and made very little effort to approximate any of the novel's concerns. McKay's *Banjo* follows a multi-national band of black drifters as they wind through the port city of Marseilles. Throughout its picaresque ramble (its subtitle is "A Story without a Plot"), the novel presents nuanced views of race, nationality, identity and culture.

The book's title refers to the name of the main character as well as the instrument he plays. And in the novel's head-on treatment of the issues of race, identity and culture that inhere to that name/instrument, the reader can see McKay's willingness to confront the complexities of those issues—to unfold them for inspection rather than neatly and insufficiently process them through a convenient series of clichés. When a fellow American ex-patriot, Goosey, hears Banjo's name and instrument, he responds: "No. Banjo is bondage. It's the instrument of slavery. Banjo is Dixie. The Dixie of the land of cotton and massa and missus and black mammy. We colored folks have to get away from all that in these enlightened progressive days. Let us play piano and violin, harp and flute. Let the white folks play the banjo if they want to keep on remembering all the Black Joes singing and the hell they made them live in."[33] Here Goosey, a self-declared "race man" (one concerned with equality for blacks), voices a series of common and reasonable objections to the stereotyped connotations of the banjo. On the surface, everything he says is true. Indeed, with Goosey's points in mind, the fact that Banjo's real first name is Lincoln heightens the racial implications.

But rather than negotiate the racial connotations of his name/instrument, Banjo's response shifts the discourse into the realm of identity: "That ain't got nothing to do with me, nigger. . . . I play that theah instrument becaz I likes it."[34] Thus he answers Goosey's pol-

ished constructions—"in these enlightened progressive times," and
"Let us play"—with the natural rhythm and phrasing of the specific
time and place of his upbringing (the American South)—"That ain't
got nothing to do with me" and "that theah instrument." Moreover,
he suggests that his own self-identity places him above or indeed outside such racial considerations. At the same time, Banjo gives no indication that he would sever his own past in order to distance himself
from past victims of racial oppression—a move that Goosey makes
when he refers to the Black Joes as "them."

And here we see McKay's illustration of the racial/cultural bind that
traps his characters. By choosing an instrument that evokes racial oppression, Banjo freely assumes and reproduces a set of hateful stereotypes. For his part, Goosey's effort to escape those oppressive
stereotypes makes his identity dependent on yet another (if opposite)
set of white expectations. In essence, Goosey's attempt to liberate his
identity from white-domination allows the white culture to once again
determine how he must behave and, in fact, who he is. Goosey is per-
petually contrary to what he perceived whites to be. Banjo, on the
other hand, is more self-actualizing, choosing to maintain the culture
and heritage of his identity, unsavory racial connotations and all. Both
approaches carry inherent benefits and sacrifices. Clearly the novel
struggles with the complexities of a serious debate on issues that faced
McKay's community in the 1920s.

And just as clearly, *Big Fella* avoids those issues. Despite the novel's
titular engagement with race and identity's many shades of gray,
Robeson insisted that the adaptation "change the film's title from
Banjo to *Big Fella* to 'avoid leading the audience to expect a sort of
"Uncle Sambo" of the cotton plantations.'"[35] Thus the film makes a
double move, away from not only racism, but also away from any ac-
tive engagement with concepts of race. Ironically, given Goosey's
comment about "Black Joes singing," Robeson's demand leads to Banjo's name becoming Joe, and the banjo is dropped in favor of his becoming a singer.

Further, while McKay's narrative drifts from place to place, much
like its deracinated characters, and resists the traditional plot arc, the
film eschews that free and loose structure. In its place it constructs
the flimsy marriage of an absurd detective plot and a clichéd marriage
plot—both of which function in service of a set of bourgeois ideals
that are utterly absent from the film's (complexly) socialist source. As
a result, in its translation to film, the social commentary novel morphs
into a comedic farce.

This perspective is true unless, of course, we decide not to view it
as a translation at all. Stam posits a view of adaptation in which it can

function as a "reading" of its source novel, pointing out, "A 'reading' can also be a critique . . . Adaptations, then, can take an activist stance towards their source novels, inserting them into a much broader intertextual dialogism. An adaptation, in this sense, is less an attempted resuscitation of an originary word than a turn in an ongoing dialogical process."[36] Extending that idea to *Big Fella*, it becomes possible to consider the adaptation as an attempt to engage McKay's novel in an ideological dialogue. But if we rely on the traditional measures of an adaptation—characters, plot, structure—*Big Fella* would seem on shaky ground as a critique-adaptation as well. For even without fidelity as a concern, the visual text doesn't fare well in engaging McKay's novel in a debate. While it amounts to a farce, its farcicality is not aimed at lampooning any of McKay's concepts. In the end, the visual text offers little engagement with its source. Worse, the seepage of its culture's latent racism into the film is now painfully obvious.

Yet an interesting possibility arises with a consideration of the film's genre. *Big Fella* is a musical. Indeed, the very fact that *Big Fella* employs the genre of the musical to adapt *Banjo* suggests that the music itself provides the richest ground for investigation. Chion views the musical genre as "decentering the system, creating imbalances and difficulties but also wonderful moments."[37] In foregrounding the musical numbers, the film pushes its story into the background. The insertion of diegetic music interrupts the flow of the film and reduces its realism. Yet the audience enters the theater aware of those interruptions, even expecting and anticipating them. Thus, in a way, the plot of the film becomes little more than a linking device for the musical numbers—a web of segues. And in that way, we can view those musical numbers as not so much decentering the system, but rather as replacing the plot as the central feature within the system of the film. The flimsy and implausible plot shifts to the background, and the film foregrounds music. At that point, narrative and music switch places and the plot becomes a device merely employed in order to make the musical numbers intelligible.

Thus, while *Shrek*'s insistence on a specific non-diegetic soundtrack functions to shift the film away from both the fairy tale and the Disney-style children's musical, *Big Fella*'s use of diegetic music actually imposes a new form *back* on *Banjo*. That is, it invites the reader to view McKay's novel as a musical. And while the shift from social protest novel to musical comedy may sound drastic, it is important to remember that *Banjo* is a novel that spends much of its time and energy putting the reader in the company of music, in addition to using that music to explore the text's major themes. Indeed, the little narrative thrust that does appear in the book owes itself to Banjo's desire to form a jazz band and perform at the bars and cafes in Marseilles's Ditch.[38] The novel also offers extended treatments of the music itself—long, jazz-like, poetic-prose descriptions of music and the effects of that music upon those who play it and those who hear it. In short, *Banjo* is a locus of music. Specifically, jazz. And as with the text in which it appears, McKay's jazz is fundamentally individual, and thus, fundamentally unstable. Viewed through the generic lens of the musical, the novel's wandering narrative can be seen as structured by and around music. Music provides a linking device for the novel's loose plot elements. And in the end, the book itself, subtitled *A Story Without a Plot*, can be read as a prose jazz arrangement.

And while *Big Fella* foregrounds music rather than uses it for subtle generic subversion, it links with *Shrek* as a film that consciously employs music as an adaptive lever. For *Big Fella* is also a locus of music. And its positioning of that music represents the film's most significant and productive adaptation. As mentioned earlier, the surface shift from novel to film offers little grist for critical discussion. However, contained within that adaptation is a parallel shift from McKay's treatment of jazz to the film's diegetic use and structural mimicking of popular music.[39] And when viewed through the lens of that specific generic adaptation, *Big Fella* provides an opportunity to explore a new intertextual direction.

This does not suggest that the film employs popular music in a way that is faithful to McKay's nuanced and complex uses of jazz. Just the opposite, in fact. Popular music—in particular, the musical number—functions in completely predictable ways in *Big Fella*. Rick Altman characterizes popular song as that which "depends on language, and is predictable, singable, rememberable."[40] So it is in *Big Fella*; song connects people, provides a sort of already-known collective back-beat that allows the film's population to come together in moments of strife, to remember themselves in moments of identity crisis, and to ground themselves in moments of drift. In all those ways, the film's popular music works in direct contradistinction to and conversation with the music of the novel. McKay's music-text produces complex questions; Robeson's, simple answers.

That said, the film's use of popular music itself is not simple. Rather, it represents a specific philosophical shift that is carried out with much more success and subtlety than the film's narrative and visual texts. With that in mind, I argue that an inspection of that musical shift yields the clearest and most cohesive philosophical blueprint for the adaptation project as a whole. Thus, in the concept of the soundtrack as an adaptive intertext, we find a space in which to listen to *Big*

Fella as a critique-adaptation of *Banjo* and as an attempt to engage its source in a dialogical process.

In *Big Fella*, we see a specific musical adaptation, a shift from the novel's jazz to the film's popular music. That shift parallels the film's adaptation of McKay's narrative. But whereas that narrative adaptation is clumsy and ineffective, the musical adaptation functions seamlessly as a method of selling/marketing a philosophy—that philosophy of collectivity, conformity and capitalism that belongs to the musical genre itself. In considering the use of popular music in recent films, Claudia Gorbman concludes, "Music belongs to a number of systems, an economy of desire. What is being marketed, to whom, and how successfully?"[41] And here we arrive at a central idea: the consideration of audience. On one hand, the film can be seen as mainstreaming McKay's marginal ideas in order to make itself marketable to a wider audience. But the shift can be seen to cut deeper as well. For music certainly participates in an economy of desire microcosmically within film. There, as will be shown shortly, the musical numbers function to stabilize and stimulate commodity markets, as well as to express and strengthen romantic attachments. And film itself can be seen to participate in a similar economy macrocosmically. That is, the shift from jazz to popular music shadows the mainstreaming of a novel as it becomes adapted into film.

We have no definitive answer as to why Paul Robeson chose to make a film based on a novel by Claude McKay. The two certainly did know one another, though nothing hints at a relationship or mutual admiration that might invite collaboration. Rather, biographers have noted a strong feeling of antipathy for McKay by Robeson's wife, Eslanda.[42] The question only becomes more confusing with the fact that the film uses the novel as an apparent jumping off point and then changes everything but the setting. Indeed, that adaptive approach suggests that the film itself considers as potentially more productive elements beyond the transcription of plot and the finding of filmic analogies for the novel's devices. Such a film demands that we look to other intertextual engagements if only to explain such odd treatment of the text that it adapts.

However, a return to Robeson's objection to the name of McKay's title character, Banjo, provides an interesting point of entry into the potential philosophy behind the film. Robeson worried that the name would get in the way of his ability to create a character believable as a contributing member of society. Robeson biographer Martin Duberman views the role as giving the actor an opportunity to portray "an ordinary but admirable black man, functioning well in a contemporary European setting."[43] That quote, taken along with Duberman's earlier quote regarding Robeson's insistence on changing the film's title, suggests that Robeson's philosophy (for the film, at least) falls far more in line with Goosey's "race-man" consciousness than with Banjo's individualism (both quoted earlier). Thus we see a sort of subtextual philosophical discourse arise between film and novel—one that parallels the Goosey/Banjo debate over the ways in which black men should participate in white hegemonic culture.[44] And the film adaptation's participation in that debate is given through its musical choices.

Read only through the lens of the novel-as-source, the discourse of *Big Fella*'s adaptation of *Banjo* seems more farcical than philosophical. However, a focus on the shift in musical genres allows us to see that, beneath the surface of its absurd farcical trappings, *Big Fella* does engage *Banjo* in what can be seen as a serious, coherent and important debate on racial identity and minority participation in hegemonic culture. The film offers a direct counterpoint to McKay's position.

The respective openings of the two texts point, through musical elements, to their general juxtaposition. In the novel, Banjo meets the band of misfits who will become his friends and introduces himself through his instrument: "Banjo caressed his [banjo]. 'I nevah part with this, buddy. It is moh than a gal, moh than a pal; it's mahself.'"[45] Here, and indeed throughout the novel, the banjo functions as a loaded phallus. Moreover, the end of that quote literally posits that phallic-symbol as Banjo's identity, thus creating a fundamentally sexually charged character at the head of a sexually charged text.

For its part, the film opens with Robeson's powerful baritone voice singing "Lazin'," and thus clearly replacing Banjo's banjo as the main instrument in the story. The loss of Banjo's ever-present phallus is compensated for, however, by the ultra-virility of Robeson's voice. Still, the sedate nature of that opening number belies the raw power of that voice. Robeson's Joe sits on a crate in a low relaxed posture. On either side of him, his friends sleep. And through the slow string arrangement, Joe goggles his eyes comically and sings a song whose refrain is, "Why get a move on / You can't improve on / Lazin'." Thus the film begins with an effort to play down those threatening aspects of black sexual presence that the novel's opening clearly flaunts. In *Big Fella*, the viewer is offered the flip-side of the black man's stereotype coin: on one side, the over-sexed walking phallus Banjo; on the other, the lazy, harmless, sleepy Joe.

But it is in their respective signature songs that the dialogic opposition of the music of the two texts becomes most evident. In the novel, Banjo's signature song, "Shake That Thing," is introduced within the conscious context of economics: "The magic thing had brought all shades and grades of Negroes together. Money. A Senegalese had em-

igrated to the United States, and after some years had returned with a
few thousand dollars. And he had bought a cafe on the quay. It was a
big cafe, the first that any Negro in the town ever owned."[46] Money
makes the Cafe African possible. And the possibility of money makes
the bar-owner hire Banjo's band to play. And play they do: "It was the
biggest evening ever at the Senegalese bar. [The band] played several
lively popular tunes, but the Senegalese boys yelled for 'Shake That
Thing.' Banjo picked it off and the [band] quickly got it. Then Banjo
keyed himself up and began playing in his own wild wonderful way."[47]
Thus the setting of and opportunity for music both rely on the capitalistic endeavor. And, initially, it works perfectly: "The magic had
brought them all together to shake that thing and drink red wine,
white wine, sweet wine. All the British West African blacks, Portu-
guese blacks, American blacks, all who had drifted into this port."[48]
Music unites a mass of diverse individuals into a single economy at the
bar. They come together; they dance together; they drink together.
Thus we see music function in its expected thematic capacity, as a sort
of *lingua franca* that liberates and tears down barriers. And in so doing,
it allows capitalism to hum along, as well.

But McKay's thematic use of music is complex. His jazz flies quickly
to another place: "Suddenly in the thick joy of it there was a roar and a
rush and sheering apart as a Senegalese leaped like a leopard bounding
through the jazzers, and, gripping an antagonist, butted him clean on
the forehead . . . The *patron* dashed from behind the bar. A babel of
different dialects broke forth. Policemen appeared and the musicians
slipped outside."[49] Thus we see jazz music begin with a capacity for
euphoric, boundary-hopping liberation. But its effect continues on
until it reaches a point of violent destabilization that disrupts all possibility of unity. Differences and inhibitions fall away. But with the inhibitions ultimately go the accepted laws of community, and violence
ensues. With that violence, difference immediately re-instates itself in
the form of chaos that utterly disrupts the business that Banjo's jazz
was hired to foster.

McKay's nuanced treatment and use of jazz finds a sharp contrast in
Big Fella's adaptive shift to popular music. The music of Joe's signature song, "Roll Up Sailorman," plays over the opening and closing
credits of the film, but the number that presents the song, lyrics and
all, appears after the kidnapping plot has been established. A rich
white boy has disappeared in the Ditch. The authorities deputize Joe
in order to find him. In service of that plot, Joe and his gang find
themselves at the cafe, owned by a character played by Eslanda Robeson, that serves as their regular hangout. Thus we see a setting—a
black-owned cafe—very similar to *Banjo*'s Cafe African. Moments ear-

lier, Joe has had a particularly slapstick run-in with his foil, Spike (Roy Emerton). The dispute spills over into this scene, and a (comical) brawl breaks out in the bar. The owner complains of the disruption to her business. And at that point, amid the fighting, Joe's girlfriend Manda (Elisabeth Welch) grabs him by the ear and pulls him to the center of the café. Manda calls to the brawling crowd, "Say boys, what do you want to hear?" The answer is unanimous: "Roll Up Sailor-man!" Following the unanimity of the request, all the patrons of the bar fall immediately under the sway of the song's anthemic rhythm. All memories of the brawl fade instantly, and the bar, moments ago a scene of mayhem, becomes a community united by song. The music literally structures the scene.[50]

Lyrically, "Roll Up Sailorman" tells the story of an anonymous sailor who comes to shore in Marseilles, his pocket full of pay. Thus the "roll" in the title represents the man's physical motion of rolling into town as well as the bank roll in his pocket. He heads straight to the Ditch where he proceeds to spends all his money in the bars. Broke by the end of the song, the sailor heads back out to sea to make more money, so he can return and repeat the process.

Musically, as mentioned, the song is anthemic—slow, regular, rhythmic strings with a healthy dose of martial percussion. During the number, the camera moves off Robeson's performance to pan the crowd, most of them sailors. They smile blankly and sway to the beat. Moments earlier, bottles were broken and tables overturned. Now everyone sits shoulder to shoulder, belting out the chorus in unison and hoisting their pints. The change is abrupt, pronounced, significant, and occurs in time with the music.

Also significant is the perfect overlap between the characters and setting of the song and the characters and setting of the cafe-audience. "Roll Up Sailorman" represents a musical exercise in containment. Out of a scene of chaos, order through music emerges. Beyond that, the casual lead-in to the number (Manda's comical pulling of Joe's ear), as well as the brawling crowd's unanimous request for and instant ability to fall into step with the song, implies that such song-as-soother scenes occur there regularly. And in that way, the cyclical action of the scene—brawl, sing/unite, drink—integrates with the cyclical action within the song—work, roll ashore, drink, return to sea. Finally, the entire number is predicated on a capitalist goal. The bar-owner's complaint of the disruption of her business serves as the catalyst for the song. Moreover, the action occasioned by the song—sailors drinking in a bar—mirrors the action described in the song. Thus the song functions to build a pliant community that will maximize an economic market.

Big Fella clearly shows the ways in which popular music can be employed to foster capitalism. Joe's rendition of "Roll Up Sailorman" restores order, and thus economic potential, to the cafe. And its contrasts with *Banjo* are telling—indeed, the respective songs will go on to function in direct inverse to one another. Still, not only the cafe-setting, but also the lead-ins to the signature songs are similar; both songs are crowd favorites and requests. However, "Shake That Thing" enters the text at a moment of unity, while "Roll Up Sailorman" enters at a moment of discord. McKay's jazz song then moves order towards chaos; Robeson's popular song moves chaos towards the re-establishment of order. Further, Robeson's number performs organically in the service of capitalism, and in that way, does not seem to serve capitalism at all. That is, Joe is not hired to perform at the café, though clearly he's done it before; rather, his song functions as a sort of public service.

The film's almost invisible link between music and commerce is quite a shift from McKay's hyper-attention to the connection. Early in the novel, one of the Ditch denizens lays out the dynamic for Banjo: "You can play all the time [in Marseilles]. . . . People will sure come and listen and the boss will get rid a some moh of his rotten wine."[51] Of course, Banjo's jazz disproves that statement, for each time he plays, violence disrupts the market. But the sentiment, though unspoken in the film, certainly applies to Joe's popular song. And in that, we can see the film's musical adaptation engaging in a philosophically based economic dialogue with the novel. While *Banjo* presents music in Marseilles as a (complex) form of racial/cultural exploitation, *Big Fella* shifts music into the position of simple universal language that functions as an entrance into the mainstream for minorities.

But the inverse drives of the genres of jazz and popular music in the texts are not confined to their potential economic effects. While capitalism functions as a conscious concern in the novel and a seemingly unconscious concern of the adaptation, both texts pay similarly representative attention to sex.

Indeed, jazz, as a genre, belongs to a sexual economy. The *OED* defines "jazz" as a term that signifies a musical genre yet can simultaneously be used "both as a verb and as a noun to denote the sex act. . . . [I]t is very likely from this usage that the term 'jazz music' was derived."[52] Further, the term "jelly roll," the type of blues played by Banjo and his band, has a specific sexual connotation: "Arising simply from the motions of sexual intercourse the term 'jelly roll' is a familiar one,"[53] and in "the Harlem slang of the 1930s, [jelly roll was] 'a term for vagina.' "[54]

Connections with sex are on the surface of Banjo's music to the point where music, racial and national identity, and sexuality merge into a single entity, as we see when the audience dances to "Shake That Thing": "It roused an Arab-black girl from Algeria into a shaking-mad mood. She jazzed right out into the center of the floor and shook herself in a low-down African shimmying way,"[55] and "The slim, slate-colored Martiniquan dances with a gold-brown Arab girl in a purely sensual way. His dog's mouth shows a tiny, protruding bit of pink tongue."[56] And with the aforementioned definitions of "jelly roll" in mind, the lyrics of "Shake That Thing," "Oh, shake that thing, / He's a jelly-roll king!"[57] make it clearly a song about sex. Finally, the novel traffics in bohemian themes that present sex casually, freely, and frequently.

But *Big Fella*'s adaptation affects a sharp shift away from any bohemian sexual ethos and right into bourgeois sensibility—a shift, moreover, led by musical numbers. At the end of the film, Joe prepares to leave Marseilles and his girlfriend Manda to take a job with the rich white family whose child he has returned safely. During Joe's going-away party (at the cafe), Manda performs "One." Backed by a slow wistful piano arrangement, Manda croons, "What though our romance becomes an ember / I know happiness for I'll remember / One kiss one sweet echo of our love / In the secret places of my heart." Designed to exploit that memory element of popular song put forth by Altman, the number works. Joe remembers the power of his feelings for the singer and remains in Marseilles. The film ends with the couple strolling along the quay, arm in arm as if walking down the aisle. Thus all conflict and tension has been resolved with the quick ease and symmetrical neatness often heard in popular song.

Indeed, it is popular music that brings the domestic arrangement to fruition. Joe's forfeiture of entry into the white hegemony (as a domestic servant) opens out into a second point of entry. That is, through the rejection of their bohemian arrangement and acceptance of the bourgeois institution of marriage, Joe and Manda represent an example of a black couple entering the white mainstream culture. Such a film representation was not common, according to the British Film Institute: "It is almost impossible to think of another film of the period that depicts a romantic involvement between a black couple."[58] Once again, we see Robeson's wish to portray black characters functioning well in a contemporary European setting. And that proper behavior is structured by the film's music. The song that reconciles Manda and Joe, "One," evokes the romantic notion of true love, a notion that exists in the heart/emotion rather than the body. It also places the central relationship in *Big Fella* within the ideal of monogamy, the ostensibly bourgeois value of one man and one woman together forever, that contrasts directly with the fundamentally individual and unstable sexual unions in *Banjo*.

Again, these contrasts do exist on the narrative surface of the film adaptation. Indeed, any careful consideration of the film must lead us to the conclusion that it functions in the capacity of a dialogical critique of its source. However, in that the narrative thrust of the text forms a light unsatirical farce, it lacks the weight with which to engage McKay's rich and complex novel in a realistic debate. But a focus on the music as the prime locus of adaptation offers productive ground for debate.

The film's shift to popular music and away from jazz accords with its philosophical position of black participation in white culture. Within both texts, all music begins with a general principle of inclusivity, but McKay's jazz leads to individuality and divisive and disruptive violence, while Robeson's popular songs lead to collectivity, capitalistic integration and a wholesale purchase of the bourgeois value-system. Further, each musical genre integrates nicely with the form of its respective text. As with the jazz it represents, *Banjo* individually wanders, loses itself, picks up seemingly random threads, struggles with control, moves in and out of euphoria, depression and violence, and ultimately just plays itself out rather than satisfy expectation. *Big Fella* works formulaically, in much the same way as a popular song: it builds from beginning to middle to end, with all the appropriate collective choruses; it exhibits and exerts control; and its traditionally structured finish provides a pay-off that carefully satisfies sentimental expectation. Finally, within the constraints of those genres, each text structures its music in order to philosophically engage in a political discourse.

Banjo offers jazz as a musical form that can subvert capitalism and, in turn, allow some of its characters to escape racial essentialization. *Big Fella* turns to popular music in an effort to support the idea that capitalism represents the best opportunity to join mainstream culture and escape racial essentialization. Indeed, as different as the texts are, they share a similar philosophical bottom line: the fundamental sameness of people, regardless of color. As a solution to the reality of the world's inability to see beyond the surface of things, *Banjo* colors whiteness: "Niggers is niggers all ovah the wul' . . . Always the same no matter what color their hide is or what langwidge they talk."[59] For its part, the film negotiates the same disconnect by white-washing blackness. If black people act/sing white, all distinctions will fall away, and they will become nothing less (or more) than functioning members of the consumer culture.

It is in the musical genres used by the texts that we see most clearly the logic of the different approaches to negotiating that surface differ-ence of skin color. It is in what we hear rather than what we see that *Big Fella* offers a thoughtful (if less nuanced) response to—and indeed, a critique of—the text that it adapts. And only by listening closely and understanding the music as a structuring device with specific cultural investments can we fully understand the overall work done by the ad-aptation.

If by the "we" in his epigram, filmmaker Alan Rudolph thinks that filmmakers are starting to think in soundtracks, then it's quite obvious that we, as critics, need to start thinking more about soundtracks. This essay represents an attempt to productively shift away from the visual narrative elements of a film adaptation. For, as critics such as Michel Chion and Thomas Leitch—but also novelists such as Christopher Bram—point out, a film adaptation of a literary text represents more than that Bluestonian move from mental to physical seeing. It is also a move into sound. Moreover, it is a move that the novel can't make. That alone should make it vital ground to cover. And the fact that the soundtrack can function as an adaptive text and produce independent meaning makes tracing the work of the soundtrack a necessary job for the adaptation critic. Bram's quotation in my epigram comes from the novelist's discussion about film adaptation that appears in the end-notes to *Gods and Monsters* (1995).[60] I've left Bram's parentheses to show that, even when the soundtrack is mentioned within the adapta-tion conversation, it is hushed, marginalized. Perhaps this look into its adaptive work can begin to remove the parentheses from our consider-ation of the soundtrack and place it, out loud, in our conversation.

NOTES

1. Thomas Leitch, "Twelve Fallacies in Contemporary Adaptation Theory," *Criticism* 45, no. 2 (2003): 149.

2. Ibid.

3. As an example of how this flattening out does not exist in other fields, consider how quickly and thoroughly critics of the novel moved beyond the concept of Hom-er's *Odyssey* as a source for James Joyce's *Ulysses*. Further, imagine how the history of the criticism would look if those critics had confined their focus to the "source" that Joyce clearly adapts. Also, though adaptation can involve any number of genres other than the novel (and film for that matter), this essay is primarily concerned with the shift from novel to film.

4. Mireia Aragay, ed., *Books in Motion: Adaptation, Intertextuality, Authorship* (New York: Rodopi, 2005), 19.

5. Roland Barthes, "The Death of the Author," *Image-Music-Text* (New York: Hill and Wang, 1977), 146.

6. Brian McFarlane, *Novel to Film: An Introduction to the Theory of Adaptation* (Ox-ford: Oxford University Press, 1996), 21.

7. While critics often use the term "soundtrack" to signify all a film's sound—voices and sound effects as well as music—my use of the term in this essay refers only to the film's diegetic and non-diegetic music.

8. Christa Albrecht-Crane's "*Lost Highway* as Fugue: Adaptation of Musicality as Film" (in this volume) begins by posing a similar question: "What might be the amplitude of adaptation theory when literature is not evoked as a major point of departure?" (244). Albrecht-Crane goes on to explore the notion that, rather than merely constructing a visual narrative, film contains the capacity for "embodying or expressing a musical sensibility, or a musical mode of movement" (248).

9. George Bluestone, *Novels into Film* (Berkeley: University of California Press, 1957), 1.

10. Ibid.

11. Leitch, "Twelve Fallacies," 153.

12. Michel Chion, *Audio-Vision: Sound on Screen*, trans. Claudia Gorbman (New York: Columbia University Press, 1994), xxv.

13. Ibid., xxvi.

14. Claudia Gorbman, *Unheard Melodies* (Bloomington: Indiana University Press, 1987), 2.

15. Arthur Knight and Pamela Robertson Wojcik, eds., *Soundtrack Available: Essays on Film and Popular Music* (Durham: Duke University Press, 2001), 5.

16. Robert Stam, "The Dialogics of Adaptation," *Film Adaptation*, ed. James Naremore (New Brunswick, NJ: Rutgers University Press, 2000), 67.

17. William Steig, *Shrek!* (New York: Farrar, Straus, Giroux, 1990).

18. *Adaptation*, DVD, directed by Spike Jonze, (Culver City, CA: Columbia, 2002) explores a similar meta-engagement, to much more theoretical fanfare.

19. "Once Upon a Time," *Shrek*, DVD, directed by Andrew Adamson and Vicky Jenson (Universal City, CA: Dreamworks, 2001).

20. This piece of music will recur throughout the film, in multiple variations. It functions as both Fiona's theme and as an often interrupted signal of the romance-path that the film seems to resist.

21. David R. Shumway, "Rock 'n' Roll Sound Tracks and the Production of Nostalgia," *Cinema Journal* 8, no. 2 (1999): 37.

22. Interestingly, and as a possible proof of the success of *Shrek*'s musical shift within the genre, since its release, no animated films have won in the category.

23. Shumway, "Rock 'n' Roll," 37.

24. In a delicious bit of irony, this song fragment appears to have been written for the film.

25. At least until the end, when the movie surrenders to the drive and engages in a full blown musical number: The Monkees' "I'm a Believer." In the same scene, we also see the return of "the book" to its place at the center of the story, as well as the classic fairy tale ending. Total restoration.

26. In an illustration of the vast range of fidelity criticism, however, Salon.com published Margot Mifflin's " 'Shrek' is not Shrek!" on May 24, 2001. The article offers classic fidelity-complaints about the film's bastardization of Steig's book. http://dir.salon.com/story/mwt/feature/2001/05/24/auti_shrek/index.html

27. Thomas Leitch addresses various aspects of that fidelity-claim in "Twelve Fallacies."

28. *Big Fella*, DVD, directed by J. Elder Willis (1937; British Lion, 2004; Urban-Works Entertainment).

29. Namely, while *Banjo* goes a long way to consciously understand, treat and move beyond the racism of its particular moment, *Big Fella* does almost nothing to escape the significant latent racism of its time.

30. Stam, "Dialogics of Adaptation," 57–58.

31. Dudley Andrew, "The Well-Worn Muse," in Narrative Strategies, (Western Illinois University, 1980). Geoffrey Wagner, *The Novel and the Cinema*, (Rutherford, NJ: Farleigh Dickinson University Press, 1975). Michael Klein and Gillian Parker, eds., *The English Novel and the Movies* (New York: Ungar, 1981).

32. McFarlane, *Novel to Film*, 11.

33. Claude McKay, *Banjo: A Story Without a Plot* (New York: Harcourt Brace, 1970), 90.

34. Ibid., 90.

35. Martin B. Duberman, *Paul Robeson* (New York: Knopf Publishing Group, 1989), 207–8.

36. Stam, "Dialogics of Adaptation," 63–64.

37. Chion, *Audio-Vision*, 184.

38. The city's bohemian, red-light district.

39. The concept of a film employing a musical structural template is explored in more depth in Albrecht-Crane's *"Lost Highway* as Fugue." There, rather than depend on literary concepts of narrative structure, Albrecht-Crane turns to "reading *Lost Highway* as an aesthetic experience akin to music" (325), specifically, a fugue.

40. Rick Altman, "Cinema and Popular Song: The Lost Tradition," *Soundtrack Available: Essays on Film and Popular Music*, ed. Arthur Knight and Pamela Robertson Wojcik (Durham, NC: Duke University Press, 2001), 24.

41. Gorbman, *Unheard Melodies*, 163.

42. Interestingly, Eslanda Robeson actually appears in *Big Fella*.

43. Duberman, *Paul Robeson*, 208.

44. That debate is still very much in play in America today. Recent statements and articles by Aaron MacGruder and John Ridley have re-polarized the discourse. In an article for *Esquire* "The Manifesto of Ascendancy for the Modern American Nigger," *Esquire*, 146, no. 6 (Dec. 2006). Ridley points to Secretaries of State Colin Powell and Condoleeza Rice as the sorts of role models that black youths should aspire to emulate, while Macgruder has referred to Powell as "Darth Vader" and Rice as a mass-murderer for their respective roles in the Bush Administration. Clearly, participation in white-dominated mainstream culture means different things for these two commentators.

45. McKay, *Banjo*, 6.

46. Ibid., 45.

47. Ibid., 47.

48. Ibid., 46.

49. Ibid., 50.

50. *Big Fella*, DVD, directed by J. Elder Willis (1937; British Lion, 2004; Urban-Works Entertainment).

51. McKay, *Banjo*, 7.

52. *Oxford English Dictionary* Online, http://oed.com/

53. Paul Oliver, *Blues Fell This Morning: Meaning in the Blues* (New York: Cambridge University Press, 1990), 109.

54. Robert McCrum, William Cran, and Robert MacNeil, eds., *The Story of English* (London: Faber and Faber, 1992), 237.

55. McKay, *Banjo*, 47.

56. Ibid., 50.

57. Ibid.

58. Stephen Bourne. *BFI Screenonline*, www.screenonline.org.uk/film/id/501396.

59. McKay, *Banjo*, 50–51.

60. Christopher Bram, *Gods and Monsters* (New York: Harper, 2005), P.S. 11.

Lost Highway as Fugue:
Adaptation of Musicality as Film

Christa Albrecht-Crane

In AN ESSAY IN 1948, THE FRENCH CRITIC ANDRÉ BAZIN NOTED, "THE problem of digests and adaptations is usually posed within the framework of literature. Yet literature only partakes of a phenomenon whose amplitude is much larger."[1] Taking a cue from Bazin, I ask in this essay what it would look like to pose the question of adaptations in a framework other than literature? What might be the amplitude of adaptation theory when literature is not invoked as a major point of departure? To ask these questions is to consider insights from contemporary theory, critical theory, and media studies in an effort to bring the field of adaptation studies more in line with some of the rigorous work done in contemporary film studies.

A first, and indispensable, move in that direction would be to question seriously the value of approaching the study of film and literature from a traditional literary perspective. This perspective involves looking at adaptations through the lens of narrative and literary factors. In discussing Brian McFarlane's structuralist approach to adaptation theory, for instance, Imelda Whelehan explains that McFarlane focuses on how narrative strategies change from novel to film. According to Whelehan, McFarlane shows how "the process of presenting a literary text on film is one in which the stock formal devices of narrative—point of view, focalization, tense, voice, metaphor—must be realized by quite other means."[2] In other words, the structure of McFarlane's approach rests on analyzing how a literary text's formal narrative devices change as the textual narrative moves into the medium of film. Significantly, the critic adopts a literary lens with which to analyze the film version of literature. For both media—original text and film—narrative devices are the focus of attention and both source text and film are reduced to their narrative apparatus. In particular, this move has significant effects on how cinema is viewed.

McFarlane, and others who employ this approach that reduces source text and film to a traditional literary apparatus, risk essentializing both literature and the cinema to assume that both media in some way embody narrative as their *modus operandi*. But as Robert Ray reminds us, the problem with this approach is that it overlooks the fact that narrative is not essential to a particular medium. Narrative can take place in any medium, and not all media—not film, and not literature—inherently include storytelling. Thus, part of the study of narrative should be investigations into the particular cultural and historical conditions that privilege certain media, at a certain time, to become the vehicle for a culture's dissemination of storytelling. Ray illustrates this point by noting that the Hollywood system is one of the most powerful (and thus also the most normalized) vehicles for transmitting narratives—*not* because the cinema inherently narrates, but because the commercialized and powerful Hollywood machine created a system of meaning in which narrative came to dominate, "turning [leading actors] into predictable signifying objects, not only through consistent cinematic use (typecasting), but also through extracinematic, semiliterary forms of publicity (press releases, fan magazine articles, bios, interviews, and news plants)."[3] In other words, the movies *became* contemporary culture's main medium for storytelling because of economic and ideological reasons.

And yet, the bulk of work in adaptation studies tends to neglect this aspect of media theory and instead analyzes cinema as if it were a rather simple extension of literature. But this neglect is itself the result of particular cultural and historical factors at work in the United States academy and in the functioning of academic professions. Adaptation studies as an academic discipline emerged in the 1960s and 1970s, as Mireia Aragay notes, "out of English literature departments, inheriting the main assumptions of the dominant New Criticism and liberal Humanism."[4] That is, from its inception as an academic discipline, the study of literature and film assumes the heritage of traditional literary study, an antitheoretical, simplistic structure that privileges the concept of the Author and High Art. Naturally, as Ray explains, this structure "sponsored the obsessive refrain of the film and literature field that cinematic versions of literary classics failed to live up to their sources."[5]

Moreover, traditionally-trained scholars in English literature departments faced three significant threats after the 1970s: market-driven pressures that generally devalued education in the humanities, a changing student population and media landscape in which movies have replaced literature as the source for storytelling, and the threat of "theory" in the wake of poststructuralism and postmodernism that seemed to attack the very foundations of traditional literary concerns (notions of authorship, originality, and textual unity, among others).

Faced with these threats, Ray notes that "fearful of seeing literature's narrative role usurped by the movies, and under the sway of New Criticism's religious reverence for 'serious art,' these critics typically used adaptation study to shore up literature's crumbling walls."[6] Interestingly, then, the discipline of adaptation studies becomes the site in which a number of factors articulate to give rise to the infamous "fidelity" approach to adaptation theory, an approach that compares/contrasts a work of fiction with its filmic equivalent to conclude that the film usually is a failure.

The overwhelming problem with this method of analysis is that the discipline really was formed as an almost reactionary move in the face of the emergence of cinema that replaced literature and the assault of new theoretical insights about texts and authorship. As Ray argues, "film and literature scholars wrote adaptation studies because New Criticism had trained them to do so."[7] Neglecting (or defending themselves against) new trends in both media culture and new academic approaches, most adaptation scholars continued to employ the conventional methods of analyzing literature and in so doing they missed a most significant factor of analysis: that cinema in general attends to different conditions and cultural formations than does classic literature. In effect, as Ray argues, since cinema functions under different determinations than literature, adaptation studies thus "made irrelevant the methods of analysis developed by 'serious literature.'"[8] As a result, the rather narrow concerns of a traditional literary approach would in time segregate adaptation studies from the bulk of media studies and film theory and relegate the discipline to the margins, in an insular and inadequate position vis-à-vis more current, more relevant film and media scholarship.

According to Ray, the focus on narrative in the study of literature and film does not attend to larger and more complex questions raised, for example, by critical theorists such as Roland Barthes, who has argued that texts across all media (not just literature and film) depend on a range of codes and conventions that are overdetermined by cultural and ideological factors. Crucially, it ignores one of critical theory's most profound insights: that all texts function in a web of radical intertextuality and that narrative is an effect of particular historical, cultural, and ideological formations. Bazin's challenge above addresses precisely this reliance on literary approaches to framing adaptation studies. Without a doubt, recently a growing number of scholars have begun to heed his argument. James Naremore's collection of essays on adaptation (*Film Adaptation*),[9] for instance, provides "somewhat less attention to formal than to economic, cultural, and political issues,"[10] as Naremore explains in his editorial introduction. This shift to considering extra-literary matters is echoed by Robert Stam, who argues in his own introduction to *Literature and Film* that adaptations are folded into a complex process of cultural and political influences that cut across different texts, media, and interpretations. Stam notes that structuralist and poststructuralist theories in particular have had a strong impact on issues of adaptation; moreover, he writes, "other theoretical movements and trends also indirectly demote the literary text from its position of overwhelming authority and thus point to a possible reconceptualization of adaptation."[11] As Stam thus argues, much theoretical acumen remains to be marshaled as we expand and enrich the traditional literary scope of adaptation studies.

In my own work to expand the conventionally literary focus in adaptation theory, I have found Stam's discussion of cinema's multidimensionality to be especially productive as a starting point. This argument links well with Ray's earlier suggestion that *narrative* cinema is the dominant function of cinema, but is by no means an inherent function. Stam argues that film employs multiple dimensions—among them the visual, aural, extra-verbal—that give the cinematic experience its abundance of expression and meaning. As he puts it, "the cinema has not lesser but rather greater resources for expression than the novel, and is quite independent of what actual filmmakers have actually done with these resources."[12] That is to say, one possible line of departure for adaptation theory would be to consider the filmic adaptation as its own site of meaning-making, independent of literary concerns or the literary source that might have inspired it. So much happens in film that attempting to bring film's meaning back to literary/narrative devices misses a range of other artistic forms that a film can also enable.

In order to more fully realize a discussion of adaptation that breaks with the usual literary tropes, then, I turn to some of the cinematic registers that have little or nothing to do with formal narrative devices. As Stam observes, "while the novel is capable of the most supple forms of ironic double-voiced discourse, film's multitrack nature makes it possible to stage ironic contradictions between music and image. Thus the cinema offers synergistic possibilities of disunity and disjunction not immediately available to the novel."[13] Interestingly, then, Stam indicates here that because of its multitrack (multidimensional) nature, film can do things the traditional novel will not do. This statement does not necessarily indict the novel and privilege film—rather, Stam helps us understand that some elements in film are just better grasped if we do not think of them in terms of traditional formal narrative as it was developed in the classical novel. In the rest of this essay I want to explore this proposition; I want to focus on a particular site of "disunity and disjunction" that, according to conventional narrative devices, offers little "sense," and yet contains a great deal of possible sense when considered according to extra-literary devices. For Stam, "cinema (and the new media) are infinitely rich in polyphonic potentialities,"[14] to the extent that "a culturally polyrhythmic, heterochronic, multi-velocity and contrapuntal cinema becomes a real possibility."[15] In other words, rather than looking for formal narrative/literary unity in film, a new object of analysis might become the identification of disjunctive and heterogeneous movements that suggest a different artistic sensibility that is not readily available if we apply traditional literary analysis to the cinema.

Thus, one of the first moves in a discussion of adaptation is to unlink the notion that a film adaptation begins with literary concerns that are transposed into film from a source novel or short story. Because of its multitrack nature, film *can* include a textual/narrative dimension, but it can also invoke non-textual artistic forms—for example, dispositions that are more dominant in other arts such as painting, poetry, or music. As Stam explains, cinema "can metaphorically evoke them by imitating their procedures."[16] As illustrations, Stam notes, "it can show a Picasso painting, or emulate cubist techniques, cite a Bach cantata, or create montage equivalents of fugue and counterpoint."[17] But film does not just emulate such artistic devices. A film works *as an artistic form of its own*. While some films, generically labeled "adaptations," often either imitate literary narratives or work mostly as literary narratives (and certainly are read as literary narratives by many adaptation scholars), other films might function as non-literary art forms. Stam explains, "Godard's *Passion* (1982) not only includes music (Ravel, Mozart, Ferre, Beethoven, Faure) but is conceived musically. It not only shows animated tableaux based on celebrated paintings (Rembrandt's *Night Watch*, Goya's *The Third of May*) but also demonstrates a painterly sensitivity to light and color."[18] What this discussion indicates is that cinema's capacity to work across multiple registers enables a potential to embody a multitude of art forms, usually more than one at one time, of which the literary/narrative is but one.

To test this argument and examine its value for the study of adaptation, I want to discuss film as embodying or expressing a musical sensibility, or a musical mode of movement. The point will be not to postulate that "music" has one essential form, but rather that one can grasp the radical multidimensionality of film by considering that it can embody, among other sensibilities, a musical dimension. As a starting point for this discussion, I will first review three essays that all consider how musicality might inform a cinematic experience.[19] In 1974, Robin

Wood writes in her essay "Written on the Wind" about Sirk's 1956 movie of the same title:

> Finally, I should talk briefly about what is the most difficult aspect of film to analyze. I suggested earlier an analogy with poetry; I hope to make this clearer rather than more obscure by adding to it the analogy with music. Sirk himself has said that his conscious model for *Written in the Wind* was Bach fugue. He talked about the acting as pared down to clean intersecting lines, like counterpoint. If *Written on the Wind* is a fugue for four voices, the sequence of the father's death is clearly the *stretto*. What I want to indicate is the obvious fact that film, like music, has a fixed duration. Hence the appropriateness to it of musical terms like "tempo" and "rhythm." We still haven't found a way of talking satisfactorily about this "musical" dimension, the direct effect of the *movement* of film on the senses, except in dangerously impressionistic terms. There is a lot of work to be done.[20]

In this very provocative passage, Wood points out that Sirk's film seems to suggest a sensibility, a mode of expression, that works in some ways like a musical composition. That is to say, in terms of how the film moves for spectators, how it creates a range of sensations, rhythms, and emotions, the work seems to invoke the form of expression similar of a musical piece, in this case a Bach fugue. Wood is also quite careful to point out that one needs to avoid "dangerously impressionistic terms" when discussing musicality in film. In other words, the argument about cinema's multidimensionality should be kept open, indeterminate; to suggest that musicality might form a productive lens through which to view the cinema does not suggest that musicality in some way should be a privileged lens, or the only lens. Essentialism, whether it is at work in traditional adaptation scholarship or in new approaches remains a problematic issue.

As a result, how can we conceive of film's musicality in non-impressionistic, non-essentializing ways? Thomas Fahy offers such an exploration in his article "Killer Culture: Classical Music and the Art of Killing in *Silence of the Lambs* and *Se7en*," in which he argues that these two films gain their expressive sense through musical form. Fahy points in particular to the scene in *Silence of the Lambs* in which Hannibal Lecter orchestrates the killing of two prison guards by first listening intently to a recording of Johann Sebastian Bach's *Goldberg Variations*, and then actually performing the killings in rhythm with the music that accompanies his movements. In other words, the music does not just play in the background but rather the film's events *become* music. Fahy says that Bach's piece forms a choice "in terms of characterization and thematic development."[21] As Stam noted above, then, the film, and in particular the character of Lecter, is conceived musically. Fahy writes, "like the make-up of this piece, all of Hannibal's actions and behaviors are highly measured. He not only sketches but also takes an artist's care in killing, presenting Boyle's body as crucifixion and a moth."[22] Interestingly, then, we have in Hannibal's character an expression of a range of behaviors and motivations that are conceived musically (and also painterly, if one considers that Hannibal displays the murdered body in the form of a crucified Christ figure). The point here is not that music forms a metaphor for characters' actions in *Silence of the Lambs*; rather, Fahy suggests that music forms *the very structure* of the film. The film's logic and movements function musically.

To further clarify this important insight, I turn to the third scholar whose work proposes that film can embody musical meaning. In his essay, "Cinema, Scored: Toward a Comparative Methodology for Music in Media," James Tobias sees "music as filmic compositional process, as aesthetic experience, as cultural identity, as tactic of differentiation or of compositional production, as image: music in these terms has tended to be left untreated, or excluded as somehow exterior to music."[23] In other words, Tobias posits that music can form the compositional logic, the methodology, of the filmic image and not just embody the "soundtrack," or an exterior, supplementary function. Music *is* the film. His case in point is Tom Tykwer's 1998 film *Lola Rennt (Run Lola Run)*, in which "the narrative of chance and intention holds together through musical texturing as rhythmic narrativity . . . The audience grasps rhythmic movement as an anchor for identification and cohesion."[24] Tobias's analysis suggests that the movie is structured perhaps like a pop song: the fast pace revolves around three "stanzas," three repetitions and variations that are slightly different in each rendition as the singer/protagonist races towards the concluding event. Indeed, each action in the movie is embedded in and carried by the rhythms of music and Lola's singing. Music becomes image. The story *is* the song, rendered in film format. As Tobias notes, musicality "provides the framework on which narrative reflexivities are hooked."[25] The film "makes sense" as a song: a rhythmic, repetitive, fast-paced series of sensations delivered by the singer/protagonist and by the image. Tobias thus considers the musicality of film, suggesting that film is felt, perhaps, rather than consciously apprehended, as we might experience effects in music.

The three scholars whose work I sketched above help us understand that film can be seen as a multi-register experience that is simply not accessible through the limited vocabulary of literary study that privileges an analysis of formal literary devices. Moreover, this argument seems particularly relevant for adaptation studies because it helps re-

lease "adaptations" from their prevalent linkage to notions of faithfulness to a source text and instead allows for fresh approaches to
thinking about the relationship between literature and cinematic adaptations. In order to flesh out some of the details of my argument I
will now turn to discussing a particular film, David Lynch's *Lost Highway* (1997), in the musical terms I have sketched above.

Judging by traditional narrative and literary criteria, *Lost Highway*
seemingly makes no sense. The plot of *Lost Highway* is truly strange,
spectral. It begins with Fred Madison, played by Bill Pullman, speeding on a highway at night, while the soundtrack plays David Bowie's
"I'm Deranged." The film then cuts to Fred's domestic life in Hollywood with his wife Renee (played by Patricia Arquette) in a tense,
unstable marriage, which becomes tenser still when anonymous video-
cassettes begin turning up on their doorstep; when Fred and Reneee
play them, the tapes reveal that someone has been entering their home
at night to record them in their sleep. In-between the tapes, scenes
vary from Fred wandering around the dark house, to Fred playing the
saxophone in a club and seeing, or imagining he sees, Renee leaving
the club with another man. In one of most bizarre scenes of the entire
movie, Fred encounters a strange man at a party, the Mystery Man,
played by Robert Blake, who asks Fred to call his own house where
Fred himself answers the phone. Back at the house, on the third anonymous tape, Fred, in an intense, short black-and-white scene, sees
himself at the foot of his bed, surrounded by a bloody and brutally
murdered Renee. Fred is thrown in jail, where we see him with intense
headaches, then in a scene that might be read as an execution scene,
followed by another odd headache experience, after which Fred gets
transformed in his cell into a young man—Pete Dayton, played by
Balthazar Getty. Now, a parallel story develops as the young mechanic
Pete, released from prison, is drawn into a web of deceit by a temptress
who is cheating on her gangster boyfriend. This woman, Alice, is also
played by Patricia Arquette, but rather than being a brunette, as Renee
was, Alice is an icy-blonde. The two men—Fred and Pete—are also
connected by a mysterious turn of events that calls into question their
very identities. Pete attempts to run away with Alice, but he turns back
into Fred in the presence of the Mystery Man. The film ends where it
began—with Fred speeding frenetically on a highway at night, again
accompanied on the soundtrack by Bowie's "I'm Deranged."[26]

Much of what the images convey on the screen escapes conventional
storytelling. The usual devices—plot, point of view, narrator, tense,
voice—are insufficient, or indeed misleading, in attempting to capture
this film's dynamic intensity.[27] It becomes obvious that the methods of
analysis developed for literature remain irrelevant when trying to

"make sense" of this cinematic experience. According to Ann Jerslev, "we should not expect to be able to make sense of this film and thus to create a sense of (narrative) certainty that the film itself so insistently denies."[28] Similarly, David Andrews notes that the film "refuse[s] to satisfy the viewer's urge for a monolithic storyline, for a narrative impelled by a univocal intention."[29] Focusing on the aspect of fantasy, Todd McGowan adds, "because the narrative of *Lost Highway* brings the logic of fantasy into the open, it necessarily strikes us as incongruous, as a film without a narrative altogether."[30] What else is going on, then, in this film? If one considers some of the lessons learned from critical theory or film studies, then *Lost Highway* does not lend itself ideally to being read through a literary approach. Even though the film is actually replete with generic narrative codes, they constantly shift, mutate, and mirror each other in a way that suggests that these codes are being rewritten at the same time that they are being cited. For instance, the first half of the film shows conventional domestic scenes between the musician Fred and his beautiful, brunette, and mysterious wife; takes are offered in classic *film noir* fashion, interrupted by conventional mystery movie plot twists (incidents with mysterious tapes, secretive glances between husband and wife, ominous background music); the stereotypical classic cinema moves then culminate in the appearance of the biggest "mystery," unapologetically personified as "The Mystery Man." The second half of the film mirrors and twists these events with even more conventionality and intertextual references to cinema. (In fact, Steve Shaviro calls this second half "largely parodic. With a knowing smirk, the film calls attention to its own unreality. Everything is cliché, lifted from romance, melodrama, or film noir.")[31] For example, in a gripping scene, a young, sexually charged Pete Dayton gazes in complete rapture as the Marilyn Monroe-type Alice steps out of a Mercedes convertible, in slow motion, sensually displaying her legs, thighs, breasts, and wavy straw-blond hair, moving in eerie rhythm with the song on the soundtrack—Lou Reed's "This Magic Moment"—which underscores (literally) the scene's seemingly magical encounter between the two archetypal lovers. And yet, even though the film is composed of seemingly conventional narrative devices, these devices do not coalesce into a narrative whole. I argue that this disharmony occurs because the film's dynamic does not follow the conventionally established narrative sequencing and narrative story arc we are accustomed to seeing in mainstream Hollywood cinema and reading in traditional literary narrative. The film's dramatic intensity does not make sense as a conventional fictional narrative, but it begins to make a different sense if we consider it as a piece of music.

As Tobias noted about *Lola Rennt*, "the audience grasps rhythmic movement as an anchor for identification and cohesion."[32] This same process seems to be at work in *Lost Highway:* a rhythmic movement seems to underwrite the film and povide an anchoring point for the viewing experience. The comparison with a Bach fugue, in fact, comes to mind and has even been suggested by Lynch himself.[33] Christoff Wolff, in his study of Johann Sebastian Bach, writes that the composer's major fugal composition, *The Art of Fugue* (containing a total of fourteen fugues and four canons), "was an exploration in depth of the contrapuntal possibilities inherent in a single musical subject. The carefully constructed subject would generate many movements, each demonstrating one or more contrapuntal principles and each, therefore, resulting in a self-contained fugal form."[34] Wolff points here to the dynamic possibilities of a musical fugue, in which a "musical subject" is being explored by way of its "contrapuntal possibilities," or its musical oppositions, generating different movements that each focus on a particular counterpoint that as a totality create a "fugal form." Noteworthy is the fact that the fugal form suggests a particular constellation of movements, made up of the main subject and its counterpoints, that forms a "totality," or a musical piece. *Lost Highway* does not narrate in the conventional sense—there's no plot other than the variation of movements, there is no character development in the conventional sense, or a thematic arch, or a logical beginning, middle, or end. And yet, the fugal form does contain a particular dynamic that works to engage a listener's senses by providing a particular assemblage of rhythms and movements.

In the following section I outline the basic structure of fugue and will in turn attempt to sketch a reading of some of the elements in *Lost Highway* as a way of approximating the film's movement to that of a fugue. In brief, according to *The Harvard Dictionary of Music*, a fugue is defined as "the most fully developed procedure of imitative counterpoint, in which the theme is stated successively in all voices of the polyphonic texture, tonally established, continuously expanded, opposed, and reestablished."[35] Already, one notices resonances in this definition with the film's structure: Pete Dayton might serve as a counterpoint to Fred Madison, the film's theme is stated successively in all voices (in Fred's wife, Dick Laurent, etc.) and is being continuously "expanded, opposed, and reestablished," particularly in the parallel story that returns in the end to the way the film began. But even beyond such a cursory comparison, *Lost Highway* seems to function the way a fugue does. Here are a fugue's main components, transposed onto the basic structure of *Lost Highway* (all quotations in this section are taken from *The Harvard Dictionary of Music*):

1. "Fugal texture requires a strict number of voices; two to six are practical, but the usual number is three or four."[36] *Lost Highway* presents two voices, or subjects: Fred Madison and Renee Madison who appear in numerous variations as countersubjects (Pete Dayton, The Mystery Man, Alice, etc.).

2. "In a fugal exposition, the subject is presented alone in one voice . . . then imitated or answered, usually in the dominant, by a second voice."[37] The film presents its subject, Fred Madison, alone at the opening of the film. We see a variation of Fred as the domestic scenes occur, and Renee appears, as the second (dominant) voice of the film.

3. "After stating the subject, each voice continues with countersubject or free counterpoint,[38] usually moving to a cadence.[39] An exposition is normally followed by an episode, the motivic material for which often derives from an aspect of the subject or countersubject."[40] In other words, a fugue presents a subject, or a voice, followed by that same subject in some sort of inversion or contrast; after that move, a "cadence" occurs, or a pause, that gives rise to a longer episodic treatment of the subject or countersubject. In *Lost Highway*, we see Fred and Renee's subjects continuously modified, or "countered," by countersubjects. Recall the intensity of the following scene: Fred and Renee lie in bed together, and Fred recounts to Renee a dream he has had; he says to her, "you were in the house . . . calling my name . . . but I couldn't find you." Cut to the Madison house, Fred's dream. We see Fred walking slowly across the living room, in a point-of-view shot, moving, searching. He stops and listens. Renee's voice is heard off-screen, "Fred, Fred, where are you?" The camera turns slowly, drifts and rises up unhurriedly, goes into the bedroom, where Renee is lying on the bed. In a voice-over, we hear Fred say, "Then there you were . . . lying in bed . . . but it wasn't you . . . It looked like you . . . but it wasn't." The camera suddenly dives at Renee's face, into a tight close-up; her face shows total fright (soundtrack accompanies this with a screeching, metallic thump). Cut to another bedroom scene. Fred is looking at Renee but it's not Renee lying next to him, but a face he has never seen before (we realize later that the face belongs to The Mystery Man); Fred moves quickly, turns on his bedside lamp, and looks again at Renee. Now her face is her own. She asks, "Fred, are you all right?" He reaches out and gingerly touches her face; Renee covers his hand with hers, and closes her eyes. Cut to fade-out, then fade-in to next scene. In this sequence, then, we can observe the movement of two voices being modified by way of counterpoint. In the dream, Fred's counterpoint picks up a motif suggested by the main subject, Fred ("I had a dream last night"), and this motif becomes the new episode (the dream itself) in which we see both Fred and Renee as countersubjects, Renee even opposed (superimposed, really) by The Mystery Man.[41]

4. "The episodic material is brought into an opposing or contrasting context, an effect often achieved by the use of harmonic sequences; once

sufficient contrast has been established, the fugue subject reenters, as a single entry or as a reexposition, in the tonic or in a related key."[42] That is to say, various episodes are used that create a sense of contrast and disparity; when this effect has been established sufficiently, the main subject of piece reappears in the form it was encountered at the beginning of the piece. The second half of *Lost Highway* can be seen as the "opposing or contrasting context" to the first half (Fred's counterpoint being Pete, and Renee being the blonde version of herself); towards the end of the film, "sufficient contrast" has been established between the voices and between the second and the first half of the film; at this point, then, "the fugue's subject reenters," as Pete turns back into Fred[43] (as a "reexposition") and the film in fact ends where it begins—the very same Fred/main subject that opened the film races down the highway at night.

The most immediate reward from this analysis of musical movement is suggested by the perception of the interplay of the various voices in fugue: the experience of multiple melodic voices at the same time that retain their unique variations while also engaging in a temporal encounter of modification, expansion, opposition, and reestablishment. In his work on Bach, Wolff explains that Bach ends his major fugal composition, *The Art of Fugue*, with three subjects in both their upright and inverted forms. According to Wolff, this turbulent movement is the most dramatic of the entire work.[44] At the end of *Lost Highway*, we see *two* subjects in both their upright and contrapuntal form—Fred and Pete, Alice and the Mystery Man—all juxtaposed in an intense, breathless manner. As Pete turns into Fred and Alice disappears into a burning barn, Fred asks the Mystery Man who she was; in turn, the Mystery Man turns the question back to Fred, all the while filming him with a video camera. It seems like Fred cannot escape the doubling and maddening representation of himself to himself. The film offers no resolution in a narrative sense, but rather ends on a heightened tone of two subjects having been repeated by inversion multiple times, in highly contrasting and intense episodes, until the piece finally finishes in a turbulent movement in which the main subject reenters.

In other words, the point under discussion here is the *emotional range* suggested by the particular structure of fugue. Writing about Italian realist cinema, Bazin said, "realism in art can only be achieved in one way—through artifice."[45] Art attempts to recreate the intensity of an experience by "artificial" means, by employing stimuli that work on our sense of touch, smell, hearing, and seeing. A musical fugue, part of a long tradition of concert music in the Western tradition, works in this space of stimuli, or perceptual affects. As I have sketched above, a fugue's focus on contrapuntal possibilities emphasizes a perception of dramatic dynamism as a subject, or multiple subjects, undergo rhythmical variations on a particular theme that is presented by way or imitations and variations. The heightened sense of tension and drama clearly resides in the juxtaposition of different voices and their interaction with and against each other. In other words, the emotional range in fugue is something like sharp tension, rhythmical variation, episodic drama—indeed, the aesthetic pleasure emanates in part from the piece's intricate formal structure. So, when Glen Gould, the celebrated pianist and Bach interpreter, says of *The Art of Fugue*, "I really cannot think of a music that moved me more deeply than the last fugue . . . it leaves the impression of an infinitely expanding universe,"[46] he does address that notion of emotional range that seems to be at the heart of fugue as an aesthetic experience.

My interest in reading *Lost Highway* by way of fugue stems from this function of cinema: that viewing *Lost Highway* is indeed an aesthetic experience that seems to focus in rendering the intricate dynamic of a problematic relationship in a contrapuntal, intensely heightened, and episodic way. The resulting effects—tension and apprehension—are arguably what a viewer might take away from the film. In that sense, the film renders by way of a particular rhythm and movement an affective experience of alienation and fear. This view suggests that film might form an aesthetic experience, akin to other forms of art (such as music) in which one perceives not narrative, but rather particular sense experiences. If a majority of adaptation scholars usually view film as a secondary narrative apparatus, inferior to the classic novel, then they risk essentializing the very medium of film and ignoring this nonnarrative potential. The affective, aesthetic experience of film on one's senses remains unaddressed. In fact, Shaviro even goes so far as to suggest that the emotional intensity presented in *Lost Highway* cannot be narrated in any conventional way. Shaviro writes that the film "is a call to leave traditional modes of storytelling, and of narrative closure, behind."[47]

The discussion above points, specifically, to considering the role of film as a sense experience, as embodied encounter. This dimension has remained largely unaddressed in discussions of literature and film. Since my overall argument poses that adaptation studies should expand its traditional purview and consider film in extra-literary terms, I now want to suggest more specifically what such an approach might look like. David Lynch offers a fitting illustration of this perspective in *Mulholland Drive* (2001). In one of the many self-reflexive scene sequences, the lovers Rita and Betty attend a performance at Club Silencio, where an actor explains on stage that everything is an illusion; a woman, Rebekah del Rio, playing herself, shot in many extreme close-ups, then lip-synchs an emotionally charged *a capella* version, in Spanish, of Roy Orbison's "Crying"; as they watch this performance, Rita and Betty are visibly shaken and begin to sob; the singer, emotionally affected by her own performance, collapses on stage and is taken away by two stage hands as the song continues to play. Betty and Rita watch the stage in rapture, still crying, enthralled by the performance and the song.[48] The point one can draw from this example is that art (theater, music, cinema) does have this powerful effect on spectators[49]—we all, at some point, are completely enthralled by the illusion, reacting in intense, bodily ways to the images/sounds/words we experience. *That* is the element of a filmic experience adaptation scholars have not addressed sufficiently when they discuss a filmic version of a novel.

Addressing this bodily experience of cinema has also remained a challenging aspect for film studies in general, but some of the most exciting contemporary work in cinema theory has started to address this issue. Barbara Kennedy, in her book *Deleuze and Cinema: The Aesthetics of Sensation*, argues that, in general, scholars have attended quite extensively to the way film has developed in terms of ideology and cultural representation. She argues that "within film theory and predominantly feminist film theory, film has been theorized through debates about representation, signification, semiotics, and structuralism."[50] That is to say, in the wake of the 1960s theory proliferation, and especially after espousing various versions of identity politics, many scholars in film and media studies have provided incisive critiques of how media representations express and perpetuate a range of ideological beliefs structured especially around the axes of gender, class, and sexuality. Kennedy asks, though, "How do we begin to understand and account for the popularity, the desires and pleasures of contemporary cinema outside these notions?"[51] In effect, Kennedy is asking questions about the affective dimension of movies and their capacity to move viewers in quite powerful ways, what she terms "the experiential characteristics of cinema."[52] She offers "a neo-aesthetics of the visual encounter of cinema" that "sees film as an 'event,' as a processual engagement of duration and movement, articulated through webs of sensation across landscapes and panoramas of space, bodies, and time."[53] Kennedy's description of this new approach to cinema seems rather appropriate in light of my analysis above of *Lost Highway*. Since that film does not lend itself to an analysis in terms of traditional literary concepts, discussing the film in terms of its "webs of sensation" takes us much farther. Like music, the film forms an experience in terms of duration and movement in the sense that particular subjects inhabit the space of two hours in various episodic encounters that are held together by a thematic thread (issues of marriage, emotional needs, jealousy and trust between two individuals). Thus, this argument suggests that the cinematic experience is, at least in part, experiential, processual: that it works incessantly on the sense and that in turn spectators react in visceral, affective ways.

While a more complete examination of this approach would exceed the purpose of this essay, I will conclude my argument with an appeal to rethink the scope and methodology of adaptation theory. It seems only logical that the discipline emerged out of concerns over literature and that literature was usually conceived in a traditional, New Critical manner by teachers and scholars who had been trained in that approach. Much good work has come from it, and to some extent this approach still holds enormous value if we want to teach students in our classes the value of traditional literature. And yet, as I have argued here, much exciting work is happening across the media theory landscape, and the "experiential" approach addressed by Kennedy deserves more attention. This approach is grounded in a poststructural focus on those dimensions of experience that exceed the work of ideology, systems of signification, and cultural/social formation of subjectivity. In no way is the work of these factors being negated; rather, theorists who work with this approach argue that in addition to such political-ideological elements, the experiential aspect of living-in-culture also comes to matter.

Thus, in terms of cinema studies, Shaviro, for example, has argued that "film is a vivid medium, and it is important to talk about how it arouses corporeal reactions of desire and fear, pleasure and disgust, fascination and shame."[54] Shaviro offers, in his study of film, *The Cinematic Body*, a discussion of film that examines how the medium of film gains its power on the viewer. In that sense, this approach asks central questions about how cinema does its work. In his very critical assessment of the state of adaptation studies, Ray notes, "confronted by our century's distinctive feature—a media industry whose shared (and oppressive) representations converge from every side to structure even our unconscious lives—we have no idea how to fight back."[55] He argues that we need to develop a more theoretically informed, more expansive apparatus with which to examine our new media landscape. We need to figure out better how new media—including film—work so powerfully (often pleasurably) on our senses, on our bodies, on our minds. Part of such work has been presented here. What I called above a "neo-aesthetics of sensation," reading *Lost Highway* as an aesthetic experience akin to music, enables a consideration of how film impacts and engages the senses and the body of the spectator as a particular event, a "real" experience. Greg Hainge notes that the deliberate dissolution of narrative in *Lost Highway* "question[s] not 'reality' itself but rather the supposed realism of the cinematic medium and its capacity for coherent representation."[56] That is to say, film is real in the sense that the film *as film* does exist; however, it exists *as film*, as a constructed entity within the cinematic medium. Because it is thus constructed, it cannot "represent" some unified whole. It's always made up, scene by scene, shot by shot. That we sometimes *perceive* it as a unified whole is precisely the power of cinema—and thinking of cinema as an aesthetic, visceral experience might help us understand better how the artifice is wrought and what makes it so powerful. This analytical insight seems to be needed particularly in the discipline of adaptation studies because this field deals with the most powerful "realism" devices our society has yet experienced: literature and film.

NOTES

1. André Bazin, "Adaptation, or the Cinema as Digest," from "Introduction: Film and the Reign of Adaptation," in *Film Adaptation*, ed. James Naremore (New Brunswick, NJ: Rutgers University Press, 2000), 19.

2. Imelda Whelehan, "Adaptations: The Contemporary Dilemmas," in *Adaptations: From Text to Screen, Screen to Text*, ed. Deborah Cartmell and Imelda Whelehan (London: Routledge, 1999), 9.

3. Robert Ray, "The Field of Literature and Film," *Film Adaptation*, ed. James Naremore (New Brunswick, NJ: Rutgers University Press, 2000), 40.

4. Mireia Aragay, "Introduction: Reflection to Refraction: Adaptation Studies Then and Now," *Books in Motion: Adaptation, Intertextuality, Authorship*, ed. Mireia Aragay (Amsterdam: Rodopi, 2006), 11.

5. Robert Ray, "The Field of Literature and Film," 45.

6. Ibid., 46.

7. Ibid.

8. Ibid.

9. Bazin's 1948 essay "Adaptation, or the Cinema as Digest," is reprinted in Naremore's collection, where I encountered it for the first time.

10. James Naremore, "Introduction: Film and the Reign of Adaptation," in *Film Adaptation*, ed. James Naremore (New Brunswick, NJ: Rutgers University Press, 2000), 10.

11. Robert Stam, "Introduction: The Theory and Practice of Adaptation," *Literature and Film: A Guide to the Theory and Practice of Film Adaptation*, ed. Robert Stam and Alessandra Raengo (Malden, MA: Blackwell Publishing, 2005), 9.

12. Ibid., 20.

13. Ibid.

14. Ibid., 21–22.

15. Ibid., 22.

16. Ibid., 24.

17. Ibid.

18. Ibid.

19. In addition to the three essays reviewed here, I want to draw attention to Glenn Jellenik's chapter in this volume. Jellenik's innovative contribution foregrounds the role soundtrack plays as an adaptive technique in its own right, rather than as a mere supplement to visual and verbal tracks. Jellenik shows that soundtrack forms a text, a meaningful entity, that directly informs the nature and feel of an adaptation.

20. Robin Wood, "Written on the Wind," in *Film Studies: Critical Approaches*, ed. John Hill and Pamela Church Gibson (New York: Oxford University Press, 2000), 24.

21. Thomas Fahy, "Killer Culture: Classical Music and the Art of Killing in *Silence of the Lambs* and *Se7en*," *Journal of Popular Culture* 37, no. 1 (2003): 31.

22. Ibid., 32

23. James Tobias, "Cinema, Scored: Towards a Comparative Methodology for Music in Media," *Film Quarterly* 57, no. 2 (2003/04): 28–29.

24. Ibid., 30.

25. Ibid.

26. *Lost Highway*, DVD, directed by David Lynch (London, UK: October Films, 1997); David Lynch and Barry Gifford, *Lost Highway*, Screenplay (London: Faber and Faber, 1997).

27. *Lost Highway* invites non-traditional readings, of course, because it almost flaunts its non-conventional structure. David Lynch also is known for defying traditional Hollywood narrative conventions. However, the analysis I provide in this essay will be relevant to film studies in general. I focus here on *Lost Highway* as my case study to more directly make my point about film's multidimensionality and the obvious difference between reading a film according to literary criteria and according to other dimensions, but this sort of analysis applies to film in general. See Kennedy for many examples of traditional narrative cinema that also lend themselves to an exploration along the lines suggested here.

28. Ann Jerslev, "Beyond Boundaries: David Lynch's *Lost Highway*," *The Cinema of David Lynch: American Dreams, Nightmare Visions*, ed. Erica Sheen and Annette Davidson (London: Wallflower Press, 2004): 156.

29. David Andrews, "An Oneiric Fugue: The Various Logics of *Mulholland Drive*," *Journal of Film and Video* 56, no. 1 (2004): 25.

30. Todd McGowan, *The Impossible David Lynch* (New York: Columbia University Press, 2007), 155.

31. Steven Shaviro, "Intrusions: *Lost Highway* and the Future of Narrative," *Paradoxa* 4, no. 11 (1998): 503.

32. James Tobias, "Cinema, Scored: Towards a Comparative Methodology for Music in Media," 30.

33. In an interview, for instance, Lynch notes that he came across a medical condition known as "psychogenic fugue," that seems to reflect to some extent Fred Madison's state of mind. Lynch notes that he likes the comparison to fugue "because it goes from one thing, segues to another, and then I think it comes back again. And so it is in *Lost Highway*" (Lynch and Gifford xix). However, Lynch is also careful not to essentialize the film and to suggest it should be read as fugue, or that he *intended* to create a comparison to fugue. See also Hughes (214) for another discussion of "psychogenic fugue." In addition, David Andrews generally argues that *Mulholland Drive*, as does *Lost Highway*, might work toward a "symphonic goal" (35), since Lynch referred to the latter film as a "psychogenic fugue." Andrews notes that the term "highlights both its narrative concern with psychosis and its formal emphasis on repetition and variation" (35). Andrews brings up repeatedly the "fugal" composition of both films, albeit in a cursory manner, to suggest that *Mulholland Drive* formally "behave[s]

according to the logic of counterpoint. Such a logic explains those repetitions in *Mulholland Drive* that resist narrative excavation" (37). Indeed, this seems to be the argument I am interested in: that a narrative reading of film risks essentializing an art form that may function in a different register, such as music.

34. Christoff Wolff, *Johann Sebastian Bach: The Learned Musician* (New York: W. W. Norton, 2001), 433.

35. *The Harvard Concise Dictionary of Music and Musicians*, ed. Michael Randel. (Cambridge, MA: The Belknap Press of Harvard University Press, 1999), s.v. "fugue."

36. Ibid.

37. Ibid.

38. "Counterpoint" is defined as "the perception of two or more melodic lines; the linear consideration of melodic lines sounding together." *The Harvard Concise Dictionary of Music and Musicians*, ed. Michael Randel. (Cambridge, MA: The Belknap Press of Harvard University Press, 1999), s.v. "counterpoint." Similarly, in *Lost Highway*, the viewer perceives two or more melodic lines in Fred/Pete and brunette Renee/blond Renee/The Mystery Man

39. A "cadence" is defined by the *Harvard Dictionary of Music* as "a melodic or harmonic configuration that creates a sense of repose or resolution. Cadences thus most often mark the end of a phrase, period, or complete composition" (105). For example, probably the most frequently used cadence is the "Amen" sung or recited at the end of Protestant hymns. The structure and function of a cadence can be readily seen in *Lost Highway:* especially the first half of the film includes a number of fade-outs and fade-ins between scenes (note the scene in which Fred returns home from the club to see Renee sleeping soundly in their bed—fade-out, fade-in—cut to scene the next day), suggesting an almost calming break between various episodes in the film. Another cadence occurs at the end of the episode I describe in the text when Fred recounts his dream to Renee. *The Harvard Concise Dictionary of Music and Musicians*, ed. Michael Randel. (Cambridge, MA: The Belknap Press of Harvard University Press, 1999), s.v. "cadence."

40. *The Harvard Concise Dictionary*, s.v. "fugue."

41. *Lost Highway*, DVD, 1997.

42. *The Harvard Concise Dictionary*, s.v. "fugue."

43. The transformation from Fred into Pete deserves more analysis and might just form the film's "high note." In brief, as Pete and Alice are on the run after committing murder, they stop in the desert. They stand in front of the car, headlights are on. Alice finds some music on the car radio. They begin to undress each other, as they dance in and out of the headlights; they sink to the ground and start making love. The lights from the car combine with the starlight, the music changes to loud and intense. Alice becomes very passionate and aggressive in her lovemaking. The headlights flare, as if the two bodies are burning up. Pete seems desperate to please her; the music on the radio goes to static, as Pete exclaims, "I want you . . . I want you." With an almost mean smile, Alice gets up into the darkness, and says into Pete's ear, "You'll *never* have me." She walks away naked to the nearby cabin. Pete turns, holding his head and shaking. When he turns to stand in the glare of the headlights, he is not Pete but Fred. Inside the car he sees The Mystery Man. In other words, this quite disconcerting scene plays out in a heightened manner the basic counterpoint movement we have seen so far: Pete and Alice engage in an episode in which their two voices interact with high intensity, first harmoniously, then quite disparately. When Pete finally tells her his inner-most desire ("I want you"), she responds with harsh disharmony and contrast ("You can never have me"). The two voices are so jarring at this point, that

the movement then switches to their counter-voices, with an even more heightened contrast. From here on, the film does not go back to Pete, but will stay with Fred's voice, whose timbre continues the sense of discord, fear, and torment to the very last image of the film.

44. Christoff Wolff, *Johann Sebastian Bach*, 433.

45. André Bazin, "An Aesthetic of Reality: Cinematic Realism and the Italian School of the Liberation," in *What is Cinema? Volume II*, trans. Hugh Gray (Berkeley: University of California Press, 1971), 26.

46. Glen Gould, "Glen Gould Talks about Art of Fugue," Internet Video, *You Tube.com*, http://vodpod.com/watch/123296-bach-glenn-gould-talks-about-art-of-fugue

47. Steven Shaviro, "Intrusions," 502.

48. *Mulholland Drive*, DVD, directed by David Lynch (Los Angeles, CA: Universal Studios, 2001).

49. Literature certainly also exhibits a powerful, visceral effect on readers. In fact, an extended argument in this chapter suggests that reading literature through a lens of traditional literary New Criticism essentializes an experience that encompasses many other aspects. This aspect has been taken up by poststructuralism most directly.

50. Barbara M. Kennedy, *Deleuze and Cinema: The Aesthetics of Sensation* (Edinburgh, UK: Edinburgh University Press, 2000), 4.

51. Ibid.

52. Ibid.

53. Ibid., 5.

54. Steven Shaviro, *The Cinematic Body* (Minneapolis: University of Minnesota Press, 1993), viii.

55. Robert Ray, "The Field of Literature and Film," 48.

56. Greg Hainge, "Weird or Loopy? Specular Spaces, Feedback and Artifice in *Lost Highway*'s Aesthetic of Sensation," in *The Cinema of David Lynch: American Dreams, Nightmare Visions*, ed. Erica Sheen and Annette Davison (London: Wallflower Press, 2004), 140.

Assemblage Filmmaking: Approaching the Multi-Source Adaptation and Reexamining George Romero's *Night of the Living Dead*

Kyle Bishop

THE ACADEMY OF MOTION PICTURE ARTS AND SCIENCES RECOGnizes only two categories of filmmaking with their Oscar awards for screenwriting—"original" and "adapted" screenplays—and film scholars often lump cinematic texts into just one or the other of these limiting binaries as well. However, in a world filled with sequels, remakes, parodies, reboots, and other kinds of adaptations, such a clear-cut dichotomy fails to address the variety of texts that can and do exist on the film screen. For instance, a movie such as Baz Luhrmann's *Romeo + Juliet* (1996) was not only based on Shakespeare's dramatic script but was also clearly influenced by the various cinematic versions of the play that preceded it. More complex examples include Mel Brooks's *The Producers* (2005), the cinematic adaptation of his Broadway musical version of his original 1968 movie of the same title, and Barry Sonnenfeld's *Addams Family Values* (1993), which is a sequel to his movie *The Addams Family* (1991), which was based on the television series *The Addams Family* (1964–66), which was adapted from a series of cartoons created by Charles Addams for *The New Yorker*, which were inspired by the classic Hollywood monster movies of the 1930s, which were derived from nineteenth-century Gothic literature. In practice, all movies fall somewhere within a complex *system* of texts, a virtual web of narratives, characters, genres, and plots that intersect at key nodal points. These points of intersection produce fundamentally intertextual movies; in other words, filmmakers draw upon multiple antecedents simultaneously to produce both "original" and "adapted" films.

Noted adaptation theorist Robert Stam argues that all films, not just deliberate literary adaptations, rely on this kind of intertextuality and that all movies are derivative on some level.[1] He views filmmaking as a kind of evolutionary mutation process that transcends the limiting perspective of strict fidelity.[2] Film scholar James Naremore similarly proposes that adaptation theory needs to engage more fully with the idea of intertextuality and Mikhail Bakhtin's sense of "dialogics" in art.[3] Both Stam and Naremore thus challenge the long-standing conception of cinematic adaptation made prevalent by prolific film theorist Dudley Andrew. In his seminal and oft-anthologized essay "Adaptation" from 1984, Andrew presents the adaptation process in terms of just three theoretical modes, which he describes in terms of transforming, borrowing, and intersecting source materials.[4] Although these rather reductive designations would prove useful for classifying and understanding straightforward, more traditional film adaptations, they ultimately prove insufficient because most films have in fact been derived from a number of disparate, if related, sources. An intertextual approach is needed, and although Claude Lévi-Strauss comes close to explaining the multi-source filmmaking process with his concept of the *bricolage*,[5] even that term implies a discordant tinkering and building rather than a more holistic blending of antecedents.

A multi-source adaptation in the cinema represents a creative process that can best be understood by interdisciplinary analogy. Most forms of art embrace a mode or genre that uses raw materials from other art works and artists in the creation of a newly constituted work. For example, two-dimensional art categorizes such a syncretic construction as a *collage, assemblage* describes the corresponding method in sculpture, and a *medley* creates a similar collection of preexisting materials in a musical score. Yet in all of these examples, the defining qualities of the source materials remain largely preserved and unaltered, being merely *reorganized* instead of *reconstituted*. The best way to understand and analyze the fusion of source material that occurs in filmmaking is through a more applicable version of the term *assemblage*, one drawn from winemaking. A talented vintner may create an assemblage wine by combining various quantities of existing vintages, blending the different flavors in an innovative way to create a unique flavor and a new drinking experience. Such an analogous perspective offers a new way to approach the cinematic adaptation process, one that could be considered a fourth mode within Andrew's matrix, but one that will ultimately be shown to replace and subsume it. Assemblage filmmaking illustrates how movies are in fact innovative and thorough blendings of multiple existing antecedents, where the different "vintages" combine in new ways to create perceptively new narratives and unique cinematic experiences.

This chapter will first explore Andrew's three adaptive modes in detail by examining the complex text system that has been created around H. G. Wells's *The War of the Worlds* (1898).[6] This analysis will both illustrate how Andrew's modes function on a theoretical level and will also expose the limitations of his reductive models and establish the need for film theorists to embrace the assemblage mode of adaptation. An investigation into the antecedental sources of George A. Romero's *Night of the Living* Dead (1968)[7] will then illustrate the practical application of this new critical approach. Although Romero's first zombie movie stands as a landmark and seemingly original movie, it actually draws upon a variety of preexisting sources that remain recognizable in themes and images, if not strictly in character or plot. A movie such as *Night of the Living Dead* synthesizes multiple antecedents; therefore, Romero's intertextual adaptation process operates on some level within all of Andrew's modes simultaneously. Such a syncretic, dialogical film illustrates the need for film scholars and critics to broaden the accepted definition of "adaptation" to include the various text systems at work behind any given movie to provide a thorough understanding of not only how that film was produced, but also to understand the cultural and historical contexts that surround that cinematic text.

RETHINKING DUDLEY'S MODES OF ADAPTATION

Motion pictures based on preceding narratives—those drawn from novels, short stories, plays, mythologies, folklore, graphic novels, videogames, true-life events, television programs, other movies, or even amusement park rides—are generally considered *adaptations*, but George Bluestone's *translations* might be a more accurate term.[8] The screenwriter, director, editor, cinematographer, actors, and others take the primary characters and the central storyline and plot from another source and re-envision the narrative as a cinematic product. Bulky text must invariably be condensed down to a workable length, subplots and other tangential materials must be simplified or removed, characters must be sacrificed or combined to save time and space, dialogue must be reworked and even created, literary concepts must be essentially recast as visual images, and entirely new material can be invented and added to take advantage of the cinematic medium. The process is understandably long and difficult, and the resulting film may bear little resemblance to the original source material. In a reductive attempt to simplify this transformative filmmaking process, Andrew has provided a theoretical spectrum of adaptation, from minor allusions to total fidelity of translation.[9]

Today's average filmgoers cannot help but be aware of these degrees of adaptation on some level, especially when a filmmaker's debt to the original source material is referenced in the opening credits or as part of the movie's marketing campaign. Douglas McGrath's *Emma* (1996), for instance, exemplifies the literal or loyal adaptation, with Jane Austen herself getting top writing credit. Such apparently "faithful" transmutations of narrative material present themselves as strict cinematic versions of classic literature, generally advertising themselves to be "based on" an original source. On the other hand, Amy Heckerling's *Clueless* (1995) is far less true to its Romantic antecedent, borrowing its general plot from Austen, but altering the setting and appearance to the point of masking the source material almost entirely. Such "liberal" adaptations give barely a nod to their antecedental texts in their title sequences, perhaps claiming instead merely to be "inspired by" an author, novel, or event. Finally, some films don't draw their narrative structures or plots from preexisting sources at all, but they do build upon established characters. The recent *Superman Returns* (2006), directed by Bryan Singer, is in this vein, where the only writing credit given to comic book author Jerry Siegel is the rather token epithet "based on characters created by."

Andrew proposes just three different approaches to understanding this variegated cinematic adaptation process. He describes this theoretical discourse, one that addresses the conversion of a text from one medium to another, as "the matching of the cinematic sign system to prior achievement in some other system."[10] On the most essential level, the signification process used by a literary text employs fundamentally different signifiers than those available to a predominantly visual one. For example, an author must rely upon written words to describe what a character is thinking or feeling, but a filmmaker may direct an actor to convey thoughts and emotions through a variety of precise facial expressions. The key to the adaptation process therefore lies in using the signifiers appropriate for the medium to invoke the desired signified concepts; these cinematic signifiers may directly mirror those from the antecedental literary text, as in the case of dialogue, or they may be entirely visual in nature, as when cinematography uses shadows instead of words to create a sense of foreboding or dread. In an attempt to illustrate the different ways filmmakers most commonly translate semiotic signs from a written to a visual medium, Andrew reduces the "modes of relation between the film and the text" to "borrowing, intersection, and fidelity of transformation."[11] An analysis of Wells's popular and well-known science fiction novel *The War of the Worlds,* along with a number of its various cinematic incarnations, will help to clarify Andrew's occasionally imprecise terminology and language and to illustrate how these rather abstract concepts translate, albeit ultimately insufficiently, into actual cinematic practice.

Andrew's presentation of his three modes of adaptation begins with the least "fidelious" relationship between two related texts. Borrowing, perhaps the most frequently occurring mode, takes place when the "material, idea, or form of an earlier, generally successful text" is employed as the filmmakers seek a certain respectability.[12] This kind of adaptation is the furthest removed from its source antecedent, with material elements being reduced to the level of light reference, homage, or even cliché. For instance, the distinctive look of *Mars Attacks!* (1996),[13] directed by Tim Burton, comes primarily from a series of Topps trading cards developed by Len Brown and Woody Gelman during the 1960s. The similar narratives told by the cards and by Burton's film feature invasions of the Earth by aliens from Mars who attack humans with advanced machines and heat rays that vaporize their targets, all signifying elements drawn from Wells's story, even though the plot has been substantially altered in both. In fact, *Mars Attacks!* "borrows" from the 1953 film *The War of the Worlds* as well by directly employing the identical sound effects for the Martian ray guns. Yet beyond these recognizable signifiers, the connections between this parody of 1950s alien-invasion movies and the nineteenth-century novel are certainly limited. Although the Martians and their weapons reflect those of earlier incarnations of the story, their primary intention is to invoke humor rather than fear and paranoia, resulting in a fundamental shift in the produced signs. In other words, the signifiers alone are "borrowed," and the resulting film has been transformed on the level of signification.

Andrew's second mode of adaptation lies somewhere between loose reference and total textual fidelity, and it proves to be the most challenging of the approaches to explain and unpack. Andrew somewhat cryptically claims that with intersecting, "the uniqueness of the original text is preserved to such an extent that it is intentionally left unassimilated."[14] In other words, with this approach to adaptation, the filmmaker strives to maintain the spirit or essence of the original text, even though the details of the narrative (characters, location, plot points, etc.) may change dramatically. To explain intersection further, Andrew references André Bazin, who describes such an adaptation as a "refraction" of the original source.[15] That is, films that intersect with their antecedents "fear or refuse to adapt" and present "the otherness and distinctiveness of the original."[16] Stephen Spielberg's 2005 *War of the Worlds* provides a good example of this mode of adaptation, for the film emphasizes those elements that were most significant to the original story—the inexplicable alien invasion, the mass destruction, the impotence of the military, and the threat to the lives of the protagonists—although many of the specific signs used to achieve those result have been changed. This adaptation and remake focuses on a single father and his children in New York City, which constitutes a clear change in the narrative's essential plot, but the film manages to retain the mood and tone of Wells's original narrative.[17] In other words, the identity of the protagonists and their geographic location may have been changed, but the story remains a terrifying depiction of the helplessness of the human race in the face of an overwhelmingly powerful alien invasion.

Andrew's final mode of adaptation addresses the kind of one-to-one relationship upon which most traditional adaptation theory focuses. With fidelity of transformation, "the task of adaptation is the reproduction in cinema of something essential about an original text."[18] Rather than focusing on just one scene, convention, plot device, mood, or style, Andrew suggests that fidelious adaptations transform or translate the source material directly from one medium to another. In other words, Andrew claims the signs used in both texts can be identical; essentially parallel signifiers are supposedly re-created cinematically to reference the same signifieds as in the original literary antecedent. This transformation must occur at the most fundamental level of creation, and Andrew emphasizes how "the skeleton of the original can, more or less thoroughly, become the skeleton of a film."[19] The 1953 version of *War of the Worlds*, directed by Byron Haskin, follows the plot and structure of the Wells text most closely of all the cinematic iterations. Although the action has been transferred to the United States, key plot points from the novel are easily recognizable—such as the mysterious cylinders, the scientist protagonist, the vaporizing heat rays, etc.—and the desired mood and tone presumably emulate the fear and paranoia inspired by Wells's original.[20]

The three modes presented by Andrew have proven popular in examining the prevalent methods of converting a literary text into a motion picture, but upon closer examination, they fail to address the complexities of the adaptive filmmaking process and the variety of cinematic texts that do exist. For instance, Andrew claims that the signifiers used by primarily literary texts can be directly recreated by a visual medium, a translation of signification that proves impossible except perhaps when the filmmaker uses dialogue or printed text directly on the screen. Instead, fundamentally different signifiers must be used, and although they may ultimately reference similar signifieds—that is, a word printed on a page and an image shown on the screen may describe and reference the same object—the signs have been unavoidably altered. Furthermore, Andrew's modes continue to fixate upon issues of fidelity, assuming a one-to-one relationship between a film and its literary origins that has almost unilaterally been challenged by current adaptation theorists, particularly Stam and Naremore. In other words, Andrew provides no framework in which to address a multi-source adaptation or an overtly intertextual film.

In his efforts to redefine the reductive binary system, Stam proposes a number of new adaptive models to replace what he sees to be the "inadequate trope" of fidelity; for instance, he suggests a "Pygmalion" approach to films that bring their source material "to life," a "ventriloqual" trope for movies that give the characters of a novel their "voice," an "alchemical" mode for films that turn "verbal dross into filmic gold," a "possession" perspective for movies that capture the spirit of the source material, and an "incarnational" model by which the "word" of a novel is made "flesh" by the film.[21] With these new modes of adaptation, Stam attempts to address the prevalent mutation of texts across different media, and he succeeds in illustrating the diversity of processes at play whenever a filmmaker translates a primarily literary text into a primarily visual one. However, like Andrew before him, Stam perpetuates the failure to consider adequately how films draw from multiple, disparate sources simultaneously; instead, even though he refutes fidelity, Stam actually continues to see the adaptation process in terms of a binary relationship between just two related texts.

In a poststructuralist world, all films must be recognized as being based on an assortment of antecedents and combining ideas, images, plot points, characters, motifs, and tropes from multiple books, stories, plays, poems, films, other works of art, and historical events. For example, a movie such as Roland Emmerich's *Independence Day* (1996)[22] may have clear thematic and plot ties to Wells's *The War of the Worlds*, making it partially an example of Andrew's borrowing, but it also features elements from disaster movies, war films, other science-fiction narratives, and popular culture. In fact, the three film versions of *The War of the Worlds* discussed above must all be considered the products of multiple influential source texts, particularly Orson Welles's sensational radio broadcast of *The War of the Worlds* from 1938, illustrated or comic versions of Wells's story, and other science fiction or invasion narratives—as well as each other. When considered from this intertextual perspective, such movies can no longer be seen as simply one side of a reductive dichotomy, but neither can they be considered totally original products. Instead, seemingly new narratives are constructed from preexisting pieces, pieces drawn from a complex system of related texts. This somewhat Frankensteinian process can best be explained by using metaphors of creation from other artistic processes.

Filmmaking is certainly not the only art form that draws from a variety of preexisting texts or inspirations. Collages are primarily two-dimensional works that incorporate newspaper clippings, photographs, or other printed media onto the surface of a painting, while assemblages work similarly on the three-dimensional level, creating architectural re-combinations of machined or other found objects. Musical compositions often "quote" or replicate tunes, melodies, and note combinations intentionally to reference other pieces of music, and a *medley* designates a piece constructed solely from other musical works. Yet in all three of these examples, the materials being re-appropriated or referenced largely retain their initial features, and thus the original significance of their signifiers. A multi-source film adaptation, on the other hand, largely loses such readily recognizable referents; therefore, the appropriation of the term *assemblage* from the art of winemaking proves more suitable. In such a context, an assemblage is a blend of wines drawn from different casks of the same or related vintages. The purpose of such a mixture can be to avoid creating too many inconsistent and dissimilar bottles of wine in the same growing season, but it can also be employed to experiment with different combinations to produce new tastes. Ultimately, although some of the original flavors would be discernible to a sophisticated sommelier, for the most part a brand new wine is created.

According to Naremore, "The study of adaptation needs to be joined with the study of recycling, remaking, and every other form of retelling in the age of mechanical reproduction and electronic communication,"[23] and the mode of assemblage filmmaking begins to address this syncretic process of translation. By appropriating the conceptual terminology of winemaking for filmmaking, the new adaptation trope of the assemblage creates a methodological structure by which a film based on multiple antecedents may be more thoroughly analyzed. As with the careful blending of related vintages of wine, the systematic combination of preexisting narrative texts and dramatic symbols resulting in the combination of a variety of related thematic, stylistic, and narrative elements likewise produces something new and original, yet with the recognizable flavor of established works. In fact, all films need to be considered as parts of an elaborate system of existing texts, and the revelation of the assemblage creative process works both to locate where any given film lies within its web of source texts and to illuminate how the movie was initially constructed. Ultimately, films need to be considered as intertextual constructions, for they all draw some inspiration from other texts, and they all contribute to the creation of the texts that follow them.

Assembling *Night of the Living Dead*

Romero and screenwriter John Russo originally conceived of *Night of the Living Dead* as a cinematic allegory inspired by Richard Matheson's 1954 novella *I Am Legend*.[24] Both narratives emphasize the isolation and destruction of a wide-scale apocalypse, featuring "a mass return from the grave of the recently dead and their need to feed off the flesh and blood of the living."[25] However, where Matheson's monsters are clearly and essentially vampires, Romero's appear as some kind of cannibalistic ghouls.[26] The two texts have other dissimilarities as well, for Romero and Russo drew from a variety of sources while creating their own uncanny tale; specifically, the existing panoply of cinematic zombie and invasion narratives, the short story "Who Goes There?" (1938) by John W. Campbell Jr.,[27] Daphne du Maurier's short story "The Birds" (1952),[28] the science fiction novel *The Body Snatchers* (1955) by Jack Finney,[29] and the film versions of these three literary texts.[30] Although *Night of the Living Dead* has a clear place in the genealogy and tradition of the invasion narrative, it resists classification as a traditionally conceived adaptation drawn from one recognizable literary antecedent. Instead, it is an assemblage—a blend of preexisting texts that combines the defining features of other narratives to create something new and original.

Although Romero's *Night* is often considered the foundational text of the zombie film tradition, the first zombie movie appeared in 1932 with Victor Halperin's *White Zombie*. This Gothic tale of voodoo and witchcraft, inspired by sensational travel narratives such as William B. Seabrook's *The Magic Island* (1929) and Universal Picture's *Dracula* (1932), established the now familiar blank stare and shuffling gait of the "living dead." Other such films followed, featuring not only voodoo zombies, as in *King of the Zombies* (1941) and *I Walked with a Zombie* (1943), but also corpses reanimated by scientific or technological means. For example, *Invisible Invaders* (1959) and *The Earth Dies Screaming* (1964) depicted hoards of reanimated human corpses used as armies by alien forces to invade and subjugate the human race, obvious sources of visual inspiration for Romero.[31] In 1966, Hammer Film's *The Plague of Zombies* returned to the voodoo roots of the monsters and firmly established the zombies' decaying appearance.[32] Yet while all of these movies clearly influenced the look and feel of *Night*, the pre-1968 zombie films generally feature the animated dead as servants or soldiers, usually controlled by a master (a voodoo priest, a mad scientist, or alien invaders).[33] *Night of the Living Dead* forever altered the subgenre by making the zombies autonomous monsters, fueled by hunger, the basest of motives and desires.

Night is now rightfully acknowledged as an essential milestone in the zombie canon, but the movie was initially conceived as part of the broader, science fiction apocalyptic tradition.[34] In fact, Romero originally considered his monsters to be "ghouls," not zombies; in his preface to Russo's 1997 novelization of *Night*, Romero never uses the "z-word," and the term doesn't appear in the film at all.[35] Instead, the monsters constitute a supernatural or a scientific invasion; although the source must be considered somewhat dubious, the news broadcasters in *Night* speculate that the corpses have returned from the dead because of interstellar radiation brought back from Venus by a NASA space probe. By thus linking the phenomenon of the living dead to outer space, Romero connects his text to the system of science fiction narratives begun by *The War of the Worlds*. Furthermore, because Romero's ghouls are simply reanimated corpses, they are not the victims of a voodoo priest or a mystical curse. That is, rather than acting on the orders of another, the creatures are merely dumb beasts, fueled by desire and instinct alone to kill, destroy, and feed. Those caught in their swarming path are either consumed or converted, and the hapless few survivors must barricade themselves inside to wait or fight back through violent means. In other words, the most famous of all the zombie movies ironically has its narrative and stylistic root in nonzombie texts.

The earliest of Romero's non-zombie antecedents comes from Campbell's "Who Goes There?," a serialized science fiction tale about a team of scientists trapped in an Antarctic research station with a malevolent alien creature that has the ability to assume human form. Even though the threat is limited to just a few of these doppelgänger monsters, Campbell's story creates a tremendous sense of dread and hopelessness by putting the protagonists in a fundamentally inescapable situation: even when confronted by the threat of death *inside*, the harsh conditions *outside* keep them trapped.[36] In *Night*, Romero shifts the signifier from an Antarctic research station to a lonely country farmhouse, but his own protagonists remain similarly confined, resulting in essentially the same sign for helpless isolation and vulnerability. Furthermore, the increasingly powerful assault of the ghouls in *Night* keeps the feckless survivors cut off from the rest of society, and as all attempts to escape fail miserably, they are eventually threatened from within, by both the reanimated dead and each other. Romero was clearly inspired by the look and feel of Christian Nyby's 1951 adaptation of Campbell's story, *The Thing from Another World* as well.[37] Although the fundamental nature of the alien creature has been changed to a single lumbering behemoth, Nyby's film still features a motley group of survivors trapped inside a remote location with a powerful killing force.

While these preexisting texts feature important developments in the invasion tradition, Romero takes his to the utmost level: that of an implicitly global apocalypse. Perhaps the most influential "end of the world" narrative of the early twentieth century is du Maurier's short story "The Birds"; Gregory A. Waller claims it to be behind not only *Night of the Living Dead*, but also the inspirational source for all post-1968 apocalyptic narratives.[38] Du Maurier's short tale focuses on a hapless family who board themselves up in their own home to escape an unexplained attack by flocks and flocks of insanely aggressive birds. Rather than dealing with just a few monsters, as in "Who Goes There?," "The Birds" features an external hoard and overwhelming odds. Romero certainly recreates this situation with *Night*'s fortified farmhouse, a direct signifying parallel to du Maurier's story, and its hostile army of ghouls. Indeed, one of the primary visual antecedents for *Night of the Living Dead* is clearly Hitchcock's 1963 adaptation of "The Birds." R. H. W. Dillard illustrates this connection by noting that "in both films, a group of people are besieged by an apparently harmless and ordinary world gone berserk, struggle to defend themselves against the danger, and struggle to maintain their rationality and their values at the same time."[39] The sequence of Mitch Brenner (Rod Taylor) nailing boards across the windows of his home is directly recreated by Romero, as are shots of the birds breaking windows and determinedly pecking away at the rudimentary fortifications.

Of course, the monsters in *Night* are much more than simple birds; Romero changes the essential signifiers of the invasion, and his zombies become decidedly uncanny because of their human appearance—some were even once known and loved by the surviving protagonists. Freud describes the uncanny as "that species of the frightening that goes back to what was once well known and had long been familiar."[40] This fear manifests, therefore, when a repressed familiarity returns in a disturbing way; the familiar (*heimlich*) becomes the unfamiliar or uncanny (*unheimlich*).[41] This casting of the "other" as the "self" can be found in two of *Night*'s assembled sources. Campbell's "Thing" has the ability to replicate itself on the cellular level; it can assume human form both physically and psychologically. Any human thus replaced by the hostile alien is indistinguishable from the others and is therefore all the more dangerous. Finney's *The Body Snatchers* also features alien invaders that look like known friends and loved ones, but act decidedly and markedly *inhuman* in their mannerisms. Romero was likely influenced by the look and feel of Don Siegel's "pod people" in his 1956 adaptation *Invasion of the Body Snatchers*,[42] because even though the ghouls of *Night* look human, they act stiff and artificial. Furthermore, Darryl Jones draws an additional connection between *Night* and *Invasion*, because in both films, traditional familial and social relationships fail to hold people together.[43] No one can be trusted, regardless of who the creatures appear to be.

These diverse texts constitute the variety of narrative flavors Romero drew upon when creating *Night of the Living Dead*, but the primary, base "vintage" comes from Matheson's novel *I Am Legend*. Romero began the filmmaking project of *Night* by drafting a short story called "Night of Anubis," an essentially Gothic tale that borrowed heavily from *I Am Legend*.[44] The screenplay that soon evolved with Russo's help featured isolated survivors, a house crudely converted into a fortress, and an army of uncanny "undead" monsters. This last characteristic is perhaps the most telling, for unlike *Night*'s other antecedental texts, *I Am Legend* features invading monsters with cannibalistic tendencies. Building on the horror genealogies of John Polidori and Bram Stoker, Matheson makes his invading force vampires, and they feast on the blood of the living to prolong their unnatural existence. Romero takes this taboo one step further; whereas Matheson's vampires only feast on blood, Romero's ghouls eat human flesh.[45] In addition, Romero taps into the allegorical themes of *I Am Legend*, using the monsters as metonymic symbols of both the dangers of contagion and modern technology and of the return of repressed desires and psychological trauma. Matheson's Richard Neville is literally haunted by both his dead wife and his former coworker, and Romero has reanimated family members kill both Barbra (Judith O'Dea) and the feckless Helen Cooper (Marilyn Eastman).

The 1964 film adaptation of *I Am Legend*, Ubaldo Ragona and Sidney Salkow's *The Last Man on Earth*,[46] represents perhaps the most influential visual source text for *Night*. Both films profit from a stark black-and-white cinematography, with much of the action taking place at night. Furthermore, although the menacing creatures of *Last Man* are technically vampires, as in Matheson's novel, they more closely resemble the zombies of earlier films, especially *White Zombie*, in their actions and movements.[47] For example, *Last Man*'s creatures are sluggish, primitive, and stupid, and they attack Robert Morgan's house with the same lack of organization and technical skill that would be seen in Romero's zombies. The interiors of the two houses are also visually similar, particularly the makeshift barricades and the boards nailed over the doors and windows.[48] The most telling visual parallel between the two films comes from the scene in *Last Man* when Robert (Vincent Price) opens his front door to reveal the disheveled form of his deceased wife Virginia (Emma Danieli), who has returned from the grave to kill him and drink his blood. This same literal manifestation of Freud's return of the repressed is recreated by Romero when the zombified Johnny (Russell Streiner) fights his way to the door of the besieged farmhouse and drags his sister Barbra outside to her doom.

Night of the Living Dead is just one example of a film adapted from multiple preexisting narratives; it features thematic, narrative, and visual elements co-opted from a variety of other sources, illustrating the limitations of Andrew's theoretical tropes of borrowing, intersecting, and transforming. Romero's landmark horror film represents an assemblage construction that blends its disparate antecedents, and this new discursive model provides critics with greater contextual insight into the filmmaker's inspirational and creative process. Yet *Night* has become more than just the end result of some dialectical synthesis—it has become a source text for a variety of other movies, from sequels to remakes to other assembled films, such as Romero's *Dawn of the Dead* (1978), Tom Savini's *Night of the Living Dead* (1990), and James Gunn's *Slither* (2006). In other words, an assembled film arises from a confluence of text systems, but it becomes part of that intertextual chain as well, perhaps even spawning a new system of its own. Therefore, with a movie such as *Night*, the cycle of inspiration and creation continues, and innovative filmmakers will keep finding new ways to recreate, re-envision, and reinvent the tried and true narratives established by other successful writers, artists, and filmmakers. The assemblage approach to cinematic adaptation studies proves an invaluable tool in understanding such diverse and syncretic film texts for two key reasons. First, it reveals how many cinematic texts that present themselves as original products are in fact adaptations constructed from existing antecedents, and second, the assemblage mode facilitates a New Historicist or culturally critical analysis of a given film adaptation.

NOTES

1. Robert Stam, "Introduction: The Theory and Practice of Adaptation," in *Literature and Film: A Guide to the Theory and Practice of Film Adaptation*, ed. Robert Stam and Alessandra Raengo (Malden, MA: Blackwell Publishing, 2005), 45.

2. Ibid., 3.

3. James Naremore, "Introduction: Film and the Reign of Adaptation," in *Film Adaptation*, ed. James Naremore (New Brunswick, NJ: Rutgers University Press, 2000), 12.

4. Dudley Andrew, "Adaptation," in *Concepts in Film Theory* (Oxford: Oxford University Press, 1984), 96–106.

5. Claude Lévi-Strauss, *The Savage Mind* (Chicago: University of Chicago Press, 1966).

6. H. G. Wells, *The War of the Worlds* (1898; Naperville, IL: Sourcebooks, 2005).

7. *Night of the Living Dead*, DVD, directed by George Romero (1968; Millennium Edition, Elite Entertainment, 1994).

8. George Bluestone, *Novels into Film* (Berkeley: University of California Press, 1966).

9. Because total fidelity of transformation between fundamentally different media is essentially impossible, the viability of Andrew's entire schema must be called into question, as shall be illustrated over the course of this analysis.

10. Andrew, "Adaptation," 96.

11. Ibid., 98.

12. Ibid.

13. *Mars Attacks!*, DVD, directed by Tim Burton (1996; Burbank, CA: Warner Home Video, 2004).

14. Ibid., 99.

15. André Bazin, *What is Cinema?* (Berkeley: University of California Press, 1968): 142, quoted in Andrew, "Adaptation," 99.

16. Andrew, "Adaptation," 100.

17. *War of the Worlds*, DVD, directed by Steven Spielberg (DreamWorks LLC and Paramount Pictures, 2005).

18. Andrew, "Adaptation," 100.

19. Ibid.

20. *The War of the Worlds*, DVD, directed by Byron Haskin (1953; Hollywood, CA: Paramount Pictures, 2005).

21. Stam, "Introduction," 24.

22. *Independence Day*, DVD, directed by Roland Emmerich (1996; Las Angeles, CA: Fox Home Entertainment, 2006).

23. James Naremore, "Introduction," 15.

24. Richard Matheson, *I Am Legend* (1954; repr., New York: Tom Doherty, 1995).

25. George A. Romero, preface to *Night of the Living Dead*, John A. Russo (Edmonton, AB: Commonwealth Publications Inc, 1997), 11.

26. Matheson builds on the tradition of Bram Stoker's *Dracula*, featuring moderately intelligent vampires that drink human blood to preserve their preternatural, undead existence; Romero's creatures lack the intellectual capacity and finesse of vampires, and they mindlessly kill and eat all living things.

27. John W. Campbell, Jr., "Who Goes There?" in *Who Goes There?: Seven Tales of Science Fiction* (1938; repr., Cutchogue, NY: Buccaneer Books, 1948), 7–75.

28. Daphne Du Maurier, "The Birds," in *You and Science Fiction*, ed. Bernard Hollister (1952; repr., Lincolnwood, IL: National Textbook Company, 1995), 281–299.

29. Jack Finney, *Invasion of the Body Snatchers* (1954; repr., New York: Scribner, 1998).

30. *The Thing from Another World*, DVD, directed by Christian Nyby (1951; Turner Entertainment and Warner Brothers Entertainment, 2003); *The Birds*, DVD, directed by Alfred Hitchcock (1963; *The Alfred Hitchcock Collection* Universal City, CA: Universal Studios, 2000); *Invasion of the Body Snatchers*, DVD, directed by Don Siegel (1956; Santa Monica, CA: Artisan Entertainment, 2002).

31. Peter Dendle, *The Zombie Movie Encyclopedia* (Jefferson, NC: McFarland, 2001), 89–91, 63–64.

32. Ibid., 135–36.

33. The only notable exception is *Zombies of Mora-Tau* (1957), which features a horde of zombies that have outlasted their creator. The creatures act out of instinct alone, following the orders of no one (Dendle 211–12).

34. The apocalypse tradition in popular literature can be traced back to Mary Shel-

ley's *The Last Man* (1826), a narrative focusing on global destruction and the resultant isolation of a lone survivor. This motif was revisited by Wells, du Maurier, Matheson, and others, and it has been the subject of much speculation in other tales of invasion and infestation as well.

35. Romero, preface to *Night*, 5–14.

36. Campbell, "Who Goes There?"

37. *Roy Frumke's Document of the Dead*, DVD, directed by Roy Frumke, *Dawn of the Dead* Ultimate Edition Disc 4 (1989; Troy, MI: Anchor Bay Entertainment, 2004).

38. Gregory A. Waller, "Introduction," in *American Horrors*, ed. Gregory A. Waller (Chicago: University of Illinois Press, 1987), 3.

39. R. H. W. Dillard, "*Night of the Living Dead:* It's Not Like Just a Wind That's Passing Through," in *American Horrors*, ed. Gregory A. Waller (1973; repr., Chicago: University of Illinois Press, 1987), 26.

40. Sigmund Freud, *The Uncanny* (New York, Penguin Books, 2003), 124.

41. Ibid., 148.

42. Robin Wood, "Neglected Nightmares," in *Horror Film Reader*, ed. Alain Silver and James Ursini (New York: Limelight Editions, 2000), 126; Waller, "Introduction," 4.

43. Darryl Jones, *Horror: A Thematic History in Fiction and Film* (London: Arnold, 2002), 162.

44. *The Dead Will Walk*, DVD, directed by Martin Perry, *Dawn of the Dead* Ultimate Edition (Troy, MI: Anchor Bay Entertainment, 2004).

45. Such macabre developments show ties to issues of the *Tales from the Crypt* graphic novels produced by EC Comics in the 1950s (Romero 12). See also Paul Wells, *The Horror Genre: From Beelzebub to Blair Witch* (New York: Wallflower Press, 2002).

46. *The Last Man on Earth*, DVD, directed by Ubaldo Ragona and Sidney Salkow (1964; Los Angeles, CA: MGM Home Entertainment, 2005).

47. Dendle, *Zombie Movie Encyclopedia*, 99.

48. Of course, *The Last Man on Earth* also constitutes a kind of assembled film text, and its look and tone would have been influenced by movies like *White Zombie* and *The Birds* as well.

"Valere Quantum Valere Potest": Adaptation in Early American Cinema
W. D. Phillips

> No man creates a new language for himself, at least if he be a wise
> man, in writing a book. He contents himself with the use of lan-
> guage already known and used and understood by others.
> —Justice Joseph Story, "Emerson v. Davies"[1]

THOMAS LEITCH, IN THE FIRST SENTENCE OF HIS CHAPTER ON EARLY
cinema in his recent book *Film Adaptation and Its Discontents* claims,
"cinematic adaptation is as old as cinema itself,"[2] and in fact we can
see at least two instances of adaptation to the medium of moving pictures as early as September 14, 1896—less than nine months after the
Lumières' well-documented first public screening of projected films.
A short program of Biograph films which opened in Pittsburgh and
continued on to Philadelphia, Brooklyn, and Manhattan as part of a
touring vaudeville company featuring Austrian strongman (and early
Edison kinetoscope subject) Eugene Sandow included excerpts from
both Washington Irving's short story "Rip Van Winkle" and George
du Maurier's gothic novel *Trilby*.[3] Adaptation in this early period,
however, was rarely a direct transposition from its literary source and
in both of these cases popular stage productions served as a—and arguably *the*—intermediate adaptive formulation. The preponderance of
intermediaries in this period, in addition to the strong intertextual
practices applied to and by the "unstable environment of popular
commercial entertainments"[4] has led early cinema scholar Tom Gunning apparently to contradict Leitch when he writes, "I would claim
that there was no such thing as film adaptation of literary works during
the first decade of the cinema's existence."[5]

As disparate as these two scholars' approaches to early moving pictures practices of adaptation seem, they are, not too surprisingly, actually quite similar upon closer inspection. Gunning's argument is
primarily that the early cinema had little-to-no interest in the integrity
of the source text and that to refer to the intertextual practices involv-

ing literary sources as "adaptation" risks the application of a term and theory(s) developed within the context of classical Hollywood cinema to a period that does not share its informing values. He proposes, then, what he feels to be a more appropriate descriptive phrase, replacing a cinema of adaptation with "a cinema of reference."[6] Leitch similarly notes that narrow conceptions of adaptation in which a given adaptation refers to "a single complete literary text" have little relevance to the films of this early period and, among other qualifying attributes, recognizes a highly selective and highly parasitic approach little interested in reproducing the armature of the narrative.[7] Both scholars, however, treat the field of adaptation in this moment as a prologue to their larger, post-1909 concerns (Louis Feuillade's *Fantômas* [1913] and D. W. Griffith's "one-reel epics" [1909–11] respectively), and both largely do so in an effort to point to the significantly different context, with respect to adaptation, that their considered film(s) emerged from. One by-product of the obligatory, if somewhat brief, discussion of adaptation in these treatments is that both scholars can thus proceed with their analyses and case studies less fettered by concerns of fidelity which they view as largely irrelevant, particularly for this moment in cinema.

However, within the context of their (as well as other recent) post-structural consideration of adaptations, these early moving pictures and their multiple referents are not radically different from classical and post-classical cinematic practices of adaptation, but rather appear as a pre-standardized instantiation of poststructural textual fluidity.[8] Adaptation in early cinema, then, can be partly understood as a sort of conceptual end point or limit case for poststructural intertextual considerations of the relationship between cinematic manifestations and the literary sources that they, in varying degrees of reference, draw upon. Therefore, in an academic environment where scholars recognize most adaptations as drawing on a number of referents and sources in dialogue with each other, the particular conditions which permit, engender, and encourage these practices, while possibly never again as overdetermined (or, conversely, underdetermined) as the period discussed here, are arguably worthy not just of consideration, but of analysis in their own right.[9] Beyond the requisite noting of the unique status of intertextuality in early cinema, neither Leitch nor Gunning, however, spends much energy analyzing the particular conditions that fostered such a unique relation between source texts and cinematic manifestations before 1909. What were the material conditions or, more specifically, the industrial, institutional, and technological structures and practices which allowed and fostered such an open relationship to the multiplicity of possible referents and—depending on one's definition—source texts? The goal of this essay is to treat one of these structures: the institutional context of early cinema—specifically the American cinema—in an effort to demonstrate its significance on filmmakers' relationship with and approach to literary (and other) source texts during this period of early motion picture production. Specifically, I will address the period marked by the cinema's inception in 1895 and the first court case, originally decided in 1909 and affirmed by the US Supreme Court in 1911, that defined legally—according to copyright law—the relationship between moving pictures and other media.[10]

Adaptation in this period is hardly the only form of begging, borrowing, or stealing that the new media and technology of cinema was engaged in. Adaptation in this period should be viewed as part of a larger field of reiterative practices such as dupes, remakes, re-enactments, and re-stagings—to name the most recognizable forms. Hence, although there are numerous examples of adaptation in this era, the preponderance of these other forms complicates a simple, or singular, application of adaptation theory in an analysis of the era's filmmaking practices. What is more, the simple linearity of the literature/film dyad is largely nonexistent in this period (again, similar to poststructural interrogations of cinematic adaptations) as studies of early cinema repeatedly address its more significant relationship to late nineteenth-century entertainment and screen cultures.[11]

With these complicating elements in mind, I recognize three aspects of early cinema as telling in the manner in which the relationship between repetition and variation was approached by early film producers.[12] First, until around 1905, American cinema's primary sites of exhibition or consumption were vaudeville theaters, whose variety format tended to emphasize the unique performance of a standard (though not necessarily standardized) act. This connection is strengthened by remembering, as well, that vaudeville served not only as American cinema's primary site of exhibition, but also that many of the first films were moving picture recordings of (shortened) vaudeville acts. The ability and ease of moving pictures to be ingratiated into this system of interchangeability will be addressed further momentarily.

The second lineage of import here is film's relation to photography, though in this context arguably less in its understanding as a mechanical reproduction than in its potential for chemical reproduction (e.g. multiple positive prints from a single negative). This brings up a point about the mechanical reproduction of early cinema that is rarely discussed explicitly (if generally understood): the dual aspects of cinema's mechanical reproducibility. First, the negative print is created through a process of mechanical reproduction that engages with issues of representation and the transformation from a material 3-dimensional "reality" into a 2-dimensional strip of celluloid (or nitrate) based in the chemical properties of the strip and its reactivity to light, which still only produces a singular entity and thus the mechanical reproduction here participates only in a 1-to-1 translation of the original; second, this singular negative print is put through a mechanical (and, importantly, also chemical) process that allows this unique negative to be reiterated multiple times, or mass-produced, annihilating any uniqueness of the resulting positive print. Though Edison had been depositing photographic representations of his films for copyright as photographs since *Record of a Sneeze* in 1894, early cinema's relation to photography was not made explicit with respect to copyright law by the courts until 1903.[13]

The third and arguably the most telling aspect here would be the prevalent, and some have argued industrially necessary, presence of the dupe and the remake.[14] Briefly, a dupe is an exact positive reproduction of a film made from a negative; though the term also describes the striking of any film print for distribution, a dupe in this context is considered to be one in which the negative was originally filmed by a different company and the copy or "duplicate" generally made after removing their proprietary markings. The remake is, in this context, a shot-for-shot reconstruction of another company's film, produced with new actors, a different camera, etc., but structured so as to emulate the first as closely as possible. A remake, in other words, is a duplication of the scene rather than a duplication of the material film.[15] With these definitions in mind, it may be worth briefly clarifying the difference between the variety required across a unique vaudeville program and the high degree of allowable repetition for specific acts that circulated among various programs or exhibition sites. Turning specifically to a consideration of film in this exhibition site, another way of approaching this issue is to consider the homogenous structure of dupes and remakes and the heterogeneous exhibition context into which they were placed. From this perspective it can be noted that they served almost exactly the same purpose due to the fact they were not compared with each other but placed into dialogue or proximity with other films and/or screen and stage practices that exhibited various degrees of difference.[16] As Jane Gaines notes in her analysis of the multiple versions of *The Waterer Watered* (1895–1899), "From the point of view of late nineteenth-century spectators and exhibitors in the United States, United Kingdom, and France, *any* watering the gardener joke was *the* watering the gardener joke."[17]

Both the dupe and the remake, as intra-media copying, and adaptation, as inter-media copying, were extremely prevalent from the very beginning of the cinema: the latter, arguably, mainly for the establishment of a market through the appropriation of known entities (e.g. vaudeville, lyceum circuit, "legitimate stage" acts on film, travelogue documents, and current events). The former, though originally employed as a means of navigating differences of technologies and camera mechanisms which required prints to be restruck or duped in order to be exhibited,[18] was increasingly utilized merely to facilitate the dissemination of a competitor's work for personal profit. Worn-out negatives could necessitate a remake, though more often they were encouraged due to the limited access to competitors' prints for duping (due to, for example, foreign sales policies) and later, after 1903, as a result of the affirmed copyright protection of films-as-photographs.

From a legal perspective, the concepts underlying adaptation, as they applied both to mechanical reproductions and artistic creations, were still in the process of being articulated within the United States legislation and judicial systems at this time.[19] Hence, the relationship between original and copy—even simply based in mechanical reproduction—had not yet been statutorily reified.[20] Until 1891 dramatic rights were not identified as the exclusive right of the original author. Moreover, the practical definition of copyrightable as it applied to "dramatic compositions" was still in flux. This situation is evidenced by two cases tried in 1892: in *Brady v. Daly*[21] the courts found that pantomime of a dramatic scene was protected by copyright, yet in *Fuller v. Bemis*[22] it was decided that a stage dance (here, in particular, representing a popular vaudeville act) was not protected under copyright legislation.[23] Early cinema, based on its close relation to vaudeville for at least its first decade then, by and large, did not legally qualify for copyright protection as a dramatic composition. As recourse, a number of film producers (particularly Edison) attempted to engage a separate aspect of cinema's tangled lineage and registered for copyrights as photographs. As this nascent media industry developed and both the form and content of its ephemeral products changed, particularly with the turn to story films, moving pictures' relationship to copyright law also changed. However, I would argue that the conceptual framework for copying and/or adapting inter-media texts did not, at least not until after *Harper Bros. v. Kalem Co.* in 1911.[24]

This *Harper v. Kalem* case is one of the four copyright suits most generally discussed with respect to the standardization of early cinema's business practices. These discussions are usually performed, to some degree, in conjunction with a discussion of the patent suits which also proliferated at the time.[25] These two fields are obviously closely related; both, in fact, find their origins as legislation in Article 1, Section 8, Clause 8 of the United States Constitution.[26] However, by the end of the nineteenth century, patent law had become more firmly ensconced in an economic/business/capitalist framework. With respect to early cinema, the shift from patent infringement suits to copyright infringement suits accompanies a changing perspective on business models and salable goods, itself tied to the standardization of exhibition (at least from a technological standpoint) such that the films no longer served chiefly to market the projection equipment and services, but were themselves increasingly viewed as the primary market good. This shift is also part of the same change in business models that led, beginning in 1903, to a redefinition of the distribution system away from film sales and toward film rentals. These four copyright suits are the 1898 equity cases Edison filed against Vitagraph, *Thomas A. Edison v. Siegmund Lubin* in 1903, *American Mutoscope & Biograph Co. v. Edison Mfg. Co.* in 1905, and the aforementioned *Harper Bros. v. Kalem Co.* in 1909.[27]

The first copyright infringement suit, from 1898, was filed alongside two patent infringement suits as part of what I call Edison's "legal shotgun" approach to market control. As there were no legal precedents specifically for moving pictures as a new medium, Edison's legal team attempted to utilize any and all forms of institutional and industrial control to dissuade competitors from encroaching on their businesses. By presenting their competitors, many of whom had been itinerant showmen and were relatively naïve with respect to turn-of-the-century big business practices, with an aggressive barrage of legalese and punitive threats, the Edison Co. obviously hoped to use scare tactic as much or more than actual court trials to reduce competition and thus assume a larger market share. In this case the scare tactic worked and Vitagraph settled out of court and the case never went before a judge; as a result no precedent with respect to copyright law was either invoked or established for the new medium.[28]

In the 1903 *Edison v. Lubin* case, Edison's legal team sued Philadelphia moving picture producer Siegmund Lubin for copyright infringement for the pirating (duping and distributing) of their film *Christening and Launching Kaiser Wilhelm's Yacht "Meteor"* (1902).[29] Lubin, in an effort to preserve the duping practice he (and others) found so lucrative, argued that Edison's copyrights were actually invalid, since photographic copyrights did not apply to moving images unless each and every frame had been submitted and registered.[30] Though the original judge found in favor of Lubin, the state appellate court found that moving pictures registered with the copyright office as photographs did enjoy protection, as such, against illegal duplication. However, as this was the first test of this practice, the majority of

moving pictures produced during the previous eight years were unregistered (Edison being the only company to register its films as photos
en masse) and it was therefore, under the law, perfectly legal to dupe
any of the many unregistered films—foreign or domestic, past or
present.[31]

With respect to the development of copyright law and its application to the cinema, there were two important aspects of the 1905 *Biograph v. Edison* lawsuit in which Biograph sued Edison for exactly
copying the subject matter of its 1904 chase film *Personal*. Edison's
remake, *How a French Nobleman Got a Wife Through the New York
"Herald" Personal Columns* (1904), appeared shortly after, and in direct
competition with, the Biograph "original"; although it adopted a significantly different title, the Edison film is nearly (though not exactly)
identical in its depicted action. The first aspect of this case that is often
addressed as consequential is the court's finding that a multi-shot film
enjoyed the same photography-based copyright protection as a single-
shot film. However, the key element for our purposes here was that
the court also decided that a film registered for copyright protection
as a photograph enjoyed *no protection* in relation to its subject matter
or story. The court did not, in this case, claim that moving pictures
could not be protected by copyright as dramatic compositions (this
was not part of the case, as *Personal* had never been registered with the
copyright office as anything but a photograph), it simply recognized
that, with respect to legal precedent, copyright protection as a photograph was a categorically different entity (and registration process)
than protection as a dramatic composition. In the wake of this decision
Biograph began to register all of its films for copyright protection
twice, once as photographs, and again as dramatic compositions.[32]

These three examples, however, still pertain only to the dupe and
the remake, or to the intra-media reiterative practices of early cinema.
I have drawn out their discussion to demonstrate, however, what I feel
to be a key contextualization for the process of adaptation employed
by filmmakers of this period, and to more clearly articulate the relationship, from an institutional perspective, between practices of intra-
and inter-media copying. Perhaps surprising, from the institutional
history provided here, the first case to test film's validity as a dramatic
composition did not result from battles within the industry (as these
others have) but rather from an outside, and increasingly competing,
entertainment industry.[33] In April, 1908, Harper & Bros., which
owned the rights to the late Gen. Lew Wallace's 1880 novel *Ben Hur:
A Tale of the Christ* and all dramatizations thereof (which they had
granted to a third party—Klaw & Erlanger—for the well-known stage
production that first appeared in 1899) sued the Kalem Co. for pro-

ducing a moving picture of the story without obtaining/purchasing the required permissions. The following year, the Circuit Court of the United States for the Southern District of New York found that although Kalem's film of *Ben Hur* (1907), as a material entity or product, did not infringe on the rights of the book's copyright holders, any *exhibition* of the film, understood by the court as a dramatic performance, did directly violate the copyright holder's exclusive rights to dramatize their work as guaranteed by statute in 1891. This lower court's decision was upheld, over the next two years, by every applicable appellate court, up to and including the United States Supreme Court in November of 1911. Thus, for the record, until 1909, although legal restrictions on the inter-media adaptation of dramatic works were "on the books" in conjunction with other forms of entertainment and media, film, as a new(er) media, had not been demonstrated legally as required to adhere. Though the final appeal was not affirmed until 1911 by the US Supreme Court, the case was appealed and affirmed in district court in 1909, after which time any film company producing a film version of a copyrighted dramatic composition could have expected to be sued for infringement. Thus, even if the recognition of moving pictures as dramatic compositions, which could therefore enter into competition with other media forms of the same, was not officially statutory until the 1912 Townsend Act, legal precedent would have indicated after 1909 that this type of film production would be an extremely risky economic venture. Still, for the decade and a half leading up to this point, filmmakers looking to produce a new work (of fact or fiction) were legally free (outside of direct duping) to adapt and appropriate any previous work or text to their own purposes and inclinations, modifying the "source text" as much or as little as suited their needs.

Though these cases did help to standardize the business practices of early cinema, I do not find them to be necessarily representative or indicative of the ideological principles on which the filmmakers were drawing in their production of dupes, remakes, and various forms of adaptation. The copyright case which I think provides the most valuable insight, as viewed through the changes to legal structures, for cultural conceptions of fidelity, originality, and the philosophical principles underlying both the laws and the media adaptations, is *Bleistein v. Donaldson Lithographing Co.*,[34] decided by the United States Supreme Court on February 2, 1903. This was not a case of dramatic composition, however, but rather a case of image infringement in which a set of three chromolithographs intended as circus advertisements had been duplicated, in reduced form, by an outside party for their own advertising purposes. The weight of precedent up to this point would have seemed to indicate that this was not an image worthy of copyright protection, as it hardly seemed to qualify under the rubric of the "usable Arts" as laid out in the Copyright Clause of the Constitution. Yet the defendant was, in fact, found to have infringed on the plaintiff's copyright. Following copyright scholar Oren Bracha, I read the decision in this case and the language used by Justice Oliver Wendell Holmes in his articulation of the majority decision as indicative of the change in the philosophical approach to copyright law which took place throughout the latter half of the nineteenth century and the first decade of the twentieth: the move from a romantic conception of the author whose originality is valuable and worthy of protection to one in which the sole role in terms of the merit evaluation of copyrightable products is assigned to the market.[35]

This development pairs well with the legal shift Jane Gaines sees as already beginning in 1884 in *Burrow-Giles Lithographic Co. v. Sarony*.[36] This case has the appearance or veneer of artist versus mass production in that Napoleon Sarony apparently won his court case and obtained clear copyright ownership of his photograph of Oscar Wilde by demonstrating the creative artistry implicit in the posing of subjects before the camera mechanism, thus supporting the romantic conception of the author as the foundation for this decision. However, upon further analysis, Gaines notes that photographers such as Sarony "sold theatrical photographs wholesale to salesman who turned around and sold them in theaters and hotels or by mail order."[37] Thus, although the Sarony case seems set up to be that of an individual photographer/artist against a mass-producing industrial lithographic company, both sides—from a position of economic interests—were engaged largely in the same process. The difference between them, then, is not one of a kind (as aesthetically based judgment would read) but rather one of degree (based on availability to the technologies of mass production). This degree of difference is condensed significantly and the false veneer of romantic author removed in both *Bleistein v. Donaldson Lithographing Co.* and *Edison v. Lubin* wherein the technologies of duplication are equally available to both and thus evaluations of legality depend wholly on either the embrace or denial of the aesthetic nature of these judgments. In both cases we see a denial of an aesthetic valuation in favor of a market-determined one. As a result, Gaines concludes, "by the [twentieth] century, intellectual property doctrine would become so accustomed to similarity that it would pretend less and less to find distinction in the work and would be satisfied more and more with the mere fact of origin in the settlement of disputes."[38]

Though Justice Holmes's decision in *Bleistein* was invoked directly by Justice Joseph Buffington in his decision on *Edison v Lubin* later that year, its significance can also be seen as registering in the treatment of copyright across media lines. This redefinition of media interactions, based on content-neutral market evaluations, indicated a changing definition to the "useful Arts" which Congress was supposed to promote and protect. Even though it first registers (in the *Edison v. Lubin* decision) with respect to cinema-as-photograph, the principles for a changing relation to cultural and entertainment products extend to later cinema-as-dramatic composition cases as well.[39] The point here is that the cultural producers first, and the law interpreters and law makers second, placed value on the "original" only to the degree that the market did: in the identification of an object profitable to imitate. This, then, became the implicit argument for protection of an original, and copyright law can be seen to come more in line with the ideology behind turn-of-the-century patent law. Filmmakers (and particularly Edison's legal team[40]) saw patent law and the two types of copyright law (image and dramatic composition) at the turn of the century as two sides of the same coin—literally.[41] The ideological underpinnings of these two, from the perspective of the judicial and legislative branches, though originally tied together in the language of the Constitution, had bifurcated over the course of the eighteenth and nineteenth centuries with patent law organized earlier around market concerns. Increasingly, in the latter half of the nineteenth century, and especially in the first decade of the twentieth, the identification of— and hence protection of—the "useful Arts" was relocated from a perspective of personal evaluation to one of market evaluation. The legal system then was "merely" coming into accordance with the perception of the two already in place in the culture of early cinema production.[42] If law interpreters increasingly understood the value of originality through the lens of a content-neutral marketplace rather than through the valorization of novelty and a reified author, they were only picking up on the interpretation and application of the relationship between reproduction and variation or fidelity and originality as it had been applied by culture producers for years.

As a consequence, any study or analysis of remakes, reenactments, or—particularly within the context of this volume—adaptation in early cinema must necessarily be framed by an understanding that they (the films and the filmmakers) were part of a culture, at least a business culture, that valued, when an item proved successful, similarity over difference and fidelity over originality. Furthermore, this conception applied equally to inter- and intra-media copying practices.[43] However, it was not due to the perception of a reified source text or a romantic notion of the author (as is implicit in most aesthetic considerations of fidelity), but to a content-neutral market evaluation of demand. This conception is a rather clear market instantiation of Leitch's argument for an approach to adaptation studies wherein "every text offers itself as an invitation to be rewritten."[44] This notion is tied, however, not to his devaluation of fidelity from an analytical perspective, in which the source text inherently possesses an "enormous and unfair" comparative advantage, but to a valuation of fidelity from a production perspective due to a market structured on reproduction and (largely) unfettered by legal statutes hindering duplication.

Perhaps we can reframe our discussion of these early filmmakers and suggest that what they were attempting to reproduce, or adapt for their own profit, was the *experience* associated with cinema. In the earliest years (the "novelty" years) this was primarily linked to the apparatus of the film itself—in the projection equipment; thus, in an effort to protect their unique experience, patent—rather than copyright—infringement suits were the commonplace. As the apparatus became regularized, and as the programs that included films were increasingly standardized, not so much in content as in form (whether as a unified lecture or a variety format), then the focus amongst producers switched to the experience as it was associated with the particular products: the films themselves. The logical endpoint in the attempt to reproduce the experience provided by a film is the reproduction of the film itself, an exact reproduction of both subject matter and technique, or the dupe; the shot-for-shot remake is the next iteration. What is commonly understood as an adaptation extends this principle of "reproduced experience" only after these other two approaches.

As poststructuralist approaches foregrounding intertextuality and the palimpsestic nature of adaptation increasingly enter the purview of adaptation scholars, and earlier questions of fidelity to a singular source text are increasingly superseded by investigations of the negotiation of pressures exerted by various referents (textual or otherwise), we, as scholars, need to develop and expand existing methodological approaches which will facilitate an understanding of not just which referents and antecedents are brought to bear on a given filmic adaptation, but also—and in some ways more importantly—the industrial, material, institutional and socio-political structures which create, engender and/or encourage these particular cinematic negotiations of "source texts." Although the periodization of my study here falls outside the classical or post-classical cinema, the institutional structures at work clearly allowed for and encouraged the particular reiterative relationships moving pictures of that era had with their media and entertainment predecessors. Though the motion picture industry's relation with source texts was forever changed as a result of *Harper Bros.*

v. Kalem Co. in 1911 (and the 1912 copyright law change that followed it), various industrial, material, and institutional structures continue to play an important role in filmmaker's particular choices at the level of adaptation. Though the degree of effect may not be as marked as that noted here, the investigation of these structures is no less warranted within more standardized industrial practices.

NOTES

1. *Emerson v. Davies*, 8 F. 615, 619 *C.C.D. Mass. 1845), qtd. in Oren Bracha, "The Ideology of Authorship Revisited: Authors, Markets, and Liberal Values in Early American Copyright," *Yale Law Journal* 118, no. 186 (2008): 202. The title of my essay ("valere quantum valere potest") also comes from Justice Story's written decision in this case (621) and can be translated: "with as much value as he can get" (Bracha, 203 n. 53).

2. Thomas Leitch, *Film Adaptation and Its Discontents: From* Gone with the Wind *to* The Passion of the Christ (Baltimore: The John Hopkins University Press, 2007), 22.

3. Charles Musser, *The Emergence of Cinema: The American Screen to 1907*, vol. 1 of *History of the American Cinema* (Berkeley: University of California Press, 1991), 150. Jonathan Auerbach, *Body Shots: Early Cinema's Incarnations* (Berkeley: University of California Press, 2007), 26.

4. Tom Gunning, "The Intertextuality of Early Cinema: A Prologue to *Fantômas*," in *A Companion to Literature and Film*, ed. Robert Stam and Alessandra Raengo (Malden, MA: Blackwell, 2004), 129.

5. Ibid., 127.

6. Ibid., 129.

7. Leitch, *Film Adaptation and Its Discontents*, 23.

8. Poststructuralism certainly provides one of the key theoretical tenets for Leitch's book-length treatment of cinematic adaptations; Gunning's essay was expanded and developed from an earlier incarnation for publication as part of Robert Stam's three volume treatment on the adaptive relationship between literature and film which was itself formulated significantly, as he notes in his introduction, in consideration of "the impact of the posts." Robert Stam, "Introduction: The Theory and Practice of Adaptation" in *Literature and Film: A Guide to the Theory and Practice of Film Adaptation*, ed. Robert Stam and Alessandra Raengo (Malden, MA: Blackwell, 2005), 8–9.

9. A similar call—or, perhaps more accurately, challenge—to adaptation studies was recently proffered by Simone Murray, though from a somewhat different perspective, in her essay "Materializing Adaptation Theory: The Adaptation Industry," *Literature/Film Quarterly* 36, no. 1 (2008): 4–20.

10. This case, known as *Harper Bros. v. Kalem Co.*, was first filed in April 1908. The first appeal was heard and confirmed in 1909. Upon further appeal, the case was ultimately heard by the United States Supreme Court on October 31 and November 1, 1911 and their decision confirming the original decision was rendered on November 13 of the same year (222 U.S. 55). Congress incorporated this judicial interpretation into the language of the copyright law the next year, in the Amended Copyright Statutes of 1912 (also known as the Townsend Act).

11. Cf. Musser, *Emergence*, 15–54.

12. Here I find a problem with the connotations attached to terminology typically used in adaptation studies, and, as a result, have replaced "fidelity" and "originality" in my early cinema context with the more encompassing terms "repetition" and "variation." This further allows me to use the same concepts and terms in my considerations of the various reiterative practices described here (dupes, remakes, as well as adaptations). As I noted in both Leitch's and Gunning's arguments and as, from an institutional standpoint I will be arguing momentarily, the concept of fidelity is ill-fitted for a socio-economic group that places little ethical or aesthetic value on the "original."

13. Peter Decherney, "Copyright Dupes: Piracy and New Media in *Edison v. Lubin* (1903)," *Film History* 19, no. 2 (2007): 110. Though *Record of a Sneeze* was published as a sequence of photographic frames in several magazines announcing the invention of the kinetoscope, it was never actually shown in public as a moving picture (Auerbach, 68).

14. For an argument of the industrial necessity of these duplicate forms, see Decherney, "Copyright Dupes," 113; Jennifer Forrest, "The 'Personal' Touch: The Original, The Remake, and the Dupe in Early Cinema," in *Dead Ringers: The Remake in Theory and Practice*, ed. Jennifer Forrest and Leonard R. Koos (Albany: State University of New York Press, 2002), 91, 95. For an older essay making the same argument, see David Levy, "Re-Constituted Newsreels, Re-Enactments and the American Narrative Film," in *Cinema 1900/1906*, ed. Roger Holman (Brussels, Belgium: FIAF, 1982), 255.

15. Forrest, following Samuel Spring, refers to dupes and remakes as literal copies and treatment copies, respectively (94). See Samuel Spring, *Risks and Rights in Publishing, Television, Radio, Motion Pictures, Advertising and the Theater* (London: Allen & Unwin, 1952).

16. I would like to thank Jason Roberts for suggesting this line of thinking in his comments on my paper at the 2008 PCA/ACA conference in San Francisco.

17. Jane M. Gaines, "Early Cinema's Heyday of Copying: The Too Many Copies of *L'Arroseur arrosé* (*The Waterer Watered*)," *Cultural Studies* 20, no. 2–3 (2006): 238, italics in original. In her analysis of multiple versions of this film (what she calls the "phenomenon of multiple singularity" [230]) she identifies versions manufactured by at least six companies across 3 countries (235–6). In addition, she claims that with the Lumières' three versions, despite exhibitor orders based on catalogue descriptions, they may have been shipped a different version depending on print availability (241 n. 12). Finally, from a somewhat different perspective, but one that still ties into this argument: "From the point of view of an audience seeking entertainment, repeat productions meant more possibilities to see a popular comedy short" (231).

18. Decherney, "Copyright," 114.

19. I think it is important to note, as Decherney recognizes, that the "pronouncements of judges and Congress . . . are always only one piece of a complex formula that steers the development of new media in one direction or another" (110). Also, Jane Gaines reminds us that the presence of laws certainly does not result in their strict adherence; citing Nancy Anderson and David Greenberg's review of Bernard Edelman's *Ownership of the Image*, she quotes: "Specifically, the acceptance of legal ideology may be uneven, depending upon the particular case at stake. People do not take law into account in carrying out their affairs. When they do, however, they do not merely follow the law. They attempt to evade it, they bend it to their purposes and assert their own interpretation of what is and should be. So, too, they may calculate the likelihood of law enforcement in organizing their conduct." (Anderson and

Greenberg, "From Substance to Form: The Legal Theories of Pashukanis and Edelman," *Social Text* 7 [Spring-Summer 1983]: 82–83, qtd. in Jane M. Gaines, *Contested Culture: The Image, the Voice, and the Law* [Chapel Hill and London: The University of North Carolina Press, 1991], 29.)

20. Although photographs were added to the copyright law by Act of Congress in 1870, the *White-Smith Music Publishing Co. v. Apollo Co.*, 209 U.S. 1 (1908) which found that player-piano rolls (mechanical reproductions in their own right) did not infringe on the musical copyright was decided as part of the Supreme Court's 1908 docket.

21. *Brady v. Daly*, 83 F. 1007 (2d Cir. 1892), *affirmed*, 175 U.S. 148 (1899).

22. *Fuller v. Bemis*, 50 F. 926 (S.D.N.Y. 1892).

23. Marie Louise Fuller filed for copyright protection for her "famous" skirt dance (as a dramatic composition) and, shortly thereafter, filed an infringement suit against a "competitor" who reproduced it at another local venue. The judge in *Fuller v. Bemis* ultimately found that the "complainant's performance" was not "a dramatic composition, within the meaning of the copyright law" (see Arthur S. Hamlin, ed., *Copyright Cases: A Summary of Leading American Decisions on the Law of Copyright and Literary Property, from 1891 to 1903* [New York: G.P. Putnam's Sons, 1904]). The inability of a vaudeville "sketch" to obtain copyright protection continued throughout cinema's early years, even as the laws were tested and adjusted in conjunction with the new media (Cf. *Barnes v. Miner*, 122 F. 480 [S.D.N.Y. 1903]). The irony here is that due to cinema's mixed/multiple lineages a moving picture reproduction of a (different) competitor's version of Fuller's skirt dance was not only filmed by the Edison Co. in 1895, but filed for (and ultimately received) copyright protection as well; adding "insult to injury," this moving picture was filed as a paper print in the Library of Congress—as per Edison's practices at the time—and was thus saved for posterity: *Butterfly Dance* (aka *Skirt Dance by Annabelle*) is now generally available on DVD collections of early cinema.

24. *Harper Bros. et al. v. Kalem Co. et al.*, 169 F. 61 (2d Cir. 1909), *affirmed, Kalem Co. v. Harper Bros.*, 222 U.S. 55 (1911). As I discuss below, intra-media copyright law had changed earlier, after *American Mutoscope & Biograph Co. v. Edison Mfg. Co.*, 137 F. 262 (D.N.J. 1905).

25. The relationship between patent law and copyright law (as well as trademark legislation) is easily notable. Jeanne Allen, for example, states: "The laws which governed intellectual property as possession underwent a process of refinement and abridgement in the nineteenth century as economic production was transformed by mechanical processes (patent law) and by modes of marketing that emphasized the reputation of the producer (trademark) and the publicity for the product (copyright)." (Jeanne Allen, "Copyright Protection in Theatre, Vaudeville and Early Cinema," *Screen* 21, no. 2 [1980]: 81).

26. Article I, Section 8, Clause 8 of the United States Constitution, known as the Copyright Clause, the Copyright and Patent Clause, the Intellectual Property Clause and the Progressive Clause, states: "The Congress shall have power. . . . To promote the Progress of Science and useful Arts, by securing for limited Times to Authors and Inventors the exclusive Right to their respective Writings and Discoveries."

27. *Thomas A. Edison v. Siegmund Lubin*, 119 F. 993 (E.D. Pa. 1903), *reversed*, 122 F. 240 (3d Cir. 1903).

28. Charles Musser, "The American Vitagraph, 1897–1901: Survival and Success in a Competitive Industry" in *Film Before Griffith*, ed. John Fell (Berkeley: University of California Press, 1983), 35–37.

29. Though Lubin was often treated in contemporary trade papers as an unethical

pirate, and many of the earliest cinema histories perpetuated this opinion, most if not all early moving picture companies engaged in duping as a means of obtaining relatively easy profits. Edison, for example, during the same period was using its contract with Vitagraph (as a result of the 1898 injunction) as a sort or legal "shield" against copyright infringement by having Vitagraph perform their duping for them.

30. At the time the United States Library of Congress Copyright Office required a fifty-cent fee along with two copies of each photograph and the accompanying registration paperwork. As such, the fee (and administrative time) required to submit every frame would have effectively nullified copyright as a means of institutional protection for moving pictures. It is perhaps worth noting briefly here that the paper copies of the films that were submitted (both before and after this decision, but all largely before the shift to copyright as dramatic composition) are what came to constitute the Library of Congress's paper print collection of early cinema and thus the attempt and ultimate application of copyright protection as a means of industrial control indirectly resulted in the archival records of these films we have today.

31. The original judge for the case indicated that he felt this was a decision for lawmakers rather than judges to decide. In the fourteen weeks (1/13/03–4/20/03) between the original court's decision in favor of Lubin and the appellate court's decision in favor of Edison when no copyright laws at all were in play there was, not surprisingly, almost a complete stoppage of new productions by all companies as producers waited out the appeal of the case (Decherney, 118). The widespread practice of duping or the exact copying of other moving pictures, however, seems to have ended when it did as much from the formation of the MPPC in 1907 and the contractual obligation to end intra-Trust duplications (stipulated by Edison—who arguably still had the most to lose, especially after contracting to distribute Pathé's films in America) as from the fear of lawsuits and the financial risks involved with continuing this practice. Thus, though it might appear the institutional changes enacted by governmental forces "righted the wrong," self-contained industrial practices appear equally contributory in this case.

32. Yet, as had occurred earlier with Edison's photographic copyrights, this policy as a protective measure was untested by the courts. Allen refers to this duality as a court-recognized, "categorical distinction between film as material artifact and film as performance" (90).

33. The industrial history offers some explanation, with the formation of the MPPC, as a patent pool, in 1907 controlling intra-media competition, at least for a moment. Furthermore, the shift from a copyright protection based in visual media (photographs) to one based in written media (dramatic composition with what Allen [86] refers to as a "notational system") was far from complete and as their copyright as dramatic composition was also untested by the courts, film producer's may not have seen any need to pursue expensive litigation at this point.

34. *Bleistein v. Donaldson Lithographing Co.*, 188 U.S. 239 (1903).

35. Bracha, 200–224.

36. *Burrow-Giles Lithographic Co. v. Sarony*, 111 U.S. 52 (1884).

37. Gaines, *Contested Culture*, 76.

38. Ibid., 77.

39. Tracing the lineage of the case law of film copyright then reveals a two-step process. The tradition of the photograph as property in United States courts made it relatively easy to distinguish motion pictures as copyrightable properties. The major early decisions were how to treat moving pictures in relation to the single-image copyright registration process of photographs: whether each frame, each shot, or multiple shots qualified via the same registration process. Each obviously applies similar

theories of ownership, but these had to be massaged for economic reasons, most notably the improbability of copyrighting each frame—and later each shot—due to the requisite accompanying copyright fee and the administrative time needed for such a level of document registration. Once this status as a single copyrightable object, filed under a single copyright (even as a multi-shot film) was established, it could then be transferred laterally to another set of legal precedents—that of dramatic composition. For an elaboration on this case history that addresses the arguments regarding single versus multiple frames and single versus multiple shots, see André Gaudreault, "The Infringement of Copyright Laws and Its Effects (1900–1906)" in *Early Cinema: Space-Frame-Narrative*, ed. Thomas Elsaesser (London: BFI, 1993), 114–22.

40. Shortly after *Edison v Lubin* Edison decided to start his own in-house legal division.

41. Jennifer Forrest notes that the "emphasis on the photographic nature of the medium shifted to the issue of the dramatization of written works, which involved a different domain of copyright law: licensing" (120n32). As I mentioned earlier, a third "side of the coin" with respect to institutional protection of industrial practices is trademark infringement suits (which was certainly part of Edison's legal "arsenal"). Although Edison was filing copyright forms for even his earliest moving pictures, the importance of these until 1902 ran a distant second behind his patents, and perhaps even behind his trademark filings. Forrest further claims that Edison only began filing copyright infringement suits (which he was willing to pay to take to court) *after* his patent suits failed to produce the market control (monopoly) he desired (99).

42. From a slightly different perspective, early filmmakers were part of the rise of industrial modernity and the growth of mass media and, as such, were part of a visual, dramatic, and business culture that was *actively redefining* cultural perceptions of originality and ownership, as well as the definition of "useful Arts" that Congress was constitutionally responsible to promote and protect.

43. Intra-media adaptations (dupes and remakes) could thus be recognized as simply being the easier of the two, as they did not require any "pesky" media-specificity adjustments.

44. Thomas Leitch, "Literature vs. Literacy: Two Futures for Adaptation Studies" in *The Literature/Film Reader: Issues of Adaptation*, ed. James M. Welsh and Peter Lev (Lanham (Maryland: Scarecrow, 2007), 29.

Contributors

CHRISTA ALBRECHT-CRANE is an associate professor and Assistant Chair in the Department of English and Literature at Utah Valley University. She teaches courses in first-year writing, advanced academic writing, critical theory, and film. Her research interests lie in the intersection of British cultural studies and French poststructuralism. She has published chapters in *Gilles Deleuze: Key Concepts and Animations of Deleuze and Guattari* and articles in *JAC* and *The Journal of the Midwest Modern Language Association*. In 2005 she co-edited a special issue of *Cultural Studies* on teaching in conservative environments.

RICHARD BERGER is currently Reader in Media and Education at the Centre for Excellence in Media Practice, Bournemouth University, UK. He coordinates pedagogic research in the Media School at Bournemouth and his other research interests include the adaptation of literature, comic books, and video games to film and television as well as blogging, fanfic, and other forms of personal expression online. In addition, Richard is an experienced broadcaster and journalist for BBC Online and BBC Radio and co-editor of *The Media Research Journal* (*MERJ*).

KYLE WILLIAM BISHOP is a third-generation professor at Southern Utah University where he teaches American literature and culture, film studies, fantasy literature, and English composition. He has presented and published a variety of papers on popular culture and cinematic adaptation, including such topics as *A Hazard of New Fortunes, Metropolis, Night of the Living Dead, Fight Club, White Zombie, Buffy the Vampire Slayer*, and *Dawn of the Dead*. He received a PhD in English from the University of Arizona in 2009, where he wrote a dissertation investigating the cultural relevance of zombie cinema.

DENNIS CUTCHINS is an associate professor of English at Brigham Young University where he teaches adaptation studies as well as American and Western literature. He has published articles on the works of Cormac McCarthy, F. Scott Fitzgerald, Louise Erdrich, Leslie Silko,

Ernest Hemingway, W. P. Kinsella, and others. In 2004 Dennis received the Charles Redd Center's Butler Young Scholar Award in Western Studies. His most recent book is an edited colletion titled *Wild Games: Hunting and Fishing Traditions in North America.*

PAMELA DEMORY is a full-time lecturer at the University of California, Davis where she works extensively with the University Writing Program. She is the editor of *Prized Writing*, an anthology of award-winning UCD student writing, and has published several essays on adaptation including: "Into the Heart of Light: Barbara Kingsolver Re-reads *Heart of Darkness* in *Conradiana*"; " 'It's About Seeing . . .' -Representations of the Female Body in Robert Altman's *Short Cuts* and Raymond Carver's Stories" in *Pacific Coast Philology*; "Faithfulness vs. Faith: John Huston's Version of Flannery O'Connor's *Wise Blood*" in the *Journal of Southern Religion*; and "Violence and Transcendence in *Pulp Fiction* and Flannery O'Connor" in *The Image of Violence in Literature, the Media, and Society.*

ANDREA D. FITZPATRICK is an assistant professor in the history and theory of art at the University of Ottawa. Her research involves issues of identity, subjectivity, politics, ethics, and war in contemporary art, especially in photographic portraiture, video art, body art, and performance art. Recent publications have addressed the art of AA Bronson, Rodney Graham, Suzanne Opton, Andres Serrano, and Andy Warhol, September 11, and have appeared in *Afterimage, Art Journal, BorderCrossings, Drain, Revue d'art canadienne/Canadian Art Review*, and *One Hour Empire.* An essay entitled "Love's Letter Lost: Reading *Brokeback Mountain*," which analyzes the short story and the film alongside Roland Barthes's *A Lover's Discourse*, is forthcoming in *Mosaic: A Journal for the Interdisciplinary Study of Literature.*

DAVID A. HATCH received his PhD from Florida State University in Interdisciplinary Modernism. His dissertation and much subsequent scholarship deal with the work of Samuel Beckett, including a recent article on Beckett's subversion of Gothic modes in *Ill Seen Ill Said.* In addition to teaching Humanities and Philosophy at Utah Valley University, David foil fences competitively and co-directs a local youth theater.

GLENN JELLENIK is a doctoral candidate at the University of South Carolina, Columbia, where he teaches Film & Media Studies and Literature. His research centers around the intersection of pop cultural and literary aesthetics.

THOMAS LEITCH teaches English and directs the Film Studies program at the University of Delaware. His most recent book is *Film Adaptation and Its Discontents: From* Gone with the Wind *to* The Passion of the Christ.

KATE NEWELL is a professor at the Savannah College of Art and Design where she teaches courses in literature, writing, and film adaptation. Her research focuses on issues of adaptation and other intersections of film, literature, illustration, comic books, and video games.

MARK O'THOMAS is Director of the Institute for Performing Arts Development (IPAD) at the University of East London where he lectures in both theatre and creative writing. He is a playwright, translator, and adapter. His translations/adaptations include *Almost Nothing* and *At The Table* for the Royal Court Theatre, *Dona Flor & Her Two Husbands* for the Lyric Hammersmith, and *Speedball* (an adaptation based on the life and works of Chet Baker) for the London Jazz Festival.

WYATT PHILLIPS is a PhD student at Cinema Studies at New York University and an adjunct professor of cinema and media culture at both NYU and College of Staten Island (CUNY). He is currently completing a dissertation on the emergence of genre in early American film. In addition to studying the theory, history, and practice of genre and adaptation, his research and pedagogical interests include international silent film and American independent cinema.

DAVID C. SIMMONS received his PhD in Humanities and Film Studies from Florida State University. His dissertation was entitled *The Dysphoric Style in Contemporary American Independent Cinema*. He co-edited and assembled a textbook for Florida State University called *Multicultural Dimensions of Film* that included two of his own articles. He has presented papers at conferences on such varied films as Alfred Hitchcock's *Psycho* and *The Birds*, Ingmar Bergman's *Persona*, Kenneth Branagh's *Mary Shelley's Frankenstein*, Darren Aronofsky's *Pi*, and Christopher Nolan's *Memento*. He is currently a professor of Humanities and Film Studies at Northwest Florida State College.

NANCY STEFFEN-FLUHR is an associate professor of humanities at the New Jersey Institute of Technology and a practicing playwright (*Heartbreaker*, 2007). In addition to her work on Ernst Lubitsch, she has written critical essays on a range of subjects including filmmakers Billy Wilder, Alfred Hitchcock, Don Siegal, and Terry Gilliam; actor Raymond Burr; and science fiction writers H. G. Wells and Alice Sheldon ("James Tiptree"). Her latest essay, "Palimpsest: The Double Vision of Exile," explores Billy Wilder's relationship to the Holocaust. She is finishing a book on Wilder that uses intertextual analysis to develop a revisionist view of his directorial style.

BRETT WESTBROOK teaches writing and American literature and film at St. Edward's University in Austin, TX, and is on the staff at The University of Texas at Austin. Recent work includes two articles on mystery writer James Lee Burke, one on masculinity and the other on ghosts, forthcoming from McFarland Press. Future projects include a study of the pirate movie as a vehicle for cinematic masculinity and learning to use fondant.

Index